Small-Business Franchises Made Simple

William Lasher, M.B.A., Ph.D., C.P.A.,
and Carl Hausman, Ph.D.

Edited and prepared for publication by The Stonesong Press, Inc.

A Made Simple Book
DOUBLEDAY New York London Toronto Sydney Auckland

A Made Simple Book
PUBLISHED BY DOUBLEDAY
a division of Bantam Doubleday Dell Publishing Group, Inc.
1540 Broadway, New York, New York 10036

Edited and prepared for publication by The Stonesong Press, Inc.
Executive Editor: Sheree Bykofsky
Editor: Sarah Gold

Library of Congress Cataloging-in-Publication Data

Lasher, William.
Small-business franchises made simple / William Lasher and Carl Hausman. — 1st ed.
p. cm.
"A Made Simple book."
Includes bibliographical references.
1. Franchises (Retail trade)—United States. 2. Small business—United States. 3. Franchises (Retail trade)—Law and legislation—United States. 4. Franchises (Retail trade)—Case studies.
I. Hausman, Carl, 1953– . II. Title.
HF5429.235.U5L37 1994
658.8'708—dc20 93-6709
CIP

ISBN 0-385-42552-X

Printed in the United States of America
January 1994
First Edition
10 9 8 7 6 5 4 3 2 1

The franchise names used in illustrative cases and examples in this book are hypothetical. Any similarity to actual businesses, franchised or not, is purely coincidental.

CONTENTS

INTRODUCTION

You can go out on your own and not be all alone out there. There's a quiet revolution going on in American small business: A franchise opens somewhere in the United States every seventeen minutes. More than half a million franchises are currently in operation.

Franchising combines the personal freedom and satisfaction of entrepreneurship with the security of forming a relationship with an experienced, proven business. In addition to receiving assistance from the franchisor in a variety of areas, you may also enjoy the recognition associated with a nationally known name.

Small-Business Franchises Made Simple is a step-by-step guide to entering the world of franchising, written with the small-business person in mind. While franchising does, indeed, involve giant restaurant and hardware chains that require large up-front cash investments, the franchise system also allows the small investor to start a business in any of a variety of profitable and interesting areas.

Why might a small-business franchise be your ticket to success? While no venture is risk-free, franchising allows you to pursue your dream with greater safety than a standard small-business start-up. If you choose your franchisor carefully, you join forces with someone who has already learned from his or her mistakes and can provide you with a proven system of doing business.

In addition, the small-business franchise allows everyone a chance at the gold ring. Retirees, young people, women, and minorities all enter on an equal footing. In his introduction to the *Department of Commerce's 1991 Franchise Opportunity Handbook*, Joe Lira, director of the Minority Business Development Agency, notes that franchising allows minority-owned businesses to enter the marketplace more easily than in the past. "There's no need to reinvent the wheel and undergo unnecessary costs to engage qualified entrepreneurs in the marketplace," Lira says. "The promise of franchising as a viable business development approach is now self-evident. It now accounts for one-third of all retail sales in the United States."

Whether your interest is in retailing, a service business, or even education, franchising may be your best route to success. We'll travel that route together in *Small-Business Franchises Made Simple.*

This book is divided into three parts: (1) the basics of franchising, (2) selecting your franchise, and (3) operating your franchise.

Chapters in Part I explain the franchise system as it exists in the United States, discuss the advantages and (sometimes significant) drawbacks of franchising, and offer a self-evaluation quiz to help determine if you have the personality, outlook, and experience that will allow you to operate a small-business franchise successfully.

Chapters in Part II lead you through the process of selecting a franchise and negotiating the deal. We'll spell out the basics of obtaining initial information about franchises, evaluating opportunities, setting the deal in motion, putting together a business plan, obtaining financing, and negotiating the franchise agreement. Part II also includes an overview of franchise law.

Part III contains detailed information about operating your franchise: locating the business, training employees, making the business grow, and coping with adversity. There's also a section on franchising your own independent enterprise.

In addition to leading you to sources of information about available franchises, we provide you with a directory of franchises that require a minimum investment of capital. You'll find that directory in Appendix A.

Throughout *Small-Business Franchises Made Simple*, we attempt to steer you away from potential hazards. While most of today's franchisors are reputable businesspeople, there are unscrupulous dealers, and we want you to have a safe and successful entry into the world of franchising.

PART ONE

THE BASICS OF FRANCHISING

CHAPTER ONE

What Is Franchising?

KEY TERMS FOR THIS CHAPTER

business-format franchising
conversion franchise
product franchising
system
trade-name franchising
turnkey operation

For most Americans, the word franchise conjures up an image of McDonald's Golden Arches or the smiling face of "Colonel" Sanders happily clutching a bucket of Kentucky Fried Chicken.

These are appropriate images, representing two of today's most successful franchised operations. Some of the big-name franchises aren't small businesses anymore. For example, it takes in the neighborhood of half a million dollars to start a McDonald's franchise. That kind of start-up capital is out of reach for many would-be entrepreneurs. However, there are literally thousands of opportunities requiring far less money on the front end, from pet stores to maid services, from auto repair shops to career counseling centers. This book will generally focus on these more accessible businesses.

Types of Franchises

Regardless of the type of product or service offered, some basic principles apply to all franchised businesses. First is the overall structure of franchising, which you must understand before you take your first steps toward becoming the owner of a franchise.

The term franchise originally comes

from the French verb *franchir,* meaning "to free." It literally means a freedom from some burden or restriction. Alternatively, it is a right or privilege. In modern commerce it has come to mean the right or privilege to conduct business using someone else's proprietary name and style.

The International Franchise Association (IFA) defines franchise as "a continuing relationship in which the franchisor provides a licensed privilege to do business, plus assistance in organizing, training, merchandising, and management in return for a consideration from the franchisee."

Franchising has actually been around for a long time, but most of us don't associate its earlier forms with what we think of as franchising today. Nevertheless, franchising has been a part of American business for over a century. The history of franchising began with the development of product and trade-name franchising. The most recent and most commonly recognized form is known as business-format franchising.

Product and Trade-name Franchising

Product franchising was started in this country in the middle of the nineteenth century; the Singer Sewing Machine Company was an early pioneer in the 1850s. Product franchising is a relationship in which a dealer signs up to sell a manufacturer's product under the manufacturer's name. The most common example is a neighborhood automobile dealership. Dealers maintain their own businesses, but take on a great deal of the identity of the manufacturer. That is, they are likely to display the manufacturer's name and logo in most of their operations and advertising. The manufacturer participates in the arrangement in order to establish a distribution network without investing its own money in showrooms.

Within broad limits imposed by the maker, dealers run their businesses any way they want to. You can see the differences when you walk into various car showrooms. Some are high-pressure operations where salespeople aggressively attack unwary customers, going to great lengths to negotiate a sale, while others are relatively low-key environments where a product is offered at a specified price, and some negotiation may be allowed, but not much.

Independently owned and operated soft-drink bottling companies are also product franchises, as are independently owned gas stations.

Trade-name Franchising

Trade-name franchising involves the use of an organization's name without the requirement that a particular product be involved. A retail store, for example, might be franchised under a certain name such as Western Auto or Ben Franklin, without being required to purchase all of its merchandise through the franchisor.

The Conversion Franchise

Another arrangement, known as the **conversion franchise,** is fairly common today. In this case, an existing business joins a chain of similar ventures operating under one franchisor. Century 21 real estate offices are a prominent example. Many Century 21 operations were previously independent real estate businesses. Their owners obtained the recognition and networking available through affiliation with a national chain.

Product and trade-name franchising have been around in a big way for years, and conversion franchising has been growing in popularity. But most of us don't think of them as "franchising." When we hear that term, we think of McDonald's and Kentucky Fried Chicken. These are examples of what is known as business-format franchising, which is the kind of franchise that interests most small-business people today.

Business-format Franchising

The essence of the **business-format franchising** arrangement is that an entire business operation is neatly delivered in a manageable package. The person going into business is known as the franchisee, while the organization providing the package is the franchisor.

The franchisee enters into the arrangement to get a ready-made business idea that has been successful in other places. The idea comes with a recognized name and a product or service that already has customer acceptance. There are instructions and diagrams on how to set everything up: signs, building designs, uniforms for employees, lists of required equipment, lists of approved vendors from whom to buy products, and equipment and much more.

Perhaps most important, the package comes with instructions on how to run the business. These instructions take the form of operating manuals and formal training; both are usually included.

A business-format franchise is very much a **turnkey operation,** meaning that the established business plans have been put in place, and all the franchisee has to do is "turn the key" to get the business running.

In summary, the business-format franchise provides the franchisee with not only the business idea, but with the **system** behind the business. By system we mean all of the knowledge, procedures, and practices that it takes to make the business work successfully.

The Value of the Business-format System

The concept of a ready-made system is tremendously important. The overwhelming majority of small-business failures aren't the result of bad business ideas. In most cases small businesses fail because the entrepreneurs don't know how to manage what they start. In a business-format franchise, the know-how comes with the package. This is an important reason why franchise failure rates are a fraction of those of unfranchised businesses.

A word of caution is also in order on this point. It is sometimes quite difficult for a prospective franchisee to determine whether a franchise opportunity does indeed provide an adequate system for running the business. Prospective franchisees must do a great deal of homework in this area. We'll talk more about how to evaluate a franchisor's system later.

Franchising in the Economy

The bulk of the sales made today through franchised businesses are in automobile retailing and gasoline sales. These are product and trade-name franchises that require a large initial investment. The fastest-growing segment of the franchise industry is the business-format franchise. It is also the most accessible for the average person who wants a career in small business. Restaurants are the most popular form of business-format franchising, followed by convenience food stores. Outside of these, the trend seems to be toward service businesses, such as travel agencies, maid services, and quick oil change service centers.

All forms of franchising together amount to roughly one-third of the retail sales in the United States, about $640 billion in 1988. Of this, auto dealers and gas stations accounted for a little over $507 billion. Roughly $133 billion came from business-format franchises, up from less than $30 billion in 1972.

Related, Nonfranchise Businesses

Certain business offerings look like franchising but aren't. A distributorship is a prime example. In a distributorship, a person has the right to sell the products of a particular manufacturer and use the company's name in advertising and promotion. In an exclusive distributorship the manufacturer agrees not to distribute through anyone else in the same geographic area. A distributorship agreement also may preclude the distributor from handling anyone else's product.

A distributorship isn't a franchise because the manufacturer doesn't help the distributor run his or her business. No guidance or training is offered, and the manufacturer doesn't receive a fee beyond the wholesale price of the product.

Some business opportunities offer a business idea and the chance to buy product but little more. These aren't franchises either. If you are looking for a franchise, you will certainly want to ensure that you are buying a genuine franchise.

Franchising and You

Many experts say that franchising is the wave of the future for small-business owners. This is due to the fact that our economy is increasingly dominated by large, powerful companies. Franchising is seen as the only way that small operators can match the name recognition, advertising clout, and operating efficiency of the big guys.

While it has much to offer, however, franchising isn't an automatic ticket to business success. Most franchisors demand hefty fees before you set up your small business and a continuing stream of royalty payments after you open. In fact, the total commitment from a small-business operator can be hundreds of thousands of dollars before the doors even open for business. In this book we will be concentrating on the smaller franchise opportunities, those in which the initial outlay is under $150,000, much of which can be borrowed from independent lenders or the franchisors themselves.

It is also important to realize that not all franchisors are reputable. There are plenty of smooth-talking operators who sell naive investors a package that doesn't exist. They collect the franchise fee and provide only a fraction of the promised support, leaving the franchisee with little knowledge and less in the way of profit.

Even reputable franchises don't always work out. There are numerous sources of confict between franchisee and franchisor, not the least of which is the loss of independence that is built into the arrangement. At the end of the day, a franchise owner doesn't get the satisfaction of saying "I did it my way!" You either do it the franchisor's way or not at all. Territorial disputes, advertising charges, and a host of other issues also can disrupt the relationship between franchisor and franchisee. (See Chapter 14 for a full discussion of some of these issues.)

Your Action Plan

Because of these potential problems, you must take the following precautions before entering a franchise agreement:

- Understand the concepts and mechanics of franchising.
- Know what franchise opportunities are available at approximately what cost.
- Know how to evaluate franchise offerings.
- Know how to determine if a match exists between your skills and desires and a particular opportunity.
- Know how to sell yourself to the franchisor.
- Understand the implications of franchise agreements.
- Know your rights under the law if things don't go as planned.

These and other parts of your action plan will be addressed throughout this book.

CHAPTER TWO

Why Franchise? The Pros and Cons

KEY TERMS FOR THIS CHAPTER

capital investment *franchise fee* *royalty*

Case in Point: Is a Franchise for You?

Will Donaldson has always wanted to run a restaurant. While not formally trained as a chef, he has worked in several restaurants, both in the kitchen and as a waiter. Moreover, he loves the work. Cooking is a challenge, and he enjoys personal contact with patrons.

However, Will has some serious concerns about opening a restaurant, primarily because he's heard that restaurants are extremely prone to failure. In his neighborhood, about eight out of ten restaurants have gone bankrupt within five years of opening.

It's a difficult situation: Will is forty; he has saved up $25,000 for his restaurant and knows he'll need to borrow $100,000 more. Naturally, he's worried about losing his entire stake. What worries him in particular is that while he knows cooking and service, there are many other things he doesn't know, such as how to meet health department codes, how to keep books, and how to administer a payroll.

What are his options? How can franchising help?

Small-Business Failure and the Franchise Concept

Business failure is a chilling fact of life for any entrepreneur. According to the Small Business Administration, almost a third of nonfranchised start-up ventures will go belly-up in their first year of operation. Another third will fail within five years. But fewer than 4 percent of franchised businesses are discontinued each year.

What accounts for the difference in failure rates? In large part, it's the fact that the entrepreneur who purchases a franchise purchases a system as well as a trade name and a product. He or she receives training, guidance in financial matters, and the added benefit of the franchisor's experience in helping to engineer dozens, hundreds, or perhaps thousands of similar start-ups across the nation.

In addition to buying a system, the small-business franchise owner buys the privilege of being part of a big business—meaning that the firm's reputation is already established and in many cases inventory will be available at the kind of bargain-rate prices usually offered only to large firms that buy in quantity. Also, the franchisor often handles national and regional advertising for the chain.

But while the operating principles of a franchise can work in your favor, they also can work against you. In this chapter we'll examine the pros and cons of dealing with a franchisor who sells you a system, the advantages and disadvantages to you when you buy that system, the ways in which the operating methods of a franchise can be restrictive to the individual entrepreneur, and some of the compromises that must be made when traveling down the two-way street of franchise operation.

Selling the System

When a firm sells you a franchise, that firm is essentially selling a method of doing business. The system—if it is a good one—is what makes the franchise successful. Why? Because the system provides comprehensive guidance in each and every facet of the business, as well as the advantages inherent in being part of a franchise network.

The Advantages of a Franchise

Let's assume, for example, that you're an expert on hardware; you know the nuts and bolts not only of nuts and bolts but of paint, building materials, plumbing, and every product connected with the business. Why, you might ask, should you pay a hefty fee and continuing royalties to become part of a nationwide chain? Here are some possible answers:

- You may be an expert on hardware but not be well versed in inventory control, advertising strategies, and employee benefits. You may not know how to set up a cash register system and keep the books. Each of these operations is as important to the success of a hardware store as knowledge of the product itself. A major franchise will help you put these business systems into place and provide you with training and continued support.
- As part of a national chain, you will be eligible to receive volume discounts. Wholesale prices are apt to be much lower

than if you were the sole proprietor of one small store.

• You'll have instant name recognition. Studies of consumer behavior show that people tend to consider standardization of goods and services a strong benefit. In the case of a hardware store, for example, it is likely that a typical consumer would feel more confident buying expensive tools at a True Value or Ace outlet than at Mom and Pop's World of Hardware.

• The links in a national chain of franchised stores have another advantage over Mom and Pop's: They are the beneficiaries of powerhouse national advertising campaigns. While individual franchise owners do, in the long run, pay for this advertising, they are buying into an advertising system that has proven its effectiveness.

• If you buy a well-known franchise, you generally are assured that the major chain will not open up a competing outlet in your territory. While there's nothing to prevent another chain or an independent operator from starting up a hardware store across the street, your status as a franchisee of a well-known firm will probably discourage competitors from locating in your immediate area.

• You're in for a much easier start-up if you sign on with a national franchise. Your questions will be not only answered but anticipated. The franchisor will know you need help in setting up your accounting system, selecting the site, outfitting the building, and hiring help. You'll receive training and assistance in all these matters.

Training is a vital factor in the franchise game, and will be examined in detail in Chapter 12. At this point simply remember that being part of a franchised chain means, in effect, that you do not have to reinvent the wheel every time you want to start a particular segment of the operation rolling.

Buying the System

Keep in mind that while a franchisor can sell a successful system, you must in fact buy that system. In other words, there's no free lunch. You're going to pay real dollars for the franchisor's name, methods, and expertise. Let's look at some of the considerations involved in making that purchase, including your capital investment in facilities, franchise fees, other start-up costs, advertising fees, and royalties.

Investment in Facilities

One of the primary costs in starting up a business is the **capital investment** in facilities. If you were starting on your own, you might choose to get by with the cheapest facility you could build, buy, or lease. Not so with a franchise: The franchisor generally will have strict requirements regarding the physical plant. Usually the owners of a franchise operation are concerned with its image (after all, image is part of the product they are marketing) and will not allow you to compromise that image with a tacky facility.

Some restaurant chains, for example, require that you invest in a high-quality building chosen from one of several designs. You cannot take liberties. The buildings must be designed to company specifications and are paid for by you. In some cases the franchisor retains ownership of the building and land, and the franchisee simply leases it over the life of the arrangement. Under those conditions, the franchisee pays the investment through the lease payment. In any event, the investment in facilities is difficult to recover if things don't work out as planned.

Franchise Fees

The initial payment for joining the franchisor's organization is called the **franchise fee.** This fee is designed to cover the franchisor's costs of recruitment and training, among other things. Franchise fees alone can be over $50,000. We're not implying that such fees are excessive, but they can be very significant expenses.

This book focuses primarily on low-cost franchises, requiring investments of as little as $2,000 to $3,000, so you need not be discouraged from franchising by the large fees charged by some of the major chains.

Other Start-up Costs

The franchise fee is only a portion of the up-front investment you'll be required to make. We've already discussed the investment in facilities. A multitude of other expenses are usually required before you can open the doors of a franchise. Much of the money can be borrowed, but the franchisee has to have a substantial chunk of assets. Burger King, for example, requires a franchisee to have as much as $300,000 in liquid assets available to get started.

While this may seem like an astronomical investment, remember that restaurants require large investments in facilities and equipment. In addition, the owners must be able to sustain a large payroll, pay for various permits and inspections, and buy a fairly large supply inventory.

Advertising Fees

As a franchisee, you'll often be expected to contribute to the national advertising effort. This might cost you 2 or 3 percent of your revenues. In addition, you will be expected to advertise locally.

Royalities

Finally, the franchisor will expect an ongoing fee based on your franchise's income. Such a fee, called a **royalty,** often is in the range of 5 to 12 percent of revenues. Keep in mind that the royalty is generally based on revenues, not profit. In a worst-case scenario you could be making $100,000 a year in revenues but spending $150,000 per year. Even though you are losing $50,000 per year, you will still be required to pay the royalty fees—which at 5 percent would be $5,000—to the franchisor.

Remember that while a franchise may involve considerable spending, it can be money well spent. If you generate a great deal of income because of name recognition, and your business runs efficiently thanks to the franchisor's business plan, it can be well worth paying the up-front fees and royalty payments in comparison to keeping all the revenue from a marginal business.

Restrictions

Franchisors impose many restrictions on their franchisees, ranging from the types of products they can sell to the design of the facility.

Let's assume, for instance, that you opened a franchised hamburger restaurant in a neighborhood in which you knew that wieners and sauerkraut would be an enormously profitable menu item. Perhaps you have several customers per day asking "What, no wieners and sauerkraut?"

In spite of this, you would probably not, under your franchise agreement, be able to offer your own menu item. Franchisors typically keep tight controls on the goods and services franchisees offer. This makes perfect sense, because standardization is what makes the franchise so appealing in the first place. Customers know what they are getting, and the national advertising campaign is geared toward selling exactly those items.

The uniformity expected of many franchisees goes beyond the nature of the inventory. You will be expected to maintain a certain level of service and sometimes will be subject to surprise inspections. If the idea of people with clipboards showing up unannounced to check on your personnel, your product, your accounting procedures, and possibly even the condition of your rest rooms bothers you, perhaps a franchise is not your best option.

Another advantage of the franchise system can turn against you: The control of your inventory supply may cost you money. While usually inventory can be purchased more cheaply because of the bulk buying power of the franchisor, things don't always work that way. An independent operator sometimes can take advantage of special sales available locally or opt for lower-quality supplies. But franchise agreements generally do not allow you to exercise these options.

Mutual Expectations

Both you and the franchisor are entering into a long-term relationship that may be made in heaven or hell. You must live up to certain standards right from the beginning. In addition to up-front cash, franchise operators will typically insist that potential franchisees have some relevant experience. They expect you to undergo fairly substantial training and pass their tests on product and service quality. They may even ask you to work for a time in an existing operation to learn the business.

If living up to someone else's expectations is exactly what you are trying to escape by opening a small business, then perhaps the franchise operation is not the ideal type of business for you. But also be aware that the benefits of the qualification standards work both ways. Often, the franchise is successful because it carefully screens prospective franchisees. In fact, if someone offers you a franchise contingent only on the availability of capital, your antennae should start tingling.

At best, a franchise that takes your money with no questions asked might be a shaky investment. At worst, it could be an outright ripoff. In either event, you could lose your life savings. One failed video-rental franchise scheme, for example, was headed by a man who happily took investors' money but failed to deliver on his promises. The national advertising campaign touted in the brochures never materialized. Support from headquarters was nil.

That's why it is imperative that both

you and the franchisor know each other and that the deal be based on a clear statement of what each party expects of the other. While you must bear the scrutiny of a franchisor's inquiry into your cash reserves, business experience, and character, you must insist on seeing a documented financial statement and a complete list of current franchise holders. (See Chapter 5.)

Case in Point Revisited

While franchising is no guarantee of success, it certainly seems appropriate in Will's case. He has a background in restaurant operation, but there's quite a bit he doesn't know. A properly selected franchise can fill in the holes in his background. He'll receive training in purchasing, inventory, and payroll, among other operations. Will knows his way around a kitchen and has experience in dealing with customers. These skills are vital for a restaurateur. If he was an expert in all other aspects of restaurant operation, perhaps an independent start-up would be appropriate. As it is, however, a franchise operation offers a much better chance of success.

CHAPTER THREE

Is Franchising for You?

KEY TERMS FOR THIS CHAPTER

decision making	*organizational abilities*
entrepreneurship	*self-starter*

Case in Point: Making the Big Decision

Josephine Costello has worked for a major corporation in an administrative capacity for fifteen years. She and her husband, Steve, have always dreamed of owning their own business. They see themselves traveling internationally, staying at the best hotels, and earning a great deal of money.

Jo is not an aggressive person and does not get along particularly well with other people. She supervises one employee but does not like the stress of dealing with her subordinate's problems.

Both Jo and her husband are relatively introverted. They enjoy spending time at home and do not enjoy their jobs a great deal. Nor do they like working long hours.

Steve has chronic high blood pressure; however, the condition is under control through medication. He was recently laid off and is currently unemployed. It was Steve who first brought up the idea of buying a franchise. Their thinking is that Steve would run the business initially with Jo maintaining her current job. After the franchise was making good money, she would quit and join him in running the business.

Is a franchise a good idea for the Costellos?

Self-evaluation

This chapter deals with self-evaluation. Read it carefully and take its message to heart—at a minimum it will help to prepare you for the problems ahead as you launch your franchised business. At the extreme, it may save you a lot of money and heartache.

Whether franchising is for you is really a two-part question. First you have to ask if small business is for you, and then you must focus on whether you'd be better off as a franchisee or as an independent business owner.

To put it another way, think of the world of business career opportunities as being divided into three categories:

- independent entrepreneur
- franchisee entrepreneur
- employee

Clearly there's a big difference between being an employee and an entrepreneur, but there's also a substantial difference between being independent and being a franchisee. A true entrepreneur doesn't do well as an employee but doesn't make a very good franchisee either.

Characteristics of an Entrepreneur

Let's talk about the broader distinction first. Should you be a small-business owner/entrepreneur or an employee? Try the following experiment. Over the next few days ask five or ten people a simple question: "Would you rather own your own business or work for someone else?" Don't explain in advance why you're asking.

Most people will respond that they'd rather own their own business. Yet only a small fraction of the population ever tries it on their own. If so many people would like to be small-business owners, why do so few actually take the plunge?

The reason is simple. When most people think of owning their own business, the image conjured up in their minds isn't consistent with reality. They imagine a successful entrepreneur relaxing behind a desk, enjoying independence, prestige, flexible hours, and wealth. Compared with their humdrum jobs, it looks pretty good.

In reality, the picture we just described is the end result of entrepreneurship—if it succeeds. The road to that success is much more arduous. **Entrepreneurship** generally means at least several years of long hours, hard work, financial sacrifice, and stress. And with all that, there's no guarantee of success.

As you read this book, you must make sure that you haven't fallen into the trap of projecting a successful conclusion without considering what you'll have to go through to get there. You must make sure you understand what you're getting into in the short run. With respect to franchising in particular, you must understand that it isn't a sure-fire route to the successful end. Franchising does improve your chances of success, but it certainly doesn't relieve you of the pressures of hard work and financial hardship.

Don't go into small business, franchised or independent, just for the end result. Go into it only if you are fascinated by the work and stimulated by the challenges you will encounter along the way, if the demanding life-style appeals to you and if you feel passionately about the business you're going to run. These are the traits that all entrepreneurs share.

The Entrepreneur Versus the Franchisee

The distinction between being a franchisee and owning one's own business hinges on the concept of independence. Franchisees really don't run their own show the way they want to; they run it the way the franchisor wants them to.

Many people hear those words but don't think through the implications. They think, "Oh, well, so all McDonald'ses look pretty much alike—no problem." But how would you react to an inspector from the franchisor showing up to check your rest rooms and kitchen? How would you feel knowing you could be put out of business if the inspector found your facilities wanting?

Or how about the franchisor insisting that you take $5,000 a month out of your pocket and spend it on advertising that you don't think you need? Or what if you have a great new product idea that you know will sell in your area, but the franchisor says you can't try it because it's just not consistent with the company's policy? These are common franchise restrictions. Not every entrepreneur can live with them.

This chapter will pose a number of questions designed to clarify whether you fit an entrepreneurial and/or a franchise profile.

The Franchisee Profile

The ideal franchisee is, no doubt, an entrepreneur. But he or she is also someone willing to take direction and operate in a relatively restricted business environment.

Over the years researchers have tried to identify the characteristics of successful entrepreneurs and franchisees. As a result, a number of questions or issues have emerged that the prospective entrepreneur should consider carefully. Your responses to these questions tend to indicate whether you have a background and personality consistent with a high probability of success in small business.

We pose some of these questions below; each is followed by a look at the implications of your answer. There are no correct answers, no score to be tallied at the end telling you whether to go for it or whether you'd be better off working for someone else. A test format would take away from the introspection that these questions are designed to stimulate.

As you answer these questions, think carefully about each issue. Record your answer, then read the explanation that follows the question. Mark those questions in which your answer indicates that you wouldn't make a good entrepreneur, and think about them again after having considered all the questions.

A preponderance of negative responses would indicate that you're not a good candidate for going into your own business. But if you're like most people, you'll fall in the middle range on most issues. In that case you may want to go ahead, but be especially careful that you really understand the nature and risks of small-business ownership. These questions can highlight the areas of entrepreneurship that will pose the greatest challenge for you.

A Self-Test for the Prospective Entrepreneur

1. Are you a **self-starter**?
   a. I generate work for myself and others.
   b. I am adept at solving well-defined problems.
   c. I complete any assignment in an outstanding way and look to my boss for the next one.

A small-business owner must have drive and initiative. He or she has to be the prime mover for getting things done day in and day out. Some people say that this is the single most important characteristic of an entrepreneur. Unfortunately, it's sometimes hard to know your own level of initiative if you've spent most of your career in a corporate job in which all of your work has originated from someone else. If you chose answer a and consistently generate your own ideas (even in a corporate setting), you have an advantage over those who wait for others to set their goals.

2. Do you like and get along with people?
   a. I have rarely met anyone I didn't like and respect.
   b. I have a few good friends, but have little interest in knowing a great many people.
   c. I'm not antisocial, but the great majority of people do not interest me.

People—primarily customers and employees—are the key to success in most small businesses. Business owners who don't genuinely enjoy interpersonal contact on a regular basis are at a distinct disadvantage. Most franchise opportunities are in service businesses where such contact is especially important. If you can honestly respond with answer a, you are better equipped to function in a small-business franchise.

3. Has your career so far been primarily in:
   a. Small business (less than 200 employees)?
   b. medium-size business (200 to 1,000 employees)?
   c. Large business (over 1,000 employees)?
   d. Government or nonprofit organizations?

The most valuable experience for your own small business is answer a, working in someone else's small business, especially in the same field. Big business and government experience can actually be a detriment, because the characteristics for success in those areas are often negatives in an entrepreneur. Further, the small-business environment must be experienced to be fully understood. If you've never been there, it's hard to know just what you're getting into.

4. Did you engage in business activity as a child/teenager?
   a. I started one or more businesses of my own.
   b. I worked all the time in a series of part-time and summer jobs.
   c. I worked when I had to.

Entrepreneurial drive shows up early; answer a is the most encouraging one. If you didn't have it when you were young, you're not likely to develop it later on.

5. How old are you now?
a. Twenties.
b. Thirties.
c. Forties.
d. Over fifty.

More successful entrepreneurs seem to start in their thirties than at other ages. This age seems to combine the requisite experience and know-how with youthful energy and enthusiasm.

6. Have you ever been fired because you didn't get along with your boss or because you found the environment stifling?
a. More than once.
b. Once.
c. Never.

Within reason, having been fired because of such difficulties is a good indication of the independence required in entrepreneurship. Entrepreneurs don't like working in someone else's structured organization, and they make waves about it. They often have trouble with authority and are vocal if they don't agree with the way things are done. Be careful though; an extreme history of firings can indicate a more serious problem. It also may indicate that you won't be able to live with a franchise relationship, which in many ways resembles working for someone else.

7. What is your main reason for considering your own business?
a. To be my own boss.
b. To earn prestige and recognition.
c. To get rich.

Answers a or b put you in the entrepreneur's profile. The most common characteristic of entrepreneurs is that they don't like working for someone else. They like to call the shots themselves. They also tend to be extroverts who crave recognition. Money is a bonus but of secondary importance.

8. How would you react if you started a business and it failed, costing you most or all of your savings?
a. I'd learn from my mistakes and start over.
b. I'd be very shaken but would eventually recover.
c. I'd be devastated. I don't know what I'd do.

Many, if not most, successful entrepreneurs have started more than once. Failure is a very real part of small business, and while franchising reduces the probability of failure, it doesn't guarantee success. It is essential that an entrepreneur be resilient. If you chose answer c, think hard about the possible consequences of owning a franchise.

9. What kind of gamble interests you the most?
a. A long shot with odds of 100 to 1 or more but with a payoff of 100 to 1 or more if you win.
b. A game in which the odds are against you (say 3 to 1) but in which you can improve your

chances of winning by developing your skill at the game.

Contrary to popular belief, entrepreneurs are not big risk takers. They don't like to gamble, but are willing to take calculated risks, as in answer b.

10. How much management experience have you had?
  a. Several years supervising a variety of people and projects.
  b. A little.
  c. None.

A small-business owner has to manage people to be successful. It's better to have made your managerial mistakes on someone else's payroll, as in answer a.

11. Do you become totally involved in your work, talking about it over meals with your family, to friends, and at parties?
  a. Yes, definitely.
  b. Mildly, but I'm not compulsive about it.
  c. No, I keep my business and personal lives separate.

The best entrepreneurs devote their entire energy to their businesses. They live, eat, drink, and sleep their business. If you don't do that and your competitor does, who do you think is likely to win? Answer a or at least b is the most positive indicator.

Some people don't have that kind of dedication, no matter what the situation. Some have it for whatever job they're doing at the moment. Some have it only for a certain field in which they're particularly interested. If you never experience an all-consuming affinity for work, think twice about small business. If you can generate this kind of enthusiasm only for a particular field, be sure that's the field your business is in.

12. Are you prepared to work eighty or more hours a week for an indefinite number of years?
  a. Yes and I'm excited about the prospect.
  b. Yes, if I have to, but I will look forward to the time when the business is secure enough for me to take it a little easier.
  c. No, that shouldn't be necessary except in the beginning. I'll work smart enough to put in reasonable hours.

Small business has been described as working sixteen hours a day to get away from an eight-hour-a-day job. Experience indicates that successful entrepreneurs work terribly long hours for many years before they get to relax. If you can't honestly choose answer a or at least b, you may want to rethink your plans.

13. When you engage in competitive activities (sports, games, etc.), what is most important to you?
  a. Winning.
  b. Playing with style, grace, and good sportsmanship.
  c. Enjoying yourself and getting a good workout.

Small business is an extremely competitive world. The best entrepreneurs focus on winning, on being better than the other guy.

14. Do you belong to and actively participate in church groups, civic organizations, social and fraternal clubs, political organizations?
   a. Yes, I'm a real joiner. I belong to five or more organizations. I go to meetings regularly, participate actively, and run for offices often.
   b. I belong to a few organizations but am not too active in most of them.
   c. No, I try to stay away from such activities as they take energy away from my work.

Successful entrepreneurs tend to be outgoing people who love social contact and genuinely enjoy meetings and groups, as in answer a. The contacts that they make in these groups are very helpful to their businesses. If you aren't already the joiner type, don't expect to change and become one when you start your own business.

15. Do you prefer to solve problems yourself, or are you comfortable with getting help and advice from an expert?
   a. I don't like reinventing the wheel. The first thing I do when faced with a problem is to look around for someone else who has already solved it.
   b. I work on things myself for a while and then look for outside help if I get stuck.
   c. I take pride in working out my own solutions to my own problems.

Effective businesspeople get the best answer as quickly as possible. That usually means looking to an expert—answer a—even if they have to pay for the advice. This is especially true in franchising, where expertise is the franchisor's largest contribution.

16. How do you handle getting several tasks done at the same time?
   a. I'm able to get a number of things under way at once, dividing my time between them. I'm able to switch my attention to the hottest item and then return to the others without losing much momentum. In fact, I enjoy the variety of having several things going at once.
   b. I find tasks yield to concentrated effort. I like to focus on one thing until it's completed, then move on to the next item.

Small-business ownership is a juggling act. You have to keep at least a dozen balls in the air all the time. If you can't divide your attention among several concurrent activities, you're almost certain to fail. Answer a is best, but this is a skill that can be learned.

17. How do you rate your **organizational abilities**?
   a. Great. I always know where I am and where I'm going, and I force the people under me to function in the same way.
   b. Fair to good. I generally know what's going on but occasionally get lost.
   c. I'm a mess.

The ability to organize people and tasks is extremely important for entrepreneurs.

A disorganized business is generally losing customers and money. If you cannot now honestly answer a or b, you probably won't become organized by buying a franchise.

18. How is your health and energy?
   a. I'm in excellent health. I have a great deal of energy and almost never get sick.
   b. I have an average level of health and energy.
   c. I have a significant health problem and am tired a lot.

Running your small business is going to be tough and stressful. If you don't have a great deal of physical and emotional strength and stamina—answer a—you'd better think twice.

19. Are you unemployed?
   a. No. I'm considering leaving my current job to start my own business.
   b. Yes, but I've been considering my own business for some time and would have quit pretty soon anyway.
   c. Yes, I was recently laid off and I thought I'd look into small business in general and franchising in particular while I'm also looking for another job.

Answer a is the most promising, while answer c can be a disaster. It's rarely a good idea to try to buy a job by starting a business or buying a franchise. If you weren't motivated to start an enterprise before you lost your job, you're probably not going to be a good entrepreneur now. In addition, getting fired can be a lot like getting divorced. You're very vulnerable for quite some time afterward, so be doubly careful before making any major commitments. (Don't confuse this with question 6. We're driving at a different issue here. It's one thing to have been fired in the past because you were too independent-minded, but it's not a good idea to think of small business as a way to create a job because you've just been let go.)

20. How do you handle conflict (as in negotiating with dissatisfied customers or firing employees)?
   a. I don't like it, but I get through it as quickly as possible and put it behind me.
   b. I rather enjoy conflict and winning by dominating others.
   c. I can't stand fights. I get through them, but it takes me days to recover emotionally.

Conflicts are a way of life in business, and in small business, the buck stops at the owner. There are conflicts with customers, suppliers, and employees all the time. In franchising, there's an added element: conflicts with the franchisor. An entrepreneur has to be able to deal with conflict and move on. Answers a and b are good indicators. Answer c may be a real problem. If you find conflict devastating, small business may be your route not to success but to a nervous breakdown!

21. How do you feel about authority?
   a. I like running my own show, but I can accept authority that I feel is legitimate.

b. I have to be able to do things my own way.

This is a key issue in franchising. A franchisee has to be willing to accept the franchisor's model of the business. If you sign the franchise agreement and can't do it the franchisor's way, you risk losing your investment. Answer a is best. It reflects an independent personality but not one so fiercely freedom loving that it cannot survive within a structure of rules. Those who chose answer b should think seriously about going it alone—without a franchise.

22. Can you make decisions?
   a. I can weigh the pros and cons and make a decision quickly. The outcome is usually pretty good.
   b. I make good decisions, but it takes me a long time. I will not be rushed in important matters.
   c. I'm uncomfortable making important decisions.

Decision making is what entrepreneurs do for a living. The ability to make reasonably quick choices and live with the outcome is an essential characteristic. Answer a is best; b is a poor second; c should raise a warning flag.

Case in Point Revisited

It should be obvious by now that the Costellos are not cut out for small business, either independent or franchised. They have a false idea of what entrepreneurship is like. They see a successful end result but have blinded themselves to the struggle involved in getting there.

Worse perhaps is the fact that they both have relatively low energy levels. Steve has a serious medical problem that would probably be made worse by stress. Further, neither has any appreciable supervisory experience.

On top of all that, Steve has just lost his job. There's strong evidence that he sees a franchise as a quick way to get back to work rather than going through the process of looking for another job. In addition, the vulnerability one feels after losing a job makes this a particularly bad time for the Costellos to make a major move such as buying a franchise.

PART TWO

SELECTING YOUR FRANCHISE

CHAPTER FOUR

Obtaining Basic Information

KEY TERMS FOR THIS CHAPTER

International Franchise Association (IFA)
Minority Business Development Agency (MBDA)
Service Corps of Retired Executives (SCORE)
Small Business Administration (SBA)

Case in Point: Starting the Search

Mel Crowley has always wanted to go into his own business, but unfortunately he's not expert in any particular field. He has a good business sense, supervisory experience, a background that includes teaching and training others, and an ability to work well with people. But he's stumped as to what business to enter. He's also a bit concerned about risk. Mel knows that most small-business start-ups fail, and he's in no hurry to do that.

At this point, he's a bit bewildered. What are the options?

Finding Reliable Information

A great deal of information relating to franchises is available, but not all of it is of equal value. Advertisements and sales material from the franchisor may or may not be reliable. Independently produced books and periodicals are generally objective, but their objectivity is no guarantee of accuracy.

In this chapter we'll provide you with a broad array of sources of information and explain how to start finding out more about particular franchises and franchising in general.

The Federal Government

When most people think of small business, they naturally think of the **Small Business Administration (SBA).** The SBA helps people who are planning to start their own business as well as those already in business. The assistance includes counseling and sometimes financial aid.

SBA Counseling

The SBA offers counseling through its specialists and through retired executives who are members of the **Service Corps of Retired Executives (SCORE)** program. The SBA offers various seminars and courses as well as some reference publications. Advice from the SBA can be useful, but there's no guarantee that the person giving the advice will be an expert in your particular business. The same applies to SCORE volunteers. That doesn't mean you shouldn't take advantage of SBA counseling; just regard the information you receive as the beginning and not the end of your search.

SBA Financial Assistance

Financial assistance from the SBA usually takes the form of loan guarantees, meaning that the SBA, in effect, countersigns your business loan at a bank or other lending institution. Such loans can be guaranteed for up to $750,000; the duration of the guarantee is seven years for working capital and up to twenty-five years for working assets (meaning real estate, fixtures, and equipment). The SBA provides few loans outright, and those are granted only under certain specified programs.

Thomas Tolan of the SBA Philadelphia office says that applicants for loan guarantees will need three-year financial projections for the franchise business, one-third of the cash investment, and proof of sufficient collateral to secure the loan. In 1992, according to Tolan, the SBA-guaranteed loans were qualified at 2¼ to 2¾ points above prime rate. Decisions, he says, usually are made within ten days.

Don't be reluctant to call the SBA. (See Appendix B for a list of SBA regional and district offices.) Remember, you've already paid for the advice with your tax dollars.

The Department of Commerce: The Minority Business Development Agency

The **Minority Business Development Agency (MBDA),** an arm of the U.S. Department of Commerce, publishes the *Franchise Opportunities Handbook.* (The government views franchising as an excellent opportunity for minorities to become entrepreneurs.) This handbook includes a section with general information about franchising, checklists of possible pitfalls, lists of other sources of information as well as governmental and private organizations that can help the franchisor.

Most of the directory consists of alphabetized listings of companies that have certified that they are equal opportunity franchisors. The listings provide summaries of the terms, requirements, and conditions under which the franchises are available. Listings are presented alphabetically categorized under forty-three headings. (See box below.)

Table 4.1 shows a sample page of listings from the *Franchise Opportunities Handbook.* Members of the International Franchise Association (see p. 28) are marked with an asterisk.

Be aware that the handbook is prepared by an independent contractor, not by the MBDA itself, and that the listing of a company in no way implies that the franchisor has been investigated or cleared by the U.S. government.

You can order the handbook through

TYPES OF FRANCHISES AVAILABLE

Here is a list of the forty-three categories in the Minority Business Development Agency's *Franchise Opportunities Handbook.* They will give you an insight into the scope of franchises available.

Automotive Products/Services
Auto/Trailer Rentals
Beauty Salons/Supplies
Business Aids and Services
Campgrounds
Children's Stores/Furniture/Products
Construction/Remodeling Materials/Services
Cosmetics/Toiletries
Dental Centers
Drugstores
Educational Products/Services
Employment Services
Equipment/Rentals
Food—Doughnuts
Food—Grocery/Specialty Stores
Foods—Ice Cream/Yogurt/Candy/Popcorn/Beverages
Foods—Pancake/Waffle/Pretzel
Foods—Restaurants/Drive-Ins/Carry-Outs
General Merchandising Stores
Health Aids/Services
Hearing Aids
Home Furnishings/Furniture
Insurance
Laundries, Dry Cleaning
Lawn and Garden Supplies/Services
Maid Services/Home Cleaning/Party Servicing
Maintenance—Cleaning/Sanitation—Services/Supplies
Motels/Hotels
Optical Products/Services
Pet Shops
Printing
Real Estate
Recreation/Entertainment/Travel—Services/Supplies
Retailing—Art Supplies/Frames
Retailing—Computer Sales/Service
Retailing—Florist
Retailing—Not Elsewhere Classified
Security Systems
Swimming Pools
Tools, Hardware
Vending
Water Conditioning
Miscellaneous, Wholesale and Service Businesses

TABLE 4.1
Franchise Company Data
***Denotes member International Franchise Association**

AUTOMOTIVE PRODUCTS/SERVICES

*** AAMCO TRANSMISSIONS, INC.**
One Presidential Boulevard
Bala Cynwyd, Pennsylvania 19004
Don Limbert, Director of Francise Development

Description of Operation: AAMCO centers service transmissions for all vehicles. Services include unique "Lifetime Warranty" for as long as customer owns car (honored at AAMCO centers throughout U.S. and Canada).

Number of Franchisees: 700 in U.S. and Canada

In Business Since: 1963

Equity Capital Needed: Approximately $48,000

Financial Assistance Available: To qualified applicants.

Training Provided: A comprehensive 5-week training course is provided at the company headquarters.

Managerial Assistance Available: Consulting and operations departments continually work with each center to insure proper operation. Technical training seminars and video tapes are available.

Information Submitted: April 1990

ABT SERVICE CENTERS
Division of ABT SERVICE CORPORATION
2339 South 2700 West
Salt Lake City, Utah 84119

Description of Operation: Alignment—Brakes—Tune-up repair centers which specialize in the one-day, high profit automobile and truck service needs. Guaranteed, fast, economical service performed in a "new" 8-bay facility, with the "right" equipment and the "right" training, is the backbone of this franchise. A strong managerial background is essential—training will provide the rest.

Number of Franchisees: 5 in 2 states

In Business Since: 1977

Equity Capital Needed: $51,000 (includes $10,000 operating capital)

Financial Assistance Available: Franchise includes 8-bay facility, signs, equipment, training with no need for additional equipment. Should a franchisee want additional equipment, financing through leasing companies, banks and ABT is available to qualified applicants. Franchisee must be financially qualified to guarantee construction.

Training Provided: 2 weeks will be spent in an ABT Service Center and at the company headquarters in Salt Lake City, Utah. This schedule will be increased if necessary. ABT operational people will then shift to franchisee's center for the training of his manpower. A grand opening will be prepared and held during this period.

Managerial Assistance Available: On a regular basis ABT personnel visit the franchisee to provide consultation in day-to-day operations and to analyze monthly progress. ABT provides operation manuals, training manuals, bookkeeping systems, insurance programs, advertising assistance and other management tools.

Information Submitted: April 1990

ACC-U-TUNE & BRAKE
2510 Old Middle Field Way
Mountain View, California 94043
Stan Shore, Chief Executive Officer

Description of Operation: ACC-U-TUNE & BRAKE centers specialize in automotive tune-ups, brakes, oil changes, air conditioning, state inspections, and other minor repair and auto maintenance services. Typical tune-up and complete lube, oil and filter change is less than $68, is done in about 1 hour while customer waits, and is guaranteed in writing for 12,000 miles. Prices include both parts and labor.

Number of Franchisees: 10 in California and 8 company-owned centers

In Business Since: 1975

Equity Capital Needed: $50,000 and approved credit rating

Financial Assistance Available: Total investment of $140,000; financial assistance available.

Training Provided: Extensive pre-opening training, classroom training (about 2 weeks) and 4 weeks on-the-job training. Training includes technical aspects of repair work, bookkeeping, marketing, customer relations, shop maintenance, sales.

Managerial Assistance Available: Complete technical manuals, advertising manuals, and operations manuals covering all day-to-day aspects of managing a profitable tune-up center.

Information Submitted: April 1990

*** ACTION AUTO, INC.**
2128 South Dort Highway
Flint, Michigan 48507
Richard A. Sabo, President

Description of Operation: Retail auto parts, service and gasoline store.

Number of Franchisees: 68 company stores in Michigan plus 2 franchises

In Business Since: 1976

Equity Capital Needed: Minimum investment of $140,000, excluding real estate.

Financial Assistance Available: None.

Training Provided: Retail sales and automotive repair—30 days (combination of classroom and store/service center).

Managerial Assistance Available: 7-week management program—time being spent in corporate office in the accounting, data processing, and personnel departments; distribution center; and store location.

Information Submitted: April 1990

AID AUTO STORES, INC.
475 Doughty Boulevard
P. O. Box 1100
Inwood, New York 11696
Philip L. Stephen, President

Description of Operation: Retail sales of automotive parts, tools and accessories.

Number of Franchisees: 88 in New York and New Jersey

any Government Printing Office, but the Boston office is one of the most efficient. You can call the Boston office at (617) 720-4180 and order by phone with a credit card; orders are mailed quickly. The cost is $16 plus a small fee for postage.

The International Franchise Association

Another must for your library is the *Franchise Opportunities Guide,* published twice a year by the International Franchise Association. The **International Franchise Association (IFA)** is a nonprofit trade organization representing more than 550 franchising companies in the United States and around the world. According to the U.S. Department of Commerce, the IFA is recognized as the spokesman for responsible franchising.

About the IFA

The IFA was founded in 1960 by a group of franchising executives who saw the need for an organization that would speak on behalf of franchising, provide services to member companies and those interested in franchising, set standards of business practice, serve as a medium for the exchange of experience and expertise, and offer educational programs for top executives and managers.

The IFA is highly selective in its membership. The association's Executive Committee must approve all memberships, and not all companies applying for membership are accepted. There are two membership categories: full membership and associate membership.

To qualify for full membership, a business must meet the following criteria:

- It must have a satisfactory financial condition.
- It must have been in business for at least two years.
- It must have at least ten franchisees, one of which must have been in business at least two years.
- It must have complied with all applicable state and federal full-disclosure requirements.
- It must have satisfactory business and personal references.

Full members are granted the use of the IFA seal in their advertising.

The associate membership category is reserved for companies that are new in franchising, that are considering franchising, or that cannot meet all of the requirements of full membership. Associate members may not use the IFA seal. They are admitted so that they can be guided by more experienced franchising companies. Like full members, their membership is contingent on adherence to the IFA Code of Ethics.

The IFA also offers international memberships to franchising organizations in other countries. Educational memberships are offered at low cost to business and law departments of colleges and universities.

The IFA historically has supported the principle of full disclosure of all pertinent information to potential franchisees. It annually distributes thousands of copies of its booklet, "Investigate Before Investing," which provides guidance for potential franchisees, and its Code of Ethics and Ethical Advertising Code are widely respected. The Small Business Administration, in its booklet "Franchise Index/ Profile," reprints the codes and the IFA's membership requirements and suggests: "It is worth a letter to the IFA requesting a copy of the International Franchise Association Membership Directory to determine whether or not the franchise you are interested in is a member. The codes themselves are reassuring."

The association traditionally has been an advocate of reasonable regulatory legislation and has actively supported legislation that would assure greater protection to potential investors. It provides thousands of persons and organizations with franchise information every year and has cooperated with the North American Securities Administrators Association (formerly the Midwest Securities Administrators Association) to develop a Uniform Franchise Offering Circular (see Chapters 5 and 7) to further uniformity in legislation and regulation throughout the states. The IFA believes such uniformity benefits the states, franchising companies, and potential franchisees.

One of the IFA's main functions is to keep members advised of changes in franchising law and regulation. The association holds an annual legal symposium, which covers franchise issues in depth, and a series of regional legal roundtable discussions covering specific legal aspects of franchising. The IFA works closely with legislators and agencies to develop laws and regulations that benefit franchising.

The IFA carries out an extensive educational program dealing with all phases of franchise management and operations. Educational meetings are held regularly throughout the year, both regionally and nationally. One of the IFA's new ventures is the establishment of an educational foundation to promote franchising courses in the nation's universities and business schools. The foundation also will provide research on franchising and act as a resource center.

A quarterly newsletter, *Franchising World,* is distributed to members and contains the most recent information about developing trends in franchising. Also circulated to IFA members is the *Current Legal Digest,* which contains updated information on the status of franchise legislation as well as summaries and analyses of the most recent decisions relating to franchising from the courts and administrative agencies. The association aims to make IFA membership connote the highest standards of business ethics and conduct.

Further information on the services and membership requirements of IFA and other organizations is provided in Appendix B.

The IFA *Franchise Opportunities Guide*

The *Franchise Opportunities Guide* lists franchisors by category. (The categories are quite similar to those in the *Franchise Opportunities Handbook*, as are the descriptive items listed.) IFA members receive larger, boldface listings in the front of each section. A useful section of the IFA guide is the "Council of Franchise Suppliers" listing, which details various firms and specialists—such as accountants, attorneys, advertising agencies, and bankers—that specialize in helping franchisors and franchisees.

While the IFA is an organization of franchisors, remember that franchisors cannot exist without franchisees, so much of what the IFA does entails some measure of mutual benefit. See Appendix B for information on ordering the guide and a catalog of IFA publications. The cost of the guide is $15 plus a small shipping charge.

What Happens Next

When you have located the franchises that look promising to you, write the company for further information. You'll receive a packet of documents and sales material. The contents of the packet will give you some initial insight into the franchisor. Interestingly, you can tell almost as much about the franchisor by reading between the lines as you can by reading the brochure. We'll tell you more about this process in the next two chapters.

Case in Point Revisited

After reading this chapter, you probably can see that there's a wealth of information available about franchising. Mel—the somewhat bewildered prospective businessman introduced at the beginning of this chapter—would probably be reassured by the availability of information on various franchises in a wide array of categories.

He also may find that he's not a bad prospect for franchising. Mel is fairly well qualified but doesn't have any particular expertise. Franchising's main appeal is that training is part of the package. By making himself an expert on the process of franchising and the kinds of franchises available, Mel can make up for his lack of expertise in any one particular business.

CHAPTER FIVE

Evaluating Franchise Opportunities

KEY TERMS FOR THIS CHAPTER

co-op advertising	*predecessor companies*
disclosure document	*sales brochure*
exclusive sales territory	*trademarks*
initial investment	*working capital*

Case in Point: Let the Buyer Beware

Ted and Dorothy Kaplan are both fifty-five years old. Ted has just retired from a career with the state government. They have $50,000 in their bank account and would like to start new careers as owners of a small-business franchise.

They've always been interested in the restaurant business, but realize they don't have the necessary capital to invest in the major franchise chains. Recently they came across an advertisement selling franchises in Bob's Rodeoboy Texas Barbecue restaurants. They called the 800 number and talked with Bob himself, who was enthusiastic and highly persuasive. Bob, whose headquarters was five hundred miles away, told Ted and Dorothy that he'd come to see them or they could come to see him.

Ted and Dorothy drove the five hundred miles to see Bob and toured his restaurant with him. Business was anything but brisk, but Bob assured them that it just happened to be a slow day. Bob showed them glossy brochures with pictures of packed Rodeoboy restaurants. He also gave them a printed sheaf of papers with small print called a disclosure document. The Kaplans looked at it briefly and filed it away for later study. Neither Ted nor

Dorothy were ever much good at paperwork, and they never did get around to studying the papers very carefully.

What particularly interested Ted and Dorothy about Bob's franchise was that they could get into business with a relatively small amount of capital. Bob said that their $50,000 was enough if they were willing to take out a loan collateralized by the equity in their home to fund the construction of the restaurant.

The first thing they had to do, however, was pay the franchise fee of $20,000. This was required before Bob could do anything for them. According to Bob, the fee paid for help in site selection, plans for the building's layout, training, and virtually unlimited help in running the business after it was open. Bob also said that there were two other people interested in a franchise in the Kaplans' area, and if one of those signed up first, Ted and Dorothy would be out of luck.

The Kaplans wrote Bob a check for the $20,000 on the spot, and returned home excited and enthusiastic about their new business. At home they began to look into real estate and bank loans. As they had expected, a local bank was willing to finance the project as long as they put up their home as collateral.

The first indication that all was not well came when Ted had a great deal of trouble getting Bob to visit and help in site selection. Eventually Bob did make a quick visit and recommended a corner lot after what seemed a very perfunctory survey.

The Kaplans have purchased the land and hired a building contractor who wants a number of questions about the plans answered before starting construction. Bob, however, is getting harder to contact. He doesn't return the Kaplans' calls, and when they do talk to him, he seems to put them off.

Ted and Dorothy are beginning to wonder just what they've gotten themselves into.

Researching a Particular Franchise

Once a prospective entrepreneur has decided that franchising suits his or her needs as a route to owning a small business, it's time to narrow the search to particular companies.

In the last chapter we discussed obtaining a broad base of information on a large number of franchisors. From this a would-be franchisee must select a limited number of firms for serious evaluation. Such an evaluation is time-consuming, so it is useful to narrow your list to three before attempting an in-depth analysis.

The first step of the study involves getting a feel for the franchisor's reputation and image. Start by asking around the industry for people who are familiar with the name. For example, suppose you are interested in a fast-food hamburger franchise but know you can't afford a McDonald's or Burger King. You come across a smaller outfit called BigBurger that seems a lot easier to get started, but you have never heard of it.

How do you begin to check out its reputation? Go down to your local McDonald's and ask the manager if she has ever heard of BigBurger. Find out who sells beef to fast-food restaurants and ask them. Call the Better Business Bureau in the town where BigBurger is headquartered and ask about its reputation. See if you can get a Dunn and Bradstreet credit report on the company. Call the Federal Trade Commission office in your area and see if any problems with the company have been reported. Check the International Franchise Association and see if the firm is a member in good standing. You can do all this while you're waiting for the material you've requested directly from BigBurger.

Be creative; ask anyone you can think of who may have any information on the company. It's amazing how quickly horror stories get around an industry. However, sometimes people are reluctant to say outright negative things to a stranger about a third party. In such a case, they'll be very hesitant to criticize, but they won't say anything positive either. Have your antennae tuned in for such responses.

You must, of course, contact the company you are interested in, and request information on its franchise program. The franchisor will generally send you a package of information by mail and also may contact you by phone. The information provided by the franchisor will include a list of active franchisees and ex-franchisees. Contact a few of them—they will be excellent sources of firsthand information.

Information from the Franchisor

The federal government and several state governments have explicit requirements regarding the information that franchisors must disclose to prospective franchisees. The information must be provided in what's called a **disclosure document.** In this chapter, we'll talk about the contents of the disclosure document and how to use it to evaluate the deal.

The Sales Brochure

The first mailing that a prospective franchisee receives from a franchisor may or may not include the required disclosure document. Many franchisors consider the federally required disclosures relatively private and send them out only after they have determined that the prospect is qualified. If that's the case, the first package you receive may be largely a **sales brochure.** It's apt to be slick and attractive, and will undoubtedly make the deal look very good.

The Disclosure Document

If, after reviewing your own findings and the initial sales information from the company, you're still interested in the franchise, follow up and get the next information packet, which will generally include the disclosure document.

You should never consider joining a franchisor's program until you've had plenty of time to evaluate the material in the disclosure document. Requiring disclosures is the government's way of protecting people from franchise confidence artists and from getting into deals they don't understand even with reputable franchisors. You must spend some time with this information, and use it wisely.

Disclosure documents must reveal roughly twenty categories of information to prospective franchisees. It is important that you study and understand the franchisor's statements in each area. Each category of information is designed to inform the reader either about the franchisor's history or about the nature of the proposed deal in areas in which abusive franchisor behavior is possible. But it is up to you to convince yourself that the information provided is true and that nothing is being held back. Therefore, you should use the disclosure statement as a starting point to ask questions of and find out about the franchisor.

A brief discussion of the implications of each of the disclosure items follows. Study these pages carefully before meeting with the franchisor's representative and certainly before making any commitments.

It should be obvious that your level of concern about truthfulness in disclosure will depend a great deal on who the franchisor is. A prospective franchisee dealing with McDonald's doesn't have too much to worry about, while someone dealing with an unknown franchisor should be very careful.

However, even when dealing with a big name, you must still ensure that you understand everything being disclosed; otherwise you may run in to some surprises. Here's an example: Some companies run outlets in the best locations themselves and only franchise outlying areas that are more difficult to run profitably. That means that you can't infer much about the success of your franchise from the general success of the business. A well-known income tax preparation firm operates in this way. As a prospective franchisee, you need to know that and factor it into your thinking about starting the business.

Timing of the Disclosure Document

An important feature of the disclosure rules involves timing. Written disclosure information must be presented at the first face-to-face meeting between the prospective franchisee and the franchisor's sales representative *or* ten business days prior to the signing of any contractual documents or the payment of any consideration (money) by the franchisee, whichever is earlier.

Furthermore, the franchisor's contract and all supporting agreements must be in the hands of the franchisee, completed and ready for signature, at least five days before the date of signature. The intent of these regulations is to prevent the sales representative from generating an artificial sense of urgency and rushing prospects into closings that they may regret afterward. It provides a cooling-off period before a firm commitment is made.

Disclosure Requirements

Disclosure documents must be prepared using one of two prescribed formats. One format is specified by the Federal Trade Commission (FTC); the other is called the Uniform Franchise Offering Circular (UFOC). A franchisor may use either format but not a combination of both. A few states do not accept the FTC format.

The formats are similar with respect to the information they require to be disclosed. The following twenty items represent the substance of the government disclosure requirements about which the franchisor must disclose information.

1. The franchisor, its affiliates, and any predecessor companies. This section identifies exactly who is involved in the deal and any other companies owned by the franchisor.

The franchisor is usually a separate legal entity set up to handle only franchising operations. That is, it is legally separate from the successful business that is being copied. Since franchisees have no dealings with the original business, this arrangement protects it from liability resulting from problems in franchising operations. There's nothing wrong with this arrangement, but it can cause confusion with respect to who owns what, what they're doing, and how long they've been at it.

In this section the franchisor must identify any businesses out of which the franchise operation has grown. These are known as **predecessor companies.** The franchisor also has to give the names and addresses of any affiliated businesses of the parent of the franchisor company.

The information about predecessor companies is important. It should reveal how long the person behind the franchise has operated this **or similar** companies. It should also indicate whether earlier incarnations of the business have failed.

If a pattern of failure emerges, watch out. Some unscrupulous businesspeople set up a business, run it for a short time, drawing out a great deal of cash, and then bankrupt it, leaving a pile of unpaid bills. They then go on to start another business. If the franchise has been developed out of a series of businesses that have been closed down, you may not want to get involved.

2. Business experience of key people on the franchisor's team. This section requires disclosure of the business experience over the last five years of the franchisor and of the key officers, directors, and managers of the franchisor company (generally limited to people with direct responsibility for franchising operations). The disclosure should include all work experience, whether related to the franchised activity or not.

It is important to understand just how much relevant experience the franchisor's people have. After all, they are claiming to be experts in the business field being franchised.

3. Litigation history. This section requires disclosure of any legal proceedings involving violation of franchise law, fraud, embezzlement, or unfair business practice by the franchisor company or any of its key people.

This is a delicate area. Only certain kinds of legal proceedings must be included. The law is aimed at disclosing actions alleging fraud, but other types of action may be omitted even though they might indicate an unsavory past. In California, state law actually prohibits listing any criminal record.

4. Bankruptcy history. This section requires disclosure of any bankruptcies of the franchisor company, its predecessor companies, or any of the key people involved in franchising operations. Disclosure is required for the past seven or fifteen years, depending on which format is being used.

Note: You should read items 2, 3, and 4 with caution. Because of the intricacies of the law and the time limits involved, it is entirely possible for relevant information to be legally omitted from the disclosure document. By "relevant" we mean information that could make a difference in a prospective franchisee's choice.

You should pointedly inquire about the entire history of every key individual on the franchisor team. Be especially diligent in ferreting out a history of bankruptcy for the individuals or for companies they control. A bankruptcy always means some creditor or investor was left holding the bag. You don't want it to be you the next time. If the franchisor or other personnel give vague responses or seem annoyed at such information requests, they may have something to hide.

5. Description of the franchise. The disclosure statement must offer a detailed description of the nature of the business being franchised, including products, services, customers, methods of operation, and business format. A discussion of the competition is also appropriate.

6. Initial fee or payment. This section requires specific disclosure of the full amount that the franchisee is required to pay at the front end of the arrangement. This is generally the franchise fee itself but may include some other sums for equipment, site, or training. The franchisor must specify how the fee is to be paid—in a lump sum or installments—and whether any of it is refundable. Watch out for terms such as fully earned. A statement that the fee is fully earned by the franchisor upon receipt means that it is not refundable even though the franchisor has done nothing to earn it yet.

7. Other fees. The franchisor is required to disclose all other fees that the franchisee is expected to make, whether to the franchisor or to a third party. The primary recurring fee in franchising is the royalty, which is usually a percent of revenues, but there are often others. A contribution to a **co-op advertising** (advertising usually controlled by the franchisor but paid for by contributions from franchisees) fund is common and usually recurring. Other expenditures include fees for equipment, real estate, site selection, and training. The obvious objective here is to prevent the franchisee from being surprised by unexpected outlays.

8. Entire initial investment. The franchisor should estimate the entire **initial investment** that will be necessary to get into business. This should include monies paid to the franchisor and related parties as well as amounts paid to third parties. For example, suppose the franchisor sells franchisees certain equipment and provides a site selection advisory service but does not get involved in the acquisition of the franchisee's real estate. The equipment would be listed as payable to the franchisor, while the real estate would be listed as payable to a landlord, with some estimate of the cost in the area under consideration.

Franchisors are not required to include **working capital** in this list of requirements. Working capital is essentially the money you have tied up in inventory and receivables less what you owe to vendors. In some businesses it can be substantial. If this item has been omitted, you should ask the franchisor for an estimate. Leaving working capital out makes the initial investment seem lower and the opportunity more attractive than it really is.

9. Obligations to purchase or lease from designated suppliers, from an approved list of suppliers, or in accordance with specifications. At one time franchisors could require that franchisees purchase product or equipment from their own firms or from designated sources with whom they were affiliated. Such arrangements were ripe for abuse, offering franchisors the chance to price the products they supplied to yield an exorbitant profit. Alternatively, they could have an affiliated supplier price in a kickback to the franchisor at the expense of the captive franchisee.

Such arrangements are now difficult under the law, though they are still possible. If a franchisor wants to require a franchisee to buy from a specific source, he or she must prove that the designated product is unique and thus essential to the business. That's hard to do for most commonplace products such as hamburgers.

The common practice today is for franchisors to require that product and equipment meet their specifications but let franchisees pick their own vendors. Alternatively, franchisors can provide a list of approved vendors, all of whom meet the required specifications, from which franchisees can choose.

All such arrangements must be disclosed in this section. Specifically, if any consideration is given to the franchisor by a supplier based on purchases by franchisees, it must be disclosed here. This would include cash payments, product in lieu of cash, or rebates of any kind.

The franchisor should discuss the reasons for the specifications, how they may change from time to time, and how approved suppliers are chosen.

10. Financing. Franchisors sometimes offer financing to help franchisees get into business. They can do this themselves or through a third party, usually a bank. If the deal is made through a bank, the franchisor may receive some consideration. The details of any financing arrangement should be disclosed in this section.

11. Obligations of the franchisor. This section addresses what the franchisee can expect in return for the required fees. The franchisor's service can generally be divided into two areas:

- services and assistance prior to opening
- services and assistance after opening

Major service issues prior to opening include the level of help provided in site selection and the nature of the franchisor's training program.

Site selection assistance varies: Some franchisors insist on picking the location, others simply approve a location chosen by the franchisee. Most business-format franchises tend to be retail business, and location can be vitally important. It is in this critical area that franchisors usually purport to be experts.

Training is the other essential ingredient in the franchise pie. It is through the franchisor's training program that the franchisee hopes to learn the secret of the business's success.

This section must disclose the full details of both these issues. A prospective franchisee is advised to pay a great deal of attention here. If the disclosure document glosses over this area, the franchisor probably doesn't have much to offer in the way of services. That is a strong indication that the franchise may not be worth considering.

The franchisor is also required to estimate the cost of any services not covered by the franchise fee. Typically the cost of travel and living during training is an incremental expense not covered elsewhere in the fees projected by the franchisor.

12. Exclusive territory and sales restrictions. The franchisor must state whether the franchisee will have an **exclusive sales territory.** An exclusive territory simply means that the franchisor will not sell another franchise or open a company-owned unit in that territory for the duration of the agreement. It's important to understand, however, that this arrangement doesn't prevent the franchisor or franchisee in another territory from selling into your territory. It's illegal under the antitrust laws to prohibit that.

A franchisee's exclusive hold on the territory is usually predicated on maintaining a certain volume of business there.

Restrictions on what the franchisee can sell also must be disclosed. For example, most food service franchises limit menu items to an approved list to ensure consistency among franchised outlets.

13. Trademarks, symbols, patents and copyrights. Registration information about **trademarks** and commercial symbols and the franchisee's right to use them must be provided. Any litigation going on must be disclosed as well.

A recognized trademark is an important element in the franchise concept. A franchisee's inability to such symbols could be a significant problem. The UFOC format requires the disclosure of information about patents and copyrights that are material to the franchised business, while the FTC format does not.

14. Obligation of the franchisee to actively participate in the business. Some franchisors allow individuals to purchase franchises as investments to be run by hired managers. Others insist that their franchisees be owner-operators, believing that there is no substitute for the enthusiasm of an entrepreneur. If this restriction applies, it must be disclosed here.

15. Modification, renewal, and termination of the franchise. This section requires disclosure of the conditions under which each party may terminate the relationship. It is particularly important to understand when the franchisor can modify or terminate the agreement. Lack of clarity in this area results in a great number of lawsuits. Here are some relevant questions:

- If the franchisor unilaterally raises the royalty fee, can the franchisee terminate the contract and not forfeit the right to continue the business independently?
- If the original contract was for ten years and everything is going well at the end of that time, does the franchisee have a right to renew or can the franchisor end the arrangement?
- If the franchisee wants to retire, can the business be sold to anyone, or must it be offered to the franchisor first? If so, at what price?

The answers to questions like these must be disclosed in this section.

16. Public figure involvement. The names of celebrities are sometimes used to market franchises. When this is done, the exact nature of the involvement of the public figure must be disclosed. Disclosure includes the compensation received by the individual for the use of his or her name, any ownership the individual has

CHECKLIST

This checklist, adapted from the Department of Commerce's Franchise Opportunities Handbook, can be helpful in structuring your analysis of one or more franchise opportunities.

The Franchise

1. Did your lawyer approve the franchise contract you are considering after studying it paragraph by paragraph?
2. Does the franchise call upon you to take any steps that are, according to your lawyer, unwise or illegal in your state, county, or city?
3. Does the franchise give you an exclusive territory for the length of the franchise, or can the franchisor sell a second or third franchise in your territory?
4. Is the franchisor connected in any way with any other franchise company handling similar merchandise or services?
5. If the answer to the last question is yes, what is your protection against this second franchisor organization?
6. Under what circumstances can you terminate the franchise contract and at what cost to you, if you decide for any reason at all that you wish to cancel it?
7. If you sell your franchise, will you be compensated for your goodwill, or will the goodwill you have built into the business be lost by you?

The Franchisor

1. How many years has the firm offering you a franchise been in operation?
2. Has it a reputation for honesty and fair dealing among the local firms holding its franchise?
3. Has the franchisor shown you any certified figures indicating exact net profits of one or more going firms that you personally checked with the franchisee?
4. Will the firm assist you with:

   a. A management training program?
   b. An employee training program?
   c. A public relations program?
   d. Capital?
   e. Credit?
   f. Merchandising ideas?

5. Will the firm help you find a good location for your new business?
6. Is the franchising firm adequately financed so that it can carry out its stated plan of financial assistance and expansion?
7. Is the franchisor a one-person company or a corporation with an experienced management trained in depth (so that there would always be an experienced person at its head)?
8. Exactly what can the franchisor do for you that you cannot do for yourself?
9. Has the franchisor investigated you carefully enough to assure itself that you can successfully operate one of its franchises at a profit both to it and to you?
10. Does your state have a law regulating the sale of franchises, and has the franchisor complied with that law?

You—the Franchisee

1. How much equity capital will you need to purchase the franchise and operate it until your income equals your expenses? Where are you going to get it?
2. Are you prepared to give up some independence of action to secure the advantages offered by the franchise?
3. Do you really believe you have the innate ability, training, and experience to work smoothly and profitably with the franchisor, your employees, and your customers?
4. Are you ready to spend much or all of the remainder of your business life with this franchisor, offering this product or service to your public?

Your Market

1. Have you made any study to determine whether the product or service that you propose to sell under franchise has a market in your territory at the prices you will have to charge?
2. Will the population in the territory given you increase, remain static, or decrease over the next five years?
3. Will the product or service you are considering be in greater demand, about the same, or in less demand five years from now than today?
4. What competition already exists in your territory for the product or service you contemplate selling?
   a. Nonfranchise firms?
   b. Franchise firms?

in the company, and the extent to which the individual may participate in the business.

17. Financial information of the franchisor. The franchisor must provide audited financial statements for the past three years. These include income statements, balance sheets, and statements of cash flow, which must have been audited by a certified public accountant. Don't confuse these with financial statements for a franchisee or projections for your business. These are the finances of the franchisor.

A very weak set of statements might give you pause about becoming part of that business.

18. Statistical information concerning franchisees. The franchisor must disclose the number of franchisees currently active and the number that have been either canceled—voluntarily or otherwise—or not renewed in the past year. In addition, the number of franchises sold but not yet in operation is required, as well as a projection of the number of units expected to be in operation by the end of one year.

The required disclosure includes the names and addresses of active franchisees. Contact a few of these on your own; don't just talk to the ones the franchisor introduces you to. It's also a good idea to talk to ex-franchisees. Find out why those people are no longer with the organization. Be especially careful if there seems to be a high turnover. It may indicate problems in working with the franchisor.

19. Franchise contractual documents.

A sample of all contractual documents that will eventually have to be signed must accompany the disclosure document.

20. Earning claims. A franchisor does not have to make any claim or statement regarding the likely earnings of a prospective franchisee. However, if such a claim is made, the basis for the projection must be disclosed in detail. That is, the disclosure must spell out the assumptions underlying the levels of sales and expenses in the earnings projection.

This is an important item. Franchise salespeople often imply that the franchises are much more profitable than they are. It's not unusual, for instance, for a franchise salesperson to quote a particular unit's performance. The unit chosen is generally among the most successful in the company. Unfortunately, that performance may not be representative of what a new prospect can expect to achieve.

You should always be on the lookout for such puffery. It happens even with otherwise reputable organizations. Insist on seeing documentation that reveals the profitability of an average operation. Even more important, you and the franchisor should try to make a realistic estimate of likely profitability given the area in which you expect to be working.

These items constitute the bulk of the disclosures required by the federal law. Some states have laws that may be more demanding than the federal rules; if that is the case in your state, the stricter rules apply. Some states also require franchisors to register before selling franchises in that state. There are no federal registration requirements.

In states where registration is required, the government may do some checking of the disclosure document, but depending solely on the government's research is unwise. In general, no one checks the validity of the information in the disclosure. As the franchisee, you are ultimately responsible for your own protection from vague or inaccurate claims.

Case in Point Revisited

Ted and Dorothy Kaplan seem to be learning an important lesson the hard way. Had they paid as much attention to the disclosure document as they did to the glossy brochure, they would have noticed that several of Bob's restaurants had failed in the past. They could then have asked him exactly what happened.

While Ted and Dorothy were visiting the restaurant, they failed to check around the neighborhood. Had they struck up a conversation with the dry cleaner across the street, they would have learned that the day they visited was not a slow day—Bob's never has much business.

In addition, had the Kaplans checked with some of Bob's franchisees, they would have found that others had had similarly negative experiences; they would have learned, the easy way, that Bob was primarily in the business of collecting franchise fees.

CHAPTER SIX

Making It Happen

KEY TERMS FOR THIS CHAPTER

initial inquiry	*motivation*
initial visit	*profile*

Case in Point: Is It Worth the Effort?

Jon Whethers has wanted to own a business brokerage for some time. He is intrigued by the process of valuing and then handling the buying and selling of companies and has always envisioned himself as a business consultant. Jon has a good commercial background, having worked as an accountant for two firms. When one of these firms was sold to a larger company, he participated in the financial end of the deal.

Jon looked through some directories and advertisements and located the Apex Business Brokerage Company, which offers franchised brokerage operations.

He wrote away for more information and received a large package by return mail. Its contents were somewhat surprising: It offered some information about Apex but asked for more about him. There was a whopping collection of forms to fill out, asking for some personal information about his background and financial situation. Further, he was asked to write an essay about his qualifications for the brokerage business.

Jon was shocked. It could easily take two full days to complete the forms. He wasn't used to being tested in order to buy something. What's the story?

An Overview of Getting Started

Suppose you've decided that franchising is for you, and you are ready to search seriously for the right franchisor. We've said a lot about qualifying the franchisor—that is, making sure the franchisor is right for you. But you also have to be sure that you're attractive to the franchisor. Good franchisors won't take on just anybody as franchisees. In order to be sure that you put your best foot forward when approaching prospects, let's look at the entire process of getting started and developing a franchise relationship:

- The basic process of the first inquiry
- How a franchisor evaluates you
- Your first contact with the franchisor

The First Inquiry

Your *initial inquiry* can be one of two basic types: You can respond to an advertisement by a franchisor, or you can make an inquiry of a franchisor who is not actively advertising but is listed somewhere in your source materials.

Evaluating Advertising

If the franchise is advertising for franchisees, that may be a bad sign. We emphasize *may* be; reputable and profitable franchisors advertise all the time, but many of the best franchisors don't need to advertise. Prospective franchisees actively seek them out, and they have more applicants than opportunities.

So scrutinize any advertisement very carefully. If it is written in honeyed language, touting the franchise in glowing terms and projecting what seem like unrealistically large profits—watch out. Legitimately profitable franchises have no need to exaggerate their claims or lard their sales pitches with superlatives.

One red flag to watch out for when you peruse ads for franchises is the overly broad appeal. Any ad that says, "Be president of your own company, king of the hill, and make enormous profits . . ." without telling you what the company is probably reflects a firm more interested in your money than in franchising a legitimate business.

Now, don't interpret this to mean that any franchise that doesn't advertise is a good bet. That's simply not so. But franchising is a peculiar business, in which an easy sell on the part of either the franchisor or the franchisee can spell trouble. Put more plainly: You don't want a franchisor who will take just anybody, and a legitimate franchisor doesn't want to sell to just anybody with a checkbook.

Writing Your Inquiry Letter

Should you find an ad or listing that piques your interest, it will provide an address and possibly a phone number. Don't just dash off a note saying "Send me all your stuff." This is a critical juncture in the franchisor's evaluation of you, and you want to make a good first impression. It's best, at this point, to write a letter that gives an impression of professionalism, describing yourself and your interest in the business.

In your letter, emphasize your strong points. From a franchisor's viewpoint, experience in the following areas is desirable:

- Management
- Teaching/training
- The field in which you are seeking a franchise
- Sales
- Small business

Your educational background is also important. The value of most of these qualifications is fairly obvious, with the possible exception of teaching/training. Franchisors in general look favorably upon applicants with some teaching in their backgrounds, because instructing employees is an important part of running a small business. Further, people who teach well tend to learn well themselves.

There are some qualifications you should probably not stress when dealing with a franchisor. For example, franchisors tend not to respond well to people with long experience as first-line supervisors of workers for large industries or business; they'd rather have someone with experience higher in the ranks of management or with small-business management experience.

Oddly, the consummate entrepreneur is not likely to be particularly welcome as a franchise applicant. Why? Because such a person might not take direction well. Some entrepreneurship is welcomed, but too much stress on your desire for independence may be viewed negatively by the franchisor.

Be sure that somewhere in the letter you speak of your high level of **motivation**. Say that you understand that the business will entail hard work and that you are willing to follow that path.

It also can be a good idea to do a little homework and tell the franchisor why you think your area would be a good one for the franchise. Check out the local demand, competition, and economy.

One caution: Avoid talking finances in the initial letter. This is not the time to bring up your capability to invest. You don't want to give away your cards now, because there may be considerable flexibility on the franchisor's part regarding financing if you are otherwise an attractive candidate. That flexibility will be lost if you tell the franchisor up front that you don't need financial help.

The Franchisor's Information Packet

What happens next? You will probably receive a return mailing that fits into one of two general types:

- A heavily sales oriented package that touts the franchise and asks relatively little about you.
- A package that presents a small amount of sales material and asks for a great deal of information about you.

The second type of package may actually be the more promising indicator of a desirable business. The franchisor has a legitimate need to know about you. He or she wants a franchisee who will reflect well on the business and contribute to its success. A request for relevant information and a commitment of time and effort on the part of the applicant is a good indication that the franchisor is a serious businessperson looking for serious, capable partners.

The package of forms you receive will probably resemble an employment application and will ask you for financial information. You may even be asked to write a brief essay. Each area of questioning serves a purpose: A legitimate franchisor will want to ascertain that you have a decent employment record and stable finances, and that you can express yourself clearly when it comes to business matters.

Why are you being put through these hoops? Because franchisors want you to sell yourself to them.

Aside from the legitimate need for more information, the packet of forms is something of a test and should be regarded as a positive factor. The franchisor does not want to become involved in a working relationship with someone who is not willing to invest a few hours in preparing an application.

After returning the forms, you'll probably receive more sales material and the disclosure documents. Now you're in a position to decide whether a personal visit is in order.

First Contact with the Franchisor

While it may be convenient for you if the franchisor offers to transport you to company headquarters and lodge you at company expense for your **initial visit,** this is not necessarily a positive sign. The all-expense-paid trip is often a tool in a high-pressure sales pitch and can be used to instill a sense of obligation in a prospect. A good franchise usually does not use such high-pressure sales tactics. A franchisor who demands that you pay for your own trip may be testing your commitment.

Using the Visit to Your Advantage

The first visit to the franchisor is your opportunity to get more information on the business. Ask tough questions. Play hardball. A legitimate franchisor is going to like that, because it shows that you're an astute businessperson, the kind he or she wants on the team.

Be sure to ask about the job histories of all the principals in the franchisor's group. Ask about bankruptcies or other legal problems of the principals. (Remember, there in some circumstances such information can be omitted from the disclosure document; you want to ferret out any of these details during the visit.) Will the franchisor be upset by your aggressive questioning? If so, that's a bad sign. A legitimate franchisor should expect to undergo the same grilling that is imposed on you.

Much of your initial or secondary visits will be devoted to negotiation. (See Chapter 10.) But a top priority when you first meet is to see if you and the franchisor mesh in terms of expectations. Come right out and ask if the firm has a **profile** of an ideal franchisee. It's better to find out in the beginning if there's a problem rather than be surprised down the road.

Why ask for a profile? Because franchisors sometimes have hidden agendas and expectations that you won't be informed of unless you ask. For example, does your experience in the restaurant business help you in your bid to obtain a fast-food franchise? Maybe not. Some fast-food franchises don't favor ex-restaurateurs because, in their eyes, it takes too long to untrain people who have developed what the franchisor feels are bad habits.

Sometimes franchisors will be candid about their biases: "We're looking for people in their mid-thirties, preferably with no children. . . ." Other franchisors will fear running afoul of discrimination laws by admitting to any sort of bias in the selection process. But use common sense: You know that these biases exist and that a franchisor does not have to let you buy in, so don't charge down dead-end streets. If you're very overweight, for example, a franchisor is not likely to sell you a weight-loss center franchise.

Finally, when you visit the franchisor, be wary of any sense of artificial urgency. If you are led to believe that you must act immediately, you may be better off letting the opportunity pass. Legitimate franchise deals rarely must be accomplished so quickly. This is a life-altering commitment for a franchisee. Don't make the decision under pressure.

Case in Point Revisited

Jon has run into a tough franchisor—tough in the sense of wanting only motivated and qualified franchisees. Apex is probably using a reverse selling technique to ensure that only the best candidates show up at their door. If Jon wants to play, he'll have to do it by their rules.

CHAPTER SEVEN

Franchising and the Law

KEY TERMS FOR THIS CHAPTER

antitrust laws	*price discrimination*
conspiracy in restraint of trade	*pricing fixing*
exclusive dealing contract	*refusal to deal*
fraudulent misrepresentation	*rule of reason*
monopolization	*tying agreement*
per se	

Case in Point: A Pricing Problem

Denise Hofstadt has been operating a Merrily Modern Miss Dress Shop franchise for five years and is doing reasonably well. Merrily Modern Miss recently sent a letter to all franchisees informing them that the company was shifting to a discount mode of operation. This involved a reduction in customer service and price cuts of approximately 30 percent below current levels. Merrily Modern Miss is confident that the expense savings and additional volume will make up for the loss in unit profits.

Denise, however, is very concerned. Her franchise is located in an upscale shopping center. She feels that a discount approach will not draw any new customers in her area. Worse than that, she's sure some of her current customers will stop coming in, since they are well-to-do women who are very status conscious and wouldn't be caught dead in a discount store.

Denise feels that the letter is threatening in tone. It "suggests" price decreases and hints at "franchise renewal problems" if the new policy is not accepted.

Does Denise have any options other than complying with the franchisor?

The Franchise Relationship in Summary

In order to understand how franchise law works, we need to have a clear picture of the nature of the franchising relationship and what is generally expected from both parties. Then we can see how abuses arise—that is, how one party can take advantage of the other.

Once we understand where and how unfair practices occur, we can look at the law and see how it attempts to prevent those unfair dealings.

Finally, we can assess how effective or ineffective the law is apt to be in protecting us from being cheated.

Let's begin by summarizing the franchise relationship, especially with respect to business-format franchises. The arrangement begins when the franchisor offers a more or less turnkey business to prospective franchisees.

The business may involve selling products made by the franchisor, but it doesn't have to. What the package does include is a recognizable logo or trade name and a documented system for marketing the product or service and operating the business. The franchisor must also offer a **continuing relationship** in which advice and management assistance are given to the franchisee in the day-to-day operation of his or her business.

In return for this the franchisee pays the franchisor an initial franchise fee and a continuing royalty, which is usually a percentage of revenues (and also often makes a contribution to a common advertising fund).

Benefits to Each Party

Why does each party participate in this arrangement? As we've already discussed, the franchisee is buying a proven business idea and method, which increase the chances of success over those of starting a similar business from scratch.

The franchisor does it for money. Franchisors make money from the franchise arrangement in several ways. It's a good idea to keep them in mind as we go on. There is:

- The initial franchise fee
- Ongoing royalties (a percentage of the franchisee's sales)
- Profits on product sold to the franchisee for resale
- Profits on equipment and supplies sold to the franchisee by the franchisor for running the business (for example, a freezer for making frozen yogurt)
- Commissions paid to the franchisor by suppliers of inventory or equipment purchased by the franchisee
- Rents on real estate owned by the franchisor and leased to the franchisee (for example, McDonald's owns the land and building at many of its restaurants, leasing the real estate to franchisees)
- Profits or commissions on real estate purchased by the franchisee

The Potential for Abuse

The franchisor and the prospective franchisee don't approach each other on an equal footing. The franchisor holds most of the cards and has been in the business for some time. The franchisee often knows little about the underlying business. The franchisor has a franchise sales staff including a specialized attorney; those people know franchising and the relevant law inside out. The franchisee has none of this expertise.

Buying a franchise is rather like buying a car from General Motors or Ford. You may be able to haggle about price a little, but you can't change anything fundamental about the product or about the way the carmaker does business.

The Franchise Agreement

When the two parties enter into a franchise deal, they sign a document called a franchise agreement. (See Chapter 10.) That agreement is a contract that dictates how the relationship will be run. Here again the franchisee is at a disadvantage. If you have never done this before, you can't anticipate all the problems that may arise. The franchisor, on the other hand, has been through it many times and knows exactly what's likely to happen. What's more, the franchisor and the firm's attorney wrote the contract, so it's going to be slanted in the franchisor's favor on every issue.

The franchisee is also at a psychological disadvantage. This is a life-altering decision, a major commitment of time and money. For the franchisor, it's just another deal.

Given this uneven playing field, it's easy to see how abuses can be perpetrated by real or phony franchisors on unwary and prospective franchisees. Let's look at some of the ways in which this happens.

Selling a Phony Business

Outright fraud is still successfully practiced today. A person or group poses as a franchisor with a franchisable business, collects a fee from several investors, and disappears. The so-called franchisor may provide the buyer with something in return for the payment, but that something is not a profitable business.

This kind of scam is usually run on the phone. An ad is placed in a newspaper promising fantastic returns on a business that sounds legitimate, and a phone number is provided. When a prospect calls, a slick salesperson sells the idea and convinces the prospect to send in a substantial fee or deposit.

Once the money is in hand, the con artist sends back some equipment of nominal value to complete his or her side of the transaction. For example, after receiving a $1,500 fee someone claiming to have a franchised cleaning service might send an assortment of vacuums and brooms along with a two-page description of how a janitorial service works. Since nothing is in writing, it's very hard to prove fraud even if the con artist can be found afterward.

The "Shell Game"

The shell game, another common scam, is a bit more complicated. It involves putting together a shell that looks like a successful business and selling franchises of it. Unfortunately, there's nothing behind the franchise documents. Here's a hypothetical case to illustrate how it works.

Joe Doe rents a storefront and puts up a sign saying "Computer Repair." Inside he puts some workbenches and a variety of electronic test equipment that he purchased inexpensively at the local secondhand store. He also picks up a few old personal computers, partially dismantles them, and spreads them around the benches.

At the same time, his brother, Tom, sets up a similar store in the next town. Next, Joe and Tom go out and find a few customers with broken computers and take them into their shops for repair. They do this on a small scale on a continuing basis.

Next, Joe has an attorney prepare an impressive-looking set of documents, including a disclosure statement and a franchise agreement, that comply with the letter if not the intent of the franchising law. He also puts together a skeletal operating manual on running a computer repair business.

Finally, Joe puts an ad in the paper advertising his computer repair franchise. The ad is aimed at electronics technicians—people who are good at repairing equipment but don't know much about business.

In time, a prospect answers the ad and comes in to see Joe about the computer repair franchise. Joe shows him the operation he has set up and claims that it's immensely profitable. He says that he's been franchising for a short time and all the franchisees are doing very well.

If the prospect wants to talk to one of the earlier franchisees, Joe takes him over to see Tom. They both claim their businesses are going great guns, but neither ever shows him any financial statements. They insist either that their finances are confidential or that the law prevents them from sharing exact financial information with prospective franchisees.

Joe also says that while only a few franchises have been sold so far, he projects having twenty in operation by year end. The prospect can get in on the ground floor if he hurries; otherwise, he may miss out, because several other people are very interested in the franchise in his area.

Joe offers the prospect a choice. He can either pay a franchise fee and open his own service, or he can buy out another franchisee whose business just happens to be for sale. Which business is that?

You guessed it: Tom's!

Technically Joe's offering does fill the letter of our definition of franchising: He has an ongoing business, a name, and the offer of his continuing help and advice. The problem is that it's only an empty shell. Joe doesn't know any more about running a successful computer repair business than anyone else. In terms of the franchising concept, Joe has nothing to sell.

If the prospect takes Joe's bait and buys, he's likely to go out of business pretty quickly. Needless to say, he doesn't get much after-the-sale support from Joe. When the prospect fails, if Joe is still around he'll claim it was the franchisee's fault, and proving otherwise will be very difficult.

Joe sells several such franchises and pockets the fees. He then lets his own operation go bankrupt and leaves the area.

Overselling

A less sinister abuse is overselling. Even a legitimate franchise can be touted by salespeople as being far more desirable and profitable than it is. If no written substantiation of the projections is offered, the franchisor has no evidence of having been led on should profits prove drastically lower than promised.

Abuses at the End of a Franchise Relationship

The end of a franchise relationship is an especially vulnerable time. Another hypothetical example will help illustrate the possibilities.

Suppose Harry has operated a BigBurger franchise for years, having built it into one of the company's most profitable operations. In fact, it's doing so well that BigBurger would like to operate it as a company-owned unit.

There are a number of ways an unscrupulous franchisor can do that. For example, an inspector can be sent into Harry's restaurant to find some technical violation of the operating manual, say a few french fries on the floor. This will happen several times. Then Harry may find that according to his franchise agreement, those seemingly minor violations are grounds for BigBurger's repossession of the franchise.

Most franchise agreements run for a long but finite period of time. At the end of that time, say ten years, there is generally an expectation that the agreement will be renewed if everything is going well. In this case, all BigBurger has to do to get Harry's business is refuse to renew the agreement. Alternatively, BigBurger could renew it on very onerous terms for Harry.

Or, as we have also seen, the franchisor might invoke a clause limiting Harry's right of assignment; that is, Harry may not be able to sell his business to anyone he wants to or leave it to his heirs. Or the franchise agreement may stipulate that the franchisor has the right of first refusal on repurchasing the franchise, or require that the franchisor approve the new owner.

Imagine that Harry dies or becomes too ill to function as the franchisee. In either case he wants the business to go to his son. Under agreements written by many franchisors, he and the family can be out of luck, since the franchisor can step in and take over the business fairly cheaply.

Other Abuses

Other abuses can occur in the course of the franchise relationship. The franchisor can sell product, equipment, or real estate to the franchisee at unfairly inflated prices. If the territorial provisions of the agreement aren't watched carefully, the franchisor can sell additional franchises in the backyard of the original franchisee. This increases total company revenue and the franchisor's fees, but divides the revenue pie into such small pieces that it becomes difficult for individual franchisees to cover overhead and earn a profit.

The Reaction to Widespread Abuses

During the 1960s and 1970s abuses such as these became rampant. Ads appeared in newspapers promising million-dollar returns on ten-thousand-dollar investments. Con artists swindled naive investors out of their life savings. As a result, franchising began to get a bad name. Knowledgeable people became so wary of fraud that legitimate franchisors were having a hard time convincing prospects they were honest. Their market was falling off due to the practices of the confidence men.

Government also became concerned about the proliferation of fraud and began moving toward legislation regulating franchises.

The result manifested itself in three areas.

In the private sector, a number of franchise executives came together in 1971 to form the International Franchise Association (IFA). The association is an attempt at self-regulation in that it promulgates a code of ethics to which member firms agree to adhere.

At the state level, California and other states passed laws aimed at making franchise fraud a lot more difficult. (To date only a minority of states have passed franchise laws.) State laws vary but tend to operate in three areas:

- They require disclosure of information to prospective franchisees.
- They may require franchisors to register with state authorities before offering franchises for sale.
- They can regulate the business relationship between franchisors and franchisees. This regulation especially concerns the establishment, modification, renewal, and termination of franchises—the times when the franchisee is the most vulnerable.

The federal government got involved in 1979, when the Federal Trade Commission (FTC) enacted Rule 436 regarding the disclosure of information to prospective franchisees. (See Chapter 5 for a full discussion of these disclosure requirements.)

The Law

Both the state laws and the FTC rule are aimed primarily at the front end of the franchisor-franchisee relationship. They attempt to prevent franchisor fraud by requiring that franchisors make certain disclosures prior to obtaining any commitments from prospective franchisees. Some state laws also regulate the relationship during the life of the agreement.

State Law

State laws, where they exist, follow the same general thrust as the federal rule, but they tend to be somewhat more demanding of the franchisor in the area of front-end disclosure. State law makes a real difference in terms of what the franchisor can get away with further down the road, especially with respect to canceling the franchise. State laws are generally binding if either the franchisor or the franchisee is located in the state with the law. The laws are usually administered by the state securities commission.

If you are operating in one of the states that does have a franchise statute, it's a good idea to consult an attorney to learn what additional protection the law gives you. However, it would also be wise not to depend on that protection very much.

Federal Law

In a nutshell, the federal rules are aimed at requiring disclosure of information about the franchise and the franchisor to the prospective franchisee before any commitments are made. They try to prevent the franchisor from telling outright lies about matters of fact. That's called **fraudulent misrepresentation.**

In addition, the rules try to prevent lies of omission. That's when the franchisor fails to tell prospects something important that they don't know enough to ask about.

Limitations of the Law

While the law can require disclosure of information, it cannot guarantee the accuracy of that information. The law does not prevent Joe Doe from opening his computer repair shell game. The law basically requires that Joe provide prospective franchisees with certain information that should enable them to figure out that he's a crook. But if prospects don't do their homework, they still won't know that they're being cheated.

Further, the law makes no judgment about the viability of the business. A business can be based on the worst idea in the world, guaranteed to fail, and be franchised perfectly legally. Someone could franchise a stand to sell salt water at the beach and be in compliance with the FTC rule.

Nor can a victim sue Joe to recover any lost money under the FTC rule; the rule permits only the FTC to bring an action. The FTC generally will do that only after receiving several complaints about Joe. In today's crowded courts, it may take years for such a matter to be resolved. By that time the money Joe stole from his victims will probably be gone. Joe may wind up in jail, but his victims will still be out their money.

Since no one checks the veracity of Joe's disclosure documents, there's no guarantee that what he claims is true. A false disclosure statement may land Joe in jail in the long run, but only if he gets caught.

As mentioned, in certain situations the franchisor is allowed to omit unsavory information that might be of great interest to a prospective franchisee and still be within the law. In California, for example, a state law specifically prohibits a criminal record from being included on a franchise disclosure document. Bankruptcies need be included only if they occurred in the previous seven or fifteen years (depending on the disclosure format). So Joe could have been bankrupt in three businesses fifteen years ago and then spent the intervening time in prison for armed robbery. In California, none of that would show up on the disclosure statement.

The bottom line is that while the law certainly helps, it by no means guarantees protection from fraud.

The Disclosure Document

The FTC Rule 436 is titled "Disclosure Requirements and Prohibitions Concerning Franchising and Business Opportunity Ventures." The heart of the rule is the Disclosure Document, which specifies roughly twenty things that have to be disclosed to prospective franchisees. (See pp. 35–42.) Actually, two formats are generally acceptable: one is spelled out by Rule 436 itself (the FTC format), and one by the Uniform Franchise Offering Circular (UFOC). This latter was developed by a group called the North American Securities Administrators Association.

A franchisor may use either the FTC format or the UFOC, not a combination of both. Eight states do not accept the FTC format: California, Indiana, Maryland,

Minnesota, Rhode Island, South Dakota, Virginia, and Washington. The UFOC is accepted in all fifty states.

The FTC document is a little simpler than the UFOC and has twenty distinct items of disclosure. The UFOC has twenty-three items, but the information required by both forms is essentially the same.

Each issue in the disclosure document is designed to enlighten prospective franchisees with respect to either the franchisor's history or to the nature of the proposed deal in areas in which abusive franchisor behavior is possible.

An important feature of the FTC rule involves the timing of disclosures. Written disclosure information must be presented at the first face-to-face meeting between the prospective franchisees and the franchisor's sales representative *or* ten business days prior to the signing of any contractual documents or the payment of any consideration (money) by the franchisee, whichever is earlier.

Furthermore, the franchisor's contract and all supporting agreements must be in the hands of the franchisee, completed and ready for signature, at least five days before the date of signature. The intent of these regulations is to prevent the sales representative from generating an artificial urgency and rushing prospects into closings that they regret afterward. It provides a cooling-off period before a firm commitment is made.

The Antitrust Laws

The United States has a set of regulations, called the **antitrust laws,** designed to maintain the competitiveness of the economy. They arose during the latter part of the nineteenth and the early part of the twentieth century. The legislation came about in response to a series of mergers among major corporations that led to a concentration of economic power in the hands of a few groups of giant companies. The groups were called trusts, hence the name antitrust law.

As the trusts gained economic power, they used unfair and often violent methods to eliminate competitors and dominate business. Once they controlled an industry, they could and did charge unreasonably high prices, to the detriment of the general public.

The antitrust laws were designed to prevent further concentration of power among the large trusts and in some cases to reverse the concentration that had already occurred. The laws set down certain regulations that impact the relationships and dealings between businesses. Although primarily aimed at large, powerful companies, the rules apply to all businesses regardless of size and can be enforced against relatively small companies. The rules tend to limit some of the things franchisors can do, and hence provide some protection for franchisees.

There are three basic antitrust laws: the Sherman Act, the Clayton Act, and the Robinson-Patman Act.

The Sherman Act (1890)

This legislation prohibits agreements or conspiracies in restraint of trade and monopolization. A **conspiracy in restraint of trade** is an agreement between businesses that would reduce the competitiveness of the economic environment. Two or more competitors agreeing to charge the same price, a practice known as **price fixing,** is a prime example. **Monopolization** is illegal if it is accomplished by some unfair means—such as intimidating customers who buy from a rival—but not if it is achieved through fair trade practices, such as offering the best product.

The Clayton Act (1914)

This act prohibits the merger of two competing firms where the result would be a substantial lessening of competition in the industry. Also prohibited are certain agreements between buyers and sellers where the result is to restrain competition.

The Clayton Act in some cases prohibits tying agreements and exclusive dealing contracts. A **tying agreement** says that a dealer will sell customers one product only if they agree to buy another as well. An **exclusive dealing contract** says that a dealer will sell to customers only if they agree not to buy from the dealer's competitors.

The Robinson-Patman Act (1936)

This act prohibits **price discrimination,** charging different prices to different customers where the result is to restrain competition.

Other FTC and State Prohibitions

In addition to the three antitrust laws, the Federal Trade Commission Act prohibits unfair methods of competition, including unfair advertising and deceptive practices. The franchise disclosure rule is an example of such a prohibition. In addition to the federal laws, some states also have rules aimed at preserving competition. Businesses operating in the respective states must follow these rules.

Categories of Antitrust Violation

Offenses against the antitrust laws are divided into two categories. Certain activities are prohibited no matter who does them or when and whether they reduce competition or not. Those activities are said to be illegal **per se**—that is, illegal on their face. The most prominent example of a per se illegal activity is price fixing.

Other activities are illegal only if they substantially reduce competition. Their legality is judged by a court under what is known as the **rule of reason**: To be illegal, the activity must unreasonably reduce competition. Mergers among competitors are a good example. A merger between two small firms in an industry containing many like-sized operators is probably permissible. On the other hand, a merger between two large companies, where the resulting enterprise will dominate the industry, will probably be viewed as a violation of antitrust law.

It is important to understand that in most cases the antitrust laws attack conspiratorial and not independent activity even though the end result may be the same. If two gas stations operate on opposite corners at an intersection, for example, it is illegal for them to agree to charge the same price for gas. However, if one station unilaterally sets a price, and the other follows the lead and sets the same price, there is no conspiracy and therefore no antitrust violation.

Antitrust and Franchising

Several activities addressed by the antitrust laws affect the relationship between franchisors and franchisees. We will briefly discuss the most important of these.

Price Fixing

It is illegal for two businesses to conspire to set prices. But suppose a franchisor feels that a high price is necessary to preserve a product's quality image. Do antitrust regulations mean that the franchisor cannot set the price that franchisees charge to control this important aspect of the business?

The answer is that it depends on how it's done. Franchisors and their franchisees may be on shaky ground if they agree to a certain price, and such an agreement may be illegal. The franchisor, however, may unilaterally declare a price and punish those who fail to adhere to it with termination. As long as the action is unilateral and there is no conspiracy or agreement, there is no violation.

An alternate method is for the franchisor to suggest a price and explain why it is important. The ultimate pricing decision is then up to the franchisee.

Refusals to Deal

Consider the following two points:

- Franchisors don't have to sell franchises to anyone who applies. They can insist that franchisees have certain qualifications.
- At the same time franchises often come with exclusive territories.

Now, suppose Sally has an exclusive BigBurger franchise in town A. Tom, who is fully qualified to be a franchisee, comes along and tries to buy a franchise in the same town. BigBurger rejects Tom because Sally already has the territory. Can BigBurger be sued on the grounds that the territorial agreement with Sally is a conspiracy in restraint of trade in that it reduces competition by preventing Tom's business from competing?

The answer to this type of **refusal to deal** isn't simple. The court would look at the nature of the business and the market in town A. It might find that the territorial arrangement enhances competition, because it makes BigBurger franchisees stronger and more able to compete with other hamburger restaurants.

On the other hand, it might find that there was plenty of room for another BigBurger franchise and that there was no good reason not to grant it. This is a case of the application of the rule of reason. In any event, antitrust law has a definite impact on this aspect of the franchise relationship.

Tying Agreements

A tying agreement exists when the purchase of one product (the tying product) is conditioned on the purchase of another product (the tied product). Suppose, for example, that Sally owns a supermarket and wants to buy beef from Tom and chicken from Mary, but Tom insists that he won't sell her his beef unless she also buys his chicken. The question becomes whether Tom's requirement unreasonably restrains competition in the market for chicken, the tied product.

The issue is complicated, and there isn't a simple answer. Tying agreements go to the heart of the franchising relationship. Franchisors feel that the franchise is a bundle of things, all of which are necessary to make the business successful.

To take another example, BigBurger might insist that franchisees buy equipment, fixtures, uniforms, meat, and buns from the franchisor to ensure a uniformly high quality among outlets. Franchisees,

IFA CODE OF ETHICS

Here is the code of ethics that all IFA members pledge to uphold:

1. In the advertisement and grant of franchises or dealerships, a member shall comply with all applicable laws and regulations and the member's offering circular shall be complete, accurate, and not misleading with respect to the franchisee's or dealer's investment, the obligations of the member, and the franchise or dealer under the franchise or dealership, and all material facts relating to the franchise or dealership.
2. All matters material to the member's franchise or dealership shall be contained in one or more written agreements, which shall clearly set forth the terms of the relationship and the respective rights and obligations of the parties.
3. A member shall select and accept only those franchisees or dealers who, upon reasonable investigation, appear to possess the basic skills, education, experience, personal characteristics, and financial resources requisite to conduct the franchised business or dealership and meet the obligations of the franchisee or dealer under the franchise and other agreements. There shall be no discrimination in the granting of franchises based solely on race, color, religion, national origin, or sex. However, this in no way prohibits a franchisor from granting franchises to prospective franchisees as part of a program to make franchises available to persons lacking the capital, training, business experience, or other qualifications ordinarily required of franchisees or any other affirmative action program adopted by the franchisor.
4. A member shall provide reasonable guidance to its franchisees or dealers in a manner consistent with its franchise agreement.
5. Fairness shall characterize all dealings between a member and its franchisees or dealers. A member shall make every good faith effort to resolve complaints by and disputes with its franchisees or dealers through direct communication and negotiation. To the extent reasonably appropriate in the circumstances, a member shall give its franchisee or dealer notice of, and a reasonable opportunity to cure, a breach of their contractual relationship.
6. No member shall engage in the pyramid system of distribution. A pyramid is a system wherein a buyer's future compensation is expected to be based primarily upon recruitment of new participants, rather than upon the sale of products or services.

however, might feel that BigBurger was selling its meat at too high a price and making an unreasonable profit on it.

The legality of the agreement turns, first, on whether meat is legitimately part of the bundle, and, second, on the effect of the agreement on competition in the market for meat.

The problems of tying agreements have led most franchisors to avoid contract clauses requiring that purchases be made directly from them. Two approaches seem to work better. The first is to provide franchisees with product specifications and allow them to find their own vendors. The second is to evaluate a number of suppliers and provide an approved vendor list to franchisees. The procedure for getting on the list is also supplied. Franchisors working under these arrangements also may offer the product for sale themselves, often providing the best prices to franchisees.

The antitrust laws tend to be of far more concern to franchisors than franchisees. Prospective franchisees should simply be aware that these laws exist and of the issues they address.

The International Franchise Association

The International Franchise Association has a Code of Ethics by which all member firms agree to operate. Remember that ethics and law are two different concepts. Codes of ethics apply only to members of the organization that promotes the code and violations are punishable only by expulsion, while law applies to everyone.

The IFA is an organization of franchisors, and critics accuse it of serving the interests of franchisors over those of franchisees. Nevertheless, the IFA Code does represent some attempt at self-regulation in the franchising industry. The articles of the code are self-explanatory.

It is easy to see that the code is vague and subject to interpretation. While undoubtedly providing some measure of benefit, it cannot guarantee that an unscrupulous individual will not take advantage of the franchise relationship.

Protect Yourself

The bottom line of all this is that franchise law is aimed primarily at the protection of the franchisee through disclosure. It is still incumbent on the franchisee to make use of the disclosed information to determine whether any deal is a good one.

As a prospective franchisee, be sure to do at least the following:

- Study the disclosure document and demand more information whenever it raises a question in your mind.
- Look for other evidence that the disclosed information is true. Look at official documents and talk to others who have dealt with the franchisor in the past.
- Study the franchise agreement carefully and understand what every clause means for your business, now and in the future, under a variety of circumstances.
- *Hire a lawyer!* Never, under any circumstances, sign a franchise agreement without competent legal advice.

Case in Point Revisited

The last point will be critical for Denise, who faced a pricing problem at the beginning of the chapter. Whether the franchisor can force her into a discount mode of operation is a difficult legal question. Denise definitely needs the help of a competent attorney. The result will depend on her franchise agreement, a court's interpretation of relevant law, and whether state laws apply. Denise should also be aware that fighting the franchisor could be expensive.

CHAPTER EIGHT

Putting Together a Business Plan

KEY TERM FOR THIS CHAPTER

business plan

Case in Point: What to Take to the Bank

Frank Ferticelli has always wanted to own his own pizza restaurant. His father ran a pizza place in New York when Frank was a boy, and he grew up in the business.

His father, however, had lost the business due to what Frank believed was poor management. The senior Ferticelli was great in the kitchen and with customers. But he never seemed to be able to handle advertising; the business's books were always a mess; and he couldn't seem to keep employees happy. The restaurant eventually closed, and Frank's dad went to work for someone else until his retirement.

After the business closed, Frank went to college and graduated with a business degree. He then continued to work in the restaurant field for other people. He is now thirty-two and wants to open his own business.

One of Frank's college buddies, Bernie Sloan, is currently the loan officer at the bank where Frank does his personal banking. Bernie has told Frank that he is sure the bank will finance the new business if he is willing to collateralize the loan with the equity in his house. Frank's experience in the food service field, and with pizza in particular, is as good as gold. It also helps that he has been a stable member of the community for many years.

In spite of all his experience, Frank is

somewhat daunted by his father's failure many years ago. He had therefore decided to buy a pizza restaurant franchise to minimize the chance of failure due to management problems. Bernie agrees and thinks the franchise will be popular in the area.

Earlier, Frank had researched franchises and settled on one that seemed especially well suited to his needs. Now he has reached a final understanding with the franchisor and signed the agreement contingent only upon securing financing.

On the morning after returning from the franchisor's headquarters, Frank gathers all of the literature together and goes to see Bernie to get his bank loan. After exchanging pleasantries and showing Bernie the franchisor's literature, Frank says, "Okay, let's get the paperwork together, and I'll sign on the dotted line."

Bernie looks a little surprised. "Frank," he says, "you haven't shown us a business plan."

Frank stares at Bernie. "Bernie," he says, "we've been talking about this idea for months. You know as much about the idea and my plans as I do. What do we need another piece of paper for?"

Bernie pushes back from his desk and sighs. "Frank, the bank just has to have a detailed business plan," he says. "Besides, you'll learn a lot by putting it together."

Why does the bank require a business plan? How does Frank go about preparing one?

What Is a Business Plan and Why Do You Need One?

A business plan is a slender notebook that tells the story of the prospective business and the entrepreneur behind it. Any entrepreneur starting a business should have a business plan. You *must* have a business plan if you expect to seek money from an outside source.

The Franchisee's Business Plan

Prospective franchisees need business plans almost as much as independent entrepreneurs do. However, putting a plan together is somewhat easier for a franchisee due to the help and information available from the franchisor. In fact, it is often available in professionally produced fliers and brochures that can be attached to the franchisee's plan. In most cases the franchisor will be able to provide a model planning format that the franchisee can complete with the specifics of his or her operation.

Further, the independent entrepreneur's biggest task in business planning is building credibility with a banker or investor. Franchisees essentially have the job done for them. In spite of these advantages enjoyed by a franchisee, it's a good idea to understand the nature and uses of business plans in the small-business world.

The Purposes of Business Planning

Business planning is the process of creating a picture, or model, of a business unit in the future. The model is made up of both verbal discriptions and numerical facts and projections, and is designed to give a reader an image of what the organization will look like as time passes. The numbers are mostly, but not entirely, in the form of financial statements. The text can describe anything from the numbers themselves, to broad strategic issues, to the handling of short-term tactical questions.

The image conveyed should be as complete as possible. Ideally it includes information on products, markets, employees, technology, facilities, capital, revenue, profitability, and anything else that might be relevant to the organization and its affairs.

The plan describes the who, what, when, where, how, and how much that make the business concept come alive in the minds of its owners and managers. A good plan is like an adventure story to an interested reader.

Business plans are prepared by large and small companies alike. Strictly speaking, plans chart where the firm is going in the future, but the document and the act of creating it have a value beyond that. A business plan serves essentially three ends: First, it helps you to set objectives; second, it explains your business to others, such as possible sources of financing, and third, it is an excellent management tool.

Setting Objectives. The planning process serves to galvanize the management team into uniting as a cohesive unit with common goals. It helps everyone understand what the objectives of the organization are, why they're important, and how they are to be achieved.

In small business, creating a plan forces the entrepreneur to think through everything that has to be done to get the business going or to keep it afloat if it's already started.

If there's more than one owner, planning helps to ensure that they're all singing from the same songbook. That is, the planning process goes a long way toward making sure that all the participants understand what they have to do and what they can expect out of it.

Explaining to Others. Second, plans are used to help explain the company's goals and methods to outsiders. Business plans for small companies are primarily tools to help entrepreneurs get their ideas funded, whether the companies are already functioning or have yet to be created.

A business plan is the single most important document in your quest for financing as a prospective franchisee. It is the document that you must present to the lender or investor as an introduction to the venture. Without submitting a plan in advance, it is usually impossible to get a serious interview with a funding source.

The plan is a little like a résumé in the job-seeking process. It has to catch the interviewer/investor's attention and get you in the door to make your presentation. Once you are there, the plan serves as a talking piece on which the evaluation of the project is based.

Managing the Business After It's Started. Business plans are marvelous retrospective devices. Owners and managers generally have an idea where they want their businesses to go, but often they can't follow a straight path to the goal.

Being in business without a plan is like traveling without a roadmap. Things are okay as long as you're on familiar ground, but if you get a little lost, you're in big trouble. A plan makes a projection of where you're going, and gives you the means of correcting your course on the way. Comparing actual performance to

A SUGGESTED BUSINESS PLAN OUTLINE

No two business plans will have exactly the same content, since no two businesses are identical. However, most will be similar in structure. Here is a suggested outline or table of contents for a plan.

Outline

A. Executive Summary (a one-page overview of the plan)
B. Table of Contents
C. Mission Statement
D. Market Identification
  - Background (as appropriate)
  - The Customer Need
  - Who the Customers Are

E. Product/Service
  - Description
  - Fit to the Market Need

F. Marketing Plan
  - Strategy/Approach
  - Location
  - Competitive Analysis
  - Pricing/Profitability
  - Buildup of the Revenue Projection from Market Assumptions

G. Operations (production/acquisition of product)
  - Sources
  - Processes
  - Equipment
  - Research

H. Management/Staffing
  - Key Players
    - Backgrounds
    - Qualifications
    - Résumés
  - Overall Personnel Requirements
  - Staffing Plan

I. Financial Projections
  - Current Financials (if appropriate)
    - Statements From the Past Three Years
    - Tax Returns
  - Projections
    - Income Statement
    - Balance Sheet
    - Cash Flows

Application of Current Request
Capital Structure (the relative amounts of the entrepreneur's money and borrowed money being used to start the business)
Contingency Plans (an outline of what will be done if things turn out worse than expected)
Appendixes
Supporting Documents
Additional Detail (as required)

plan is the best way to understand your problems and come up with solutions. A plan is truly a roadmap for running a business.

The Components of a Business Plan

Business plans typically have a fairly standard structure. We can think of the structure as a table of contents with various chapter headings. Plans tend to have most of the same chapters, usually called sections. For example, they all have one section showing financial projections, one on marketing, and one on management.

Major Business Issues

Each section of the plan addresses a major business issue or function; such as marketing, finance, or production. It's useful to think of each section as a component, and understand that a plan must have all of its components to work, just as an automobile must have all of its components—engine, wheels, brakes, and so on. This isn't as obvious as it may seem, because while all cars need wheels and engines, not all businesses have the same functions. A plan for a retail business won't have a section on manufacturing, and a plan for a manufacturing business won't have a section on store layout. But the preparation of a good business plan entails the understanding that the functions that do apply to a particular business are all integral parts of it that work together to make the business go. Proper treatment of all the right issues is essential if the plan is to stand on its own.

The business planner's job is to write a description under each subject heading that will give a reader an understanding of what the business is all about and what it is expected to become.

Basic Building Blocks

A business plan has two fundamental ingredients: words and numbers. How these elements are integrated will determine the success of the document.

A plan that's all words, promises, and discussions gives the reader a sense of imprecision. It leaves the feeling that while the idea may be good, the author probably won't be very effective in implementing it. On the other hand, too many numbers can be confusing and irritating, especially if they aren't adequately supported by explanatory text.

Major Divisions of the Business Plan

An excellent business plan can be divided into three major parts:

- Mission Statement
- Descriptive Sections
- Projected Financial Statements

Mission Statement. The mission statement gives the reader a quick overview of what the business is and why it's worth his or her time and investment.

The statement should be relatively short but establish in definite terms why a business opportunity exists. It should explain the kind of business you're proposing, what customer need is being satisfied, who the target customers are, and what methods will be used to satisfy their need.

The mission is never to make money. The mission relates to the fundamental nature of the business, and why it's a good idea here and now.

Descriptive Sections. The descriptive sections explain how you'll make the business work. Each section addresses a separate department or feature of the operation, such as production or marketing. Descriptions use both words and numbers but tend to be mostly words.

Projected Financial Statements. The financial statements are packaged in a separate section and consist of a standard set of statements, the Income Statement, the Balance Sheet, and the Statement of Cash Flows. The statements are projections for the future, but include recent history if the company already exists.

A business plan's financial statements involve making assumptions about the level of business that the franchised outlet will do over time, and translating these into pro forma (projected) accounting statements.

If the franchisor doesn't offer assistance in that area, a franchisee unfamiliar with finance may need the help of an accountant. However, an inexpensive book on business planning and a little diligent effort may suffice. (See Appendix B.) Financial statements must be tied to the assumptions expressed in the descriptive sections of the plan, and the relationship of numbers to text must be easy for the reader to understand.

For example, suppose that in your marketing section you projected selling one hundred units in your first month and an increase of ten units a month thereafter. You also project that price will drop by 2 percent a month due to increasing competition. Further, you think the mix between standard and deluxe model units, which sell at different prices and margins, will shift seasonally. At the same time your production section predicts a cost decrease of 3 percent per month as you build up volume and experience.

All these changes are expressed in the dollar figures of your financial statements by means of some complicated arithmetic. If you simply present these results without support, you'll confuse and anger your readers. They have to be able to verify without difficulty that your figures on unit sales, price, and cost assumptions are consistent. Otherwise, they'll lay your plan aside and look at someone else's.

Length and Level of Detail. How long should a business plan be? There isn't any set answer, but a few guidelines are appropriate.

Larger, more complicated businesses require longer, more detailed plans. A $20 million start-up requires more justification than a restaurant in a shopping center. In terms of complexity, a manufacturing proposal is generally longer than a retail idea requiring the same level of investment.

The plan needs to have enough substance to explain adequately what's going on. But bigger isn't necessarily better. A plan that is too long and complex puts people off. How do you package detailed thought, research, and analysis into something that looks spirited and easy to read?

The answer often lies in backup that is bound separately. Keep the basic plan document between twenty and sixty pages, and expand on each section as required in an appendix that readers can ask for if they want it.

The Whole Package

Any time there's a business plan, there's a presentation to go along with it. In fact, we can look at the entire business plan as consisting of at least four pieces:

- The Business Plan document
- Prepared appendixes carrying greater detail
- The presentation
- Additional information in the planner's head

Everything you know about your business doesn't go in the plan. But as a successful planner, you will have thought out answers to almost any question that might be asked about your business. Preparing those answers is just as much a part of business planning as writing the plan document itself.

How Financial People Will Read Your Plan

People who evaluate business plans for funding may have to sift through a hundred plans a week. The process is similar to that of reviewing résumés sent in response to employment advertisements. Evaluators can't read every document carefully—they don't have that much time—so they eliminate most of the candidates on the basis of a brief reading. The interesting ones are put aside and read more carefully later. How do you make sure you get on the read-more-carefully-later pile?

The first thing evaluators look at is the **executive summary.** That gives them an overview of what the business is all about. If it's well written, it tells financial people all they need to know at this point about the qualitative aspects of the business. On the first pass evaluators rarely, if ever, look at the detailed sections describing the business and the market approach.

The next thing analysts look at is the financial projections, especially the cash line. That shows how the funding is to be used and where the money to pay it back will come from. Next they'll check the balance sheet and income statement to see if the assumptions made about the account balances that lead to the cash projections are reasonable.

Finally readers will take a look at the background of the entrepreneur and the management team and make a quick judgment of their quality and character as businesspeople.

In short, people try to very quickly grasp three things:

1. What the business is
2. How much money is involved and how it's used
3. Who's behind it

It's a very good idea to put the best pieces of news you've got about each of these things in the Executive Summary. If the summary is done right, your plan is sure to get a careful reading on the evaluator's second pass and put you in line for funding consideration.

Case in Point Revisited

Just a closing word about Frank's pizza venture. It should be clear that no matter how qualified you are and how well you know your banker, you still need a business plan.

In Frank's case the plan should be fairly easy to put together. The descriptive information about the business can come from the franchisor's brochures and other documentation, and Bernie has already given Frank an indication that the bank will lend based on certain collateral.

Frank's plan won't have to be as detailed and convincing as it would if he was not known at the bank, but he must still put together a formal document.

CHAPTER NINE

How to Get Financing

KEY TERMS FOR THIS CHAPTER

bond
collateral
covenants
debt
equity
executive summary
general partnership
limited partnership
limited liability
secured, unsecured
term

Case in Point: Can Joe Get Started?

Joe Logan is ready to get serious about opening an instant printing franchise. He's put a great deal of effort into research and has found a reputable franchisor. Negotiations have gone well and Joe feels satisfied with the franchise agreement. He's also carefully researched the market for printing services in his area and believes there is a vacant niche for a firm supplying small businesses in an industrial park near his home.

Joe's biggest problem at the moment is financing. The venture requires a total of $150,000 to get started. This includes the purchase of all the equipment, an initial inventory of paper and supplies, rent, and enough spare cash to operate for the first six months even if early business is slow. The equipment, which is fairly standard in the business, costs $80,000.

Unfortunately, the franchisor offers no help with financing other than an information packet that will inform backers about the nature of the business.

Joe has $25,000 in savings and owns his own home. His parents are reasonably well off and might lend him a few thousand dollars, but he hasn't a clue as to how to pull together the rest of the $150,000. Joe does know that banks are reluctant to lend to brand-new businesses such as the one he proposes.

Does Joe have to give up his dream until he saves up more money? That could take ten years!

When a prospective franchisee is close to a deal with a franchisor, it's time to line up financing.

There's a little of the "chicken and the egg" in this situation. You really can't get a franchised business funded without a firm franchise agreement, but you wouldn't want to sign an agreement until you were sure you could secure all the financing necessary to get the business's doors open.

Most financial sources will work with a franchisee on the basis that the funds are contingent on reaching a satisfactory agreement with the franchisor.

The total amount of funding necessary should be developed in the financial projections of your business plan with the help of the franchisor. This estimate must be developed very carefully to ensure that you don't run out of cash while your business is getting started. The franchisor, if reputable, has been through this before and should be able to tell you almost exactly how much you'll need. Don't forget working capital and money to allow for delays in getting started.

Before going further, let's review some basics concerning the forms that funding can take and a few of the more important rules of the game.

Financing Basics

Money provided to small businesses generally comes in the form of either debt or equity. Larger firms sometimes raise money using sophisticated financial instruments that are essentially a combination of debt and equity; these are not available to most entrepreneurs. Let's talk about debt and equity in turn.

Debt

Debt simply means a loan. A bank or other lending institution loans your business money with the expectation of being repaid the full amount plus interest at a specified rate. The two major forms of debt are ordinary loans, which can carry a variety of repayment terms, and bonds.

Bonds are a device that allows a number of people to loan money to a company in one transaction. Suppose, for example, a firm wants to borrow $1 million. It can't find any one source willing to loan that much, but it can find a thousand people each willing to loan it $1,000. Rather than make up a thousand different loan agreements, the firm issues $1 million of bonds. Each person who buys a bond for $1,000 is lending the company that amount. (We say that lenders "buy" bonds even though they are lending money.) Few small companies can issue bonds, so we won't dwell on them. Most of what follows is applicable to both loans and bonds.

Term. Loans come in a variety of forms. The most important distinction about a loan is its **term**, meaning the length of time over which it must be repaid. Loans are generally classified as follows:

Short term	one year or less
Intermediate term	one to five years
Long term	longer than five years

Lenders generally expect the term of the loan to be matched to the use of the money. If you want a loan to buy equipment that will last twenty years, the banker will expect to make a long-term loan. On the other hand, if you need money to see you through a brief period when your receivables and inventory exceed your collections, the banker will want to lend short term. The expectation is that long- and intermediate-term money will be repaid out of profits, but short-term money will be repaid as soon as you collect your receivables.

Most short-term loan agreements have what's called a clean-up clause, which stipulates that the borrower must be out of short-term debt for at least sixty days each year. This is to be sure that the short-term money is really being used for short-term purposes.

Most lenders consider term an element of safety. A short-term loan is more secure than a long-term loan. That's because a bank makes a judgment about a borrower's financial condition at a given point in time. In a short-term loan there isn't much time for the borrower's condition to deteriorate a great deal. Anything can happen in the long run.

Payments. Most loan agreements require the payment of interest and principal over the term of the loan. Lenders will sometimes give a business a period in which principal repayments don't have to be made, but interest is always collected regularly.

This is an important feature of loans. The interest must be paid whether your business is making any money or not. In fact, this requirement to pay interest increases your risk of failure, because an unserviced loan can put you into bankruptcy.

Covenants. Most business loans have **covenants** attached. Covenants are clauses in the loan agreement that limit the way you can run your business while the loan remains outstanding.

Lenders insist on covenants to ensure the safety of their investment. A typical covenant might be that the company cannot pay dividends to stockholders during the life of the loan. In addition, the agreement may preclude you from drawing or borrowing money from the business, or it may limit the compensation paid to officers.

Clearly, these rules are designed to ensure that the company's cash is used to service the loan first, before it can be paid to owners. Covenants can also restrict the day-to-day operations of the firm.

If a covenant is broken the loan is in default, just as it would be if payments weren't made. Most loans have an accelerator clause that says that if the loan goes into default, the entire principal becomes due and payable immediately. This means that a lender can generally force a defaulted borrower into bankruptcy immediately.

Collateral. Lenders to small businesses generally feel that the businesses themselves are too risky to justify loans. The lenders therefore require that some marketable asset back the loan. In other words, if the company defaults on the loan, the asset becomes the property of the bank. The proceeds from the sale of the asset then pay off the loan. Such an asset is called **collateral.**

Collateral can be an asset owned by the business, or it can be something you own outside of the business, such as your house.

Long-term loans that are used to buy equipment or real estate are usually collateralized by those assets themselves. Short-term loans to cover inventory and receivables are often partially collateralized by that inventory and those receivables.

Generally, the collateral value of an asset is a fraction of its original market value. In other words, if a machine costs $1 million, a bank would probably not lend more than $600,000 toward buying it based on the machine's value as collateral.

It's easy to see the reasoning behind this practice. If the borrower defaults and the bank winds up with the machine, it would have to be disposed of as used equipment. Clearly, a used machine is worth a lot less than a new one. Further, the bank would have to absorb any selling expenses involved.

Thus, to buy an asset with a loan collateralized by that asset, you generally have to put in some of your own cash as well. This is similar to residential mortgages and car loans, which are collateralized by the houses and cars they are used to buy but usually also require some of our own cash, called a down payment. The down payment is also called our **equity** in the asset, meaning what we own, as distinguished from what the bank owns.

A collateralized loan is also said to be **secured** by the asset. A loan without collateral is called an **unsecured** loan. Lenders generally make unsecured loans only to businesses that have substantial track records of profitable operation.

Limited Liability. Many people have a misconception about the idea of **limited liability**, which is associated with the corporate form of business organization. A corporation is a legal entity that does business as if it were a person. It is owned by stockholders who are legally separate from the corporation and its business. This separation of owners and their personal assets from the business and its assets is the essence of the corporate form of business organization.

Theoretically, if a business that is a corporation fails (or is sold), creditors can look only to the assets of the business for recovery of their debts and not to the assets of the owners. This implies that if a bank lends to an entrepreneur whose business is incorporated, the entrepreneur's personal assets are safe in the event of the business's failure.

Unfortunately, it doesn't work that way in real life. In order to avoid losing their depositors' money when lending to small businesses, banks invariably require the entrepreneur's personal guarantee of the loan along with the business's agreement to repay the money. The entrepreneur's personal guarantee puts all of his or her personal assets at risk.

As a practical matter, the limited liability associated with incorporation is a myth for entrepreneurs engaged in running their own businesses.

Control. An advantage of debt as opposed to equity financing is that, under normal circumstances, a relatively small amount of control over the business is given up. If covenants are negotiated carefully and aren't unreasonable, they don't get in the way of normal operations at all.

Equity

Equity means an ownership interest in the business. In a corporation, an equity investor gets stock. If the business is not a corporation, an equity investment means taking on a partner of some kind.

There are basically two kinds of partnerships, general and limited. The simplest and most common is the general partnership. Limited partnerships are complex financing devices.

General Partnerships. A **general partnership** is intended to be a working relationship between two or more people. General partners usually participate in the running of the business and share in the profits, although not necessarily on an equal basis. They also usually contribute funds toward getting started, but again not necessarily equally.

General partners also share in the liability for the business's debts and any damage that the business may do to others. That means that their personal assets are at risk for the business.

These features make taking on a general partner an awkward way to raise money, if that's all you want out of the deal. New partners are likely to want some control in return for their money and the risk they're taking. As an entrepreneur, on the other hand, you may not be interested in giving up that control. General partnerships are appropriate if you want someone's expertise and help as well as his or her money. These partnerships are easy to form, requiring only a comprehensive agreement between the partners.

Limited Partnerships. A **limited partnership** is a special legal device designed to let people invest in businesses without being involved in management and without taking on personal liabilities beyond their initial investment.

A limited partnership has two kinds of partners: There is at least one general partner who runs the business, and there are any number of limited partners who invest only money. The limited partners have no say in how the business is managed and are not liable for the debts of the business beyond their investment. Limited partnerships are popular in real estate investment enterprises. These partnerships are legally complex, however, and should not be considered without the advice of a lawyer.

Stockholders. If the business is a corporation, an equity investment is accomplished by selling stock to investors. Investors are usually most interested in common stock, because it carries voting rights, which offer a say in how the company is run. Stockholders vote to fill seats on the board of directors. That board, in turn, appoints management, which runs the company.

A person or group owning a minority of stock in the company is unlikely to be able to elect any directors and may insist on being given a seat on the board as a prerequisite to buying in.

Other kinds of stock don't carry voting rights. Although these are called equity, they really aren't, since they don't offer a share in the control of the company. Equity investors in incorporated small businesses, especially start-ups, are unlikely to be interested in anything other than common stock.

Control. Unlike debt, accepting equity investment can mean that an entrepreneur gives up a substantial amount of control of the business. Investors often have little interest in day-to-day operations under normal conditions, but they can become very difficult in bad times if they feel that their investments are in jeopardy.

Equity Versus Debt from the Investor's Perspective

Investing in an entrepreneur's new business is a risky proposition for either unsecured lenders or stockholders. In either case, if the business fails investors are likely to lose their money. The results of the two investment methods are quite different, however, if the business does well.

The equity/stock investor enjoys the potential for substantial gain if the business is successful due to appreciation in the value of the stock. Lenders, on the other hand, do not share in that success; they simply get their money back with interest. Therefore, investors are more likely to put their money into a risky small start-up via stock than via a loan. The downsides are about the same, but the upside is substantially better with equity.

As a practical matter, franchisees aren't likely to interest unrelated equity investors in their businesses. The nature of most franchises simply isn't conducive to that kind of speculation. Franchises are, however, a realistic way to get financial participation from friends and relatives.

Sources of Financing and How to Deal with Them

One basic financing fact should be understood at the outset if you are interested in starting your own business, whether franchised or independent. This fact is:

Most of the money behind small-business start-ups comes from the entrepreneurs themselves and from family and friends.

That is not to say that financing cannot be had, but a big chunk of the money generally has to come from the entrepreneur's savings or the liquidation of other assets. It's rarely realistic to assume that you can start your own business without any money of your own.

Outside of family and friends, the traditional sources of funds for start-ups and relatively new businesses are banks for debt and venture capital for equity and, in the case of franchises, the franchisors themselves. As we will discuss, few start-ups have the characteristics that interest venture capitalists. That's especially true of franchises. Most successful funding comes out of banks.

Help in Financing from the Franchisor

Franchisors often provide assistance to their franchisees in securing financing. The nature of that assistance varies a great deal. In what follows we'll discuss a few of the ways franchisors are sometimes willing to help.

Financing by the Franchisor. Franchisors are occasionally willing to loan money directly to particularly promising franchisees. Generally only the largest and most successful franchisors do this, and only if the prospective franchisee is unlikely to be able to secure financing through conventional channels.

Further, the offer is likely to be limited

to a particular group of people. For example, a franchisor might offer financing to a limited number of members of a minority group as part of an affirmative action program.

Financing by the Franchisor Through Real Estate Ownership. Franchisors will sometimes provide partial financing by purchasing and developing the real estate under the franchisee's business. The franchisee then leases the facility from the franchisor during the life of the agreement.

This arrangement saves the franchisee from having to raise a lot of money to acquire the real estate, but it also makes the operation the franchisor's business in the long run. In some cases, this is the only way the franchisor will do business. As we'll see in Chapter 14, real estate ownership is a powerful control exercised by franchisors.

A Bank Relationship Provided by the Franchisor. Another common way that franchisors help with financing is by providing a ready-made banking relationship. The franchisor may regularly do business with a particular bank. That bank is therefore already comfortable with the franchisor and the business concept.

Under such conditions, the bank may provide a more or less ready-made financing package for a new franchisee joining the operation. The franchisee will have to qualify as a good credit risk, but most of the basis for the relationship goes back to the franchisor.

If a financing package or financing assistance is offered by a franchisor, it will be promoted up front as a positive part of the relationship. Otherwise, a franchisee must go it alone.

Funding from Banks

Banks do make a great many loans to small businesses. The trick to getting such a loan is to understand the bank's motives and concerns.

What the Bank is Looking For and Why. When a bank considers a business loan, it looks for three crucial things:

1. The existence and stability of cash flows sufficient to make interest and principal payments and/or collateral
2. A proven market with a credible plan for reaching it
3. The competence and experience of management

The reason banks look at these factors is that they indicate security and stability. Bankers invest other people's money and are essentially not big risk takers. Furthermore, the bank's reward system isn't consistent with risky investments. The bank doesn't share in profits if the venture goes well, but it stands to lose its principal and interest if things go badly.

Guidelines for Approaching Banks. Now that we've clarified the bank's motives, we can set down some general guidelines that are of help in getting a business loan whether your business is brand new or has been around for a while.

First it's helpful to understand two things. One, the bank wants to make loans. That's the business it's in, and it's a competitive business. Check the rosters of your local Rotary, Kiwanis, and Lions clubs. You'll find bankers on all of them.

Why? Because banks want to be involved in the business community and make loans to local businesses.

Two, about 75 percent of loans to small businesses are made by small and medium-size banks. That says that your chances are better with a bank that's small enough to value your business.

Keep in mind that the banking relationship is a two-way street. You need bankers, but they need businesspeople like you too.

Approach. When approaching a bank, seek an opportunity to make a complete, thorough presentation to your loan officer.

Don't imagine you can do that by just walking in cold and pulling out your business plan. The first time you go into the bank, try to identify the loan officer, meet him or her briefly, and set up a second meeting. That is when you will present your plan, so be sure enough time is blocked out for you to get through the entire presentation.

You may want to leave a copy of your plan with the loan officer to look over before your meeting.

Information Requirements for a Commercial Loan. All banks have their own loan application forms. You will have to fill out their forms regardless of the fact that a great deal, if not all, of the information that's asked for is in your business plan. It's a good idea to pick up the forms early and have them completely filled out prior to your presentation with a loan officer.

Commercial bankers work from this package of information. Applicants need to be sure that all the material is readily available to the loan officer.

The loan information required by most banks is fairly similar. It can be roughly summarized as follows.

Company/Business Information

1. A description of the nature and operation of the business. If the business is already in operation, a brief summary of its history.
2. The general plan for the future operation of the business, including a summary of how the proposed loan will help the company meet its goals.
3. The exact amount and purpose of the loan. People don't like to make general-purpose loans to businesses. The money should be for a specific purpose.
4. Proposed repayment terms. Show how you plan to repay the loan and interest and where the cash will come from.
5. The capital structure of the business after the loan is made; in other words, how much of the company's total capital will be from debt and how much will be from equity.
6. Details of any leasing agreements that the company has already entered into or contemplates, especially if they are not reflected on the financial statements.
7. The collateral being proposed for the loan. Banks are unlikely to make uncollateralized business loans to new businesses or to businesses and entrepreneurs they don't know well.
8. Insurance coverages carried on the business. List insurance policies for both the business itself and its owners.
9. Breakdown of assets owned by the

business, including inventory, fixtures, equipment, and real estate. Include information on any intangibles considered of value, such as patents, licenses, and goodwill.

10. Current and prior years' financial statements. Go back at least three years if the company or its predecessor has been around that long. Include balance sheets, cash flow statements, and income statements.
11. The company's federal tax returns for at least the past three years.
12. Projected financial statements for at least the next three years. Provide the first year in monthly detail and subsequent years in quarterly detail. All three statements are required, but the order of importance is cash flow first and balance sheet second. Accounting profitability as reflected on the income statement isn't as important to a bank as cash.
13. Summary of the assumptions that underpin the financial projections.
14. A worst-case scenario. In other words, a contingency plan. If things don't go as the business owner plans, how does the bank get its money?

Personal Information on the Business Owners

15. Professional qualifications, including complete work history and education. This is essentially a résumé with references the loan officer can contact.
16. Credit history and references. The loan officer will also get credit bureau reports.
17. Personal financial statements stressing your net worth. This includes money in banks with verifiable account numbers, the value of your home, if you own it, the amount of your mortgage, the value of your cars, and outstanding loans thereon.
18. Copies of your income tax returns for at least the previous three years.

Two points should be made about loan information and your relationship with the loan officer. First, most of the information a loan officer needs will already be included in a well-prepared business plan. Second, the value of arriving for your meeting with all the information assembled and well organized can't be overemphasized. When you come prepared, you will gain credibility and will be perceived as competent and efficient.

Your Own Investment—Equity. The bank doesn't really separate the business and the entrepreneur, regardless of whether the company is incorporated. In small business, banks lend primarily to the person.

The entrepreneur's general character and experience are both important. From the bank's perspective, the best experience an entrepreneur can have is a track record of successful small-business management in the industry in question.

Banks prefer to lend to existing businesses with some operating history rather than to start-ups. They will lend to start-ups if the business and the person look good, the loan is collateralized, and the company shows substantial equity, meaning that the entrepreneur has a fair amount of his or her own money invested in the business.

The entrepreneur's own investment is important for two reasons. First, investors, including banks, feel, probably rightly, that people tend to manage and safeguard their own money more carefully than someone else's and that a business has an extra margin of safety and energy when the owner/operator's money is on the line.

Second, if the business starts losing money, owner equity is lost first before debt money. Equity therefore cushions the bank's money against operating losses.

Attitude. Attitude is crucial in dealing with a bank. You should strive to create the impression that you would like the loan but don't really need it. To loan officers, an impression of desperation signals a possible loan default. Wanting the money for bigger and better things, on the other hand, signals prosperity and a successful business relationship.

Borrow Enough. Be careful to borrow enough money—make sure your figure has been calculated to cover all your needs and contingencies. Also, be careful of a banker who is willing to make a loan but won't lend you a sufficient amount. It's very bad for a banking relationship and for your business's health if you accept a loan for a given purpose and then go back and request more money for the same purpose.

When applying for a loan, document carefully how you arrived at the amount you're requesting. If the loan officer suggests that you borrow significantly less, it might be a good idea to consider another source.

Perseverance. Don't be discouraged by a refusal. Try to learn something from the experience. Determine what you might have done to cause the loan committee to turn you down. But also keep in mind that you may not have done anything wrong.

Refusals are sometimes made for reasons that have little to do with the applicant. For example, the bank may already have too many loans in your type of business. There are also times when loan money is just tight, and there isn't much around for anyone. On the other hand, if you get six or eight refusals, it might make sense to rethink the whole idea and/or approach.

Stay in Touch. Once you get a loan and establish a relationship with a bank, keep the loan officer informed about how you're doing. When their businesses aren't doing as well as they'd hoped, people tend to be reluctant to share the bad news, especially with their backers. But remember, bankers don't like surprises, especially bad ones. Keep your loan officer informed in good times and bad, and your banking relationship will be one of your biggest assets.

SBA Loans. The Small Business Administration (SBA) is a government agency that promotes small business in the United States through loans and other types of support. But SBA loans are misunderstood by many people. With few exceptions, the SBA does not loan government money to businesses; it guarantees loans made to small businesses by banks.

This government guarantee lowers the bank's risk, thereby allowing it to charge a slightly lower interest rate. The key point is not the rate, however, but the fact that some businesses are perceived as too risky to get bank financing without that guarantee. In order to get an SBA loan, you must already have been turned down by all available conventional channels.

To investigate SBA loans, contact the Small Business Administration office in your area. Look in the phone book for local listings or see Appendix B in the back of this book for regional offices.

The Five C's of Credit. Banks and other credit-granting organizations are often said to make funding decisions based on the Five C's of Credit. It's a good way to remember how banks think.

1. **Character** refers to the probability that borrowers will attempt to pay off their debts, that they intend to pay off the loan, and that their intention is serious.
2. **Capacity** refers to the borrowers' ability to pay, as determined by the lender.
3. **Capital** refers to the general financial condition of borrowers, as reflected in financial statements.
4. **Collateral** refers to the assets that are offered as security.
5. **Conditions** refers to general economic conditions and circumstances in the borrowers' particular industry or geographic area. The best of businesses can fail in the worst of times.

Venture Capital

A great deal has been written about venture capitalists and venture funding. However, few new business propositions have the characteristics that will attract venture interest. A few words of explanation are appropriate.

What Venture Capitalists Look For. Venture capitalists are interested in companies with a potential for very rapid and sustained growth. Rapid and sustained means an annual rate of 40 or 50 percent compounded for five or six years.

That kind of performance is generally associated with a new market. Suppose, for example, someone invents a new product that is met with an instant demand—then long-term supergrowth is possible. The market for the product grows immediately, and firms in the business can grow with it. Integrated circuits, cellular phones, personal computers, and new medical drugs are examples of products where such growth was possible.

Contrast these with a more typical business, such as a restaurant. In order to grow, a restaurant has to take business away from other restaurants, and that's unlikely to happen at unusually high rates.

Supergrowth opportunities tend to come about in high-technology areas and less commonly in lower-tech industries. Federal Express is a good example of a low-tech business that experienced spectacular growth.

Franchises. It should be clear that a franchised outlet is unlikely to meet the growth characteristics required by the venture capital business. Franchises are tried and true ideas that are likely to do well, but unlikely to experience explosive growth.

Other Sources of Money

Occasionally entrepreneurs find private sources of either debt or equity funding. These so-called angles are typically wealthy individuals looking for an unusual investment opportunity. This kind of financing is hard to find; it generally depends on having some personal contact or a nonbusiness relationship with the investor.

Ask your accountant or banker if he or she knows of anyone who might be interested. Personal financial planners sometimes have such leads among their clients.

Vendors are an often overlooked source of limited amounts of short-term money. If eager to do business, a vendor may extend credit on sales to your business. It never hurts to ask.

Case in Point Revisited

Can Joe Logan raise enough money to get into the printing business, or does he have to put it off until he can save up a lot more?

Well, he might be able to pull it off if he's willing to take a lot of risk. He lives in a house whose market value is approximately $155,000 and carries a mortgage of $100,000. Joe's equity in the house is therefore about $55,000. A bank will probably lend about 80 percent of that figure if Joe is willing to put up the house as collateral. That's $44,000.

In addition, the printing equipment is said to be fairly standard. That means it could be sold on the used equipment market if the business failed. Given that, a bank would probably give Joe a loan to buy it collateralized by the equipment itself. However, that loan is unlikely to be more than, say, 70 percent of the price of the equipment, which was $80,000. That's $56,000.

So, thus far Joe's funding stacks up like this:

Equipment based loan	$ 56,000
House based loan	44,000
Savings	25,000
	$125,000

That leaves a shortfall of $25,000 to get to the required $150,000. Can Joe borrow that much from his parents or other friends and relatives? If he can, he can get started.

Joe's position would be, to say the least, tight. If he fails, he loses everything, including, perhaps, the goodwill of his family. Further, if the $150,000 turns out to be not quite enough, he's tapped out, unlikely to be able to borrow more.

It takes a real entrepreneurial spirit to go for it under these conditions, but it can be done.

CHAPTER TEN

Negotiating the Deal

KEY TERMS FOR THIS CHAPTER

assignment
book value
confidentiality agreement
covenant not to compete
development
franchise agreement
franchise fee
independent contractor
inspections
operating manual
right of first refusal
royalty payment
term
territory
trademark

Case in Point: The Renewal Blues

Terri Hanson has been running a FurryFriends Pet Store franchise for eight years and has built it into a highly profitable operation. Her original franchise contract had a ten-year duration, and the wording concerning renewal was quite vague.

Terri knows another franchisee, Ted Cohen, in a nearby city. Ted just lost his franchise, and the franchisor is now running the store as a company operation. This is a shock to Terri, because Ted's outlet has always been one of the best run and most profitable in the entire chain.

Terri is suddenly wondering what will happen when her franchise comes up for renewal in two years. Will FurryFriends renew? Will she be fairly compensated if they don't? If they don't will she be able to continue to operate an unfranchised pet store in the same location?

The Franchise Agreement

The legal document that controls the franchise relationship during most of its life is a contract between the parties called the **franchise agreement.** Franchisee/franchisor negotiation centers on the terms of this document.

During the negotiating process, the franchisee needs to:

- Be sure that the franchise agreement is specific enough that nothing is left out.
- Understand thoroughly all of the implications of all of the terms in the agreement.

Reading the Fine Print

The franchise agreement is prepared by the franchisor and offered to prospects along with the whole franchise package. Since such contracts are prepared by franchisors and their attorneys, they tend to favor the franchisor on every conceivable issue. Franchisors argue that they need to protect the quality and consistency of their products and services. This is a reasonable argument, but the contracts that emerge are so one-sided that they open the door to abusive behavior later on. In his book *Franchise Selection*, attorney Raymond Munna has described the typical franchise agreement as "a license to destroy."

Many people in our society sign formal contracts without reading or thoroughly understanding the fine print. We do that when we buy insurance, cars, even houses. Don't do it this time. It could cost you everything you have. *Read the entire agreement and be sure you understand it, with all its implications, thoroughly*. Don't let an enthusiastic sales presentation push you into things that might unreasonably tie you up later. Remember, some of the contractual issues can cost you the business ten years down the road.

What's Negotiable?

With respect to negotiation, the first question that comes to mind is this: How flexible are the franchisors? Unfortunately, the answer is generally, not very. If the franchisor has a large business and a substantial number of outlets already in place, he or she isn't likely to change the contract much. On the other hand, a new franchisor who is struggling to get started may be more open to negotiation.

In any case, it's a good idea to try to improve on the contract as presented. Some people take unreasonable opening positions, expecting to give up a lot in negotiations. You want to make sure your franchisor isn't following this strategy—and if he or she is, you want to hone down those unreasonable points.

It also may help to talk to other franchisees about their contractual experience with the franchisor.

It is imperative that you employ an attorney at this point, ideally, someone with some experience in franchise law. The average general-practice attorney does not have this experience.

Be sure your attorney explains the implications of every clause in the contract to you in plain English. *Don't sign a contract that is going to control your professional life without legal advice!*

Typical Franchise Agreement Provisions

Most franchise contracts address several specific and very important issues. What follows is an explanation of why each of these clauses is significant and what its implications are. This list, however, is by no means definitive. Your contract may contain other clauses that are not covered here.

Introduction and Grant of the Franchise

This section identifies the parties involved and explains the nature of the business being franchised and the franchise relationship. It summarizes the reason for the contract. It may also reference other documents, such as the disclosure statement or the franchisor's operating manual. Be careful that seemingly casual language here doesn't commit you to something specified in one of those other documents.

Term and Renewal

Most franchise agreements cover a specified length of time, or **term,** although a few run indefinitely. A typical term is ten years.

Franchisees generally consider the deal a lifelong partnership and therefore expect renewal to be a matter of course at the end of the term. However, the contract may severely limit the franchisee's rights in this area.

Also, unless the contract gives the franchisee the right to renew under the old terms and conditions, renewals are likely to be under the terms and conditions being offered to new franchisees at that time. This often means a higher royalty rate.

It is at renewal time that the franchisor is most likely to attempt to get rid of an unwanted franchisee. Be careful of contract terms that would allow the franchisor to take the business at a price below market value if there is no renewal. That gives the franchisor a big incentive not to renew.

Try for wording that guarantees renewal as long as you're conducting the business reasonably successfully.

Trademarks, Trade Names, and Commercial Symbols

A **trademark,** an emblem or a name that belongs exclusively to a product or service, provides an identity to the franchisor's business. Trademarks are crucial to the franchising concept, because they provide for a uniform recognition of the product or service by the public. Trademarks are owned by the franchisor and licensed to the franchisee during the term of the contract only.

The franchise agreement generally will specify how the franchisee may use the trademarks and that such use must be discontinued in the event of termination of the contract.

Trademarks are registered nationally for interstate commerce and locally for regional businesses. It is therefore possible that an out-of-town franchisor's trademark may already be taken in your area by an unrelated local business. This can be a disaster, because if you can't use the franchisor's name and logo, all co-op advertising (advertising paid for in part by the franchisor) will be useless to you. Be sure your attorney checks availability in your local area.

Relationship of the Parties

Most franchise agreements state that the franchisee is an **independent contractor,** that is, an independent businessperson who has contracted for the services provided by the franchisor. The franchisee is not an employee or an agent of the franchisor. That means franchisor and franchisee are responsible for their own debts and liabilities, and neither can incur debts and responsibilities for the other. Neither can enter into contracts on behalf of the other.

Fees

This clause spells out the fees to be paid by the franchisee to the franchisor. There are usually two fees, the initial **franchise fee** and the **royalty payment.** The agreement should state how the initial fee is to be paid—in a lump sum or in stages. The royalty fee should be very precisely defined. If it is to be a percentage of revenues, the term revenues should be clearly defined, as sales of some items are sometimes omitted in the definition. The percentage should be specified, and any provisions for changes should be laid out.

Consequences of late or missed payments also should be spelled out. For example, does a missed payment void the contract or just incur late charges?

Changing the royalty payment percent is a critical issue. Many contracts state that this decision is the unilateral right of the franchisor. In such a contract, the franchisor can arbitrarily kill a franchisee's business at any time.

Territory

Franchises are often granted a **territory** in which the franchisee is licensed to operate. The contract language should explicitly state that the franchisor will not sell other franchises or open a company-owned unit within that territory. Be careful of contract terms allowing the establishment of operations designated as development, model, pilot, and the like. These can be slick ways to open a competing operation if yours turns out very well.

It is important to understand that an exclusive territory does not prevent other franchisees located outside of it from selling to customers within it; an agreement to prevent such sales would be illegal under U.S. antitrust law.

Be sure you understand exactly how your territory is defined, because territorial disputes are common in franchising. Here, for example, is a common problem:

> Town A sits astride the line separating County X and County Y but is mostly in County X. The town contains the only significant population for miles around. Joe wants a Modern Meticulous Maid franchise for Town A, but the agreement says that his territory is County X. The franchise salesman says not to worry; they always work by county, because maps are readily available and easy to read. Everyone understands, promises the salesman, that Joe's territory is Town A.
>
> A year or two later, the company sells another franchise in County Y, which competes head-to-head with Joe for the same customers. And suddenly the franchisor remembers only the letter of the contract.

This kind of confusion is especially likely in big cities, since metropolitan areas are divided into political units—towns and counties—that often have little relation to population or business patterns.

Site Selection and Development

The retail nature of most business-format franchises makes site selection critically important. One of the benefits that a successful franchisor offers is expertise in choosing a location. How that expertise is to be applied should be spelled out in the contract. Details of the arrangements vary significantly. At one extreme franchisors insist on selecting the site themselves; at the other they simply exercise a veto power over locations proposed by the franchisee.

The particular arrangement must be spelled out in detail and enforced. Site selection and development often arise as issues of contention in lawsuits after a franchisee has failed. If part of the reason for failure is alleged to be a poor location, it makes a big difference who actually chose it.

Expertise in site selection is frequently oversold by franchisors, who sometimes simply contract a commercial real estate agent in the area to do the work for them. In such a case, the agent may be motivated by commissions to select a site that may not be consistent with your best interest. Also, although real estate agents may know the local market best, they may not be familiar with the demographics that make your business successful.

Development refers to transforming a chosen site into a working business location. This involves financing and construction. Some franchisors provide a turnkey operation; this means they do the development and turn the finished product over to the franchisee, who either buys or leases it.

Others are less involved in the project and may simply inspect the facilities to make sure they are up to standard. The exact level of involvement of the franchisor must be spelled out in detail in the agreement.

The franchise agreement usually specifies a deadline by which the site development must be complete. Once the agreement is signed, the franchisor wants the franchisee to get into business as soon as possible. It is incumbent upon the franchisee to ensure that the time frame for completion of the site is realistic. (Construction always seems to take longer than expected.) The deadline is usually negotiable.

Image and Conduct of Business

Franchisors have an interest in ensuring that all franchisees maintain a consistently high quality public image. This image is composed of a multitude of things, such as cleanliness, courtesy, hours of operation, and staffing. All this is in addition to product quality. Contracts invariably contain a provision in which the franchisee agrees to live up to the franchisor's standards of performance on items of importance to the company's image. The standards themselves are usually detailed in the franchisor's operating manual.

Also, the franchisee agrees to submit to inspections to verify that the standards are being met.

This clause has created what is possibly the largest single area of dispute in franchising. In the past, franchisors have used the clause to terminate unwanted franchises at will. They could always send an inspector into an operation and find some minor technical violations of a vaguely worded operating manual such as a paper towel on the floor, when the manual says the rest room will be kept "clean." They could then use these violations to terminate the contract.

This abuse led several states to enact "good cause" legislation that prevents franchisors from terminating or failing to renew franchises without reasonable cause.

You should be very careful that you understand how the franchisor has used this clause in the past and what protection is available in your state.

Products and Services to Be Purchased by the Franchisee

Franchisors argue that they must be able to assure themselves that the product or service provided to the public by franchisees is of a consistently high quality. In order to do this, they maintain that they must control the inputs used by the franchisees. In extreme cases, the franchisor insists on selling inputs to the franchisees and builds such a clause into the franchise agreement. Clearly, this presents the franchisor with an opportunity for unfair dealing. If the franchisee must buy from only one source, that source can charge exorbitant prices.

Fortunately, the requirement that franchisees buy directly and only from franchisors runs afoul of the antitrust laws in the United States. Therefore today's contracts rarely contain such a strict requirement.

Franchisors can, however, ensure quality levels by requiring franchisees to purchase inputs that meet their written specifications. This can be done in two ways. Franchisors can provide either the specifications or a list of approved vendors whose products meet specifications.

An opportunity for abuse still exists under these terms. Specifications could be so restrictive that only the franchisor's own product or that of a particular vendor would meet them. In such a case, unfair prices could again be exacted, either by the franchisor or by the vendor, who in turn gives a kickback to the franchisor. Such arrangements are illegal, but it takes a court action to put a stop to them.

Training

Training is a key element in the franchise formula. It is what enables a person with limited experience in a field to become a successful franchisee. Nearly all franchise arrangements offer training of some sort, with the details spelled out in the franchise agreement. It's a good idea to look at the training facilities and documentation to be sure that the program actually offered is consistent with what is spelled out in the agreement.

The training program can be the source of a great deal of contractual confusion. To minimize that possibility, be sure that you know the answers to the following questions before signing up.

- Is the training at the home office or your site?
- Is there an additional charge for training?
- Who pays for travel and living expenses during the training period?
- Can additional people attend? At what cost?
- What happens to the contract and any money you've paid if you fail to complete training?
- After opening, is there a continuing

training program for the franchisee? For employees?
- How much of the training is self-study, through manuals?
- What are the qualifications of the instructors?
- How much training is required, and what is optional?

Operating Manuals, Confidentiality

The franchisor's **operating manual** is at the heart of the franchising concept. It tells you how to run your small business. It also contains most of the franchisor's trade secrets and is therefore highly confidential.

The franchise agreement normally will make reference to the operating manual in a number of places, and will require that you sign a **confidentiality agreement** with respect to its contents. You also may need to have your employees sign confidentiality documents. Typically such an agreement requires that franchisees agree not to divulge the contents of the manual to anyone else, not to copy the manual, not to use its secrets in any other business, and to return it at the end of the franchise relationship.

Many contracts have a separate clause dealing with confidentiality. This serves to emphasize its importance.

If possible, prospective franchisees should study the operating manual carefully before signing up. Make sure there is some substance to its content. Unfortunately, determining this is difficult if you're not overly familiar with the business beforehand.

Advertising

Contractual provisions regarding advertising generally fall into two areas:

1. The franchisor's right to determine how and where the franchisee advertises
2. The amount of money the franchisee must spend on advertising

In the first area, it is both reasonable and typical that franchisors demand the right to approve or design all advertising. Advertising has a tremendous impact on public image, which is something a franchisor has a legitimate right to protect. Imagine, for example, the result if a family restaurant franchisee decided to run ads featuring naked women!

Franchisors sometimes want to dictate the media used for local advertising. That can create a problem if the rates in a particular area or the effectiveness of the medium are substantially different from those that the franchisor has experienced elsewhere. A reasonable franchisor should be negotiable on this issue.

Regarding money: Franchisors often require that specified amounts be spent on advertising on a regular basis. Expenditures are usually stated in terms of percents of revenue but may also be dollar figures. Expenditures come in two forms:

1. A contribution to a national or regional co-op advertising fund
2. Local spending handled by the franchisee alone

The total budget can be as high as 10 or 15 percent of the franchisee's revenues.

A franchising abuse commonly found in the past involved co-op advertising. Funds were collected from franchisees but used for purposes other than common advertising. Sometimes the uses weren't even to the benefit of franchisees. The practice resulted in the formation of trusts to administer co-op advertising funds. Such trusts sometimes are administered by committees of franchisees as well as the franchisor.

The franchise agreement should spell out the details of the advertising program and specify how much the franchisee is required to spend. It should also specify how and under what conditions those amounts can be changed. It's a major problem, for instance, if the franchisor can unilaterally raise the percentage contribution to co-op advertising. It's also a major problem if you have to continue to advertise heavily even if the expense forces you to run at a loss.

Inspections, Audits, and Financial Reports

In order to enforce their quality standards, most franchisors require that franchisees submit to periodic physical and financial **inspections** on short notice or without any notice. The physical inspection involves gauging quality in product or service. A financial inspection is called an audit and consists of a review of the company's books by an accountant. The audit's purpose is to verify the franchisee's revenue to be sure that the calculation of royalties is correct.

Inspections, audits, and reports are reasonable requirements, but they can be costly and time consuming. Some franchisors try to make the franchisee bear the cost of audits, especially if they are conducted by outside public accounting firms. Try to avoid this contingency; it can be very expensive.

Inspections tend to tie up management's time. It's a good idea to try to negotiate a limit on their frequency.

Managerial Assistance

In their marketing effort, franchisors often claim to have all the answers to problems that franchisees encounter and to be ready and willing to share those answers on a continuing basis. In practice, figuring out why a franchisee is in trouble and what to do about it costs money, and franchisors, like everyone else, are careful about what they spend.

Franchisees should insist that the contract be clear on what the franchisor will do to help them and on what that help will cost. If a company consultant is available, the franchisor will probably charge for his or her services as well as expenses. Make sure the rates are spelled out in advance.

Assistance can be especially important around the start of a business. The weeks just before and just after opening tend to spawn the most problems, especially if the franchisee has limited experience in the industry. Franchisors frequently offer help during that time. Try to get it nailed down in the contract.

Financing and Financing Assistance

Franchisors occasionally offer financing to franchisees and more frequently offer assistance in getting financing from other sources.

If financing is to be provided, be sure you know and have in the agreement how much is available and at what interest rate. Also spell out the consequences of a missed or delinquent payment—don't risk losing your entire business because you're a little late on the mortgage payment. When it comes to lending money, the franchisor won't be any nicer than a bank if you can't pay it back.

Franchisors frequently claim that they provide assistance in obtaining financing. That generally means they will help you fill out the loan application and provide a packet of information on the business for you to submit to the bank. They occasionally have a bank relationship on which you can piggy-back. That's a real help, but ultimately you have to qualify for your own loan.

Covenant Not to Compete

Franchisors don't like the idea of people leaving the organization and starting a competing business, often using what they learned by working in the franchise. They attempt to keep this from occurring by inserting a clause in the contract in which the franchisee agrees not to compete with the franchisor or other licensees. This is called a **covenant not to compete.**

The clause is intended to be binding during the life of the contract and for some period after termination. It is often limited to a specific geographic area.

Court decisions have limited the effectiveness of covenants not to compete. In general, a blanket covenant is not enforceable. In other words, although you may agree never to work in another fast-food restaurant again, anywhere, the court is unlikely to enforce that provision. On the other hand, your agreement not to open a hamburger restaurant in Phoenix for two years may be enforceable.

Keep in mind that a covenant not to compete affects your employment options in the event that the franchised business doesn't survive. That can be especially important if all of your prior work experience is in the industry that you're franchising into. Don't agree to a covenant not to compete without consulting your attorney about its likely effect on you.

Assignment of the Franchise, Right of First Refusal

Assignment means the transfer of ownership of the franchise through sale or other means. Transfers other than sale can occur due to the owner's death or disability, or a divorce.

Franchisors naturally want to ensure that their franchises remain in the hands of qualified franchisees. Therefore, they usually put restrictions into the agreement on whom the franchisee can transfer the business to. This reasonable requirement can result in serious problems for the business owner.

The most common restriction is that the transferee must be approved by the franchisor. This is indeed reasonable, but be sure the conditions for approval are specified and not left unilaterally up to the franchisor. They should be the same conditions that the original franchisee had to meet.

A related requirement is that only a qualified franchisee can run the business. This becomes important if the original franchisee becomes disabled or dies. Does a spouse or child then qualify to continue the business? If not, many agreements read that the franchise must be sold to a qualified operator. A similar situation can occur in cases of divorce. The spouse who keeps the business in the property settlement may not be the one who was qualified as a franchisee.

Contracts can be abusive in this area if they specify an unfair disposition of the business. For example, the agreement might say that in the event of the franchisee's death or disability, the business is to be sold to the franchisor at book value. **Book value** is the value of the assets minus the liabilities on the company's books, usually a fraction of its true worth. Such clauses actually have been written into contracts, and they amount to stealing the business from the heirs of the franchisee.

A related and very common clause grants the franchisor the **right of first refusal** to buy the business if the franchisee wants to sell. Under this clause, if the franchisee has a buyer at, say, $200,000, he or she must offer it to the franchisor for the same price first. Only after the franchisor refuses can the first sale proceed.

A clause restricting assignment also impacts the franchisee's right to incorporate the business. Incorporation involves transferring ownership to a separate legal entity, the corporation, and corporations don't meet the qualifications for being a franchisee; only people do. This usually results in the requirement that the qualified franchisee remain the major stockholder in the corporation. It also may require the franchisor's approval for the sale or transfer of stock.

Termination

At one time, franchisors could terminate a relationship unilaterally. This was a source of numerous abuses resulting in the passage by some states of "good cause" statutes. These require a reasonable cause for termination regardless of what the contract says. You should avoid any contract that doesn't spell out the conditions under which the franchisor can terminate the agreement. Reasonable and common causes include:

- Failure to follow the operating manual
- Failure to follow other contract terms
- Conviction for a felony
- Nonpayment of fees
- Death or disability
- Unauthorized sale of the business
- Abandonment of the business
- Bankruptcy (in combination with other faults on the part of the franchisee, as federal bankruptcy law prohibits bankruptcy alone from being used as a cause of termination)

Vague language should always be avoided. To return to our earlier example: What is a "clean" rest room or kitchen? Clean by whose definition? In addition, a contract should always provide you with a reasonable time in which to cure deficiencies before they can be used as grounds for any action against you.

Upon termination, the ex-franchisee is generally obligated to:

- Return all proprietary materials to the franchisor
- Destroy all symbols of the franchised business

- Cancel state trade-name registrations
- Pay all amounts due to the franchisor
- Stop operating under the franchisor's identity

Be sure you understand whether the contract allows you to continue operating the same business without the franchisor's identity in the event of termination.

Case in Point Revisited

The experience of Terri's friend Ted certainly indicates that FurryFriends may not be a completely ethical franchisor. Terri may be headed for trouble when her franchise agreement comes up for renewal in two years.

Unless the state in which Terri does business has good cause legislation, it is entirely possible that FurryFriends will be able to take over her franchise.

If she owns the real estate or the lease in which she operates, she may be able to continue to run the business as an independent pet store if the agreement is not renewed. If the franchisor owns the real estate, it may be able to take over operations and pay Terri nothing.

The real solution, unfortunately, lies in hindsight: The question should have been clarified before signing. Perhaps Terri could have negotiated better wording in the renewal clause. If not, she could at the very least have surveyed other franchisees to see if a pattern of abuse existed.

PART THREE

OPERATING YOUR FRANCHISE

CHAPTER ELEVEN

Selecting Your Location

KEY TERMS FOR THIS CHAPTER

break even	*drive-by*	*radius site, situs*
contribution customer profile	*fixed cost*	*traffic*
demographics	*location analysis*	*variable cost*
		walk-by

Case in Point: Location, Location, Location

Harvey Botz is ready to lock up the deal to buy a BigBurger franchise for his community or one nearby. He wants to be in the fast-food business and has chosen BigBurger after long and extensive research.

BigBurger's franchise advertisements said that site selection assistance would be provided. When Harvey first approached BigBurger, he thought that meant some kind of sophisticated, mathematical analysis to select a site that would virtually guarantee success. In other words, Harvey expected the franchisor to do the job for him. He was taken aback to find that assistance was provided in the form of one person on the headquarters staff who reviewed and approved sites proposed by the franchisees themselves.

The location expert was an older gentleman named Ralph who seemed about ready for retirement. Reviewing location decisions was only one of several things he did. Ralph was quite candid. He said that he would make sure Harvey didn't make a gross blunder in location, but that was about all. Knowing the difference between a good location and a great one was up to Harvey alone.

In spite of that disappointment, Harvey feels that BigBurger is overall the best deal around. And he's determined to go through with the project.

But picking a location suddenly is his biggest problem. He's never done it before, and doesn't even know what to consider.

Location Analysis: A Science or an Art?

There's an old saying in retailing and commercial real estate circles: "The three most important things in determining a business's success are location, location and location." Is this true? Well, it often is, but sometimes it isn't. While location is absolutely critical to some businesses, it's less important to others. A good location generally means one that's convenient to get to and has high customer traffic. But better locations usually cost more to rent or own. To arrive at the best decision for your business, you must balance a location's quality against its cost.

People often talk about location analysis as if it were an exact science, as if there were some secret formula that could guarantee selection of the perfect spot for a business. In reality, there's no such formula. Location analysis is a matter of sifting and organizing a great deal of data and then making an informed decision. In the end it comes down to personal judgment. Of course, experience helps, and people who specialize in commercial real estate tend to have developed insights that beginners lack. Franchisors also may have developed an expertise in locating their own particular type of business as well.

This chapter doesn't present "the answer" to the location dilemma. Rather, it will point out a number of things that you should consider and weigh carefully in making your decision.

The Nature of Location

Location, also called **site** or **situs,** really has three dimensions. First, it's important to consider the community in which a business is located. The question is whether the people and businesses there have a demand for the product or service your business offers. For example, you wouldn't want to put a high-tech computer store in a low-income, rural, or blue-collar community.

The second issue involves location within the community. That is, once you've determined that a market for your product or service exists in a given area, the question of exactly where you put it has to be answered. You want to locate somewhere within the community that will maximize your attractiveness to customers. This is related to the nature of your product or service.

Finally, in franchising the idea of location is somewhat related to the territory assigned to you by the franchisor.

The Role of the Franchisor

The part played by franchisors in site selection varies a great deal. Most franchisors in businesses where location is important advertise that they offer "assistance" in site selection. Prospective franchisees should be sure that they understand in the beginning exactly what they can expect from their franchisors in the site selection area and what it will cost.

Probably the most common franchisor practice is to provide a review and approval process for sites selected by franchisees. The approval responsibility may be vested in a committee or in a single person at headquarters. This policy, of course, puts most of the burden on the franchisee. In some cases, the home office approval may do little more than catch extreme blunders on the part of franchisees.

At the other extreme, franchisors do all the work and make site selections themselves. Some are very proud of their ability to chose successful locations. In these cases, franchisors often take an ownership interest in the real estate and lease it to the franchisee while he or she is in business. Franchisors intending to develop an area may even acquire a site and begin building an outlet before finding a franchisee to operate it. If franchisors do a lot of work in site selection, it's important to understand whether that effort is included in the franchise fee or if separate reimbursement is expected.

Some franchisors claim that they will provide site selection assistance and then simply contract the job out to a local commercial real estate agent after the franchisee is signed up. This can create a problem, because the local agent may know the market for property in the vicinity but may not be familiar with the characteristics of the business in question. Real estate agents are also commission motivated—they try to move their own listings first because they get a higher commission that way. The customer may never see another listing that's actually a better deal.

Type of Business

Not all businesses are equally location sensitive. If you're a chimney sweep, people don't care where your office is because they generally don't go there. They just need to know you're in the area and will come when they call you. The same is true for a great many service businesses: Employment agencies, maid services, plumbers, and so on, don't depend on a specific location within a town for their success. They do, however, have to be sensitive to the community's overall demand for their product or service. A maid service, for example, won't do well in an industrial area or in a low-income residential district. A fast-food restaurant, on the other hand, is dependent not only on how many potential pizza or hamburger eaters there are in town but also on how convenient it is for people to get to the restaurant.

Territory

A territory or an exclusive territory involves the franchisor's guarantee not to sell another franchise or open a company operation in the area granted by the territorial agreement.

Territories are usually defined in relation to population statistics or maps. For example, it wouldn't make sense to place a hamburger restaurant somewhere and say its territory is the surrounding area within a five-mile radius if no one lives in that radius. More typically the franchisor would look at a map showing population statistics and find an area in which, say, 20,000 people live. It would then define that area as a territory in which a franchisee could locate the business. An exclusive territory would mean that the franchisor would agree not to sell another franchise or open a company unit in that area.

A territorial agreement in no way prevents a competing hamburger or other fast-food operation not associated with the franchisor from opening in the area.

Be Sure of What's in Your Territory

When you buy a franchise, you are essentially buying a territory. You must be very careful about the nature of that territory. An illustration will make the point.

Suppose you're interested in a Magic Mouse Pizza franchise and live in a city in which several successful Magic Mouse outlets already exist. Assume Magic Mouse is a combination pizza restaurant and children's amusement center that attracts young families with small children. You approach Magic Mouse, which tells you that territories are granted based on population districts containing 25,000 people, and yes, there is one district still open in your town. Excited beyond words, you rush to Magic Mouse's headquarters, which is located in another state, and sign up.

Upon your return, you build your restaurant and open the doors to find only a slow trickle of business, a fraction of what the other franchisees in your area do. What went wrong?

You probably failed to notice that your territory consisted entirely of neighborhoods populated by couples who are middle age and older. The people in your territory don't have small children, and thus no need for a Magic Mouse restaurant.

The age, income, and life-style characteristics of a population, known as **demographics,** are extremely important to the designation of a territory and the selection of a location.

Community

Choosing a viable community for a business involves taking a hard look at population, demographics, and competition.

Population

The first step is determining if enough potential customers live in an area that you can reasonably expect to service.

First decide how far people will drive to obtain the kind of thing you sell. For example, for fast food it might be five miles, for bedspreads and draperies it might be ten or fifteen.

Once you've determined your **radius** of business, look at some potential sites and draw circles of that radius around them on a map. Examine who is in the circle. The real question is not how many people but how many potential customers are within that radius.

Demographics

In order to answer that question, you have to develop a **customer profile** for your business. A profile is a listing of the important characteristics of a buying unit, usually a household. These include age, family size, income, and other relevant characteristics. A profile might look something like this:

Age	30–45
Family size	4–5
Income	\$30–\$40,000
Education	high school grad, some college
Children's age	Teens

The franchisor should have this kind of information on people who buy its product. Ask for the information and use it.

Next you have to get some idea as to whether the people in your area match the profile. Demographic information for census tracts is available in larger public libraries. The town hall or county seat may have some information as well.

Be careful of subtle traps. Not everything shows up in the profiles. Consider, for example, the difference between a university town and one supported by an auto assembly plant. Ages, family sizes, and incomes might be fairly similar, but other basic traits will probably be very different. A fast-food restaurant might do well in either place, but what about an art gallery, a bicycle shop, or a health food store? These would probably do better in the college town. On the other hand, an auto parts store, a motorcycle shop, or a body builder's gym might fare better in a blue-collar environment.

Competition

Competition has to be considered in addition to the customer base. How many similar businesses are already there? A town may be able to support several fast-food operations, but two health food outlets will probably kill each other. The franchisor should be a valuable source of information on what constitutes a saturated market.

To make the community decision, look at profiles, competition, and demographics, but also walk around a lot with your eyes open, to see the nature of the environment and the people who live there.

Site Location

The final location question involves choosing a specific site within a community. The first thing to address here is the importance of your location to your customer. If your customer doesn't need to come to you, then exact location may not be too important. Many service businesses are like that. They depend on advertising and telephone contact to reach the customer, then the service is brought to the customer's home or place of business.

Location is important to a majority of franchised businesses. Business-format franchises tend to involve products that are sold to walk-in or drive-in customers. The industry is dominated by food service businesses, especially fast food, but there are a significant number of other retail establishments as well.

Traffic

Retail location revolves around the idea of **traffic,** of which there are two types, **walk-by** and **drive-by.** Traffic is the reason for the success of many stores in modern shopping malls. The mall draws a great deal of traffic based on its large anchor stores as well as a large number of smaller establishments. Small stores that wouldn't have a chance in outside locations can do well in malls because of all the customers walking by. People don't go to the mall specifically to visit the small store, but as they walk past they do stop in and buy.

A location must be visible and accessible. If you're on a road with high traffic, but it's difficult to get off the road and into the store, the traffic won't do you much good. The speed of drive-by traffic is important too. A car going 25 mph has a better chance of seeing your business and stopping than a car doing 55 mph.

There are two issues involved in traffic, quantity and quality. Quantity is a matter of number: How many people walk by or drive by in a day? You can figure that out by standing in front of a location and counting for a few days. Be sure to do it on different days of the week. Weekday count is likely to be different from weekend count. You may want to hire a reliable teenager to do it for you.

Quality—the issue of how many passersby are potential customers—is more difficult to determine. The concept of quality traffic is best illustrated by an example.

An entrepreneur opened a decorator art gallery in a suburban strip center. He located among three established businesses: an upscale restaurant, a women's health studio, and a large supermarket. He thought success was guaranteed because of the traffic to these other establishments. In particular he reasoned that women do most home decorating, that they would be going in and out of the spa and the supermarket and would stop into his store.

Unfortunately, the gallery owner had miscalculated: He found that women going to the spa tended to change into exercise clothes at home, drive to the spa, park, and run almost head down from their cars to the studio. They returned the same way. They were not about to go shopping in their leotards!

Supermarket shoppers behaved similarly, but probably for different reasons. Once a woman has parked in the supermarket's lot, she tends to go directly to the store and then directly home. There's no time to shop for art while the ice cream's melting.

The point of this story is that traffic made up of people who aren't potential customers doesn't count. Walk-in customers for an art gallery or a gift shop need to come from people who are leisurely cruising around even if they're not shopping for specific items.

Assessing the quality of traffic is a tough judgmental call, but it needs to be done if you're going to maximize your probability of success.

Break-even Analysis and Traffic Counts

Break-even analysis is a useful technique for calculating the viability of a retail location. Remember that better locations with more quality traffic are more expensive to lease or buy. The best example is an indoor mall. The traffic is high, but so is the rent. Break-even analysis is a way to estimate whether the sales generated by the traffic will cover the additional overhead.

Fixed and Variable Costs

To conduct a break-even analysis, the first thing to do is look at your monthly budget and divide all your costs into two categories, fixed and variable. A **fixed cost** is one whose dollar amount doesn't change with your level of sales, such as rent. The store can sell more or less product and the rent stays the same. (Some retail leases charge a percentage of sales over a certain amount in addition to a base rent. In that case only the base rent is a fixed cost. These are called percent leases.)

In the case of a **variable cost,** the dollar amount changes with the level of sales, for example, the wholesale cost of product. (The increasing portion of the rent in a percent lease is also a variable cost.) Suppose, on the average, you buy goods for 45 percent of what you sell them for. That is, for every dollar of sales you pay the wholesaler 45 cents. If your sales are $100, your cost is $45; on sales of $200, your cost is $90. We would then say that your variable cost is 45 percent of sales and your **contribution** is 55 percent, meaning that out of every dollar of sales you get to keep 55 cents to contribute to profit and overhead.

In a store fixed costs typically include rent, utilities, property taxes, depreciation, and the salaries of salespeople and management. (Be sure to include a salary for yourself.) Variable costs probably include only the wholesale cost of goods and freight.

The Break-even Volume

Now suppose your total overhead, or fixed cost, is $4,000 a month. The question is: How much do you have to sell to **break even,** that is, to have total revenue just equal total cost?

The answer is relatively simple. If 55 cents of each dollar of sales is a contribution to overhead, how many of those dollars do you have to earn to cover your $4,000? To get the answer, divide $4,000 by .55:

$$\$4{,}000/.55 = \$7{,}272.73$$

That is, you have to sell $7,272.73 worth of product just to break even. This won't give you any profit or return on your investment in the business, but you won't be losing money either. We'll round the number to $7,300 for convenience in the rest of this chapter.

Required Traffic Count from Break-even Volume

Now let's work backward to traffic count. Suppose the franchisor tells you that the average sale in one of his or her stores is $25. That means you have to make at least 292 sales transactions during the month ($7,300 divided by $25 = 292). By watching other stores, you figure out that one walk-in customer out of three buys something. That means you have to have 876 walk-ins a month (292 × 3 = 876). You also observed other similar stores or franchise locations and estimate that one walk-by out of twenty comes into the store. That would imply that you need somewhere in the neighborhood of 17,520 walk-bys a month (876 × 20 = $7,520). If you're open seven days a week, that means you need at least 584 walk-bys in an average day (17,520 ÷ 30 = 584) to survive. To make a profit will take more.

How do you tell if a location will provide that kind of traffic? Quite simply, stand there and count for a few days. Remember, however, to allow for traffic quality. All the walk-bys in the world won't help if they're not potential customers for your product.

And since you pay a higher rent for higher traffic, your break-even point is higher as well in a prime location. Analyze your options carefully. Talk to local real estate professionals and a local banker before making a location decision.

Case in Point Revisited

Harvey has a lot to consider in locating his BigBurger franchise. He has to reevaluate the demographics in his town as well as the existing competition. He'd also better take a close look at how his territory is defined. There's no substitute for hard work when looking for a site.

His first step should be to contact an experienced commercial real estate agent in the area. He should also get his banker's thoughts on the issue.

A caution is appropriate with respect to real estate agents. Be sure to contact an experienced commercial agent rather than someone in residential sales. Commission-driven salespeople will try to get your business even if they have very little commercial experience, but an agent who sells houses is likely to know absolutely nothing about selecting business property.

CHAPTER TWELVE

Training: The All-Important Element

KEY TERMS FOR THIS CHAPTER

continuing training
grand-opening training
operations manual
pre-opening training
training center
training manual

Case in Point: Going Back to School

Charlie Dudley has been interested in an automotive service franchise for years. He has an affinity for cars and wants to make his living in some way associated with the field.

Unfortunately, Charlie has never had much experience in the business end of automobiles. Cars have always been a hobby, but he's worked for a large electronics company as an accountant for years. Further, Charlie considers himself only a mediocre mechanic. His interest has always been in the performance and appearance end of autos.

Nevertheless, Charlie is determined to get into the automotive field. He knows he hasn't got the resources to acquire anything as grand as a car dealership, so he's been looking into franchises for mufflers, brakes, and transmissions.

Charlie has a serious concern. As an accountant, he knows the importance of a business's supporting functions, such as finance, personnel, and attracting customers, and he doesn't know anything about these areas in the automotive industry. He also realizes that he doesn't have a deep enough technical knowledge about how cars work and are maintained. In other words, he's going to have to learn a lot.

Charlie's concern revolves around

whether he can depend on the franchisor to teach him enough to run one of its businesses effectively. Perhaps the franchisor expects franchisees to have prior automotive business experience, and Charlie will be in over his head from day one.

How can Charlie assess whether a franchisor's training program will be adequate to cover his needs? Should he go back to school first to learn a little more about mechanics?

The Role and Importance of Training

Training is a central element in the concept of franchising. Unfortunately, its importance is often overlooked or misunderstood by prospective franchisees who take learning how for granted.

Franchising involves transferring proven business formats from experts (franchisors) to beginners (franchisees). Part of that format is the system for running the business. Simply opening a restaurant that looks like a McDonald's doesn't make it a McDonald's. The owner has to know how to run the place like a McDonald's. Franchisors always give new franchisees an extensive how-to book, called the **operations manual,** but it isn't enough. Running a franchised business successfully requires a great deal of training, which the franchisor should provide.

To put it another way, when you purchase a franchise, you deserve more than just the right to run a business like the franchisor's. You deserve to be *taught* to run the business as the franchisor does. The teaching is a fundamental part of the deal. Unfortunately, it's a part that's hard to judge from the outside, and easy for franchisors to cut corners on.

You should study the franchisor's training program very carefully and give it significant weight in your overall evaluation of the opportunity. Learning by doing is a poor substitute for formal training before your doors are open.

The Consequences of Poor Training

Lack of know-how, especially in peripheral, support areas, can sink a business more quickly than anything else. Small businesses usually don't fail from lack of knowledge about the business's product or service. They fail from lack of knowledge about other facets of running the company.

For example, people who open restaurants generally know how to cook. The reason so many restaurants fail so quickly is that their owners don't have enough knowledge about the other parts of running a restaurant: finance, inventory control, site selection, advertising, and personnel management.

People buy franchises because franchisors have successfully pulled all these things together into a manageable package. But the knowledge has to be transferred through training. Franchisees need training even if they have industry experience, because they're rarely experienced in all aspects of running the show.

Evaluating Training

Because so many different kinds of business are franchised, there aren't any absolute rules by which you can measure the quality and effectiveness of a franchisor's training program. There are, however, some general practices and observations that can provide a structure for your thinking as you evaluate the training provided.

The Franchisor's Training Function

Franchisors should have a formal training department within their organization. That department should be headed by a senior employee with extensive experience in the business. Sometimes a person with strong educational credentials can be appropriate if he or she is backed up by a technically qualified staff. The point is that training should be a senior function within the franchisor organization.

If training is run by a junior person and stuck off in a subdepartment somewhere, there may be cause for concern.

Facilities and Staff

There should be a separate **training center** or training facility. The center can be located anywhere; it doesn't necessarily have to be at headquarters. Some companies have regional centers while others do everything at a central location.

Regional centers are more convenient for geographically dispersed franchisees, especially if training is continuous after the business is open. However, a central location allows the franchisor to concentrate its efforts and present a more sophisticated training product. Either arrangement can be quite effective.

There should be a full-time staff involved in training, although this may be difficult for a small franchisor just getting started in franchising operations. The staff should have appropriate credentials and experience in the subjects they're teaching.

What to Look for While Visiting

While visiting the franchisor, ask to inspect the training facility and observe a class or two in session. Ask yourself the following questions:

- Is the facility clean and well maintained?
- Is the equipment installed adequate to simulate field operations?
- Do the staff appear knowledgeable, motivated, and professional? Are they appropriately dressed?
- Do the students appear to be of an appropriate caliber?

Documentation

The entire training program should be well documented in printed material. Each course should have an associated **training manual** or book that lays out the subject matter. The book should serve as a supplement to the classroom work. Each manual should have a table of contents and be easy to read and follow. Be careful of a manual that's too technical for you to understand if you open to a random page and begin to read.

Franchisors generally offer a basic course for beginning franchisees. This basic course is the heart of the program. (The training program may or may not include other courses in specialized areas.) Examine the syllabus and training manual for the basic course carefully. It should include sections on the following:

- Introduction, background
- Finance and accounting, record keeping
- Marketing and sales
- Operations, service, production
- Personnel management

Keep these points in mind as you tour and evaluate the franchisor's training program. Remember that it is not uncommon for salespeople to oversell the training program.

Types of Training

There are generally three major classifications within franchisee training:

- Pre-opening training
- Grand-opening training
- Continuing training

In **pre-opening training,** the new franchisee gains basic exposure to the business. **Grand-opening training** might more properly be called grand-opening assistance, as the trainer generally comes to the franchisee at that crucial time. **Continuing training** is ongoing and ranges from substantial to nonexistent. We'll talk briefly about each.

Pre-opening Training

The weeks and months prior to opening the doors for business are very busy for the new franchisee. You must get everything ready for the launch including financing, facilities, and advertising. In addition, you must attend the most intensive period of training the franchisor offers.

Pre-opening training is virtually always at the franchisor's training center. It generally lasts for at least two weeks, but in some cases it may be as long as eight weeks. The program is usually a combination of classroom work and hands-on experience in a simulated business environment.

The nature of the training depends on the nature of the business. A food service franchise should have a classroom kitchen in which to work, while tax preparation would be entirely a classroom exercise.

Ideally, classes are kept to twelve or fifteen students to enhance the learning experience and build a strong relationship between the franchisor and franchisees. The training materials may include lectures, slides, audio and video tapes, and instructional manuals.

It is important to understand who may attend pre-opening training and at what cost. Typically training for the franchisee is included in the franchise fee. Attendance by more than one owner or by employees is negotiable; the franchisor generally charges for additional attendees. Living expenses during training are usually the responsibility of the franchisee.

Grand-opening Training

In many franchised lines of business, the grand opening is a crucial event. A restaurant is a good example. People watch the building going up and try the new eatery within a few days of opening. Their experience on that first try dictates whether they'll come back. It is therefore in the best interest of both the franchisee and the franchisor to make sure the first days go well, and that quality and service are as good as they can be at the outset.

Of course, there are other businesses in which the first days aren't so critical. A temporary help agency, for example, isn't likely to open its doors to an onslaught of customers.

Where the grand opening is critical, franchisors often send a trainer to the franchisee's site to help him or her get started. The trainer may arrive a week or two prior to opening and stay a week or more afterward. The trainer's stay can extend as long as several weeks if there are problems in getting the business to run smoothly.

The trainer's function in the period around opening is to assist the franchisee in any way possible and to train the staff. This should be done with the franchisee, who will be doing most of the staff training in the future.

Be sure you understand who pays for the cost of grand-opening training/assistance before signing up. Some of this service is usually included in the franchise fee, but if an excessive amount of help is required, the franchisee may be expected to pay for it.

Continuing Training

Franchisors don't have a consistent policy regarding ongoing training. Some do none at all, while some offer a series of courses and seminars on a variety of specialized topics. The most sophisticated have regularly scheduled offerings that franchisees can take advantage of on a planned basis.

Franchisors that hold periodic meetings of their franchisees usually include optional training sessions in the meeting programs. This practice is similar in style to conventions or meetings held by professional associations.

In most franchised businesses, field representatives visit franchisees on a regular basis. Most ongoing training is delivered through these field visits. Field representatives provide expert advice on virtually any area of operations in a one-on-one environment with the franchisee and employees.

Franchisees often view the field representative's visit as an unwelcome inspection, but the rep's role as trainer should not be overlooked.

Case in Point Revisited

Our best advice for Charlie is to be up front with the franchisor about what he does and doesn't know. In addition, he needs to take a very hard look at the franchisor's training program. Do the materials seem to teach what he needs to learn? Or is the program a cursory review for those who are already familiar with the business? Charlie needs to do some careful evaluating of how his needs mesh with the training provided by the franchisor.

CHAPTER THIRTEEN

Making Your Business Grow

KEY TERM FOR THIS CHAPTER

trading area

Case in Point: Is This All There Is?

Kyle Valentine is ready to open an equipment rental franchise. He has chosen to franchise from RedyRents Inc. in spite of the fact that it is a new franchisor. RedyRents has three company-owned outlets and only two other franchisees. The company-owned operations have been in business for over five years, but the franchisees have been at it only for about eight months.

Kyle realizes that the offering is riskier than other more established franchises, but he is convinced that the people behind the company are honest. The big advantage of RedyRents is cost. Because they are trying to break into franchising, the owners are willing to get the first five franchisees established very cheaply. In fact, they seem to be subsidizing these first start-ups to some extent. Kyle's total investment will be less than half of what it would have been with one of the larger chains.

The other side of the coin is that RedyRents' franchising package is not yet adequately developed. Training largely consists of working in a company store for a month. Beyond that it's somewhat haphazard.

What worries Kyle even more is that the

business support features of the franchise system aren't documented for easy understanding by a franchisee. Whenever he asks RedyRents' owner Bob Hamilton about advertising, bookkeeping, or inventory control, Bob gives him a detailed description of the way the company-owned stores operate now. Kyle finds such lectures confusing, and there is little in writing to study.

Kyle has no background in business operations either on the job or academically. In college he majored in literature, and has always worked for a large publishing company on the editorial staff.

The other two franchisees seem to be doing well, but both have business backgrounds. One was previously an accountant, and the other worked in small business for years.

Kyle realizes that the problem is as much his as RedyRents. If the company had developed a franchisee profile, he probably wouldn't fit because of his inexperience in business. Nevertheless, he doesn't want to pass up what may be the opportunity of a lifetime.

Operations and Growth: The Franchisor's Role

Virtually all reputable franchisors offer a good blueprint for running operations. That is, they offer good training and instruction on providing the business's product or service once a customer comes along.

Marketing and Administration

Likewise, virtually all franchisors offer some advice on marketing. However, the value of that advice can range from excellent to poor.

The largest and best-known franchisors manage most of the marketing and advertising effort. For example, you don't see many locally produced, customized ads for McDonald's or Burger King. Franchisees contribute to co-op advertising and may place some ads of their own, but the overall advertising program is orchestrated by the franchisor.

At the other extreme are franchises that leave local marketing and advertising entirely up to franchisees. Some specify that franchisees spend a certain percent of revenues on advertising; others don't even require that.

Franchisors are even less consistent in the guidance they offer on managing the administrative functions necessary for a successful business. These functions include sales, marketing, finance, personnel, and inventory control. Sadly, some franchisors provide little help in these areas. No implication of disreputability is intended. Newer, smaller franchisors have often not had the opportunity to develop these features of their package.

In short, franchisors sometimes set people up in business and train them well in the production area but neglect to give adequate instruction in the peripheral aspects of running a small business. By peripheral we mean marketing and administration. Administration further breaks down into finance/accounting and personnel.

This is especially true of smaller, low-investment franchises. The implicit assumption seems to be that the franchisee should already know how to manage the administrative end of a small business, and that the franchisor should be responsible only for imparting the secrets of the particular business being franchised.

Unfortunately, that assumption is often not valid. Most small-business failures are not associated with a lack of product or service knowledge. They are more frequently the result of a lack of management ability in attracting customers, keeping records, managing money, and handling people. Franchised businesses are not an exception to that rule. If the franchisor's system fails to include detailed training and support in these areas, they can become vulnerable spots in the franchisee's business.

Evaluate Your Own Needs

As a prospective franchisee, you should evaluate the franchisor's support in these peripheral areas of business management and decide if you need extra training. If the answer is yes, it's advisable to look into a course in small-business management at a local community college. Such courses are offered at many schools. The cost can be substantial at private schools but is usually nominal at public institutions.

Don't underestimate the importance of this additional training. If you've never worked in or owned a small business before and you don't have a degree in business administration, it is unlikely that you will be able to manage the peripheral elements of a small company effectively. This won't necessarily lead directly to failure, but it will significantly decrease your chances of success.

Let's look at some of the problems that come up in these administrative areas. These are only a sample of the types of challenges you might encounter, but this discussion will give you an idea of what to expect.

Marketing and Advertising

Sales is the key element for most small businesses. Without customers you haven't got anything. But how do you reach the customers out there and convince them to buy from you? Most businesses do that through advertising. But many small-business people waste a great deal of their advertising dollars, because they don't use them efficiently.

Trading Area

The first thing to do as an advertiser is determine your **trading area.** That's the geographical area from which customers are drawn. For most franchises that area is relatively limited, probably a radius of five to ten miles around the business. The first principle of advertising is to avoid spending money on advertising to people outside of that area. That's not always easy. Newspaper advertising is one instance where it can be difficult.

Consider this example. Your business is a specialty shop in a small town that is a suburb of a larger city. The town is eleven miles from the city and has a population of 15,000, while the city has a population of 250,000. Most of the town's residents read the city newspaper; the town probably has a weekly paper, but people don't read it very carefully. How do you reach your market?

Even though everyone in town will read your ad if you put it in the city newspaper, you probably don't want to do that. The cost will be prohibitive, and probably over 90 percent of the paper's readers live outside your town and thus aren't potential customers. That advertising is totally wasted. Yet many small-business owners in such a situation also will tell you that advertising in the local paper is ineffective. So where do you advertise?

Media

The answer generally lies in a mix of media. Some ads in the local paper are appropriate. Also try signs, coupons, direct mail, and fliers. Local radio advertising can be fairly cheap, although it usually covers too wide an area as well. Sometimes the major paper divides its coverage into regions. Check out the cost for your region. It will be more reasonable, but probably still pretty high.

Small-business advertising is a trial-and-error process. You have to experiment to see what works. It's important to ask your customers what brought them into your store. That's the only way you'll really be able to tell what advertising is working for you and what isn't. Also keep careful records of sales and traffic on a daily basis. See if there's an upswing in business immediately after a certain kind of advertising appears.

A word about the Yellow Pages: Ads there generally don't draw well for small businesses. You get a free one-line listing along with your business phone. Take that, and resist the phone company salespeople's pressure to buy a larger ad.

Writing Effective Advertising

Every advertisement should answer three questions for readers:

- Why should they buy the product?
- Why should they buy it from you?
- Why should they buy it now?

Let's consider each of these in turn.

Why Should the Customer Buy the Product? Your ad must sell the benefits or image of your product, not the item itself. Big companies learned that lesson long ago. Does Kodak advertise film? Yes, but if you look closely at the ads, you'll see that they really sell memories. Does Cadillac sell cars, or does it sell prestige with transportation as a by-product? You can probably think of a dozen examples. Design your ad to appeal to the underlying motivation that will lead people to buy what you're selling.

Why Should the Customer Buy from You? You can't just say "I'm in business, buy from me." Customers have to be given a reason to change from whomever they've been buying from in the past. You've got to be better, faster, cheaper, offer training, more variety, longer hours, or better service. Something has to distinguish you from the competition, and that distinction must be called out in your advertising.

Why Should the Customer Buy Now? People are creatures of inertia. They procrastinate about most purchase decisions until they have to buy. Your ad has to give them a reason to get off the sofa and come buy your product or service now. That incentive is best applied through some offer that's going to expire if the customer doesn't act right away. Sale prices or limited stocks of particularly desirable merchandise are common devices. The idea is to impart a sense of urgency to the customer. Auto dealers learned this lesson years ago. Did you ever see one that isn't having a sale?

Books, Records, and Tax Regulations

The most important rule in this area is to be careful and get professional help if you don't know what you're doing. A decent accounting system is relatively cheap to acquire, and you don't need a certified public accountant to set it up for you. There are bookkeeping services that offer a few hours a week of a clerical person's time. That level of expertise will be adequate for keeping books and records for virtually any small business. Take the results to a tax preparer at the end of the year and stay on the right side of the law.

If you have some expertise and a personal computer, you can get an accounting package at your local software store and do the job yourself.

A word of caution in the area of withholding taxes is appropriate. If you employ people, you'll have to withhold money from their pay and remit it to a federal depository (a designated bank) on a regular basis. Be sure you do this in strict accordance with government regulations. New businesses have lots of cash needs. It's tempting to use today's withholding dollars to satisfy some of those needs and expect to catch up on the federal deposit next month.

Avoid that temptation. Not paying your income tax is bad news, but not remitting employees' withholding is a disaster. It's money your employee owes to the government. If you don't pay it, you're stealing it from Uncle Sam, and the IRS takes a dim view of that.

Expansion

Everyone's goal is to grow and expand, but even in terms of growth there are pitfalls that should be avoided. The main danger is expanding too fast. It's perfectly possible to go out of business while earning a hefty profit.

Here's an example of how it can happen. Sally Lewis has a business that sells kitchen utensils to retailers on credit. Sally's business buys raw material inventory, and employees apply some hand labor to produce the finished products, which are then sold.

Sally's start-up was a rousing success. In the first month she sold out her entire finished inventory. In the second month she figures that she can sell twice as much as she did in the first, and orders raw materials accordingly.

Because she's new in business, her supplier demands cash in advance. Sally uses the last of her cash to purchase inventory, expecting to collect on her sales of last month in short order. Unfortunately, Sally's expected collections don't materialize. Her customers are slow payers. She'll get her money eventually, but probably not for another sixty days.

Sally is in a real bind. All her cash is tied up in inventory and receivables. She hasn't any money to pay her employees to convert the existing inventory into salable product. Sally goes to the bank for a loan, but she has no collateral and is turned down. Her business fails for lack of cash even though she was earning great accounting profits and had a tremendous future in terms of customer acceptance and demand.

This scenario is not unusual in small businesses. Expansion has to be handled carefully.

Case in Point Revisited

Should Kyle go ahead and open his RedyRents franchise in spite of the fact that he's not comfortable with all of the details of the business? Maybe, but he's taking a risk if he does.

Kyle definitely needs extra training. He should take a course on small-business management while he's getting ready to open. A beginning course in accounting and bookkeeping wouldn't hurt either.

Above all, we'd suggest that he be up front with the franchisor about his concerns and see if Bob thinks his lack of business knowledge is a manageable problem or a show stopper. If it's the former, perhaps Bob will offer some extra help until Kyle catches on. Maybe in the rental business, these things aren't as bad as they seem to Kyle's uninitiated eyes. On the other hand, maybe he's walking into a disaster. If so, it's better for Kyle to find out before investing rather than after.

CHAPTER FOURTEEN

What to Do When Things Go Wrong

KEY TERMS FOR THIS CHAPTER

breakaway franchise
breaking away
documentation file
refusal to renew
termination

Case in Point: Diminishing Returns

Harriet Henderson has owned a Mighty-TidyMaid Cleaning Service for six years, but she is increasingly unhappy with the services she is getting from the franchisor. Harriet pays royalties on gross income every month and contributes to cooperative advertising. But she rarely sees any advertising that she feels will directly benefit her.

She has come to understand the business very well and has not had to turn to the franchisor with a question for three years.

The franchisor did give her some help during start-up and probably is partly responsible for her success, but in retrospect Harriet's not sure that she couldn't have started the business on her own, given her previous work experience. Now she feels that the franchisor is simply receiving money and has been justly compensated for the initial help many times over. Does she have an option?

Franchisor-Franchisee Relations

Ideally, the franchise relationship is friendly and characterized by mutual support, trust, and respect. Most issues in good relationships are governed by common sense and by the franchise agreement. If both parties fully understand what the franchise agreement says, the relationship usually flows smoothly.

However, even harmonious relationships between reputable franchisors and dedicated, enthusiastic franchisees can deteriorate over time. This is especially true if one or both parties aren't receiving a reasonable return on their investments and efforts. In such a case there can be a tendency for each party to blame the other for any problems that arise. There are many ways in which the relationship can become rocky, and disputes can arise over the terms and conduct of the agreement.

When franchisors and franchisees argue, it generally isn't a fair fight. The odds are stacked in favor of franchisors, who have vastly more economic power than franchisees. Their legal positions are one-sided too, as we saw in Chapter 7. Franchise agreements are written to favor the franchisor in virtually any dispute that may arise. As a result, franchisors can outlast and outfight franchisees on most issues.

Legal Recourses

Sometimes franchisors press their advantage too far, creating situations so intolerable to franchisees that they are inclined to sue. Suppose, for example, that a franchisor wants to sell franchisees a product that is clearly required in the process of doing the franchised business. Franchisees, however, maintain that an equivalent product is available from other sources at a lower price, and some resist purchasing directly from the franchisor.

It can be illegal for the franchisor to require that franchisees buy his or her product under threat of termination. But suppose it is merely "suggested" that the product be so purchased? Franchisees might well feel that the "suggestion" is a thinly veiled threat amounting to coercion, effectively an illegal requirement that they do business in a certain way. If discussions and negotiation don't resolve the conflict, the franchisees may feel their only option is a lawsuit. The question then becomes: How can the underdog franchisees best equip themselves to take on the powerful franchisor in court?

Why a Documentation File?

It's almost axiomatic that if you contemplate a lawsuit against the franchisors, you will need a good attorney. In addition, however, your position will be helped a good deal if you maintain a detailed **documentation file.** This file is simply a documentation of all transactions and interactions with the franchisor and its agents. Then if you want to bring allegations of contractual overreaching on the part of the franchisor, this file will serve as your evidence that such a pattern of actions occurred.

If a franchisor commits actions that amount to acting outside the contract or the law, two things have to happen for an injured franchisee to win in court:

1. The franchisee has to establish that the illegal or noncontractual actions occurred.
2. The court has to find that the franchi-

sor's actions constituted a violation of the law or of the contract—for example, that the suggestion that franchisees purchase an item exclusively from the franchisor was indeed a threat.

So, for instance, if the franchisor's suggestion was delivered in a private conversation, it's unlikely that the franchisee will be able to prove coercion because it will be difficult to prove how, and even if, the threat was made. On the other hand, if the suggestion was made in a letter, or there were witnesses present at the conversation, the fact of the suggestion can be established and the court can determine its implications.

Contents of the Documentation File

A documentation file should contain at least the following:

- Copies of all agreements between the parties.
- Dated copies of all franchisor written requirements, such as accounting and reporting, pricing policies, buying policies, territorial issues, quotas, fees, and threats or pressure tactics.
- Copies of all documents received from the franchisor.
- Written explanations of unfair actions and requirements.
- Written records of promises made by the franchisor.
- Records of names of people attending meetings with the franchisor.
- Records of franchisee's refusal to agree to contested requirements.
- Other documents as appropriate.

Even with a complete file, beating a strong franchisor in court is a tough job. In most cases the franchisor has enough good legal advice to avoid actions that will get it in trouble. Ultimately, the franchise agreement controls the relationship. That's why it's so important that you understand what you are getting into before signing the agreement.

Common Problems and Areas of Dispute

Certain aspects of the franchise relationship tend to cause problems more frequently than others. James L. Porter and William Renforth, writing in the *Journal of Small Business Management,* in 1978, identified co-op advertising, inspections, volume requirements, territorial disputes, royalty payments, fees, and restrictions as among the more common disputes.

Some franchisees seem to have more legal problems than others. People who have not previously run a business of their own are prone to disputes, as are individuals who did not seriously review the franchise agreement with an attorney. Nevertheless, even with the most carefully understood agreement, things can go awry. Here are some areas most vulnerable to disputes between franchisor and franchisee.

Co-op Advertising

Franchise agreements frequently require two kinds of advertising from franchisees. They must spend a certain amount of money themselves on local advertising, and they must contribute a certain amount to a joint co-op fund, which is administered by the franchisor. Franchisees often feel that they are not receiving their fair share of benefits from the co-op fund. This is especially common when the franchisee is pioneering in a new area or the franchisor is relatively new in the business.

There have been cases in which unscrupulous franchisors appropriated the co-op advertising funds for other purposes.

Inspections by the Franchisor

Franchisors generally have the right to inspect franchisees' places of business and evaluate them on their compliance with the operating manual. The inspections and the violations found can seem arbitrary. Minor technical violations have been used as ways to terminate an unwanted franchisee. In all fairness, however, something that seems unimportant to a franchisee may be legitimately significant in the eyes of the franchisor.

Volume Requirements

Franchisors often insist that franchisees do a minimum level of sales each year. The minimum acceptable level is sometimes set lower in the first year or two to allow for start-up. Failure to achieve the required sales level can be a cause for contract termination. Franchisors generally will want franchisees to boost low sales by staying open longer, advertising more, or doing special promotions. Franchisees may not feel that such actions are warranted.

Territorial Issues

The parties often don't agree on what the territory of the franchisee is. The problem can be especially difficult in urban areas where political boundaries as drawn on maps don't reflect population patterns. A county line, for example, can go right through a densely populated area. A franchisee assigned a particular county often claims rights to the entire population center, leading to trouble when the franchisor later sells another franchise in the adjacent county.

Royalty Payments

Franchisees can come to feel that royalty payments are excessive for the amount of support given by the franchisor. Franchisors, on the other hand, may feel that rising costs have made the original royalty payment schedule too low. Franchise agreements often give the franchisor the unilateral right to raise the royalty. Such an action nearly always causes friction.

Additional Service Fees

Suppose you are having a problem with some aspect of running the business, a problem that is somewhat out of the ordinary. You turn for help to the franchisor who says, "Yes, we've run into that before and have a solution. We'll send someone out to help you for $10,000 plus expenses."

You are shocked. Your understanding of the agreement was that the franchisor would provide all available knowledge for the franchise fee and royalties.

Restrictions on Products, Prices, or Services

A franchisor's restrictions on the types of products or services a franchisee can offer, or on pricing of those products and services, also can create friction between the franchisor and franchisee.

Suppose Rhoda Smith's BigBurger franchise isn't doing well. Her restaurant is in a Hispanic neighborhood, where tortillas are much more popular than burgers. Rhoda projects that she can save the business by adding tortillas and several other ethnic items to the menu.

However, the franchise agreement specifies that the franchisor must approve any new menu items. BigBurger refuses to approve the tortillas, because it will make Rhoda's menu inconsistent with the other franchise outlets.

Rhoda feels that this is an arbitrary and perhaps fatal blow to her business. Further, she argues that the problem location is at least part BigBurger's responsibility, since the company provided site selection assistance.

Restrictions on Other Activities of the Franchisee

Another BigBurger franchisee is doing well and wants to open a PizzaPlenty franchise nearby. However, the BigBurger agreement contains a covenant not to compete, which BigBurger invokes, claiming that pizza is a competing fast food. The franchisee feels that pizza isn't really in competition with burgers and that the second franchise wouldn't affect BigBurger at all.

Termination of the Franchise Relationship

Attitudes about business relationships tend to change over time, and franchise relationships are no exception. There's a honeymoon period in the beginning, during which both sides are happy with one another. The happiness is particularly intense if the franchise is growing rapidly. Later each side's expectations change and the relationship can deteriorate into a series of conflicts and disputes.

The ultimate solution to a rocky relationship is termination of the agreement. Under different conditions, termination can be favored by one side and opposed by the other. Let's look at some situations in which one side or the other wants out.

Termination by the Franchisor

A franchisor may want to get rid of a particular franchisee for any of a number of reasons:

- The franchisee has been especially difficult and demanding for a long time.
- The franchise meets minimum volume requirements, but the franchisor feels that a better manager could get more out of it.
- The unit is very successful and profitable. The franchisor would like to run it as a company-owned operation.
- The franchisor simply wants to sell the franchise again, in order to pocket another fee.

Termination by the franchisor can come about in two ways: overt **termination** (simply calling an end to the relationship before renewal time) and **refusal to renew.** Either one can be devastating to the franchisee who has spent years building up the business. It can mean the loss of current wealth and most future income potential. Franchisor-initiated termination has been a major abuse of the franchise system in the past.

The franchisor's termination rights are largely governed by the franchise agreement. The contract may say the franchisor can terminate or refuse to renew arbitrarily and unilaterally, and in most states that is legal. Look out for such a clause when reading and negotiating your agreement.

Franchisees have some protection against arbitrary termination in some states, such as California, which have passed "good cause" statutes. As mentioned earlier, these laws require that a franchisor have reasonable cause before terminating a franchisee, regardless of what the contract says. Courts can determine what is reasonable and what isn't.

Prospective franchisees should always find out from their attorneys what protection, if any, their state laws afford.

The best way to avoid being dropped is to insist that conditions for termination be built into the contract. Demand that the contract state that in order to be terminated, you must be in breach of the agreement. Also, structure the contract so that renewal is a right if you meet reasonable conditions of successful operation of the franchise.

Such provisions are especially important if your state doesn't have good cause laws. Unfortunately, many strong franchisors won't agree to such modifications of their contract. If you want to play, you have to do it on their terms. If that's the case, find out how many franchisees they've terminated in the past and why. The franchisor must tell you that; it's part of the federal disclosure requirement. (See Chapter 5.) Be sure to verify what the franchisor tells you by contacting some current and past franchisees on your own.

Termination by the Franchisee

Franchisees can become disenchanted too. This often happens after several years when the franchisee feels that the royalties being paid are greater than the value of the benefits received.

Donna Kelly, for instance, has a DynamicDonut franchise that was successful from the start. After a while, however, she comes to feel that:

- She knows all that DynamicDonuts can teach her about the doughnut business.
- Her customer base is established in the neighborhood and customers would continue to buy from the store whether it was DynamicDonuts or Donna's-Donuts.
- She can get all the products she buys from Dynamic elsewhere.
- Her past payments to Dynamic more than justly compensate the company for what she learned and for its help in getting started.
- Some of Dynamic's rules are counterproductive.

In short, Donna would like to keep the business but terminate the franchise relationship. This is called **breaking away.** Donna's business can be called a **breakaway franchise.** Dynamic doesn't like losing a franchise, but what is worse, from its point of view, is the possibility that Donna may start selling Donna'sDonut franchises herself.

Franchisees break away in one of two ways.

1. They may try to provoke termination by breaking the franchisor's rules.
2. They may drift away by ceasing to participate and stopping royalty payments.

In any case, breakaway franchisees must deidentify with the franchisor by taking down franchise signs and trademarks.

Breakaways can be bad news for the franchisor, mainly because of the loss of royalty revenue. Franchisors attempt to prevent breakaways by writing clauses into their contracts that restrict the franchisee's ability to operate the business after termination. The most common such clause is the covenant not to compete (see Chapter 10), in which the franchisee essentially agrees not to run a similar business for a specified period of time in the geographic area of the franchise.

Unfortunately for franchisors, the enforceability of such clauses varies a great deal between states. In some states such clauses are almost useless. Cessation of the use of the franchisor's identifying marks is always required, but the breakaway operators usually don't view that as a drawback or else they wouldn't break away in the first place.

A strong franchisor defense against breakaways is control of their real estate. A BigBurger franchisee who is leasing a building from BigBurger will have a hard time breaking away if BigBurger doesn't want a competing business in the building.

Breaking away poses difficult legal problems. Franchisees tempted to undertake a breakaway should consult an attorney before trying anything that would damage the franchise relationship.

Selling the Franchise

Another way out of an unhappy relationship is selling the business. Here again the franchise agreement dictates whether this will be a reasonable solution or a disaster for the franchisee.

Most franchise agreements restrict the franchisee's right to sell the business. The least difficult restriction may be that the franchisor must simply approve the buyer according to the same criteria that were used to qualify the franchisee in the first place. However, restrictions can be structured so as to effectively preclude the sale to virtually anyone.

Franchisors can also repurchase franchises. Here again, the terms of the franchise agreement will apply. Be careful that you don't agree to a contract that permits or requires sale of the business to the franchisor below market value.

Franchisors often have the right of first refusal in the agreement. That means that you have to offer it first to the franchisor for repurchase on the same terms you would offer anyone else.

Case in Point Revisited

Harriet Henderson, the owner of the cleaning service, may have some justification in believing that the franchisor has been more than compensated for any services provided. And the franchise arrangement may no longer be particularly important to her. Perhaps the value of the business is no longer based on the franchisor's trademark but on Harriet's reputation, reliability, and standing in the community.

In a service business, like Harriet's, the real estate ownership is not a particularly important factor. The location and style of Harriet's office don't matter much to her customers.

What may be important is whether she signed a covenant not to compete, and if she did, how binding it is in her state. If the agreement Harriet signed with the franchisor includes a binding covenant, she may not be able to operate an independent cleaning service in the area for some time. In that event she'd be stuck with MightyTidyMaid until the expiration of the agreement.

However, if there is no covenant, or it's not binding, Harriet would probably have little trouble in striking out on her own. Of course she'd have to reidentify herself, but that would be fairly easy.

In any event, she definitely needs the advice of a lawyer.

CHAPTER FIFTEEN

Franchising Your Business: A View from the Franchisor's Perspective

KEY TERMS FOR THIS CHAPTER

blueprint for franchise operations *franchise plan*

Case in Point: To Franchise or Not to Franchise?

Harry Bartelli comes from an Italian family with a long tradition of fine cooking. The tradition didn't involve professional food preparation, but the entire family seemed to revolve around the kitchen. Young Harry developed an early interest in food and went through a professional, two-year cooking school after high school. Subsequently he worked in a series of restaurants until he had earned the right to be called chef.

Harry opened his first Italian restaurant, the Bella Napoli, twenty-five years ago at the age of thirty-two. The business was reasonably successful from the start, but there were a number of tough years before it became truly established. Harry worked very hard during those years, often putting in eighteen-hour days. But he seemed to have a knack for running a restaurant, and the business prospered.

After ten years, he opened a second Bella Napoli. It too prospered, but only after a slow start. There were many more long days during which Harry poured his energy into the second restaurant. Five years later he added a third unit, which developed similarly to the first two, requiring a large amount of personal attention from the boss.

Harry is now fifty-seven. He and his wife are reasonably well off, but by no means rich. The restaurants more or less run themselves now and provide the Bartellis with a good income. They finally have some leisure time and are able to travel and enjoy their grandchildren.

A friend recently told Harry about franchising, saying he thought the Bella Napoli had the potential to become a substantial chain. Harry wasn't sure about this. He had always thought that his restaurants' success was largely due to his personal skill in the kitchen and with customers. But he admitted that the franchising idea seemed to have some merit.

Harry doesn't really want to take on a major new venture at this point in his life. He would not, for example, consider opening a fourth Bella Napoli. It would simply be too much work for the potential additional income it would offer.

Further, he knows that restaurants often fail. A fourth unit might not succeed if he made a mistake on location or some other facet of the business. He could easily lose most of his savings in such an event, and he certainly doesn't need that.

On the other hand, franchising the Bella Napoli might be a way to make a great deal of extra money without much effort on his part. Harry envisions running an ad in the paper and having several eager franchisees pay him for his expertise. He could train them in a few weeks in his own kitchens and advise them if they ran into trouble. They would pay him a franchise fee and royalties, and if they failed it would be their loss and not his. It would be like picking up money off the street, and Harry doesn't want to pass it up.

Advantages of Franchising Your Business

Not every successful business is a candidate for franchising. A franchisable business has certain characteristics of replicability that are far from universal. In addition, the owner of a franchised business has to be able to deal with the additional managerial problems inherent in a franchise organization. These are not insignificant demands.

However, there are several big advantages to being a franchisor; most of them revolve around money.

Profit

The single biggest advantage of franchising a business is the potential profitability involved. Most of the success stories one hears about franchising involve franchisees becoming millionaires. Although that happens, it's fairly rare. It's more likely that the franchisor will become a millionaire. Successful franchisors collect a hefty franchise fee at the front end of each relationship and a steady stream of royalties thereafter. That money comes in whether individual franchisees are successful or not.

Franchisors can make money on sales of product and equipment to franchisees. As we've pointed out earlier, it's generally illegal to require franchisees to buy your products if similar ones are available elsewhere. Nevertheless, franchisors often are able to put together a better deal for their franchisees than anyone else, and still turn a handsome profit for themselves on what essentially becomes a captive market.

Franchisors also can get into real estate operations by owning the land under their outlets and leasing it back to the franchisees. That practice can generate big returns.

Rapid, Low-Risk Expansion on Limited Capital

Suppose someone has a business that's a huge success and also determines that there's a potential to expand into many locations across the country. However, each new location requires a significant capital investment to get started and also needs a bright, dedicated, and enthusiastic manager to guarantee its success.

That makes internal expansion a slow, difficult process. First, there are limits on the amount of money that the original company can raise. Second, it's hard to get good management to work cheap. Paying a top-flight executive to open each outlet might sink the operations financially before they got started.

Franchising solves both of these problems. Enthusiastic, dedicated people will contribute their own money to getting outlets started and work for peanuts until things become successful.

For these reasons a franchised business can grow at a very rapid rate with owners investing almost no money of their own. Of course, the original owner has to give up a good share of the profitability, but that would be the case if stock were sold to finance internal expansion anyway.

Expansion through franchising is also relatively risk free. To expand internally, a business generally has to take on a great deal of debt or sell more equity (stock) to finance the new operations. In such a situation, if the new sites fail they may well take the original business down with them.

With franchising, the original business can be separated from franchising operations and go on relatively untouched in the event of the failure of the outlets.

Empire

The satisfaction of running a big show is a real motivator for some people. Franchising can offer these people a business empire.

Disadvantages of Franchising

In spite of all the potential benefits, there's a dark side to the franchising picture if things don't go smoothly or work out well. Here are a few of the problem areas.

Effort and Expense with No Guarantee of Success

Putting together a franchise program that has a reasonable chance for success requires considerable effort and substantial sums of money.

It involves developing a prototype unit, an operations manual, a training program, and a marketing program. The required disclosure documents and a standard franchise agreement must be prepared. Finally, staff to manage the enterprise, at least a director of franchise sales, must be hired.

As with most business projects, if you decide to franchise your business, you have to make the effort and spend the money with no guarantee of success.

Ongoing Trouble and Effort

Running a franchised organization is a substantial job. You have to keep doing everything you were doing with respect to the original business and manage franchise operations as well. In addition to managing headquarters marketing and training departments, you have to manage the relationship with your franchisees. A great deal of effort is required to keep them happy.

Lost Profit

While a successful franchised location contributes to the franchisor's wealth, the contribution is substantially less than would be made by a company-owned operation at the same location. This is the other side of the expansion-without-capital coin. Franchisees are cheaper than your own operations, but you have to share the profits with them.

Responsibility for Other People's Future

Franchisees put a great deal of faith in franchisors. They often quit jobs and sink their life savings into the new businesses. They do this based largely on the claims that you, the franchisor, make in order to sell franchises.

Inevitably, some franchisees don't succeed. Those who fail can suffer financial ruin. The franchisor has to bear some of the responsibility for that. Did you screen the applicants carefully enough? Did you provide enough support at the right times? If you have a sensitive conscience, such doubts could cause you sleepless nights.

Lawsuits

If franchisees do fail, they probably won't blame it on themselves. It's human nature to blame failure on someone else. Franchisees, of course, want to blame the franchisor. If they've got a reasonable case, they'll sue. Fighting a lawsuit can consume a great deal of your time and money.

Breakaways

A breakaway franchisee can go off on his or her own after taking advantage of a franchisor's training. (See Chapter 14.) When that happens, the franchisor not only loses the breakaway's royalty stream, but also picks up a new competitor who can damage the remaining business.

Is Your Business Franchisable?

The first thing to do as a prospective franchisor is examine your business to determine if it is a likely candidate for successful franchising.

A franchisable business is one in which the replication of relatively small units makes sense. That lets out most manufacturers, for example. If a factory produces something that can be shipped nationwide, it doesn't make sense to create more small factories as a means of growth. A bigger factory that can turn out more product or the addition of new distributors are better ideas in that case.

The franchisable business also must be something that can be learned by a person of average skill and intelligence in a relatively short time. For example, a highly specialized craft such as woodworking, which takes years to learn, is not a good candidate.

Good franchises are usually businesses that serve a limited geographical area and are not in competition with other businesses that are far away. Fast-food restaurants are a classic example, but so are printing services, employment agencies, and a variety of automotive services.

There's no set rule, but the farther you stray from these guidelines, the less likely your business is to be a viable candidate.

Franchising Operations

Once the decision is made to franchise a business, franchising operations have to be designed and documented. This is a good time to consider hiring a consultant and a lawyer. People who know what they're doing can save you a lot of time and money in the long run. At a minimum, the following elements have to be considered.

Prototype Unit

The business to be franchised has probably grown in a less-than-optimal fashion. In other words, the existing business provides the basic idea, but if you could design it from scratch knowing what you know today, you'd probably make some changes. These changes need to be incorporated into the design for the optimal unit, which is what will be franchised. Design changes might be in the areas of floor layouts, equipment, organization modifications, and many others.

Floor plans, site selection guidelines, and staffing levels are among the many areas to be addressed in designing a prototype unit.

Operations Manual

The operations manual is the franchisees' bible. It tells them everything they need to know about how to run the business on a day-to-day basis. As the owner of the original business, however, you probably don't have one. All that information is in your head. The manual has to be designed and written to cover everything from getting started to procurement, to operations, to marketing, to personnel management.

Training Program and Facilities

Franchisees expect and deserve to be trained in your business methods; they can't get everything out of a book. Before getting started, you have to design a complete training program and at least document the pre-opening training course by deciding and writing down what is to be taught in how many lessons, by whom and where. The student's training manual should be written. Early training sessions can be conducted at your original location. A separate facility doesn't have to be established right away.

Marketing Program

A marketing program has to be developed to reach prospective franchisees. Initial advertising is required to locate them and a high-quality, professional information package is needed to keep them interested and enthusiastic. Screening guidelines need to be developed to select the most promising candidates. Finally the whole thing must be put into practice. That calls for a franchising staff, or at least a director of franchise sales.

A marketing plan should be established to forecast the number of units that will be sold over the first three years. Revenue and cost figures should be based on this projection.

Initial and Continuing Support

Franchisors are expected to provide initial as well as ongoing support and advice to franchisees. The exact level of this support needs to be defined. What will you as franchisor do as a matter of course, and what services will you offer for an extra charge?

It is particularly important to define how you will assist in site selection. It's also important to get an understanding of what you will do to help if a franchisee starts to get in trouble. All of these decisions should be laid out as policies and included in the franchise agreement.

Fees

A reasonable fee schedule has to be worked out that is consistent with the true value of your business ideas and your expected contribution to the franchisee. Fees also must be consistent with the practices of the industry.

An unrealistically high fee schedule will choke off demand for your franchise, especially in the early stages where the value of your offering is unproven. On the other hand, fees that are too low will fail to cover the costs of doing franchise business.

Initial fees should be set based on the planned number of outlets over the first few years of operation. Don't try to cover all your franchising costs with income from one or two franchisees.

The Franchise Agreement

A prospective franchisor needs to prepare a formal franchise agreement to serve as a starting point for negotiations with future prospective franchisees. Franchisees will expect you to have such a document prepared; don't disappoint them.

The contract's terms should be in your favor, as it is your opening position. However, a new franchisor won't have the negotiating clout of a McDonald's or Burger King, so you may have to be willing to give in on some points.

The advice of a lawyer is absolutely mandatory in preparing a franchise agreement. Try to find an attorney experienced in franchising.

Legal Entity Setup

It's a good idea to legally separate franchise operations from the original business. That way if the franchising business gets into trouble—for instance, if it is sued successfully—there's a good chance of saving the original business. Have a lawyer do this for you.

The Franchise Plan

An outline for executing all these steps should be put into a business plan for franchising operations. This is usually called the **franchise plan** or the **blueprint for franchise operations.**

Compliance with the Law

One of the most important things a new franchisor must do is comply with the provisions of Federal Trade Commission Rule 436 and any state laws that may be applicable. The FTC rule (see Chapter 7) requires preparation of a disclosure document that meets the requirements of the law.

Don't try to create a disclosure document using only this book as a guide. Proper handling of the disclosure rules is a complicated legal issue and requires the advice of an attorney, preferably one with franchise law experience.

It should be clear from all this that franchising a business takes quite a bit of effort and money if it's to be done right. To do it halfway makes failure likely. Study the decision carefully.

Several books written entirely from the franchisor's perspective are available. Be careful, however: They are written by consultants who have a vested interest in having business owners go into franchising. That's when they hire franchising consultants!

Case in Point Revisited

What about Harry Bartelli and the Bella Napoli? Should he franchise or not?

Right now he obviously doesn't have a realistic picture of what it will take to do the job right. Franchising won't be easy, it will take a lot of work, and he will have to put some money at risk to try it.

There's also some question as to the franchisability of Bella Napoli. Upscale gourmet restaurants aren't particularly replicable. They're too dependent on the skill of the chef and the style and class of the wait staff.

Further, if Harry is ready to start taking it easy, he may not want to get into anything as ambitious as franchising.

APPENDIX A

Small-Business Franchise Opportunities

This appendix contains summary information on over three hundred low-investment franchise opportunities, drawn from the *Franchise Opportunities Handbook* published by the U.S. Department of Commerce. These have been culled from more than a thousand franchises and generally represent those in which the franchisors' estimated equity requirements for franchisees were $50,000 or less. Not listed here are most offerings with only a few franchisees, many of those in which all the franchisees were in one state, and those requiring special licenses, such as in optometry or nursing.

This list is intended as a convenient source of small-business franchise opportunities. Inclusion here in no way reflects an endorsement of the opportunity or the franchisor.

You will notice that although food service businesses dominate modern franchising, few are listed here. That's because even a modest restaurant generally costs several hundred thousand dollars to get started. The kitchen requires a heavy investment. An exception is a sandwich shop, where no cooking is done.

Convenience stores are another unusual opportunity. A few chains finance the whole operation, including the store and the inventory. In such cases franchisees are required to invest very little of their own money.

You should realize that an equity capital requirement of $50,000 generally doesn't mean that you can get into the business for that amount. In most cases you need that much cash and may be able to borrow the rest. Some franchisors, however, seem to have interpreted the term equity capital requirement as meaning total cost to get started. Read each entry carefully.

An asterisk before a franchise name indicates IFA membership.

AUTOMOTIVE PRODUCTS/SERVICES

* AAMCO TRANSMISSIONS, INC.
One Presidential Boulevard
Bala Cynwyd, Pennsylvania 19004
Don Limbert, Director of Franchise Development

DESCRIPTION OF OPERATION: AAMCO centers service transmissions for all vehicles. Services include unique "Lifetime Warranty" for as long as customer owns car (honored at AAMCO centers throughout U.S. and Canada).

NUMBER OF FRANCHISEES: 700 in U.S. and Canada

IN BUSINESS SINCE: 1963

EQUITY CAPITAL NEEDED: Approximately $48,000

FINANCIAL ASSISTANCE AVAILABLE: To qualified applicants.

TRAINING PROVIDED: A comprehensive 5-week training course is provided at the company headquarters.

MANAGERIAL ASSISTANCE AVAILABLE: Consulting and operations departments continually work with each center to ensure proper operation. Technical training seminars and videotapes are available.

INFORMATION SUBMITTED: April 1990

ACC-U-TUNE & BRAKE
2510 Old Middle Field Way
Mountain View, California 94043
Stan Shore, Chief Executive Officer

DESCRIPTION OF OPERATION: ACC-U-TUNE & BRAKE centers specialize in automotive tune-ups, brakes, oil changes, air conditioning, state inspections, and other minor repair and auto maintenance services. Typical tune-up and complete lube, oil and filter change is less than $68, is done in about 1 hour while customer waits, and is guaranteed in writing for 12,000 miles. Prices include both parts and labor.

NUMBER OF FRANCHISEES: 10 in California and 8 company-owned centers

IN BUSINESS SINCE: 1975

EQUITY CAPITAL NEEDED: $50,000 and approved credit rating.

FINANCIAL ASSISTANCE AVAILABLE: Total investment of $140,000; financial assistance available.

TRAINING PROVIDED: Extensive pre-opening training, classroom training (about 2 weeks), and 4 weeks on-the-job training. Training includes technical aspects of repair work, bookkeeping, marketing, customer relations, shop maintenance, sales.

MANAGERIAL ASSISTANCE AVAILABLE: Complete technical manuals, advertising manuals, and operations manuals covering all day-to-day aspects of managing a profitable tune-up center.

INFORMATION SUBMITTED: April 1990

AL & ED'S AUTOSOUND
516 Monterey Pass Road
Monterey Park, California 91754
Michel Odie, Sales Manager

DESCRIPTION OF OPERATION: Al & Ed's Autosound sells, installs and services mobile electronics products such as cellular telephones, auto security devices, and car stereos. Turnkey retail stores.

NUMBER OF FRANCHISEES: 11 in California

IN BUSINESS SINCE: 1954

EQUITY CAPITAL NEEDED: $45,000, complete franchise $93,000 to $165,000.

FINANCIAL ASSISTANCE AVAILABLE: Yes.

TRAINING PROVIDED: 4-week training program in sales, administration, and technical procedures. 2 weeks at corporate location and 2 weeks in-store location.

MANAGERIAL ASSISTANCE AVAILABLE: Training and installations manuals provided. Franchisor locates sites, offers continuing field consultation in problem solving, and keeps franchisee abreast of innovations and changes in industry. Franchisor assists in marketing strategy and trends.

INFORMATION SUBMITTED: April 1990

AMERICAN TRANSMISSIONS
38701 Seven Mile Road
Suite 105
Livonia, Michigan 48152
John F. Folino, President

DESCRIPTION OF OPERATION: American Transmissions centers service all types of transmissions, foreign or domestic. Specially trained mechanics are on-site.

NUMBER OF FRANCHISEES: 17 in Michigan and Ohio

IN BUSINESS SINCE: 1979

EQUITY CAPITAL NEEDED: Approximately $83,000 depending upon location.

FINANCIAL ASSISTANCE AVAILABLE: Personnel from American Transmissions can arrange for financial assistance, or franchisee has the option to acquire his own outside financing.

TRAINING PROVIDED: A 2-week training program is offered which directs the new franchisee in management, advertising techniques, warranty and adjustment procedures, etc. This program consists of classroom and on-site training. Additional training programs and refresher courses will be made available on a regular basis.

MANAGERIAL ASSISTANCE AVAILABLE: The home office continually works with the franchisee and his operation. Complete manuals are provided which cover operation, marketing, inventory, etc.

INFORMATION SUBMITTED: April 1990

AMMARK CORPORATION
10 West Main Street
Carmel, Indiana 46032
Curtis J. Butcher, President

DESCRIPTION OF OPERATION: Service, installation, and repair of automobile transmissions. Only area franchises available with the right to subfranchise in your area.

NUMBER OF FRANCHISEES: 29 franchise locations in operation in Indiana, Ohio, Kentucky, and Florida

IN BUSINESS SINCE: 1974

EQUITY CAPITAL NEEDED: Operating capital of $2,000 per bay and the ability to obtain loan to pay for franchise, parts, equipment and inventory.

FINANCIAL ASSISTANCE AVAILABLE: AmMark Corporation works closely with franchisee in attempting to locate outside financing sources.

TRAINING PROVIDED: Initial training of from 2 to 4 weeks is provided for each new franchisee.

MANAGERIAL ASSISTANCE AVAILABLE: The company will provide up to 12 hours of consultation and technical services per year without charge to the franchisee; additional consulting services will be provided when a suitable fee has been agreed upon. The company will sponsor at least one seminar each year for franchise managers.

INFORMATION SUBMITTED: May 1990

APPEARANCE RECONDITIONING CO., INC.
12833 Industrial Park Boulevard
Plymouth, Minnesota 55441
Daniel Almen, President

DESCRIPTION OF OPERATION: Appearance Reconditioning Co., Inc., offers a complete service to the ever-expanding used car market that reconditions the auto interior or wherever vinyls, plastics, cloth, and leather are found. The priority of the Appearance Reconditioning Co., Inc., is to provide its franchisees with continued support.

NUMBER OF FRANCHISEES: 6 in 6 states

IN BUSINESS SINCE: 1977

EQUITY CAPITAL NEEDED: $13,500 minimum

FINANCIAL ASSISTANCE AVAILABLE: A total investment of $25,000 is necessary for an Appearance Reconditioning Co., Inc., franchise. The minimum of $7,500 is needed with financing available to qualified franchisees. (An approved vehicle must be obtained, which is not included in the franchise package.) The balance, if financed, is payable over 3 years. Franchise has option to arrange own outside financing.

TRAINING PROVIDED: A 1-week training course must be completed before each franchise is in operation. Within 30 days of completion, a representative from the home office provides the franchisee with continued training. The home office provides constant support with each of its franchisees.

MANAGERIAL ASSISTANCE AVAILABLE: Appearance Reconditioning Co., Inc., provides continual management support in areas of market awareness, inventory control, bookkeeping, advertising, and technical guidelines. A manual of operations and training is provided and each franchisee is expected to know it thoroughly. Problem solving is offered at any time for each franchisee.

INFORMATION SUBMITTED: May 1990

APPLE POLISHING SYSTEMS, INC.
6103 Johns Road, Suite 102
Tampa, Florida 33634
Jimmy Morrison, National Sales Manager

DESCRIPTION OF OPERATION: Apple Systems, Inc., is a unique paint sealant for use on automotive, marine, and aviation vehicles. We have a full line of products to be applied on both commercial and individual vehicles, with up to a 5-year warranty.

NUMBER OF FRANCHISEES: 3,000 in the United States

IN BUSINESS SINCE: 1979

EQUITY CAPITAL NEEDED: $5,000

FINANCIAL ASSISTANCE AVAILABLE: Call the company.

TRAINING PROVIDED: Intensive 3-day mandatory training class is scheduled for all new franchisees and personnel.

MANAGERIAL ASSISTANCE AVAILABLE: Apple Systems provides continual management assistance and training sessions to review and update sales and marketing techniques and to disseminate other information and training to assist franchisees.

INFORMATION SUBMITTED: May 1990

ATLAS AUTOMATIC TRANSMISSION, INC.
10303 Northwest Freeway
Suite 201
Houston, Texas 77092
Doug Fletcher, Vice President of Marketing

DESCRIPTION OF OPERATION: Service and repair of automobile transmissions, automatic and standard.

NUMBER OF FRANCHISEES: 26 in Texas

IN BUSINESS SINCE: 1964

EQUITY CAPITAL NEEDED: $30,000 to $50,000

FINANCIAL ASSISTANCE AVAILABLE: Atlas Transmission can work with franchisee to locate outside financing sources if needed.

TRAINING PROVIDED: 2 to 4 weeks of initial training provided for new franchisee.

MANAGERIAL ASSISTANCE AVAILABLE: The home office provides field consultation and managerial assistance on as-needed basis.

INFORMATION SUBMITTED: May 1990

AUTO ONE ACCESSORIES AND GLASS, INC.
580 Ajax Drive
Madison Heights, Michigan 48071
Michael Daniels, President

DESCRIPTION OF OPERATION: Auto One Appearance and Protection Centers specialize in the service and installation of auto and truck replacement glass, burglar alarms, running boards, sunroof tops, rustproofing, paint sealant, fabric protection, and a complete line of automotive accessories. Glass suppliers, tooling, sealant compounds, technical data, marketing are provided by Auto One.

NUMBER OF FRANCHISEES: 28 in 2 states, Michigan and Florida

IN BUSINESS SINCE: 1963

EQUITY CAPITAL NEEDED: $40,000 to $70,000

FINANCIAL ASSISTANCE AVAILABLE: None.

TRAINING PROVIDED: 1 week at corporation, 1 week at operational shop, 1 week on their site with follow-up assistance as needed.

MANAGERIAL ASSISTANCE AVAILABLE: Auto One provides continuing management assistance in sales, marketing, and technical operations. Field service managers are on staff to support franchisees. Technical manuals and operations manuals are continually updated. Advertising assistance is always available.

INFORMATION SUBMITTED: May 1990

AUTO VALET, INC.
7110 Blondo Street
Omaha, Nebraska 68104
Marge Johnson, President

DESCRIPTION OF OPERATION: Auto Valet offers full-time or part-time opportunities for an individual. We offer to the public a guaranteed paint protection for the vehicle, guaranteed interior protection, dry cleaning for the interior, under-coating, rust proofing, and other detail services. The dealer can be mobile or have a store location. Also offering window tinting and sun roofs.

NUMBER OF FRANCHISEES: 11 in 5 states

IN BUSINESS SINCE: 1978, starting franchising in 1982

EQUITY CAPITAL NEEDED: From $3,000 to $25,000

FINANCIAL ASSISTANCE AVAILABLE: None.

TRAINING PROVIDED: On-the-job training, in house as well as on location.

MANAGERIAL ASSISTANCE AVAILABLE: Management, advertisement, and marketing assistance.

INFORMATION SUBMITTED: April 1990

BRAKE WORLD AUTO CENTERS
2640 Hollywood Boulevard
Hollywood, Florida 33020
Gerald D. Hopkins, President

DESCRIPTION OF OPERATION: Brakes, alignment, front end repairs, mufflers, and other light repairs.

NUMBER OF FRANCHISEES: 15 in Florida

IN BUSINESS SINCE: 1970

EQUITY CAPITAL NEEDED: $25,000

FINANCIAL ASSISTANCE AVAILABLE: Will hold mortgage on balance.

TRAINING PROVIDED: On-the-job training in all phases of operation.

MANAGERIAL ASSISTANCE AVAILABLE: Managerial assistance provided in any way possible.

INFORMATION SUBMITTED: April 1990

CAP-A-RADIATOR SHOPS OF AMERICA, INC.
dba CAP-A RADIATOR SHOPS
2879 Long Beach Road
Oceanside, New York
Joseph Fels, President

DESCRIPTION OF OPERATION: Cap-A Radiator Shops are clean, attractive shops located in high-traffic areas designed to appeal to the retail customers for service of auto radiators, heaters, and air conditioners.

NUMBER OF FRANCHISEES: 7 in New York

IN BUSINESS SINCE: 1971, franchise business established 1980

EQUITY CAPITAL NEEDED: $24,000

FINANCIAL ASSISTANCE AVAILABLE: Franchisor is willing to render assistance to franchisee in locating outside financing.

TRAINING PROVIDED: Franchisor offers a complete 2-week training program at company headquarters, which includes training in technical and managerial aspects of operating a Cap-A Radiator Shop. Franchisee will also receive 1 week of training and assistance at his location.

MANAGERIAL ASSISTANCE AVAILABLE: Franchisor offers many managerial and technical aids including complete operating manual (describing proper operation of a Cap-A Radiator Shop), textbooks on technical aspects of the business, advertising and merchandising programs, and a sustained program of cooperation for the duration of the franchise.

INFORMATION SUBMITTED: May 1990

CLEANCO INC.
8018 Sunnyside Road
Minneapolis, Minnesota 55432
James A. Trapp, President

DESCRIPTION OF OPERATION: Truck washing—mobile units and drive-thru. A complete chemical wash.

NUMBER OF FRANCHISEES: 16 in Minnesota, Wisconsin, Illinois, Georgia, and Florida

IN BUSINESS SINCE: 1963

EQUITY CAPITAL NEEDED: $20,000

FINANCIAL ASSISTANCE AVAILABLE: None.

TRAINING PROVIDED: 1 week full training in Minneapolis, Minnesota.

MANAGERIAL ASSISTANCE AVAILABLE: Ongoing in all areas of the franchise.

INFORMATION SUBMITTED: May 1990

* COTTMAN TRANSMISSION SYSTEM, INC.
240 New York Drive
Fort Washington, Pennsylvania 19034
Greg Mowry, National Sales Manager

DESCRIPTION OF OPERATION: Cottman Transmission Centers repair, service, and remanufacture automatic transmissions for wholesale and retail trade. Operator does not need previous automotive experience.

NUMBER OF FRANCHISEES: 129 throughout the United States and Canada

IN BUSINESS SINCE: 1962

EQUITY CAPITAL NEEDED: $35,000 (total cost: $97,500)

FINANCIAL ASSISTANCE AVAILABLE: A financial package designed to aid franchisee in loan negotiations with lending institutions.

TRAINING PROVIDED: 3 weeks training at the home office and 1 week training at operator's location. Continued assistance through operational support.

MANAGERIAL ASSISTANCE AVAILABLE: The home office continually works with each operator on all phases of operation, advertising, sales, management, employee relations, remanufacturing techniques, etc.

INFORMATION SUBMITTED: May 1990

* DR. VINYL & ASSOCIATES, LTD.
13665 East 42nd Terrace South
Independence, Missouri 64055

DESCRIPTION OF OPERATION: Dr. Vinyl franchisees provide a mobile wholesale service to the auto dealership community in their franchise territory. The service includes vinyl, leather, and dashboard repair to car interiors and tops as well as complete recoloring of vinyl and leather, either to match or change colors; also installation of pin stripes, side moldings, and other cosmetic add-ons.

NUMBER OF FRANCHISEES: 100 in 30 states

IN BUSINESS SINCE: 1972

EQUITY CAPITAL NEEDED: Minimum franchise is $20,000, which includes all materials and training but does not include necessary vehicle.

FINANCIAL ASSISTANCE AVAILABLE: Qualified applicants may receive financing assistance up to 40 percent of the required investment.

TRAINING PROVIDED: 2 weeks of training is required by the franchisor at the Kansas City headquarters. Franchisee is responsible only for room and board during training interval.

MANAGERIAL ASSISTANCE AVAILABLE: All managerial and technical assistance is provided during the 2-week training period in Kansas City, Missouri. Technical, sales, accounting, and business practices are included.

INFORMATION SUBMITTED: April 1990

ENDRUST INDUSTRIES
1725 Washington Road
Suite 205
Pittsburgh, Pennsylvania 15241

DESCRIPTION OF OPERATION: Engaged in establishing dealerships for Endrust Auto Appearance & Detailing Centers. Services include wash, wax, interior cleaning, detailing, rustproofing, undercoating, sound deadening, exterior paint protection, fabric protection, car alarms, etc. Can be established as a separate center or a supplement to a present automotive business.

NUMBER OF FRANCHISEES: 80 dealerships

IN BUSINESS SINCE: 1969

EQUITY CAPITAL NEEDED: $30,000

FINANCIAL ASSISTANCE AVAILABLE: None.

TRAINING PROVIDED: Company training in all phases of operation, ongoing support.

MANAGERIAL ASSISTANCE AVAILABLE: All that is required by dealer.

INFORMATION SUBMITTED: April 1990

FANTASY COACHWORKS LTD
6034 S. Lindbergh
St. Louis, Missouri 63123
James Smoot, Jr., President

DESCRIPTION OF OPERATION: A new concept in automotive retailing, the "Auto Boutique" features practical and functional motoring accessories for all cars, vans, imports, and pickups, plus designer wearables for the driving enthusiast. Packaged in "high-fashion" themes. Professional installation available.

NUMBER OF FRANCHISEES: 25 in 4 states

IN BUSINESS SINCE: 1975

EQUITY CAPITAL NEEDED: $20,000 per single unit

FINANCIAL ASSISTANCE AVAILABLE: Finance package preparation assistance.

TRAINING PROVIDED: 2 weeks intensive training at an existing boutique, operations manual, bimonthly newsletter, site selection, and grand opening planning and assistance.

MANAGERIAL ASSISTANCE AVAILABLE: Managerial assistance provided in advertising, public relations, promotions, accounting/bookkeeping, co-op buying, product testing, sales, personnel, periodic visits from company field consultants.

INFORMATION SUBMITTED: April 1990

GUARANTEED TUNE UP
101 Eisenhower Parkway
Roseland, New Jersey 07068
William Okita, President

DESCRIPTION OF OPERATION: Automotive tune-up and automobile repair service business.

NUMBER OF FRANCHISEES: 7 in New Jersey, New York, North Carolina, and Pennsylvania

IN BUSINESS SINCE: 1984

EQUITY CAPITAL NEEDED: Turnkey operation approximately $96,000; $25,000 cash, and balance financed, to qualified investors.

FINANCIAL ASSISTANCE AVAILABLE: Will assist in securing outside financing.

TRAINING PROVIDED: An intensive 1-week training program is provided for shop managers, mechanics, or owners.

MANAGERIAL ASSISTANCE AVAILABLE: Continuous managerial assistance is provided in all phases of operation to ensure proper operation of the business.

INFORMATION SUBMITTED: May 1990

JIFFIWASH, INC.
P. O. Box 2489
San Francisco, California 94126
Merle Akers, President

DESCRIPTION OF OPERATION: Service institutional clients at their locations, washing, brushing, and cleaning their fleet of vehicles from a Jiffiwash mobile unit equipped with patented pressure-washing equipment. Work is done mostly in the evenings and on weekends when rolling stock is parked in their respective yards.

NUMBER OF FRANCHISEES: 31 now—exclusive franchises in 10 states

IN BUSINESS SINCE: 1959

EQUITY CAPITAL NEEDED: $5,000–$25,000

FINANCIAL ASSISTANCE AVAILABLE: Franchisee is to arrange own financing for the purchase price. $5,000–$20,000 is needed to purchase a Jiffiwash franchise. The additional $5,000 is necessary to defray initial operating expenses for the first 6 months the franchisee is in business, or until such time sufficient revenue is generated for the franchisee to be self-sufficient with positive cash flow.

TRAINING PROVIDED: 1 week of on-site training with established Jiffiwash Dealer washing vehicles and making sales calls. Optional: a visit to the home office in San Francisco for additional sales training and a training period at the Jiffiwash machine shop to acquaint franchisee with Jiffiwash patented equipment. Franchisee to pay all expenses incurred during training period.

MANAGERIAL ASSISTANCE AVAILABLE: Jiffiwash will do all accounting functions on behalf of franchisee until the franchise is terminated. Jiffiwash will conduct periodic sales campaign in and around the area serviced by franchisee. Franchisee is to follow up leads thus generated, calling on interested parties selling the Jiffiwash Mobile Washing Service in and around his service area. Jiffiwash machine shop is available for technical assistance during normal shop hours. All equipment received by the franchisee is covered by a 90-day warranty. After the warranty period, replacements will be shipped, at cost, to franchisee to keep the equipment working on-the-job.

INFORMATION SUBMITTED: May 1990

MALCO PRODUCTS, INC.
361 Fairview Avenue
P. O. Box 892
Barberton, Ohio 44203
J. Ginley

DESCRIPTION OF OPERATION: Distributorship to sell complete line of automotive chemical specialties including cleaners, oil additives, brake fluid, etc., to service stations, garages, new and used car dealers, and industrial outlets. He is assigned a territory that can support him. The distributor and his men travel the area using step vans, selling to the above accounts.

NUMBER OF FRANCHISEES: 430 throughout the United States

IN BUSINESS SINCE: 1953

EQUITY CAPITAL NEEDED: $6,000 for inventory investment only.

FINANCIAL ASSISTANCE AVAILABLE: None.

TRAINING PROVIDED: Thorough field and product training in the distributor's area by regional sales manager. Periodically during the year the regional sales manager spends time with the distributor and salesmen for training both in product knowledge and field training.

MANAGERIAL ASSISTANCE AVAILABLE: Distributor sales meetings are held twice a year for further training. Complete managerial assistance provided through company personnel and field representatives.

INFORMATION SUBMITTED: May 1990

MILEX OF AMERICA, INC.
4914 North Lincoln Avenue
Chicago, Illinois 60625

DESCRIPTION OF OPERATION: Milex service centers provide written warranties on all work performed. Although tune-ups and brake services are the mainstay of the operation, other car care services may be offered subject to Milex approval. Milex shops are equipped with the latest computerized diagnostic equipment to give an exclusive Milex diagnosis. Milex franchisees come from many different walks of life; some have a mechanical background, others do not.

NUMBER OF FRANCHISEES: 32 in Illinois

IN BUSINESS SINCE: 1972

EQUITY CAPITAL NEEDED: $35,000 minimum

FINANCIAL ASSISTANCE AVAILABLE: The total investment range is $119,500, depending on the equipment needed in the location. Milex Finance Department will assist the franchisees by recommending procedures by which such loans previously have been obtained and will counsel in preparing any applications or presentations necessary to submit to the lending institutions or government agencies.

TRAINING PROVIDED: Prior to the opening of a center for business, a new franchisee must attend Milex's comprehensive training program, which takes place in a classroom and/or service center for a period of 24 working days.

MANAGERIAL ASSISTANCE AVAILABLE: Since 1972, most principals of Milex have been successfully owning and operating auto care service centers specializing in tune-ups and brakes. Continuous managerial and sales counseling is provided throughout the life of the franchise. The Operations Division will put special emphasis on counseling the franchisees during their first year in business. Ongoing counseling in such areas as advertising, accounting, complete operating procedures manuals, and forms and directions is provided.

INFORMATION SUBMITTED: May 1990

MING OF AMERICA, INC.
7526 Metcalf
Overland Park, Kansas 66204

DESCRIPTION OF OPERATION: Automotive beautification and protection services, including Ming Mirror Finish, complete appearance reconditioning, Ming custom rust protection.

NUMBER OF FRANCHISEES: 43 in the United States and 2 countries

IN BUSINESS SINCE: 1968

EQUITY CAPITAL NEEDED: $49,600–$68,800

FINANCIAL ASSISTANCE AVAILABLE: Ming of America, Inc., will assist in preparation of loan application and in locating sources of financing.

TRAINING PROVIDED: 3-week mandatory training program for manager and 1 employee at the corporate training center. 1-week training provided on-site at time of store opening.

MANAGERIAL ASSISTANCE AVAILABLE: Technical and managerial support is provided on a continuing basis, including operations manuals, on-site inspections, and updated technical information.

INFORMATION SUBMITTED: May 1990

MIRACLE AUTO PAINTING
Division of MULTIPLE ALLIED SERVICES, INC.
Century Plaza One Building
1065 East Hillsdale Boulevard
Suite 110
Foster City, California 94404

DESCRIPTION OF OPERATION: Miracle Auto Painting offers quality body repair work and baked enamel auto painting with a written guarantee at a volume-producing low price. Miracle provides high-quality, rapid service and lowest cost through the production line process. Assistance is provided to the franchisee in site selection, equipment installation, and sales promotion. Supplies and materials are available through Miracle's volume purchasing.

NUMBER OF FRANCHISEES: 46 in California, Oregon, Arizona, Nevada, and Texas

IN BUSINESS SINCE: 1953

EQUITY CAPITAL NEEDED: $35,000 minimum

FINANCIAL ASSISTANCE AVAILABLE: The franchisee usually needs a minimum of $79,000 cash to establish the business on a profitable basis.

TRAINING PROVIDED: A 4-week training course is scheduled for new franchisees. Two weeks of the training is at a Miracle location and 2 weeks at the franchisee's location. Training covers systems and procedures for production painting and bodywork as well as sales and business procedures. Miracle operates training centers in San Mateo and Foster City, California.

MANAGERIAL ASSISTANCE AVAILABLE: Miracle provides continuing consultation not only for production techniques and procedures but also for sales and business management, accounting and record keeping, and employee recruiting and training.

INFORMATION SUBMITTED: April 1990

MOBILE AUTO TRIM, INC.
10500 Metric Drive
Dallas, Texas 75243
C. F. "Butch" Davis, Jr., President

DESCRIPTION OF OPERATION: Mobile Auto Trim, Inc., provides the franchisee the opportunity to offer their prospective market area with one of the most complete mobile reconditioning and trim concepts in the country. Services include body side molding, pin striping, custom dye for carpet, vinyl, and leather surfaces, vinyl repair, trunk reconditioning, auto paint chip repair, windshield repair, etc. No prior experience required; methods and techniques highly effective toward success.

NUMBER OF FRANCHISEES: 15 in Texas, Oklahoma, Louisiana, Arkansas, Indiana, and Michigan plus 10 company-owned

IN BUSINESS SINCE: 1981

EQUITY CAPITAL NEEDED: $10,000 minimum

FINANCIAL ASSISTANCE AVAILABLE: Total investment for a Mobile Auto Trim franchise operation is approximately $25,000. Investment includes $15,000 franchise fee and $10,000 equipment and supplies.

TRAINING PROVIDED: Complete 3-day administrative orientation required at home office in Dallas, Texas, followed by a 4-week field training program. Training program includes establishment of customer base, familiarization with product line, and how to professionally and proficiently perform the range of services offered through Mobile Auto Trim.

MANAGERIAL ASSISTANCE AVAILABLE: In addition to initial training program outlined above, Mobile Auto Trim provides continual management services for the life of the franchise (i.e., bookkeeping, advertising, inventory control). Complete manuals of operations, solving any problems of the franchise operation. Dissemination of new methods and products as they are tested and become available.

INFORMATION SUBMITTED: May 1990

MOBILE TRIM TEAM
1239 Braselton Highway
Lawrenceville, Georgia 30243
Ken Clark

DESCRIPTION OF OPERATION: Company has a wide variety of repair services and complete upholstery to new and used car dealers, restaurants, motels, hotels, hospitals, or wherever there is work to be done.

NUMBER OF FRANCHISEES: 18 in 8 states

IN BUSINESS SINCE: 1972

EQUITY CAPITAL NEEDED: $28,000–$29,500

FINANCIAL ASSISTANCE AVAILABLE: None.

TRAINING PROVIDED: 3 weeks minimum in shop and field training.

MANAGERIAL ASSISTANCE AVAILABLE: Ongoing seminars in all phases of operations.

INFORMATION SUBMITTED: May 1990

* MOTRA CORP.
4912 North Lincoln
Chicago, Illinois 60625
Werner E. Ament, Chairman of the Board

DESCRIPTION OF OPERATION: MOTRA Transmission Service Centers provide transmission rebuilding and repair services with warranties from 6 months to lifetime. MOTRA Centers provide free 23-point diagnostic Motra checks. MOTRA will make recommendations as to the equipment requirements for each center. Franchisee does not need a mechanical background.

NUMBER OF FRANCHISEES: 42 in Illinois, Arizona, and Florida

IN BUSINESS SINCE: 1980

EQUITY CAPITAL NEEDED: $17,500

FINANCIAL ASSISTANCE AVAILABLE: The total investment is $89,500 depending on the equipment needed in the location. MOTRA will assist the franchisee by recommending procedures by which such loans previously have been obtained and will counsel in preparing any applications or presentations necessary to submit to the lending institutions or government agencies.

TRAINING PROVIDED: Prior to opening center for business, franchisee must attend MOTRA's comprehensive training program.

MANAGERIAL ASSISTANCE AVAILABLE: The principals of MOTRA have over 30 years of successful experience in owning and operating transmission shops, and continue to own and operate MOTRA Centers. Continuous managerial, technical, and sales counseling is provided throughout the life of the franchise. The Operations Division will put special emphasis on operators during the first year in business. Ongoing counseling in such areas as advertising and accounting is provided. Complete operating procedure manuals and forms and directions are provided. Operations director and other representatives are available to counsel franchisees through MOTRA's Operations Division.

INFORMATION SUBMITTED: May 1990

NOVUS WINDSHIELD REPAIR AND SCRATCH REMOVAL
10425 Hampshire Avenue South
Minneapolis, Minnesota 55438
Gerald E. Keinath, President

DESCRIPTION OF OPERATION: Using the exclusive NOVUS patented process, professionally trained franchisees repair, rather than replace, stone-damaged windshields. NOVUS franchisees are the experts in windshield repair and offer a money-saving service to fleets, insurance companies, government agencies, and consumers. Franchisees work out of their home or from a fixed location. NOVUS has also developed a process for removing scratches from windshields and other laminated glass.

NUMBER OF FRANCHISEES: 600

IN BUSINESS SINCE: 1972

EQUITY CAPITAL NEEDED: Approximately $10,000

FINANCIAL ASSISTANCE AVAILABLE: None.

TRAINING PROVIDED: 5-day factory training at the NOVUS international headquarters includes technical training, sales and marketing classes, and seminars on general business operations.

MANAGERIAL ASSISTANCE AVAILABLE: Ongoing technical sales assistance provided by professional staff. Newsletters, conventions, regional meetings, and ongoing research and development are included.

INFORMATION SUBMITTED: May 1990

PLUG BUGGY, INC.
7501 Gynor Avenue
Van Nuys, California 91406
Edward R. Hier, President

DESCRIPTION OF OPERATION: Mobile auto parts distribution (auto parts store on wheels). Selling auto parts wholesale to repair garages, service stations, and dealers both foreign and American from an attractive, well-organized van in a protected area.

NUMBER OF FRANCHISEES: 10 in California and Hawaii

IN BUSINESS SINCE: 1970, franchised since 1979

EQUITY CAPITAL NEEDED: $27,500

FINANCIAL ASSISTANCE AVAILABLE: Franchisor will assist in obtaining franchisee his own financing.

TRAINING PROVIDED: Product knowledge, product identification, sales, accounting, buying and selling.

MANAGERIAL ASSISTANCE AVAILABLE: Ongoing field assistance, technical assistance from franchisor and manufacturers' representatives.

INFORMATION SUBMITTED: May 1990

SAF-T AUTO CENTERS
R & R ENTERPRISES, INC.
209 Forbes Avenue
New Haven, Connecticut 06512
Richard G. Bilodeas, President

DESCRIPTION OF OPERATION: SAF-T Auto Centers is an owner-operated auto repair shop offering steering, suspension, brakes, mufflers, lubrication, and minor repair. Our main effort is to give good mechanics a business opportunity to capitalize on their trade. Ability, skill, and talent to do auto repair are a prerequisite.

NUMBER OF FRANCHISEES: 9 in 2 states plus 1 company-owned

IN BUSINESS SINCE: 1978

EQUITY CAPITAL NEEDED: Minimum $32,500—maximum $65,000

FINANCIAL ASSISTANCE AVAILABLE: Assistance in third-party financing to qualified applicants.

TRAINING PROVIDED: 1 week in your franchise on site geared toward managerial aspects and administrative operations. Ability, skill, and talent to do auto repair are a prerequisite.

MANAGERIAL ASSISTANCE AVAILABLE: Ongoing.

INFORMATION SUBMITTED: April 1990

* SPARKS TUNE-UP, INC.
1400 Opus Place, Suite 800
Downers Grove, Illinois 60515

DESCRIPTION OF OPERATION: Tune-ups are an $8.7 billion market in the United States; under-the-hood is a $23.6 billion market. Sparks intends to be a major player in this market while providing engine diagnostics, fuel injector cleaning, air conditioning servicing, radiator flush and fill, and lube and oil changes to the motoring public. GKN purchased Meineke in 1963 and has been the driving force behind their growth since that time. Sparks was acquired by GKN Automotive in 1987.

NUMBER OF FRANCHISEES: 132 in 29 states

IN BUSINESS SINCE: 1981

EQUITY CAPITAL NEEDED: $50,000

FINANCIAL ASSISTANCE AVAILABLE: The franchisee is responsible for the total investment of $127,834. Sparks' finance department will assist the franchisee by recommending procedures by which such loans have been previously obtained, and will assist in preparing any applications or presentations necessary to be submitted to lending institutions or government agencies.

TRAINING PROVIDED: An intensive 3-week training program is scheduled at the Corporate Headquarters, and another 3 weeks of training at the franchisee's Sparks center by a full-time Sparks Tune-Up, Inc., employee when the center opens.

MANAGERIAL ASSISTANCE AVAILABLE: Sparks Tune-Up, Inc., provides continual management services for the life of the franchise in such areas as advertising, inventory control, and accounting. Complete operating procedures manuals, technical manuals, forms, and directions are provided. An operations director and field representative are available to work closely with the franchisee both by phone and by visiting the centers regularly to assist whenever needed. Sparks' operations department will hold regional meetings and conventions for the franchisees, and conduct marketing and product research to assure the best service available to our customers.

INFORMATION SUBMITTED: April 1990

STAR TECHNOLOGY WINDSHIELD REPAIR, INC.
P. O. Box 724706
Atlanta, Georgia 30339
David A. Casey, General Manager

DESCRIPTION OF OPERATION: The franchisor develops, owns and operates, and authorizes franchisees to operate and own mobile and fixed windshield repair business using franchisors' registered trademarks and exclusive ADP windshield repair system. Many franchises are operated as mobile service units in conjunction with an answering service and post office box for mailing and collection of receipts. The primary business of the franchise is the mobile repair of rock-damaged windshields, guaranteeing the windshield against further breakage for the life of the windshield. Complete customer satisfaction is guaranteed. The income base is primarily provided by service to commercial fleets, car sales lots, auto rental, insurance-independent motorists.

NUMBER OF FRANCHISEES: 140 in 38 states

IN BUSINESS SINCE: 1983

EQUITY CAPITAL NEEDED: $14,000 to $35,000, includes franchise fee, all equipment and materials, training and city setup, and 3 months personal expenses.

FINANCIAL ASSISTANCE AVAILABLE: 70 percent down payment required. Franchisor will finance remainder to persons with approved credit.

TRAINING PROVIDED: An intensive 2-week training course is mandatory: 1 week at the national training center in Boulder, Colorado, and 1 week in the franchisee's territory setting up working accounts with a certified corporate senior technician. Training manuals, operations manuals, account cross-reference catalogues, a complete bookkeeping system, all equipment and accessories, complete uniform package, all printed materials, continuous newsletters, and follow-up marketing support are included in the franchise package.

MANAGERIAL ASSISTANCE AVAILABLE: A full-time corporate staff is available to provide technical assistance, counsel, and marketing guidance as needed. A full-time national account marketing department is in effect. Seminars and advanced training are available full time. An annual convention is held.

INFORMATION SUBMITTED: May 1990

* TIDY CAR INTERNATIONAL, INC.
P. O. Box 7024
Troy, Michigan 48007-7024

DESCRIPTION OF OPERATION: The Tidy Car format is specifically designed to meet the needs of today's on-the-go, quality-conscious consumer by offering a spectrum of automotive detailing services and accessories that range from those performed on a low cost, while-you-wait basis to full service long-term appearance with protective warranties.

NUMBER OF FRANCHISEES: 121

IN BUSINESS SINCE: 1976

EQUITY CAPITAL NEEDED: $41,700–$59,000

FINANCIAL ASSISTANCE AVAILABLE: None.

TRAINING PROVIDED: The 4-week training period is comprised of extensive schooling in all services offered in addition to management techniques. Ongoing training is also available via schools, seminars, and national meetings.

MANAGERIAL ASSISTANCE AVAILABLE: With site selection, lease negotiations, display setup, and inventory requirements. Product orders can be placed with home office personnel who also arrange shipment; marketing staff assists with advertising selection and placement while field staff visit and work with the franchisee on an ongoing basis.

INFORMATION SUBMITTED: April 1990

ULTRA WASH, INC.
2335 Naomi Street
Houston, Texas 77054
Brian Peskin, President

DESCRIPTION OF OPERATION: A state-of-the-art mobile pressure washing franchise specializing in truck fleet washing at the customer's location. All equipment, training, and initial supplies are included. An on-site salesman will come to franchisee's area to secure sales of $75,000.

NUMBER OF FRANCHISEES: 32 in 6 states

IN BUSINESS SINCE: 1981, franchising since 1984

EQUITY CAPITAL NEEDED: $25,000 cash. Total franchise is approximately $54,000.

FINANCIAL ASSISTANCE AVAILABLE: Sources provided.

TRAINING PROVIDED: 2-week training at corporate headquarters in Houston, Texas, plus 1 week on location. Sales specialist goes to franchisee's area to assist in securing sales. Ongoing support is continual in the form of monthly newsletters, videotapes, etc.

MANAGERIAL ASSISTANCE AVAILABLE: Over 15 years fleet washing experience. Mr. Peskin has been a manager with a Fortune 500 company. Our sale's expertise numbers over 12 in selling this service to truck fleet managers. We have over 5 man-years in equipment design, and the washing equipment can bring in more sales per system than any other competitor due to its vastly reliable design.

INFORMATION SUBMITTED: April 1990

AUTO/TRAILER RENTALS

A.I.N. LEASING SYSTEMS
501 Burnside Avenue
Inwood, New York 11696
Garry Rothbaum

DESCRIPTION OF OPERATION: An automobile and equipment leasing franchise. A.I.N. provides training, marketing plan, and all necessary lease financing.

NUMBER OF FRANCHISEES: 265 nationwide

IN BUSINESS SINCE: 1980

EQUITY CAPITAL NEEDED: $25,000

FINANCIAL ASSISTANCE AVAILABLE: None.

TRAINING PROVIDED: 4 days of training covers marketing and merchandising.

MANAGERIAL ASSISTANCE AVAILABLE: Ongoing support and assistance.

INFORMATION SUBMITTED: May 1990

AMERICAN INTERNATIONAL RENT A CAR
One Harborside Drive
Boston, Massachusetts 02128

DESCRIPTION OF OPERATION: American International is a worldwide network of car rental operations servicing customers at airport, suburban, and downtown locations. All outlets are franchised-owned; there are no corporate locations.

NUMBER OF FRANCHISEES: The American International network consists of over 1,300 locations in more than 25 countries throughout North America, Europe, the Middle East, South America, and the Caribbean.

IN BUSINESS SINCE: 1968

EQUITY CAPITAL NEEDED: Varies with size and location of the territory. Average initial franchise investment: $50,000.

FINANCIAL ASSISTANCE AVAILABLE: Arrangements are discussed on an individual basis.

TRAINING PROVIDED: Initial training available at the corporate headquarters location. Complete operations manuals are provided and updated by the Systems Office. Ongoing consultation and assistance will be provided as needed.

MANAGERIAL ASSISTANCE AVAILABLE: The management team at American International assists new franchisees in selecting sites, financing and managing their fleets, analyzing financial statements, obtaining corporate accounts and government contracts, and local marketing and advertising. American International has standardized everything their franchisees need, including signs, rental agreements, uniforms, and promotional materials.

INFORMATION SUBMITTED: May 1990

PRACTICAL RENT-A-CAR
705-B Yucca
Boulder City, Nevada 89005
Bert Frost, General Manager

DESCRIPTION OF OPERATION: Practical Rent-A-Car is America's alternative car rental agency. We offer affordable car rental franchises to people committed to service. New car prices make new car rentals prohibitive for the majority of people; renting used cars is right for the 1990s.

NUMBER OF FRANCHISEES: 13 in 6 states

IN BUSINESS SINCE: Practical Rent-A-Car was trademarked in Canada in 1984. Micro Instrument Corp of Rochester, New York, purchased the United States rights to the trademark in March 1989.

EQUITY CAPITAL NEEDED: $12,500 to $275,000

FINANCIAL ASSISTANCE AVAILABLE: None.

TRAINING PROVIDED: Mandatory training program conducted at the franchisee's location or at corporate headquarters. The training program covers general policies, fleet purchasing and management, rental counter management, financial information, record keeping, personnel, customer relations, and advertising and promotion.

MANAGERIAL ASSISTANCE AVAILABLE: On-site opening assistance, continuing management, marketing, operation, and technical assistance to franchisee and employees.

INFORMATION SUBMITTED: April 1990

BEAUTY SALONS/SUPPLIES

* COMMAND PERFORMANCE
Baldwin Park
7 Alfred Street
Woburn, Massachusetts 01801
Dennis Brown, C.O.O.

DESCRIPTION OF OPERATION: Precision haircutting and styling salons for men and women. Company encourages owner-operators.

NUMBER OF FRANCHISEES: 90 in 30 states plus 130 company-owned

IN BUSINESS SINCE: 1976

EQUITY CAPITAL NEEDED: Total cost to purchase, construct, and open salon: $41,500 to $124,500.

FINANCIAL ASSISTANCE AVAILABLE: Various combinations of approved leasing and financing alternatives.

TRAINING PROVIDED: In addition to recruiting and training the salon's manager and staff, the franchisor conducts a comprehensive 30-hour initial training course for its franchisees in all phases of operations, advertising, promotion, legal and financial considerations.

MANAGERIAL ASSISTANCE AVAILABLE: In addition to initial site selection, lease negotiations, hiring and training of staff, and construction advice, the franchisor furnishes continuing management, marketing, operational, and technical assistance to franchisee and his/her employees.

INFORMATION SUBMITTED: May 1990

JOAN M. CABLE'S LA FEMMINA BEAUTY SALONS, INC.
3301 Hempstead Turnpike
Levittown, New York 11756
John L. Wagner, Vice President

DESCRIPTION OF OPERATION: Joan M. Cable's La Femmina Beauty Salons, Inc., offers qualified applicants franchises to operate retail ladies' beauty parlors under its name. La Femmina offers total service to women with complete haircare and grooming services including manicures, pedicures, and facials, using only the highest-quality name-brand products—all at affordable prices and convenient hours for today's active women.

NUMBER OF FRANCHISEES: 7 in New York/Long Island areas

IN BUSINESS SINCE: 1974

EQUITY CAPITAL NEEDED: Total investment ranges from $27,265 to 33,265

FINANCIAL ASSISTANCE AVAILABLE: Franchisor will possibly assist franchisee in obtaining appropriate financing or franchisor may offer a portion of such financing for the purchase of all necessary machinery and equipment.

TRAINING PROVIDED: The training program shall last no less than 5 days and provides the franchisee with the certain knowledge to assist the franchisee in the operation of the La Femmina Beauty Parlor. Throughout the training program, which will be held on a one-to-one basis, such topics as payroll, advertising, insurance, products, and scheduling will be discussed in conjunction with the direct use of the operations manual.

MANAGERIAL ASSISTANCE AVAILABLE: Joan M. Cable's La Femmina Beauty Salons, Inc., provides continual and ongoing training and management service for the term of the franchise in areas of bookkeeping, advertising, workshops, seminars, and promotional programs, all on an as-needed basis.

INFORMATION SUBMITTED: April 1990

THE MANE EVENT FRANCHISING CO., INC.
dba AUTUMN ROSE HAIR DESIGNERS
225-A Main Street
Farmingdale, New York 11735
Lee Meyer, President

DESCRIPTION OF OPERATION: The franchise offered is for the establishment and operation of a hair care salon featuring traditional "beauty parlor" services, such as full sets, in addition to basic haircutting, styling, and hair care services, at a designated location under the name Autumn Rose Hair Designers. The marketing emphasis of the franchise salons is haircutting and styling for women as the primary market target, although services are available to men. Personalized attention in a relaxing atmosphere is stressed. Private-brand hair care products packaged under the name Autumn Rose are also featured at franchise salons for retail sales to customers.

NUMBER OF FRANCHISEES: 4 in New York

IN BUSINESS SINCE: 1979

EQUITY CAPITAL NEEDED: Initial estimated total cost, including initial franchise fee, ranges between $24,945 to $56,250.

FINANCIAL ASSISTANCE AVAILABLE: Initial franchise fee of $9,500 may be paid in installments. Most installment payment plans require the franchisee to pay at least $3,500 upon signing the franchise agreement, at least $1,500 upon signing the sublease for the franchise premises, and the balance of the initial franchise fee by no later than 3 months after the franchise salon opens for business. However, in individual cases different payment plans may be available.

TRAINING PROVIDED: Initial training is in 2 parts: hands-on training at a company-owned location and on-site assistance at the franchise location following the opening of the franchise business to the public. The length of the initial training program varies in individual cases depending on the franchisee's prior business and trade experience. Training covers all aspects of the Autumn Rose franchise system. There is no training fee (fee is included in initial franchise fee), except the franchisee is responsible for all personal expenses incurred in attending the training program. An unlimited number of employees and managers of the franchisee may attend the initial training program.

MANAGERIAL ASSISTANCE AVAILABLE: The franchisor will periodically inspect the franchise premises to provide on-site operations assistance. Franchisees will be provided with the names of recommended suppliers for equipment, signs, fixtures, nonproprietary supplies, and materials. The franchisor may periodically make available advertising plans and advice and in-shop merchandising materials for franchisees' local use and may assist in designing special advertising and promotional programs for individual market regions. The franchisor will periodically offer free optional and mandatory workshops for franchisees and their employees in haircutting and hairstyling and may hold franchisee conferences to discuss sales techniques, training of personnel, performance standards, advertising programs and merchandising procedures.

INFORMATION SUBMITTED: May 1990

SNIP N' CLIP
6804 West 75th Street
Overland Park, Kansas 66212
Ronald M. Mitchell

DESCRIPTION OF OPERATION: Family haircut shops.

NUMBER OF FRANCHISEES: 26 franchised plus 30 company-owned

IN BUSINESS SINCE: 1982

EQUITY CAPITAL NEEDED: $35,000. The Snip N' Clip investment package includes all equipment and leasehold improvements for a finished, turnkey operation.

FINANCIAL ASSISTANCE AVAILABLE: None.

TRAINING PROVIDED: Offering up-to-date workshops in hairstyling, retraining, and communications. Periodic visits by Snip N' Clip supervisory personnel to all shops will keep shops and staffs up to date on the latest trends, hairstyles, products, and specific promotions.

MANAGERIAL ASSISTANCE AVAILABLE: Use of operations manual to ensure consistency of operations.

INFORMATION SUBMITTED: April 1990

* THIRD DIMENSION CUTS, INC.
8015 Broadway
Everett, Washington 98203
Rob Jurries, New Development Director

DESCRIPTION OF OPERATION: Third Dimension Cuts offers a unique design and no-appointment-style hair salon for men and women with a concept that appeals to the largest segment of the population. You need not be a hairstylist to own or operate.

NUMBER OF FRANCHISEES: 13 plus 31 company-owned in Alaska, Idaho, Washington, Oregon, and Utah

IN BUSINESS SINCE: 1979

EQUITY CAPITAL NEEDED: Approximately $25,000

FINANCIAL ASSISTANCE AVAILABLE: Investment in between $65,000 to $120,000 of which approximately $25,000 is start-up capital for franchise fee, down payments, grand opening advertising, and start-up capital, depending on financial arrangements.

TRAINING PROVIDED: Training is done at the nearest location or 3D headquarters and consists of 25 to 120 hours training in all aspects of the operation; all manuals and operation formulas are provided.

MANAGERIAL ASSISTANCE AVAILABLE: Third Dimension Cuts offers handbooks, manager manuals, and continued hairstyling training from company representatives, plus national company training from products companies throughout the life of the franchise.

INFORMATION SUBMITTED: May 1990

BUSINESS AIDS & SERVICES

ADVANTAGE PAYROLL SERVICES
800 Center Street
P. O. Box 1330
Auburn, Maine 04211

DESCRIPTION OF OPERATION: Franchisees provide a complete payroll and payroll tax filing service to small businesses. Small computers in the franchised offices are linked to the company's computer center in a unique shared distribution of responsibilities.

NUMBER OF FRANCHISEES: 22 in 13 states, 1 company-owned

IN BUSINESS SINCE: 1967

EQUITY CAPITAL NEEDED: $13,000–$20,000 including equipment, franchise fee, and training. Additional working capital for personal living expenses required.

FINANCIAL ASSISTANCE AVAILABLE: $5,000 at 10 percent over 4 years. No payments required during the first year.

TRAINING PROVIDED: Up to 2 weeks at company headquarters with a minimum of 10 days in field. Ongoing service and support.

MANAGERIAL ASSISTANCE AVAILABLE: Ongoing.

INFORMATION SUBMITTED: April 1990

AFTE ENTERPRISES, INC.
13831 Northwest Freeway
Suite 335
Houston, Texas 77040
Ken Jaeger

DESCRIPTION OF OPERATION: Computerized bookkeeping, tax, and business consulting service. Proven method of acquiring clients.

NUMBER OF FRANCHISEES: 13 in 7 states

IN BUSINESS SINCE: 1986

EQUITY CAPITAL NEEDED: $5,000

FINANCIAL ASSISTANCE AVAILABLE: None.

TRAINING PROVIDED: 2 weeks training.

MANAGERIAL ASSISTANCE AVAILABLE: Continuous guidance and support by all company personnel when and as needed. Regular contact by phone and through the mail during the life of the agreement.

INFORMATION SUBMITTED: April 1990

AIT FREIGHT SYSTEMS, INC.
1350 North Michael Drive, Suite D
Wood Dale, Illinois 60191
Herbert L. Cohan, Director of Corporate Development

DESCRIPTION OF OPERATION: Air freight forwarder offering expedited air and surface transportation services.

NUMBER OF FRANCHISEES: 5 in 5 states plus 1 company-owned in Illinois

IN BUSINESS SINCE: 1979

EQUITY CAPITAL NEEDED: Costs vary from $10,000 to $30,000 depending on locale. Contact company for full particulars.

FINANCIAL ASSISTANCE AVAILABLE: None.

TRAINING PROVIDED: At corporate headquarters and at franchisee's location as needed.

MANAGERIAL ASSISTANCE AVAILABLE: Continuous management guidance during the life of the franchise agreement in such areas as accounting, policies, procedures, operations, and sales.

INFORMATION SUBMITTED: April 1990

ALL AMERICAN SIGN SHOPS, INC.
1460-A Diggs Drive
Raleigh, North Carolina 27603
Doug Lipscomb, Director of Marketing

DESCRIPTION OF OPERATION: Retail sign shop specializing in small signs. Concept puts you in business with minimum capital and reduces overhead expenses. 24-hour service for the consumer.

NUMBER OF FRANCHISEES: 14 in 6 states

IN BUSINESS SINCE: 1984, franchising since 1987

EQUITY CAPITAL NEEDED: $30,000–$50,000, franchise fee $10,000

FINANCIAL ASSISTANCE AVAILABLE: Equipment leasing assistance available.

TRAINING PROVIDED: Yes.

MANAGERIAL ASSISTANCE AVAILABLE: Ongoing.

INFORMATION SUBMITTED: April 1990

ALLAN & PARTNERS
603 Lawyers Building
428 Forbes Avenue
Pittsburgh, Pennsylvania 15219
Allan L. Hyman, General Partner

DESCRIPTION OF OPERATION: Executive marketing, outplacement, résumé services to corporate and private sector clients.

NUMBER OF FRANCHISEES: 2 in 2 states

IN BUSINESS SINCE: 1972—franchise operations since 1984

EQUITY CAPITAL NEEDED: $30,000

FINANCIAL ASSISTANCE AVAILABLE: None.

TRAINING PROVIDED: Initial year's start-up training approximately 30 days and approximately 10 days' training each succeeding year. All selected franchises are appointed senior consultants and receive, with no additional cost, a complete set of training, operations, and client information manuals which outline company policy and operations methods; computerized résumé reference files; 2 weeks of initial training plus 1 week of advanced training in Pittsburgh, Pennsylvania; periodic field training in the franchisee's office as needed. Training and individual assistance continue through experienced home office personnel and senior partners to be assigned in the future.

MANAGERIAL ASSISTANCE AVAILABLE: Each franchisee is trained in the use of PAAR Plan-A job search program for professional, executive, technical, and other white-collar workers that is based on effective and proven marketing and communications procedures. Full assistance is provided continuously to franchisees and their clients by home office personnel. In addition, the company provides professional writing, research, and computer support services to franchisees and their clients.

INFORMATION SUBMITTED: May 1990

* AMERICAN ADVERTISING DISTRIBUTORS, INC.
234 South Extension Road
Mesa, Arizona 85202
Al Shindelman, Managing Director, Franchise Operations

DESCRIPTION OF OPERATION: American Advertising Distributors, Inc., has trademarked techniques, methods, experience, and know-how in establishing a professional direct mail business. Franchisee shall have the exclusive marketing license for a particular territory. The company has complete 80,000-square-feet facilities for the printing and production of coupons and other mailing pieces, for nationwide delivery.

NUMBER OF FRANCHISEES: 111 in most states

IN BUSINESS SINCE: 1976

EQUITY CAPITAL NEEDED: $25,000 to $50,000

FINANCIAL ASSISTANCE AVAILABLE: None.

TRAINING PROVIDED: 4 weeks comprehensive training: 2 weeks at company's home office, 1 week at a similar operation, and 1 week in the licensee's territory by an authorized trainer.

MANAGERIAL ASSISTANCE AVAILABLE: Provided in training school. Further training at regional sessions 2–3 times per year. Also, national convention once a year. Support network to guide franchisee through various stages of growth.

INFORMATION SUBMITTED: March 1990

AMERICAN BUSINESS ASSOCIATES FRANCHISE CORP.
475 Park Avenue
New York, New York 10016
Jerome P. Feltenstein, President

DESCRIPTION OF OPERATION: ABA offers a unique system for executive networking councils. Each franchise operates 5 councils in a specific geographic area. A business category can be represented by only one company so there is no competition.

NUMBER OF FRANCHISEES: 11 in 3 states

IN BUSINESS SINCE: 1983

EQUITY CAPITAL NEEDED: $25,000–$80,000

FINANCIAL ASSISTANCE AVAILABLE: 60 percent financeable.

TRAINING PROVIDED: 1 week intensive training, working with existing ABA councils and ABA representatives.

MANAGERIAL ASSISTANCE AVAILABLE: ABA offers continual advisory services, as well as financial administration, and national and public relations.

INFORMATION SUBMITTED: May 1990

AMERICAN COLLEGE PLANNING SERVICE, INC.
94B Jefryn Boulevard East
Deer Park, New York 11729
Richard A. Simeone, President
Randy G. Romano, Vice President

DESCRIPTION OF OPERATION: ACPS Planning Centers help families afford the high cost of a college education. Services help parents of college-bound students, regardless of income, to quality and apply for maximum college funding.

NUMBER OF FRANCHISEES: 9 in 5 states

IN BUSINESS SINCE: 1984

EQUITY CAPITAL NEEDED: Total investment $20,000

FINANCIAL ASSISTANCE AVAILABLE: None. The company will assist franchisees with financing arrangements.

TRAINING PROVIDED: 1 week training at company's training center. Ongoing training and assistance at the company's training center and at franchise center location.

MANAGERIAL ASSISTANCE AVAILABLE: ACPS provides complete managerial assistance in all phases of operation including franchisee's pre-opening and start-up, marketing, training, accounting, and day-to-day operations. Complete manuals are provided.

INFORMATION SUBMITTED: April 1990

AMERICAN HERITAGE AGENCY, INC.
Heritage Building
104 Park Road
West Hartford, Connecticut 06119

DESCRIPTION OF OPERATION: Wedding consulting business furnishes services tailored to the needs of the brides-to-be.

NUMBER OF FRANCHISEES: 6 in Connecticut, Massachusetts, and New York

IN BUSINESS SINCE: 1925

EQUITY CAPITAL NEEDED: $500–$10,000

FINANCIAL ASSISTANCE AVAILABLE: Financing of up to 50 percent of the franchise fee provided credit standards can be met.

TRAINING PROVIDED: 12 days of formal classroom training and on-the-job training at established office; up to 30 days' training at franchisee's own office; periodic briefings and meetings.

MANAGERIAL ASSISTANCE AVAILABLE: Liaison officer available to help in solving problems, expanding operations, and suggesting improvements.

INFORMATION SUBMITTED: May 1990

AMERICAN INSTITUTE OF SMALL BUSINESS
7515 Wayzata Boulevard, Suite 201
Minneapolis, Minnesota 55426

DESCRIPTION OF OPERATION: The American Institute of Small Business is a publisher of books and educational materials on small business and entrepreneurship and provides seminars on how to start and operate a small business. Publications including books and software are sold to individuals, libraries, companies, secondary and postsecondary high schools, colleges, and universities. Seminars are offered to individuals wishing to set up their own small business.

NUMBER OF FRANCHISEES: 5

IN BUSINESS SINCE: 1985, in franchising since 1988

EQUITY CAPITAL NEEDED: $5,000

FINANCIAL ASSISTANCE AVAILABLE: None.

TRAINING PROVIDED: The American Institute of Small Business provides training at their home offices and conducts the first seminar on how to set up and operate your own small business in the city of the franchisee. A prompter book and materials are provided. Literature on all books and educational materials are supplied.

MANAGERIAL ASSISTANCE AVAILABLE: The Institute provides all necessary management assistance relative to the company's manner of doing business.

INFORMATION SUBMITTED: April 1990

AMERISPEC HOME INSPECTION SERVICE
1507 West Yale Avenue
Orange, California 92667
Sheilah Hyman, Vice President, Sales

DESCRIPTION OF OPERATION: Residential inspection services offered to home buyers, sellers and referral services (i.e., real estate brokers).

NUMBER OF FRANCHISEES: 85

IN BUSINESS SINCE: 1987

EQUITY CAPITAL NEEDED: Capital requirement $5,300–$12,250 plus working capital. Franchise fee ranges from $12,900 to $18,900.

FINANCIAL ASSISTANCE AVAILABLE: None.

TRAINING PROVIDED: Required to complete 2-week intensive management institute at corporate headquarters.

MANAGERIAL ASSISTANCE AVAILABLE: Complete operations. Technical and business development manuals. Ongoing marketing assistance.

INFORMATION SUBMITTED: May 1990

AN INTERNATIONAL WORLD OF WEDDINGS, INC.
12012 S.E. 122nd Avenue
Portland, Oregon 97236
Francine M. Hansen, President

DESCRIPTION OF OPERATION: The company's principal business is as a franchisor of business opportunities to own and operate bridal consulting and wedding design firms, not only planning and creating traditional Christian ceremonies but also creating custom ethnic and religious ceremonies for Hindu, Buddhist, Jewish, and Muslim brides and coordinating a variety of formal occasions, such as proms, balls, cotillions, and anniversary parties. The rental of bridesmaid gowns, wedding gowns, and other formal women's attire also included in the franchise.

NUMBER OF FRANCHISEES: 4 in Oregon and 3 in Washington

IN BUSINESS SINCE: 1973

EQUITY CAPITAL NEEDED: $17,500–$31,500

FINANCIAL ASSISTANCE AVAILABLE: None at present.

TRAINING PROVIDED: A 1-week training program includes comprehensive training for 2, covering all aspects of wedding, consultation, planning, and design. The training is conducted by 7 qualified instructors in Portland, Oregon, teaching not only traditional American wedding planning but also the planning of many authentic ethnic or religious rituals, including but not limited to the Hindu, Buddhist, Jewish and Muslim weddings.

MANAGERIAL ASSISTANCE AVAILABLE: Complete support system including confidential operations manuals, training manuals, full-color photo presentation manual, initial supply of brochures, fliers, coupons, newspaper slick ads, business cards, and VHS tape to assist franchisee in selling the service. Regional representatives to assist in ongoing advice and counseling, and a newsletter with the most up-to-date information in the wedding industry. Regional and/or national advertising through a cooperative effort in combining our advertising dollars.

INFORMATION SUBMITTED: May 1990

BINEX-AUTOMATED BUSINESS SYSTEMS, INC.
4441 Auburn Blvd., Suite E
Sacramento, California 95841
Walter G. Heidig, President

DESCRIPTION OF OPERATION: Binex licenses offer a broad range of computerized services to small and medium-size businesses. Services include financial reports, general ledgers, accounts receivable, accounts payable, job cost, and payroll. Specialized computer services are also available, and you can develop your own. You may operate your business in various ways from a bookkeeping office to a full computer service. The computer programs are licensed to you for use on your computer or a central Binex computer. Complete small business computer sytems may be installed in your client's office.

NUMBER OF FRANCHISEES: 60 in 21 states, Canada, and New Zealand

IN BUSINESS SINCE: 1965

EQUITY CAPITAL NEEDED: $8,500. The fee covers training, manuals, and start-up supplies. No expensive equipment is required.

FINANCIAL ASSISTANCE AVAILABLE: A computer can be purchased for $2,000. Lease arrangements available if a computer is purchased.

TRAINING PROVIDED: Home study course and 1 week home office. Individuals may return for further training as needed.

MANAGERIAL ASSISTANCE AVAILABLE: Support is provided on a continuous basis. Frequent newsletters are sent out covering a variety of subjects including business operation, marketing, technical, taxes, etc. New programs and services are developed, documented, and made available regularly to all licensees. Periodic regional meetings provide upgrading and review.

INFORMATION SUBMITTED: April 1990

* THE BUILDING INSPECTOR OF AMERICA
684 Main Street
Wakefield, Massachusetts 01880
Larry Finklestone, Director of Marketing

DESCRIPTION OF OPERATION: The Building Inspector of America is a national organization of home and building inspection consultants. The service is used primarily by buyers of homes, condominiums, and property investors. It is designed to alert buyers to potential problem areas as well as show buyers how to maintain their property and possibly save money by conserving on energy.

NUMBER OF FRANCHISEES: 73 in 27 states

IN BUSINESS SINCE: 1985

EQUITY CAPITAL NEEDED: $15,000 and up depending on size of territory

FINANCIAL ASSISTANCE AVAILABLE: None.

TRAINING PROVIDED: Intense 2-week in-field and in-franchisee. Audio and videotapes provided. Workbook on sales promotion and advertising is included.

MANAGERIAL ASSISTANCE AVAILABLE: Extensive ongoing market research for franchisee benefit. Report-writing clinics and sales training and promotion workshops run several times a year at corporate headquarters. Regular newsletters, slide show programs, national referral system in place.

INFORMATION SUBMITTED: April 1990

BUSINESS CONSULTANTS OF AMERICA
Affiliate of: HORIZONS OF AMERICA
P. O. BOX 4098
Waterbury, Connecticut 06714
Gregg Nolan, Franchise Director

DESCRIPTION OF OPERATION: Franchisor offers time-tested practice, dealing with advisory services for small and medium-size business operations. Training in services to include: management, market, tax advisory, and financial advisory services. Additional training to include programs for mergers/acquisition, business brokerage, and franchise coverage. Franchisor provides a client lead service through a computer hookup to franchisee's office.

NUMBER OF FRANCHISEES: 26 in 11 states

IN BUSINESS SINCE: 1973

EQUITY CAPITAL NEEDED: $20,000 plus $5,000–$10,000 working capital. Computer equipment optional.

FINANCIAL ASSISTANCE AVAILABLE: Assistance with bank/government financing/franchisor financing.

TRAINING PROVIDED: 3 weeks intensive training at franchise headquarters, 1 week at franchisee's office, followed by 2 months cassette courses packaged by franchisor and other professional organizations. Continuing franchisor advisory newsletters and tapes. Fully computerized national listing and consulting service.

MANAGERIAL ASSISTANCE AVAILABLE: Technical and advisory services at discretion of franchisee. Continued services on an as-needed basis from franchisor. Additional memberships arranged in professional associations.

INFORMATION SUBMITTED: May 1990

CARING LIVE-IN'S, INC.
214 East 72nd Terrace
Kansas City, Missouri 04114
George Fetekamp, President

DESCRIPTION OF OPERATION: Consultation and referral service for elderly.

NUMBER OF FRANCHISEES: 10 in Missouri, Texas, Kansas, Ohio, and Florida

IN BUSINESS SINCE: 1982

EQUITY CAPITAL NEEDED: $10,000–$15,000

FINANCIAL ASSISTANCE AVAILABLE: None.

TRAINING PROVIDED: 4 days of training in all phases of operation.

MANAGERIAL ASSISTANCE AVAILABLE: Ongoing consultation.

INFORMATION SUBMITTED: May 1990

CA$H PLUS
4020 Chicago Avenue
Riverside, California 92507
Jerry E. Todd

DESCRIPTION OF OPERATION: Check cashing service and related services.

NUMBER OF FRANCHISEES: 11

IN BUSINESS SINCE: 1989

EQUITY CAPITAL NEEDED: $40,000

FINANCIAL ASSISTANCE AVAILABLE: None.

TRAINING PROVIDED: As much time as necessary at company-owned store and follow-up at location.

MANAGERIAL ASSISTANCE AVAILABLE: From beginning to end. We assist, coach, train, help, do whatever is necessary to put you into business. Protected areas, follow-up, country managers, a complete system to assure your success.

INFORMATION SUBMITTED: April 1990

* CHECK CHANGERS
2 West Madison
Suite 200
Oak Park, Illinois 60302
Ted Malone, Operation Development Manager

DESCRIPTION OF OPERATION: Check cashing centers.

NUMBER OF FRANCHISEES: 12 plus 47 company-owned

IN BUSINESS SINCE: 1964, franchising 1989

EQUITY CAPITAL NEEDED: $21,500 start-up cash. $50,000–$70,000 total investment.

FINANCIAL ASSISTANCE AVAILABLE: None.

TRAINING PROVIDED: Complete training in operating a check cashing center.

MANAGERIAL ASSISTANCE AVAILABLE: Continuous.

INFORMATION SUBMITTED: June 1990

CHECKCARE ENTERPRISES, INC.
3907 Macon Road
Columbus, Georgia 31907
Michael Stalnaker, Vice President, Franchise Development

DESCRIPTION OF OPERATION: Checkcare Systems' franchisees provide a check guarantee and verification service for its members. The system utilizes proprietary sales, collection, and administrative software with data line to franchisor.

NUMBER OF FRANCHISEES: 30 in 8 states

IN BUSINESS SINCE: 1983

EQUITY CAPITAL NEEDED: $30,000

FINANCIAL ASSISTANCE AVAILABLE: Limited financing available to qualified individuals.

TRAINING PROVIDED: Complete 1 week training program at home office.

MANAGERIAL ASSISTANCE AVAILABLE: On-site support and evaluation as necessary.

INFORMATION SUBMITTED: April 1990

* COMMUNICATIONS WORLD INTERNATIONAL, INC.
14828 West 6th Avenue
Suite 13B
Golden, Colorado 80401
Aletha Zens, Franchise Director

DESCRIPTION OF OPERATION: Sale and service of business telephone systems to companies with 2 to 250 employees.

NUMBER OF FRANCHISEES: 61 in 16 states

IN BUSINESS SINCE: 1979

EQUITY CAPITAL NEEDED: $40,000, $10,000 cash and $30,000 line of credit, for sales franchise. $100,000, $40,000 cash and $60,000 line of credit for master franchise.

FINANCIAL ASSISTANCE AVAILABLE: Yes.

TRAINING PROVIDED: Initial 5 days at company headquarters, involving administrative and product knowledge. On-site quarterly, yearly national conference/convention.

MANAGERIAL ASSISTANCE AVAILABLE: Continuous technical help via 800 number. Managerial support, researching acceptable product lines; providing sales advice. Business telephone centers are established in each city to provide administrative, service, and demonstration backup.

INFORMATION SUBMITTED: April 1990

* COMPREHENSIVE ACCOUNTING CORPORATION
2111 Comprehensive Drive
Aurora, Illinois 60505
John F. Kean

DESCRIPTION OF OPERATION: Comprehensive franchises, independent accountants to provide a monthly computerized accounting, bookkeeping, tax, and business consultation service to small- and medium-size businesses of all types. Services include complete computerized preparation of monthly balance sheets, operating statements, general ledger and payroll ledgers, accounts receivable, and job cost statements. Comprehensive trains its franchisees to use the Comprehensive Client Acquisition System. The franchisee can build his practice as fast as he is able to grow and maintain quality service.

NUMBER OF FRANCHISEES: Approximately 240 in 40 states and Puerto Rico

IN BUSINESS SINCE: 1949; licensing since 1965

EQUITY CAPITAL NEEDED: $25,000 initial franchise fee; $20,000 deferred franchise fee.

FINANCIAL ASSISTANCE AVAILABLE: The initial franchise fee is paid in cash. The $20,000 deferred franchise fee and $10,000 computer equipment may be financed.

TRAINING PROVIDED: The franchisee is required to complete a 4-week course at the corporate headquarters after sufficient home study preparation in Comprehensive's production methods. Training at corporate headquarters is divided equally between production and marketing. In addition, a postgraduate course lasting 1 week is given in the corporate headquarters.

MANAGERIAL ASSISTANCE AVAILABLE: Comprehensive provides, on an ongoing basis, a consultant for production, marketing, and practice management and a data processing consultant. Each consultant is available by phone or in person for each franchisee. Also provided are detailed production procedures and methods, client reporting forms, plus sales aids for use in obtaining accounts, one professional firm portraying Comprehensive's service to prospective clients, desktop visual for client presentation, sample computer financial statements, and various sales brochures. Comprehensive gives the franchisee the benefit of Comprehensive's experience gained through current licensees who are providing services for 20,000 monthly accounting, bookkeeping, tax, and business consultation service clients. A management information system provides statistics monthly and annually of continuing education and interchange of ideas. Other seminars are conducted for franchisee's staff and clients.

INFORMATION SUBMITTED: May 1990

COMPUTER CAR
131-61 40 Road
Flushing, New York 11354
Rod Barfield, President

DESCRIPTION OF OPERATION: Quality transportation service provided with sedans and limousines to corporate clients within New York City and the surrounding metropolitan area.

NUMBER OF FRANCHISEES: 190

IN BUSINESS SINCE: 1987

EQUITY CAPITAL NEEDED: $12,000

FINANCIAL ASSISTANCE AVAILABLE: None.

TRAINING PROVIDED: 80 hours of training both in the classroom and on the road. This includes company procedure, map skills, etc.

MANAGERIAL ASSISTANCE AVAILABLE: Management personnel is available to help the franchisees with their record keeping and having their franchise expense paid directly from their earnings.

INFORMATION SUBMITTED: May 1990

CORPORATE FINANCE ASSOCIATES
1801 Broadway
Suite 1200
Denver, Colorado 80202
Robert Prangley

DESCRIPTION OF OPERATION: Financial consultants on loans, mergers—acquisition brokers. For executives only.

NUMBER OF FRANCHISEES: 48 in 18 states plus 2 international offices.

IN BUSINESS SINCE: 1956

EQUITY CAPITAL NEEDED: $35,000 for operating capital

FINANCIAL ASSISTANCE AVAILABLE: No financial assistance except for sources for loan and venture funds.

TRAINING PROVIDED: For executives—one on one. Operating manuals are provided. Semiannual seminars and periodic regional meetings. Total of 8 training days annually.

MANAGERIAL ASSISTANCE AVAILABLE: Ongoing—case by case training.

INFORMATION SUBMITTED: April 1990

CORRECT CREDIT CO. OF HOWELL, INC.
P. O. Box 537
Howell, New Jersey 07731
Pat Fasano, President

DESCRIPTION OF OPERATION: Credit restoration service. Each office is approximately 500 square feet with 2½ salespeople, who see clients in their homes 6 days a week.

NUMBER OF FRANCHISEES: 8 in Pennsylvania, Massachusetts, Florida, and Georgia

IN BUSINESS SINCE: 1983

EQUITY CAPITAL NEEDED: $6,500, total fee $19,500

FINANCIAL ASSISTANCE AVAILABLE: Approximately $3,000–$5,000 operating capital needed for office and advertising for first 6 weeks. A portion of the investment finances to qualified applicants—$11,000.

TRAINING PROVIDED: In-out office training for 1 week and follow-up at franchisee's office whenever needed.

MANAGERIAL ASSISTANCE AVAILABLE: Always available to assist franchisees whenever needed.

INFORMATION SUBMITTED: April 1990

DEBIT ONE, INC.
9387 Dielman Industrial Drive
St. Louis, Missouri 63132
Arthur Cohen

DESCRIPTION OF OPERATION: Debit One offers a unique concept in bookkeeping services. Our mobile vans are a custom-designed office with computer and software used to travel to the client's place of business where their bookkeeping is done "at the door of their store."

NUMBER OF FRANCHISEES: 65 in 26 states

IN BUSINESS SINCE: 1983

EQUITY CAPITAL NEEDED: $44,025 minimum plus $5,000 operating capital.

FINANCIAL ASSISTANCE AVAILABLE: Franchisee provides no financial assistance, but the $26,025 for the vehicle and equipment can be financed through local banks or leasing company.

TRAINING PROVIDED: Intensive 80 hours' mandatory training course is scheduled for all new franchisees and/or their personnel. 56 hours of training are conducted at the home office and 24 hours are held in franchisee's territory.

MANAGERIAL ASSISTANCE AVAILABLE: Debit One provides continued management service. Complete manuals of operations (computer and sales) and directions are provided. A director of franchisees is available to work closely with franchisee and to assist in solving problems. Debit One provides a bimonthly newsletter in order to keep the franchisees up to date on any software changes, changes in tax laws, etc.

INFORMATION SUBMITTED: May 1990

DIXON COMMERCIAL
INVESTIGATORS, INC.
728 Center Street
Lewiston, New York 14092
E. L. Dixon, President

DESCRIPTION OF OPERATION: Complete range of credit and collection services. Territories available by city or state/province (U.S. and Canada locations available).

NUMBER OF FRANCHISEES: 6 in New York, Pennsylvania, Ohio, California, and Canada.

IN BUSINESS SINCE: 1956

EQUITY CAPITAL NEEDED: $5,000

FINANCIAL ASSISTANCE AVAILABLE: None.

TRAINING PROVIDED: 1 or 2 weeks head office training. Continuous supervision and aid afterward.

MANAGERIAL ASSISTANCE AVAILABLE: Franchisee is trained in all areas of credit collection. Franchisee is in continuous contact with head office.

INFORMATION SUBMITTED: April 1990

DYNAMIC AIR FREIGHT, INC.
1732 Old Minters Chapel Road, Suite 100
Grapevine, Texas 76051
E. G. McGuire

DESCRIPTION OF OPERATION: Dynamic Air Freight is an air freight forwarder, transporting a customer's cargo from pickup at the point or origin to delivery at destination. The company's purpose is to provide effective and efficient air freight forwarding services to businesses, industry, institutions, and governmental entities.

NUMBER OF FRANCHISEES: 20 in 10 states and 3 countries

IN BUSINESS SINCE: 1978

EQUITY CAPITAL NEEDED: $30,000

FINANCIAL ASSISTANCE AVAILABLE: $307,500 for qualified individuals. The company offers to finance up to three-quarters of the franchisee's initial license fee. The company does not offer financing for any other purpose relating to either the establishment or operation of the franchise business.

TRAINING PROVIDED: 2-week mandatory training program is provided all new franchisees and their management personnel. Training program is conducted at both the company's headquarters and the franchisee's outlet.

MANAGERIAL ASSISTANCE AVAILABLE: Dynamic provides continual administrative and managerial assistance for the life of the franchise business. Complete manuals of operations are provided each franchisee.

INFORMATION SUBMITTED: April 1990

ECONOTAX
a/k/a Taxpro, Inc.
5846 Ridgewood Road, Suite B-101
Jackson, Mississippi 39211
James T. Marsh, E.A., or Chip Johnson, E.A.

DESCRIPTION OF OPERATION: ECONOTAX provides the public with a full range of professional tax services, including tax preparation, audit assistance, electronic filing, and refund anticipation loans. ECONOTAX franchisees find their practices compatible with a wide range of financial service, bookkeeping, small business service, and other endeavors.

NUMBER OF FRANCHISEES: 56 offices in current operation

IN BUSINESS SINCE: 1965, franchising since 1968

EQUITY CAPITAL NEEDED: Initial franchise fee is $2,500. Computer adequate to run tax software recommended. Estimated other start-up costs are $500 to $1,500.

FINANCIAL ASSISTANCE AVAILABLE: Partial financing of computer hardware, software, and initial franchisee fee available.

TRAINING PROVIDED: ECONOTAX provides a course for franchisees and employees in tax preparation and tax law. Franchisees are provided an initial practice management seminar at the company's offices. ECONOTAX sponsors accredited continuing professional education seminars and courses, regular updates and bulletins, and maintains a toll-free hotline.

MANAGERIAL ASSISTANCE AVAILABLE: Assistance is provided in the provision of advertising and marketing materials; recruiting, hiring, and training programs; work scheduling and internal controls and procedures; resolution of tax questions; electronic filing, RAL, and computer support; and general management assistance.

INFORMATION SUBMITTED: April 1990

EGAL, Inc.
12345 West 95th Street, Suite 203
Lenexa, Kansas 66215
Timothy J. Watkins

DESCRIPTION OF OPERATION: EGAL, Inc., is a home inspection and radon screening franchisor, offering home inspection and radon screening for residential real estate. No office is required; it can be operated out of your house and EGAL supplies you with most materials and equipment needed to start the business.

NUMBER OF FRANCHISEES: 16

IN BUSINESS SINCE: 1987

EQUITY CAPITAL NEEDED: $12,800

FINANCIAL ASSISTANCE AVAILABLE: None.

TRAINING PROVIDED: 1 week to 10 days' training is required at EGAL's home office.

MANAGERIAL ASSISTANCE AVAILABLE: We will assist you in areas of management of the business.

INFORMATION SUBMITTED: April 1990

E. K. WILLLIAMS & CO.
8774 Yates Drive, Suite 210
Westminister, Colorado 80030
David H. Hinze, Franchise Director

DESCRIPTION OF OPERATION: EKW is a business management service specializing in the "how-to" of maximizing small-business profits through a network of franchised offices. This network of local offices provides the most up-to-date accounting, tax, and business counseling services plus a wide range of computer services to independently owned businesses. EKW has developed and marketed recordkeeping systems for small businesses, and these systems and the business management services EKW offers have received the endorsement of numerous organizations that represent potential management service clients.

NUMBER OF FRANCHISEES: 301 franchised offices in 50 states

IN BUSINESS SINCE: 1935 and franchising since 1947

EQUITY CAPITAL NEEDED: Will vary by market. Minimum $40,000.

FINANCIAL ASSISTANCE AVAILABLE: None.

TRAINING PROVIDED: A 3-week initial training course is conducted at EKW national training center to instruct in the day-to-day business operations and techniques. Field training sessions are conducted throughout the year.

MANAGERIAL ASSISTANCE AVAILABLE: After the initial training course EKW field staff provides on-site follow-up counseling, assistance, and guidance in all phases of business operations manuals, and EKW conducts field training sessions throughout the year. National marketing department works to secure endorsements of national companies that represent potential clients to the franchisee. Computer system software for processing client work is supported from the corporate office by an in-house staff of data processing professionals.

INFORMATION SUBMITTED: April 1990

FOCUS ON HOMES MAGAZINE
GUIDES PUBLISHING, INC.
One Anderson Avenue, Dept. FOH
P. O. Box 133
Fairview, New Jersey 07022
Louis C. Fernandez, President

DESCRIPTION OF OPERATION: *Focus On Homes* is a free pictorial "houses-for-sale" magazine whose main advertisers are the real estate agencies in your territory. No previous experience necessary. We produce the complete magazine for you. Complete training and protected territory.

NUMBER OF FRANCHISEES: 10 in 5 states

IN BUSINESS SINCE: 1980

EQUITY CAPITAL NEEDED: $1,800 license fee

FINANCIAL ASSISTANCE AVAILABLE: None.

TRAINING PROVIDED: Complete training and continuous support.

MANAGERIAL ASSISTANCE AVAILABLE: Continuous assistance via telephone "hotline" and periodic bulletins.

INFORMATION SUBMITTED: May 1990

FRANKLIN TRAFFIC SERVICE, INC.
5251 Shawnee Road, P. O. Box 100
Ransomville, New York 14131
Richard D. Dearborn, Manager Sales/Franchising

DESCRIPTION OF OPERATION: Franklin Traffic Service, Inc., is a prominent company providing its nationwide clientele with audit and payment of freight bills, management reporting, management services, and complete industrial traffic services.

NUMBER OF FRANCHISEES: 6 in New York, Pennsylvania, and Georgia

IN BUSINESS SINCE: 1969

EQUITY CAPITAL NEEDED: $19,000–$25,000

FINANCIAL ASSISTANCE AVAILABLE: $11,000–$14,000 required in advance. Financing on balance to qualified applicants.

TRAINING PROVIDED: Intensive 3-week, mandatory training program for all new franchisees. Training consists of in-house programs and time in the field with an existing franchisee.

MANAGERIAL ASSISTANCE AVAILABLE: Franklin Traffic Service maintains a bona fide interest in all franchises. Manuals of operations, forms, and directions are provided. In-the-field assistance is provided on a regular basis. Franchisees benefit from all new marketing concepts that are developed. Franklin sponsors regular franchise meetings, and continually upgrades and maintains the highest level of quality possible.

INFORMATION SUBMITTED: April 1990

* GENERAL BUSINESS SERVICES, INC.
20271 Goldenrod Lane
Germantown, Maryland 20874-4090
Robert Pirtle, President

DESCRIPTION OF OPERATION: General Business Services franchised business counselors provide financial management, business counseling, tax planning, and computer services to small businesses and professionals. Supported by the GBS national office, franchisees provide clients the proper record keeping system, guaranteed correct tax return preparation, computer services, and financial planning services. GBS provides its business counselors and their clients with continuous training and support. The franchisee can be operated as either a sole proprietorship or corporation.

NUMBER OF FRANCHISEES: Hundreds nationwide

IN BUSINESS SINCE: 1962

EQUITY CAPITAL NEEDED: Franchise fee is $25,000 (Plan I) or $15,000 (Plan II). Should also have sufficient operating capital for living expenses and for business start-up period—will vary by individual.

FINANCIAL ASSISTANCE AVAILABLE: None.

TRAINING PROVIDED: Initial and continuous training is provided. Approximately 32 days' training provided during the first year and approximately 17 days' training each year thereafter. GBS business counselors are trained in all aspects of counseling, client acquisition, and operating an independent business based on GBS's 25-plus years experience. All new franchisees receive without additional expense: (1) a 4-volume operations manual containing all operating instructions, company policies, and procedures; (2) 2-week basic training institute and 1-week advanced training institute at GBS's national training center; (3) 1-week individual training in the franchisee's own marketing area by an experienced business counselor; (4) necessary sales aids, client servicing, and practice management forms; and (5) 12 days' ongoing training and individual guidance through assigned field support manager.

MANAGERIAL ASSISTANCE AVAILABLE: In addition to local assistance provided by an experienced field support manager, a staff of over 100 in the national office is available for managerial assistance and technical support as required; 20 continuing support services are provided franchisees: e.g., annual series of seminars for professional development and continuing education; business management self-study services; lending library of books, tapes, and pamphlets; sales brochures, client advertising, and ongoing public relations program; toll-free numbers for order placement, computer assistance, and tax advisory services; ongoing communications through biweekly and monthly newsletters and field-represented President's Advisory Council.

INFORMATION SUBMITTED: April 1990

HOMES & LAND PUBLISHING CORPORATION
dba HOMES & LAND MAGAZINE
1600 Capitol Circle SW
Tallahassee, Florida 32310
Ken Ledford, Vice President, Sales

DESCRIPTION OF OPERATION: Nation's largest publisher of community real estate magazines. Magazines are black/white or color and contain property listings of real estate companies. Franchisees sell advertising space to real estate brokers and distribute the magazines in the community. Separate franchises offered for quality magazines and for economy magazines.

NUMBER OF FRANCHISEES: 300 under contract in 35 states

IN BUSINESS SINCE: 1973

EQUITY CAPITAL NEEDED: $6,000 for quality magazine; $1,500 for economy magazine.

FINANCIAL ASSISTANCE AVAILABLE: None.

TRAINING PROVIDED: 1-week orientation at company offices, including instruction in production, sales, and financial management; field assistance provided for initial sales.

MANAGERIAL ASSISTANCE AVAILABLE: Operating manuals and sales aids provided. Regional meetings and annual sales convention provide opportunities for further training and interaction. Home office technical assistance is provided by telephone; sales assistance is available from district sales managers.

INFORMATION SUBMITTED: May 1990

HOMEWATCH CORPORATION
2865 South Colorado Boulevard
Denver, Colorado 80222
Paul A. Sauer, President

DESCRIPTION OF OPERATION: A checking and sitting service that provides attentive care for people's homes, pets, and elderly people. Homesitting 24 hours or overnight, companion sitting, and in-home personal services (errands), odd jobs, and handyman services.

NUMBER OF FRANCHISEES: 26 in 11 states

IN BUSINESS SINCE: 1973

EQUITY CAPITAL NEEDED: Initial fee is $6,000. The total investment not to exceed $10,000. Area development available.

FINANCIAL ASSISTANCE AVAILABLE: Financial assistance available for multiple sales or large franchises.

TRAINING PROVIDED: 4-day (mandatory) training

program at corporate office or on-site. Bookkeeping and advertising/marketing manuals. Continuous support and consultation, bimonthly newsletters, and voice and video cassette telephone helpline.

MANAGERIAL ASSISTANCE AVAILABLE: Continuous assistance available whenever needed. Newsletters, regional seminars, and national convention.

INFORMATION SUBMITTED: April 1990

* HOUSEMASTER OF AMERICA, INC.
421 West Union Avenue
Bound Brook, New Jersey 08805
Robert J. Hardy, President

DESCRIPTION OF OPERATION: HouseMaster of America is an organization of home inspection professionals. Qualified technical people conduct the inspections, while marketing-oriented people run the business end. Home buyers who want to know the condition of perhaps the largest investment of their lifetime are the primary users. There are no inventory requirements and no need for fancy office space. Suitable for ownership by men and women alike.

NUMBER OF FRANCHISEES: 115 in 35 states

IN BUSINESS SINCE: 1979

EQUITY CAPITAL NEEDED: $17,000–$35,000, depending on the number of owner-occupied homes in area.

FINANCIAL ASSISTANCE AVAILABLE: It is advised that an additional $10,000 to $15,000 is needed to get started. Sources of financial assistance are provided by the franchisor.

TRAINING PROVIDED: 3-day orientation training for the person who will run the business, 5-day technical training course for the designated technical director. Also provided are (1) sales and promotion manual, (2) operations manual, (3) technical training manual.

MANAGERIAL ASSISTANCE AVAILABLE: Ongoing counseling in all aspects of the business. Administration of referral system (WATS Line), advertising, publicity and promotion programs, regular newsletters, both technical and sales, as well as bulletins, trade digests. Periodic seminars. Both technical and marketing research and development. A warranty program.

INFORMATION SUBMITTED: April 1990

IDENT-A-KID SERVICES OF AMERICA, INC.
8430 Sixth Street North
St. Petersburg, Florida 33702
Robert King, National Director

DESCRIPTION OF OPERATION: The IDENT-A-KID program provides parents with a laminated child I.D. card containing a child's photograph, physical description, and fingerprint. In case of an emergency, parents can provide the card to law enforcement or others to help in the quick, safe recovery of their child. Total turnkey package is $12,500 including computer, camera, assembly equipment, supplies, etc.

NUMBER OF FRANCHISEES: 80 total, 70 in the United States, 10 in Canada

IN BUSINESS SINCE: 1986

EQUITY CAPITAL NEEDED: $12,000 total turnkey operation

FINANCIAL ASSISTANCE AVAILABLE: None.

TRAINING PROVIDED: 3 days at the franchisee's home.

MANAGERIAL ASSISTANCE AVAILABLE: Telephone assistance, information releases, and newsletter.

INFORMATION SUBMITTED: April 1990

INCOTAX SYSTEMS, INC.
P. O. Box 1380
Lake Worth, Florida 33460
Richard B. Vondrak, President

DESCRIPTION OF OPERATION: Incotax Systems is a volume, multiunit tax service system. It has developed an outstanding method of providing high-quality, accurate tax returns to the public at a minimum cost.

NUMBER OF FRANCHISEES: 15 in Florida and 3 in Arizona

IN BUSINESS SINCE: 1967

EQUITY CAPITAL NEEDED: $15,000

FINANCIAL ASSISTANCE AVAILABLE: $10,000 of equity capital is prorated throught the first year of operation.

TRAINING PROVIDED: Complete management and tax preparation training for 2 persons is conducted by the home office. Complete cost of training, including air fare, hotel, etc., is included in equity capital.

MANAGERIAL ASSISTANCE AVAILABLE: Continuous home office inspection and management training is conducted. Home office consultation and management suggestions are made to all franchisees, complete procedural manuals and forms are furnished franchisees as well as monthly news bulletins.

INFORMATION SUBMITTED: May 1990

INNOVATIONS IN CORPORATIONS, INC.
3333 Veterans Highway, Suite C-527
Ronkonkoma, New York 11779
David E. Gorman, President

DESCRIPTION OF OPERATION: Singles' matchmaking business. Calculated couples matchmaking parties use a new, innovative process to compatibly match hundreds of singles within minutes. Our parties virtually replace dating services.

NUMBER OF FRANCHISEES: None. Previously sold licenses.

IN BUSINESS SINCE: 1983

EQUITY CAPITAL NEEDED: $10,000–$25,000

FINANCIAL ASSISTANCE AVAILABLE: None.

TRAINING PROVIDED: Training begins at franchisor's New York offices and continues at area parties. Further training is then provided at franchisee's location during grand opening period.

MANAGERIAL ASSISTANCE AVAILABLE: Complete operations manuals are provided. Innovations in Corporations also provides management assistance in such areas as advertising, location referrals, system updates, policies, and procedures.

INFORMATION SUBMITTED: March 1990

INTERNATIONAL MERGERS AND ACQUISITIONS
4300 North Miller Road
Suite 220
Scottsdale, Arizona 85251
Neil D. Lewis, President

DESCRIPTION OF OPERATION: International Mergers and Acquisitions is a national affiliation of members engaged in the profession of servicing merger and acquisition-minded companies on a confidential basis. Our program embraces all aspects essential to a successful merger or acquisition.

NUMBER OF FRANCHISEES: 38 in 15 states

IN BUSINESS SINCE: 1970

EQUITY CAPITAL NEEDED: $10,000 minimum

FINANCIAL ASSISTANCE AVAILABLE: A total investment of $10,000 is necessary.

TRAINING PROVIDED: Quarterly regional creative work sessions, plus orientation sessions for each new member as needed.

MANAGERIAL ASSISTANCE AVAILABLE: International Mergers and Acquisitions provides complete procedures and operations manual, forms, and product research to all members.

INFORMATION SUBMITTED: May 1990

* JACKSON HEWITT TAX SERVICE
224 Groveland Road
Virginia Beach, Virginia 23452
Walter Ewell, Vice President, Franchise Development

DESCRIPTION OF OPERATION: A Jackson Hewitt Income Tax franchise will offer computerized income tax preparation, bookkeeping, and other related services. Franchisees are licensed to use the Jackson Hewitt System, which includes proprietary software, accounting methods, merchandising, equipment selection, advertising, sales and promotional techniques, personnel training, and other related matters.

NUMBER OF FRANCHISEES: 224 nationally

IN BUSINESS SINCE: 1960

EQUITY CAPITAL NEEDED: $16,000–$30,000 (estimated) including initial franchise fee.

FINANCIAL ASSISTANCE AVAILABLE: Jackson Hewitt, Inc., will not offer financing to any franchisee, either directly or indirectly.

TRAINING PROVIDED: Prior to franchisee's commencement of business, Jackson Hewitt, Inc., will provide a minimum of 5 days of training in all aspects of the operation and management of a Jackson Hewitt Income Tax Franchise, including the use of the computerized tax programs. In addition, annual refresher training is provided.

MANAGERIAL ASSISTANCE AVAILABLE: Jackson Hewitt, Inc., will provide assistance in advertising and marketing, recommendations and advice concerning site selection, ongoing advice and guidance as requested by franchisees concerning operations and tax problems as well as new and improved techniques and operating methods, business procedures, management and promotional materials, and updated software programs.

INFORMATION SUBMITTED: April 1990

K & O PUBLISHING
P. O. Box 51189
Seattle, Washington 98115-1189
Warren E. Kraft, Jr., President

DESCRIPTION OF OPERATION: K & O Publishing franchises a special interest newspaper called the *Bingo Bugle*. The franchisee has the opportunity to become the editor and publisher of his/her own newspaper even with no previous publishing experience. This publication is extremely popular with bingo players. The *Bingo Bugle* is America's largest group of bingo newspapers.

NUMBER OF FRANCHISEES: 52 in 20 states and District of Columbia

IN BUSINESS SINCE: 1982

EQUITY CAPITAL NEEDED: $2,000–$10,000

FINANCIAL ASSISTANCE AVAILABLE: None.

TRAINING PROVIDED: Franchisor provides a 2-day seminar.

MANAGERIAL ASSISTANCE AVAILABLE: An operation

manual and ongoing assistance are provided by franchisor.

INFORMATION SUBMITTED: April 1990

* MAIL BOXES ETC. USA
5555 Oberlin Drive
San Diego, California 92121
Anthony W. (Tony) DeSio, President & CEO

DESCRIPTION OF OPERATION: Postal, business, and communication centers. Provides more than 30 services to consumer, small and home-based businesses in the following areas: mailbox service with 24-hour access, mail receipt and forwarding, rapid air shipping/receiving, parcel packaging and shipping, telephone messaging, copy and printing service, secretarial service, electronic mail, wire services and fax network, office supplies, notary, passport photos.

NUMBER OF FRANCHISEES: 1,200 in 44 states, Puerto Rico, Canada, Mexico, and Japan

IN BUSINESS SINCE: 1980. Public company since 1986 traded on NASDAQ as (Mail).

EQUITY CAPITAL NEEDED: Individual franchise—$43,000–$73,000 (includes $13,000–$31,000 leasehold improvements and $10,000–$15,000 working capital).

FINANCIAL ASSISTANCE AVAILABLE: Yes.

TRAINING PROVIDED: Combination of classroom at MBE University and in-store training. Individual franchise—2 weeks at corporate and 1 week at franchise location. Area franchise—2 weeks at corporate and 2 weeks at franchise location.

MANAGERIAL ASSISTANCE AVAILABLE: Initial assistance provided in setting up turnkey operation including site selection, lease negotiation, facility design, construction management (optional), setup of facility, grand opening promotional assistance. Continuing assistance in local store marketing, advertising and public relations, promotions and new profit center development. Monthly newsletter and quarterly video newsletter.

INFORMATION SUBMITTED: May 1990

MONEY BROKER ONE
230 East Wheeling Street
Suite 101
Lancaster, Ohio 43130
Raymond A. Strohl, President

DESCRIPTION OF OPERATION: Money broker offering loans and financing to individuals, businesses, and churches for financing almost any worthwhile project. We offer real estate loans and business loans, and there is no upper limit on the size of the loans. We also act as a business broker helping people and companies purchase and sell businesses.

NUMBER OF FRANCHISEES: 10 in Ohio, Florida, California, Pennsylvania, Louisiana, Missouri, and New York

IN BUSINESS SINCE: 1983

EQUITY CAPITAL NEEDED: None

FINANCIAL ASSISTANCE AVAILABLE: Yes.

TRAINING PROVIDED: Varies, depending on the background and experience of the franchisee.

MANAGERIAL ASSISTANCE AVAILABLE: Perpetual assistance as needed.

INFORMATION SUBMITTED: March 1990

MR. SIGN FRANCHISING CORP.
159 Keyland Court
Bohemia, New York 11716
Herb Miller, Vice President of Franchising Administration

DESCRIPTION OF OPERATION: Sign business. Mr. Sign offers a unique concept in custom sign making—computerized vinyl/sign making services for both business and residential communities. Franchisees can offer a selection of over 100,000 different types of signs, and they can duplicate supplied artwork, such as a business customer's logo. The high quality, reasonable price and relatively quick turnaround of a Mr. Signs' sign is particularly appealing to the business and residential community.

NUMBER OF FRANCHISEES: 103 in 26 states

IN BUSINESS SINCE: 1985

EQUITY CAPITAL NEEDED: $50,000

FINANCIAL ASSISTANCE AVAILABLE: Franchisor assistance in financing.

TRAINING PROVIDED: Mr. Sign provides the franchisee with the entire computer equipment package, including proprietary copyrighted software, start-up inventory of supplies, a comprehensive 3-week training program, and substantial ongoing technical and marketing support.

MANAGERIAL ASSISTANCE AVAILABLE: Turnkey operation, including design and layout specification, site review, review of lease, grand opening package, sales and marketing manual and portfolio, total administration kit.

INFORMATION SUBMITTED: April 1990

THE OFFICE ANSWER
One SeaGate
Suite 1001
Toledo Ohio 43604
Steven B. Hanson

DESCRIPTION OF OPERATION: By joining The Office Answer team, you'll offer telephone answering, typing, facsimile, copies, shipping, and more. Because of Office Answer's exclusive telephone answering equipment, you'll be able to offer telephone answering by company name at a cost to you of only $3 per line per month. Your clients will also be able to receive their mail and have the use of a desk and an office to return calls, open mail, etc. A real Office Answer.

This business is ideal for adding to an existing business or can be opened in almost any location in just a matter of weeks. Because you'll cater to business clients, your business can be operated successfully during normal business hours.

NUMBER OF FRANCHISEES: 5 in 5 states

IN BUSINESS SINCE: 1988

EQUITY CAPITAL NEEDED: $12,000 total package

FINANCIAL ASSISTANCE AVAILABLE: Telephone system, computer, furniture, etc.

TRAINING PROVIDED: Training to be conducted at corporate headquarters in Toledo with all expenses including travel and lodging paid for. Franchisee get hands-on training, all necessary manuals, and extensive marketing and advertising assistance.

MANAGERIAL ASSISTANCE AVAILABLE: Continuous in all phases of operation.

INFORMATION SUBMITTED: May 1990

* THE PACKAGING STORE, INC.
8480 East Orchard Road
Englewood, Colorado 80111
Richard T. Godwin, President

DESCRIPTION OF OPERATION: Custom packaging and shipping service. Wholesale and retail sales of packaging supplies.

NUMBER OF FRANCHISEES: 335 in 40 states

IN BUSINESS SINCE: 1980

EQUITY CAPITAL NEEDED: $30,000–$40,000

FINANCIAL ASSISTANCE AVAILABLE: None.

TRAINING PROVIDED: Intensive, 1-week mandatory training session for all new franchisees and their employees in an authorized training store and opening assistance at franchise store.

MANAGERIAL ASSISTANCE AVAILABLE: The Packaging Store provides continual management service for the life of the franchise in the areas of advertising and marketing, operations, and management reviews. Complete manuals of operations, forms, and directions are provided. Field managers are available in all regions to work closely with franchisees and visit stores regularly to assist in solving problems. The Packaging Store sponsors meetings of franchisees and conducts marketing and product research to maintain high Packaging Store consumer acceptance.

INFORMATION SUBMITTED: April 1990

PADGETT BUSINESS SERVICES USA, INC.
160 Hawthorne Park
Athens, Georgia 30606
Hub Brightwell, Jr., Franchise Division

DESCRIPTION OF OPERATION: PBS grants licenses to individuals who desire to operate their own accounting, income tax, and business counseling practice, utilizing the unique forms and successful systems of operations developed by the franchisor. The PBS franchisee remains, at all times, in control of his practice, subject only to quality control and performance prescribed by the franchisor. The franchisee markets small to medium-size businesses located in an area that franchisee is able to service from his assigned territory.

NUMBER OF FRANCHISEES: 93 in 23 states and 11 in Canada

IN BUSINESS SINCE: 1965, franchising since 1975

EQUITY CAPITAL NEEDED: The PBS franchise fee is $14,500 with an additional training fee. First year operating capital is also necessary.

FINANCIAL ASSISTANCE AVAILABLE: Yes—through a local financial institution.

TRAINING PROVIDED: The franchisor offers an initial 3-week training program. The first week of this program consists of training in the PBS systems and client services with emphasis on establishing and working with a large number of monthly clients. The second week consists of training in the PBS marketing techniques and the third week is held in an established franchise working with the office owner, employees, clients and prospective clients. A fourth week will be in field training conducted by a home office representative.

MANAGERIAL ASSISTANCE AVAILABLE: PBS offers 2 seminars annually. One is a thorough 3-day income tax seminar, the other is a 2-day update on PBS procedures and new marketing techniques. There are no charges for these seminars. A year-round income tax answering service is also included. Special visits to each franchise office are made to examine additional needs of franchisee and to update PBS forms, tax procedures and marketing advice. Retraining and new employee training are also available at no cost to the franchisee.

INFORMATION SUBMITTED: April 1990

PARSON-BISHOP SERVICES, INC.
7870 Camargo Road
Cincinnati, Ohio 45243
Lou Bishop, President

DESCRIPTION OF OPERATION: P-B's executive franchisees market P-B's guaranteed effective, low-cost accounts receivable management, collection, and cash flow improvement plans. These exclusive plans provide solutions to an ongoing, basic business need. More than 90 percent of businesses are prospects. Build equity from long-term, repeat customers. You must have a sales, marketing, or management background and be qualified to call on upper level management in corporations of all sizes.

NUMBER OF FRANCHISEES: 43 franchisees with 58 territories in 23 states

IN BUSINESS SINCE: 1973

EQUITY CAPITAL NEEDED: $23,000–$29,500

FINANCIAL ASSISTANCE AVAILABLE: None.

TRAINING PROVIDED: 1-week classroom training at home office. Two training visits to franchisee's area in first 6 months. National and regional seminars quarterly. Continuous one-on-one support.

MANAGERIAL ASSISTANCE AVAILABLE: Constant advertising, marketing, and public relations support plus videos and manuals. Computerized franchise management system.

INFORMATION SUBMITTED: April 1990

PDP, INC. (Professional Dynametric Programs)
400 West Highway, Suite 201
Box 5289
Woodland Park, Colorado 80866
Bruce M. Hubby, President

DESCRIPTION OF OPERATION: PDP provides a statistically based system that promotes effective in-house management and employee development. Franchisees train and implement the PDP System into small, medium and large client organizations. Applications of the PDP System include identifying motivators and stressors, reducing stress, opening lines of communication, job matching and selection, conflict resolution, team building, and job performance improvement.

NUMBER OF FRANCHISEES: Total of 26: 21 in 12 states, 4 in Canada, and 1 in Australia

IN BUSINESS SINCE: 1978

EQUITY CAPITAL NEEDED: Franchise fee of $29,500 plus $5,000–$10,000 working capital.

FINANCIAL ASSISTANCE AVAILABLE: None.

TRAINING PROVIDED: 1 week at home office, with overflow handled on weekend if necessary. Includes overview, philosophy of PDP training, hands-on implementation, marketing, pricing, and operation.

MANAGERIAL ASSISTANCE AVAILABLE: Home office staff is readily available to offer support in areas of program operation, data interpretation, and client implementation. PDP's in-house research department provides field representatives and clients with up-to-date research information. Annual conferences/and regional meetings promote effective sales presentations and system applications.

INFORMATION SUBMITTED: April 1990

PENNYSAVER
80 Eighth Avenue, Suite 315
New York, New York 10011
Allan Horwitz, President

DESCRIPTION OF OPERATION: A free publication offering advertisers total market coverage of the households and businesses throughout the community. Usually delivered by mail, the *Pennysaver* is recognized as the number-1 local shopping guide throughout the U.S. Because the *Pennysaver* has no wasted or duplicated circulation and little editorial, the advertiser receives more circulation, and at a lower cost than with any daily or weekly newspaper. Many *Pennysavers* have started out in garages and basements, and have grown into multimillion-dollar publishing empires.

NUMBER OF FRANCHISEES: Over 300 throughout the United States

IN BUSINESS SINCE: 1973

EQUITY CAPITAL NEEDED: $19,900 with a money-back guarantee

FINANCIAL ASSISTANCE AVAILABLE: Yes. 80 percent financing to qualified applicants.

TRAINING PROVIDED: 8 days of classroom, in-field and on-site training for franchisees and their employees. Teaches how to sell *Pennysaver* advertising, acquire co-op ads from manufacturers, profit from barter, service accounts, design ads, layout the publication, distribution, and bookkeeping. Includes confidential operations manual, audio and video tapes, training films, and video-taped role playing sessions.

MANAGERIAL ASSISTANCE AVAILABLE: Continuous assistance provided by the home office. Includes our unique "head start" program to get you off to a flying start with $1,000 free printing, a direct mailing to your prospects by the company, and our special charter advertising program to produce immediate income for the franchisee and his advertisers. In addition, the company contributes $1,000 per each new franchise plus 12 percent of all royalty fees for direct mailings, sweepstakes, and other promotions, funded 100 percent by the company to produce greater profits for all franchisees.

INFORMATION SUBMITTED: April 1990

PEYRON ASSOCIATES, INC.
P. O. Box 175
Sellersburg, Indiana 47172
Dan Peyron, President and CEO

DESCRIPTION OF OPERATION: Company licenses others to prepare tax returns in leading department and discount stores nationally. Prefer people already in tax return prep business but will train others. Minimum investment $2,000, which includes location, furniture, equipment, signs, advertising, training, and complete warranty package; $1,000 for each additional location. No restrictions on area or number of locations. Company also offers electronic filing and refund loans nationally. Subfranchising permitted but not required.

NUMBER OF FRANCHISEES: 400 units in about 30 states

IN BUSINESS SINCE: 1960

EQUITY CAPITAL NEEDED: Minimum $500

FINANCIAL ASSISTANCE AVAILABLE: None.

TRAINING PROVIDED: Locally by any tax return prep school, college, course, etc.

MANAGERIAL ASSISTANCE AVAILABLE: Monthly newsletters for tax return prepared the year round plus separate tax newsletter for clients, warranty backup for mistakes, audits, technical assistance on tax matters, etc. Also pay operators for audit work covered under warranty.

INFORMATION SUBMITTED: May 1990

PILOT AIR FREIGHT CORPORATION
Route 352
P. O. Box 97
Lima, Pennsylvania 19037
John J. Edwards, President

DESCRIPTION OF OPERATION: Pilot provides the service of handling air freight shipping requirements of their customers both domestically and internationally.

NUMBER OF FRANCHISEES: 70 in 29 states, Canada, and Puerto Rico

IN BUSINESS SINCE: 1970

EQUITY CAPITAL NEEDED: $10,000–$30,000 determined by market

FINANCIAL ASSISTANCE AVAILABLE: None.

TRAINING PROVIDED: 2 weeks classroom, Pilot headquarters, with emphasis on operation, customer service, sales, and accounting procedures.

MANAGERIAL ASSISTANCE AVAILABLE: Ongoing communications with corporate headquarters and visits by Pilot regional managers.

INFORMATION SUBMITTED: 1990

P.K.G.'S, INC.
4394 Glendale-Milford Road
Cincinnati, Ohio 45242
Thomas R. Sizer, President

DESCRIPTION OF OPERATION: P.K.G.'s is an established and nationally recognized industry leader in a unique service business. P.K.G.'s provides both retail and commerical packaging and shipping services for customers wanting to pack and ship anything anywhere in the world. This proven concept provides a "hassle-free" retail store environment for sending an overnight letter or a baby grand piano. Our pickup services for both retail and commercial/industrial customers provides for a total full-service packaging and shipping program.

NUMBER OF FRANCHISEES: 75 in 20 states

IN BUSINESS SINCE: 1983

EQUITY CAPITAL NEEDED: Approximately $47,765

FINANCIAL ASSISTANCE AVAILABLE: Yes—financing available to qualified individuals through equipment and cabinetry leasing program.

TRAINING PROVIDED: P.K.G.'s provides each franchisee with a 3-phase training program. Initial training phase is a franchise orientation and development program. Second phase is a comprehensive multimedia hands-on training program for retail store owners, managers, and employees consisting of business operational instructions, franchisors' objectives, policies and procedures, utilization of all equipment and packaging technology involved in the operation of the franchise business. Extensive training in packaging, shipping, and customer service, marketing and advertising. Phase 3 involves in-store training and commercial sales and marketing on site in franchise owners retail location.

MANAGERIAL ASSISTANCE AVAILABLE: P.K.G.'s provides each franchisee with field operations consultation and assistance on a continuing basis including demo site analysis, site selection, lease negotiations, turnkey store setup and development, marketing and advertising programming and planning, operations planning, and routine field visits.

INFORMATION SUBMITTED: April 1990

PRIORITY MANAGEMENT SYSTEMS, INC.
500 108th Avenue, NE, Suite 1740
Bellevue, Washington 98053
Tee Houston-Aldridge, Manager, Franchise Marketing

DESCRIPTION OF OPERATION: Priority Management is the one management training franchise in North America. Franchisees work with busy professionals and instruct them in the development of personal effectiveness skills.

NUMBER OF FRANCHISEES: 125 in 38 states, 48 in Canada, 44 international in 7 countries

IN BUSINESS SINCE: 1984

EQUITY CAPITAL NEEDED: $35,000 including franchise fee

FINANCIAL ASSISTANCE AVAILABLE: None.

TRAINING PROVIDED: 2-week intensive training in the "Priority Management" program, 6 days in-house plus 1 week in-field. Minimum 3 follow-up training sessions each year.

MANAGERIAL ASSISTANCE AVAILABLE: Teach franchisee the "Priority Management" program. Sales techniques, presentation skills, marketing methods, bookkeeping, general business management skills. Work with franchisee on sales calls, conduct (at franchisee's request) first 2 workshops.

INFORMATION SUBMITTED: April 1990

PROPERTY DAMAGE APPRAISERS, INC.
P. O. Box 9230
Fort Worth, Texas 76107
John Tate, Vice President-Franchise Operations

DESCRIPTION OF OPERATION: Property Damage Appraisers, Inc., grants franchises to highly qualified automobile damage appraisers in cities with sufficient business potential to provide a good income for the franchisee.

NUMBER OF FRANCHISEES: 185 in all states except Montana, South Dakota, and Wyoming

IN BUSINESS SINCE: 1963

EQUITY CAPITAL NEEDED: $5,000–$15,000

FINANCIAL ASSISTANCE AVAILABLE: None. Property Damage Appraisers does not sell franchises. We provide all forms, procedure manual, advertising materials, and marketing service. Equity capital required is needed to purchase office equipment, automobile, insurance, etc., necessary to start a business.

TRAINING PROVIDED: No formal training program is provided as only experienced appraisers are considered.

MANAGERIAL ASSISTANCE AVAILABLE: Through a staff of regional managers we provide at least 2 weeks of intensive marketing support when an office opens. A bookkeeping system is provided at no cost to franchisee and is installed by a company accounting representative. Periodic visits are made by regional managers to market services of all franchisees.

INFORMATION SUBMITTED: April 1990

PROVE CONSUMER REPORTING SERVICES
A Division of the Taylor Group
4806 Shelly Drive
Wilmington, North Carolina 28405
Lorraine Taylor, President

DESCRIPTION OF OPERATION: Since 1974, Prove Mystery Shoppers have been monitoring the quality of service employees provide patrons and provide an operations review for management along with suggestions and ideas on how to improve customer service. Training seminars provided on site for clients in all customer related areas.

NUMBER OF FRANCHISEES: 35 franchisees

IN BUSINESS SINCE: 1974

EQUITY CAPITAL NEEDED: Franchise fees from $14,500 to $39,500.

FINANCIAL ASSISTANCE AVAILABLE: To qualified buyers.

TRAINING PROVIDED: 10-day intensive training program consists of classroom and field training. Includes operational and training manuals, video and audio aids.

MANAGERIAL ASSISTANCE AVAILABLE: Additional and ongoing training and updates provided periodically or upon request.

INFORMATION SUBMITTED: April 1990

PROVENTURE, INC.
79 Parkingway, Box 7169
Quincy, Massachusetts 02169
Leo F. Meady, Chairman

DESCRIPTION OF OPERATION: Professional business brokers—specializing in the listing and sale of medium-priced going businesses. Also represent franchise companies in the sale and location of their franchised units.

NUMBER OF FRANCHISEES: 6 plus 1 company-owned in Massachusetts and New Jersey. Seeking franchisees for all areas of the U.S.

IN BUSINESS SINCE: 1979

EQUITY CAPITAL NEEDED: $15,000 franchise fee plus about $30,000 for working capital.

FINANCIAL ASSISTANCE AVAILABLE: None.

TRAINING PROVIDED: Intensive classroom training program for 1 week in Quincy, followed by on-the-job training in franchisee's own office. Assistance offered in recruiting and training commissioned sales staff. ProVENTURE prefers that franchisees (or their associates) have real estate licenses, or they obtain one as soon as possible.

MANAGERIAL ASSISTANCE AVAILABLE: Continued training and management assistance for all franchised units. Parent company coordinates the distribution of "VENTUREIist" to all offices. "VENTUREIist" contains all the listings of all local offices. Participating franchisees share proportionately in the sale of business listed by one office and sold by another.

INFORMATION SUBMITTED: May 1990

* RECOGNITION EXPRESS INTERNATIONAL, LTD.
31726 Rancho Viejo Road, Suite 115
San Juan Capistrano, California 92675
Dennis Hunt, President

DESCRIPTION OF OPERATION: Recognition Express franchise owners manufacture and sell corporate recognition and specialty advertising products—personalized badges, nameplates, plaques, awards, office signage, buttons, lapel pins, to name a few. Recognition Express is the oldest and largest chain of full-service recognition shops. Our owners have been providing service to medium and large corporations. Our customers include Hilton Hotels, Century 21 Real Estate, Baskin-Robbins, Rotary, Mary Kay Cosmetics, etc. Recognition Express dealers operate from a commercial location. Our shops feature state-of-the-art showrooms and do light manufacturing with the latest technology including computer engraving, automatic hot stamping, and automatic pinning machines. In addition, other items are offered that are purchased from approved trade suppliers.

NUMBER OF FRANCHISEES: 70 throughout the U.S. and in 9 countries

IN BUSINESS SINCE: Founder began manufacturing name badges in 1972. BadgeMan franchises were first awarded in 1974 to part-time, home-based owners who manufactured name badges only. Recognition Express units tested since 1981, franchised since 1983.

EQUITY CAPITAL NEEDED: $30,000

FINANCIAL ASSISTANCE AVAILABLE: A total investment of $75,000 to $100,000 is needed to cover opening inventory, equipment, franchise fee, training costs, start-up promotion and advertising, as well as working capital. Financing can be arranged.

TRAINING PROVIDED: An intensive training course is conducted for the new owner at the home office. A field development person will help you in your new shop during opening. He will insure that you are capable of developing your business properly.

MANAGERIAL ASSISTANCE AVAILABLE: Complete ongoing support and managerial assistance in all phases of the business.

INFORMATION SUBMITTED: May 1990

* SARA CARE FRANCHISE CORPORATION
1612 Lee Trevino
Suite 8
El Paso, Texas 79936

DESCRIPTION OF OPERATION: Sales of Sara Care Service franchise—specializing in temporary companion and home support personnel. Provides companion care, sleepovers, baby/child sitters, house sitters, hospital sitters, pet sitters, plant/garden sitters, drop-ins (companion, teens, pets, house) and subcontracting services to all home health agencies and hospitals. We pride ourselves in being the largest franchisor of specialized services in the United States and the first company specifically organized to concentrate in the field of home support personnel.

NUMBER OF FRANCHISEES: 46 in 18 states

IN BUSINESS SINCE: 1978, franchising since 1983

EQUITY CAPITAL NEEDED: Capital requirement about $48,000.

FINANCIAL ASSISTANCE AVAILABLE: None.

TRAINING PROVIDED: A 5-business day intensive management training program at corporate headquarters. Training will continue even after the opening of your office to sharpen your skills and to make certain that your new business is operating as efficiently as possible. You even have the option of 1 week of on-site training at your location.

MANAGERIAL ASSISTANCE AVAILABLE: You will have an effective support system behing you at corporate headquarters every step of the way. You will receive instructions and constant updates in the use of all Sara Care manuals and forms in addition to training in recruiting, interviewing, and applicant processing techniques as well as detailed training and handling customer requirements.

INFORMATION SUBMITTED: May 1990

SELECTRA-DATE CORPORATION
2175 Lemoine Avenue
Ft. Lee, New Jersey 07024
Robert Friedman, President

DESCRIPTION OF OPERATION: Computer dating has been around since Art Linkletter started playing matching games with a Univac Computer in the late 1950s. But that was just for laughs. Today it's for love and money, with a score of computer-dating firms throughout the country reporting brisk business. Selectra-Date, one of the pioneers, now offers a complete turnkey package that makes it possible for any reputable individual with a sound business or professional background to enter this fascinating work. Since all computer processing is handled entirely by the company, no technical knowledge is required.

NUMBER OF FRANCHISEES: 9 in 10 states

IN BUSINESS SINCE: 1967, oldest existing franchise operational since 1969

EQUITY CAPITAL NEEDED: $7,000–$10,000

FINANCIAL ASSISTANCE AVAILABLE: The total required investment for promotional material, initial advertising, franchise fee, and forms and stationery is $9,000, of which Selectra-Date will finance $3,500 for qualified franchisees. In addition the franchisee should have sufficient capital to adequately equip his office and to see him through the first 30 days of operation.

TRAINING PROVIDED: A full-time Selectra-Date executive thoroughly trains each franchisee in all phases of the business during the first week he is in operation.

MANAGERIAL ASSISTANCE AVAILABLE: Selectra-Date furnishes continuing individual guidance and support in all phases of the franchisee's operation.

INFORMATION SUBMITTED: April 1990

SHIPPING CONNECTION, INC.
7220 West Jefferson Avenue, Suite 305
Denver, Colorado 80235
Betty Russotti, Vice President

DESCRIPTION OF OPERATION: Shipping Connection is a retail convenience center that provides complete packaging and shipping services to the general public. Dealing with both business and individuals, you can literally ship any item, any size, any place in the world. This business was founded by ex–United Parcel Service management personnel who will provide you with the packaging and shipping techniques recommended by the NSTC. The franchise locations also offer fax service, copies, gift wrapping, and the sale of all types of packaging materials.

NUMBER OF FRANCHISEES: 18 in Colorado, Kansas, Ohio, Minnesota, New Jersey, North Carolina plus 1 company-owned

IN BUSINESS SINCE: 1982; franchising since January 1987

EQUITY CAPITAL NEEDED: $32,000–$46,000 (includes $14,500 franchise fee plus working capital).

FINANCIAL ASSISTANCE AVAILABLE: Lease options on $7,000 in equipment, WAC.

TRAINING PROVIDED: An extensive 2-week training program provided at national headquarters in Littleton, Colorado, 1 week on site.

MANAGERIAL ASSISTANCE AVAILABLE: Site selection and lease negotiation assistance. Decor and equipment package. Franchisee is set up with negotiated discounts from suppliers and freight carriers. Co-op advertising program, continual follow-up and ongoing support, detailed operations manual.

INFORMATION SUBMITTED: May 1990

* SIGN EXPRESS
Clark Corporate Park
6 Clarke Circle
P. O. Box 309
Bethel, Connecticut 06801
Laurie Wright, Vice President

DESCRIPTION OF OPERATION: Company offers complete sign center that offers 24-hour service. Signs are made by a signmaking computer and scanner, using 3M graphic materials, with complete design functions. Signs include indoor and outdoor signs, vehicle lettering, magnetic signs, banners, business signs, trade show exhibits, illuminated signs, etc. No prior experience is required.

NUMBER OF FRANCHISEES: 22 in 10 states; 1 in Mexico

IN BUSINESS SINCE: 1985, franchising since 1988

EQUITY CAPITAL NEEDED: $50,000

FINANCIAL ASSISTANCE AVAILABLE: Company provides full equipment financing.

TRAINING PROVIDED: 3-week comprehensive training in sign center operations, full business and marketing training; 2 weeks at company headquarters; up to 1 additional week on location with owner.

MANAGERIAL ASSISTANCE AVAILABLE: Regular on-site visits to sign center owners; toll-free assistance, newsletters, conferences, and workshops.

INFORMATION SUBMITTED: May 1990

* SMI INTERNATIONAL, INC.
(SUCCESS MOTIVATION INSTITUTE, INC.)
1600 Lake Air Drive
Waco, Texas 76710
James Sirbasku

DESCRIPTION OF OPERATION: The company's international franchise organization markets specialized management, sales, and personal development programs to individuals, companies, governments, and other organizations. Materials are printed and recorded, using modern learning methods, personal goal setting, and management by objective techniques.

NUMBER OF FRANCHISEES: Approximately 2,000 in 50 states and 26 foreign countries

IN BUSINESS SINCE: 1960

EQUITY CAPITAL NEEDED: $20,000

FINANCIAL ASSISTANCE AVAILABLE: Financial assistance available.

TRAINING PROVIDED: Complete training program in printed and recorded form furnished with initial investment; continuous home office sales training and sales management seminars available monthly. Field sales training also available in many areas.

MANAGERIAL ASSISTANCE AVAILABLE: Continuous sales consultant assistance provided by home office to distributors through use of monthly mailings, telephone, and prompt response to mail communications.

INFORMATION SUBMITTED: April 1990

TAX MAN, INC.
674 Massachusetts Avenue
Cambridge, Massachusetts 02139
Robert G. Murray, President

DESCRIPTION OF OPERATION: Preparation of individual income tax returns. Interested in franchisees in New England only.

NUMBER OF FRANCHISEES: 15 company-owned units

IN BUSINESS SINCE: 1967

EQUITY CAPITAL NEEDED: $4,500 minimum plus means of support for first 2 years.

FINANCIAL ASSISTANCE AVAILABLE: Advertising support. Bookkeeping income opportunity for rest of year.

TRAINING PROVIDED: Tax preparation training (8 weeks). Tax office management training (3 days).

MANAGERIAL ASSISTANCE AVAILABLE: Complete tax advice, management assistance, site selection, advertising, and marketing.

INFORMATION SUBMITTED: May 1990

TAX OFFICES OF AMERICA
Box 4098
Waterville, Connecticut 06714
Gregg Nolan, Franchise Director

DESCRIPTION OF OPERATION: Income tax preparation for individuals and small businesses. Thorough training program, exclusive territories. Estate planning and business consulting services.

NUMBER OF FRANCHISEES: 15

IN BUSINESS SINCE: 1966

EQUITY CAPITAL NEEDED: Approximately $12,000 plus $7,500 working capital.

FINANCIAL ASSISTANCE AVAILABLE: Financing arranged through Horizons of America, Inc., parent company.

TRAINING PROVIDED: About 2 weeks' training provided at Waterbury headquarters, 2 weeks at franchisee's location, plus a mail order course. If available in franchisee's area, the company pays all expenses to a special training course set up by a nationally known organization.

MANAGERIAL ASSISTANCE AVAILABLE: Company always available for counseling, plus on-site office organization.

INFORMATION SUBMITTED: May 1990

TV NEWS
COMMUNITY PUBLICATIONS OF AMERICA, INC.
80 Eighth Avenue
New York, New York 10011
Allan Horwitz, President

DESCRIPTION OF OPERATION: *TV News* is an award-winning free community publication combining the 7-day readership of a *TV Guide* with the community saturation of a shopper and the efficiencies of scale of a major national publication. *TV News* is an exciting editorial product that attracts readers, while the low advertising rates and concentrated circulation attract the advertisers. The publisher of *TV News* was formerly the sales strategy planner for the *Wall Street Journal*. As a leader in the publishing field, he has been interviewed by Barbara Walters on *20/20* and appeared as a panelist on the *Phil Donahue Show*.

NUMBER OF FRANCHISEES: 7 in New York, and in South Carolina with no solicitation and no advertising

IN BUSINESS SINCE: 1973—*TV News* is a successful, respected and highly profitable publication, company-owned in New York. We stopped franchising in 1981 and began this new program in 1990.

EQUITY CAPITAL NEEDED: $19,900 with a money-back guarantee.

FINANCIAL ASSISTANCE AVAILABLE: Yes—80 percent financing to qualified applicants.

TRAINING PROVIDED: 8 days of classroom, in-field and on-site training for the franchisees and their employees. Covers how to sell *TV News*, how to get co-op advertising, financial leverage through barter, servicing of accounts, distribution, ad design, layout, and accounting. Includes extensive training manual, audio and video cassettes, numerous films, and videotaped role-playing sessions.

MANAGERIAL ASSISTANCE AVAILABLE: Continuous assistance provided by the home office. Includes our unique start-up program to get you off to a flying start, with $1,000 of free printing, a direct mailing to your prospects by the company, and our special charter advertising program to produce immediate income for the franchisee and his advertisers. Also the company contributes $1,000 for each new franchise purchased plus 12 percent of all royalty fees for direct mailings, sweepstakes, and special promotions to make the franchisees more successful.

INFORMATION SUBMITTED: April 1990

TV TEMPO, INC.
P. O. Box 420215
Atlanta, Georgia 30342-0215
M. Usman Mirza

DESCRIPTION OF OPERATION: TV Tempo, Inc., offers a unique system of "free" weekly television and cable TV scheduling and home entertainment guides. Each associate publisher (franchisee) owns and operates his/her local edition of *TV Tempo* magazine, which is distributed "free" in high-traffic retail areas. Individual associate publishers place advertising around Saturday-through-Friday television scheduling listings and readership features such as crossword puzzle, horoscope, and movie descriptions. No need for expensive equipment, fixtures, or offices. Excellent cash flow and low operational costs. Excellent localized guides.

NUMBER OF FRANCHISEES: 199 in 25 states

IN BUSINESS SINCE: 1975

EQUITY CAPITAL NEEDED: Approximately $35,000 up depending on the population of associate publisher area.

FINANCIAL ASSISTANCE AVAILABLE: None, interim financing only.

TRAINING PROVIDED: 5 days of intensive classroom training in fundamentals of business operation. Follow-up field training at the actual site assisting the associate publisher to put into operation the techniques of a successful operation. Classroom training available on repeated basis for associate publisher, if needed. Periodic seminars conducted by home office.

MANAGERIAL ASSISTANCE AVAILABLE: TV Tempo, Inc., offers guidance and assistance to franchisee on a continuing basis to enhance franchisee's ability and skills. Basic managerial control is always within the control of the associate publisher's business operations. Advertising rates are in the control of the associate publisher.

INFORMATION SUBMITTED: May 1990

TWP ENTERPRISES, INC.
11128 John Galt Boulevard, Suite 512
Omaha, Nebraska 68137
Sanford Friedman, President

DESCRIPTION OF OPERATION: *The Wedding Pages* (TWP) is a wedding planner (250-page book) that contains an advertising section for local area advertisers. The local advertisers receive a monthly listing of brides-to-be names, addresses, phone numbers, and wedding dates, making this the most targeted direct marketing tool available in the wedding market today. Franchisee sells the local advertising.

NUMBER OF FRANCHISEES: 90 in 15 states and Washington, D.C.

IN BUSINESS SINCE: 1982

EQUITY CAPITAL NEEDED: $15,000 minimum

FINANCIAL ASSISTANCE AVAILABLE: None.

TRAINING PROVIDED: 2-day in-house training at home office in Omaha, Nebraska. 1 week in market with franchisee or franchisee's sales force for field training.

MANAGERIAL ASSISTANCE AVAILABLE: Franchisor provides support for all questions regarding sales and servicing of the markets. Updating and creation of products is done constantly to maintain a quality product. Franchisor publishes the advertising section and the books.

INFORMATION SUBMITTED: May 1990

VIDEO DATA SERVICES
24 Grove Street
Pittsford, New York 14534
Stuart J. Dizak

DESCRIPTION OF OPERATION: Videotaping services, legal, real estate, social, inventories, and film and tape transfers.

NUMBER OF FRANCHISEES: 206 in 42 states

IN BUSINESS SINCE: 1980

EQUITY CAPITAL NEEDED: $18,000

FINANCIAL ASSISTANCE AVAILABLE: Assistance in local banking financing.

TRAINING PROVIDED: 3-day school and continuous correspondence training.

MANAGERIAL ASSISTANCE AVAILABLE: Marketing, technical consulting, and co-op advertising.

INFORMATION SUBMITTED: April 1990

WEDDING INFORMATION NETWORK, INC.
11128 John Galt Boulevard
Omaha, Nebraska 68137
Kenneth L. Nanfito

DESCRIPTION OF OPERATION: *The Wedding Pages* is a complete marketing program reaching the $28 billion wedding market. It is based around The Wedding Pages, a 160-page wedding planner, and a directory of local area advertisers. The book is distributed free to brides-to-be. Through the distribution, a list of brides and grooms-to-be is compiled. Involves the sale of space advertising and the list.

NUMBER OF FRANCHISEES: 76 in 37 states

IN BUSINESS SINCE: 1982

EQUITY CAPITAL NEEDED: $20,000–$75,000 depending on market and area.

FINANCIAL ASSISTANCE AVAILABLE: None.

TRAINING PROVIDED: 2-day seminar in Omaha and 1 full week in the franchise market. Ongoing support provided.

MANAGERIAL ASSISTANCE AVAILABLE: Operations manual detailing operation is provided and updated on an ongoing basis. Consulting on sales techniques, record keeping provided at owner's request.

INFORMATION SUBMITTED: April 1990

WESTERN APPRAISERS
Division of WEST/APP, INC.
P. O. Box 215742
Sacramento, California 95821
Bert F. Baumbach, President

DESCRIPTION OF OPERATION: Western Appraisers provides material damage appraisals, total loss evaluation, and mechancial failure inspections to major insurance companies, lending institutions, and fleet operators.

NUMBER OF FRANCHISEES: 33 in 7 states

IN BUSINESS SINCE: 1960

EQUITY CAPITAL NEEDED: $7,500–$15,000 depending on population count of area desired.

FINANCIAL ASSISTANCE AVAILABLE: None; exceptions may be made under certain circumstances.

TRAINING PROVIDED: Intensive 4-week training period at one of our California training offices prior to franchisee opening business.

MANAGERIAL ASSISTANCE AVAILABLE: West/App, Inc., provides continued management service for the life of the franchise in such areas as work product quality control, customer development, and profit structure. Many services such as medical insurance, manuals, and printing can be purchased from West/App, Inc., at a considerable discount. Semiannual training seminars are also provided.

INFORMATION SUBMITTED: April 1990

CLOTHING/SHOES

ATHLETIC ATTIC MARKETING, INC.
P. O. Box 14503
Gainesville, Florida 32604
C. J. Collins, Director of Franchise Sales

DESCRIPTION OF OPERATION: A retail sporting goods operation specializing in the sale of active-wear apparel, athletic footwear and related sporting goods (racquetball, tennis, soccer, etc.).

NUMBER OF FRANCHISEES: 145 in 40 states, District of Columbia, Puerto Rico, New Zealand, and Japan

IN BUSINESS SINCE: 1974

EQUITY CAPITAL NEEDED: $15,000 for franchise fee. $125,000–$175,000 total investment. Minimum $45,000 cash required.

FINANCIAL ASSISTANCE AVAILABLE: No financial assistance is provided by the franchisor; however, all necessary information for loan applications is available.

TRAINING PROVIDED: Training program includes 1 week of classroom instruction in all aspects of store operations and 1 week of in-store instruction at franchisor's training store.

MANAGERIAL ASSISTANCE AVAILABLE: Assistance includes, but is not limited to, the following: site selection, lease negotiations, store design, basic construction drawings, product mix assistance, opening suppliers accounts, accounting systems, inventory systems, on-site opening assistance, complete operations manual, advertising manual, local advertising materials, national advertising and publicity support, monthly management and newsletters, annual sales meetings.

INFORMATION SUBMITTED: May 1990

FASHION CROSSROADS
2130 North Hollywood Way
Burbank, California 91505
Bob Deutsch, Director of Franchise Development

DESCRIPTION OF OPERATION: FASHION CROSSROADS (formerly Mode O'Day Company) presently operates and licenses women's apparel specialty shops. These stores specialize in popular and moderately priced merchandise in size ranges that may include junior, misses, and large sizes. Licensees do not purchase inventory from FASHION CROSSROADS; all FASHION CROSSROADS inventory is placed in licensee's store on consignment.

NUMBER OF FRANCHISEES: Approximately 250 in 27 states

IN BUSINESS SINCE: 1933

EQUITY CAPITAL NEEDED: Variable—estimated range: $15,000 to $30,000 to cover initial license fee, lease deposit, leasehold improvements, equipment and fixtures, working capital, insurance, and security deposit.

FINANCIAL ASSISTANCE AVAILABLE: No merchandise investment, all merchandise supplied on consignment. Licensee pays FASHION CROSSROADS for merchandise after it has been sold to the ultimate consumer. FASHION CROSSROADS requires a security deposit from all licensees.

TRAINING PROVIDED: Mandatory training is conducted at the National Training Center of FASHION CROSSROADS. FASHION CROSSROADS customarily provides a 2-week training period for each new licensee by company trainers. There is no charge to licensee for training. Additional licensee training is provided in the form of FASHION CROSSROADS continuous in-store training program, which is based on periodic visits by the licensee's field consultant, a FASHION CROSSROADS employee, and various training materials prepared by FASHION CROSSROADS. The licensee's field consultant will visit the licensee's store at regular intervals in order to provide the licensee with guidance concerning operation and management of store.

MANAGERIAL ASSISTANCE AVAILABLE: FASHION CROSSROADS agrees from time to time to provide and make available to licensee retail operations assistance and supplies. The assistance provided by FASHION CROSSROADS shall include, but not be limited to, training of licensee; supervision and assistance in store leasing, store operation, personnel management, inventory control, advertising, sales promotion, and window display; providing without additional charge store improvement plans, layout plans, advertising productions, seasonal window backgrounds, window signs, interior signs, and merchandise bags; and making available insurance, store fixtures, gift boxes, sales checks, bookkeeping supplies, and other miscellaneous items. Licensee is not required to make use of any or all of these services in order to obtain merchandise on consignment.

INFORMATION SUBMITTED: April 1990

FASHION LTD.
P. O. Box 51273
Jacksonville Beach, Florida 32240
W. H. Bonneau, President

DESCRIPTION OF OPERATION: We offer over 3,000 designer and brand-name fashions, footwear, and accessories at below-wholesale pricing. You are able to offer your customers current season styles at 25 to 75 percent savings, and all inventory is guaranteed to sell. We offer site selection, lease negotiation, design fixturing, and inventory control. We will tailor a theme store of your choice to fit your budget.

NUMBER OF FRANCHISEES: 73 units

IN BUSINESS SINCE: 1985

EQUITY CAPITAL NEEDED: $25,000–$100,000

FINANCIAL ASSISTANCE AVAILABLE: We will assist in a business plan.

TRAINING PROVIDED: Complete training is provided at licensee's store location for 1 week in hiring, merchandising, pricing control, and customer relations.

MANAGERIAL ASSISTANCE AVAILABLE: Managerial assistance is continued as long as purchasing is through Fashion Ltd. since licensees have the option of purchasing from anyone.

INFORMATION SUBMITTED: April 1990

FLEET FEET, INCORPORATED
1555 River Park Drive, Suite 102
Sacramento, California 95815
Sally Edwards, President/CEO

DESCRIPTION OF OPERATION: Retail, active name-brand shoes, apparel, and accessories with a strong emphasis on a health-oriented fitness life-style. Owners must be actively involved in physical fitness.

NUMBER OF FRANCHISEES: 35 locations in 11 states

IN BUSINESS SINCE: Retail business 1975, franchise since 1978.

EQUITY CAPITAL NEEDED: $25,000–$50,000

FINANCIAL ASSISTANCE AVAILABLE: Financial advice and assistance in preparing papers and business plan for financial institution. The total capitalization costs range from $85,000 to $125,000.

TRAINING PROVIDED: Strenuous 2-week training program in Sacramento and 1 week on-site assistance before store opening. Ongoing support with manuals, computerized accounting package, workbooks, toll-free telephone consulting, national buying programs, and more.

MANAGERIAL ASSISTANCE AVAILABLE: Ongoing weekly bulletin, "Fleet Feet Weekly Memo," to announce inventory and management news. Weekly phone calls to each franchise to offer assistance. Warehouse facilities that offer franchises inventory goods. Franchisee/franchisor meetings three times annually to improve managerial, technical, and other business skills. Discount buying programs.

INFORMATION SUBMITTED: April 1990

* GINGISS INTERNATIONAL, INC.
180 North LaSalle Street
Chicago, Illinois 60601
John Heiser, Vice President

DESCRIPTION OF OPERATION: Specialists in the sale and rental of men's formal wear.

NUMBER OF FRANCHISEES: 208 in 36 states

IN BUSINESS SINCE: 1936 franchising since 1968

EQUITY CAPITAL NEEDED: $40,000–$95,000

FINANCIAL ASSISTANCE AVAILABLE: Through external sources franchisor arranges and guarantees $65,000 financing for opening inventory.

TRAINING PROVIDED: 2-week comprehensive training at Gingiss International Training Center in Chicago approximately 1 month before center's opening. 1 week on-site training during initial opening week. Regular visits by training directors and various department heads on a continuing basis.

MANAGERIAL ASSISTANCE AVAILABLE: Franchisor provides regular visits by field training advisors, a comprehensive instructional manual, periodic bulletins, semiannual meetings.

INFORMATION SUBMITTED: April 1990

THE MARK-IT STORES, INC.
316 Yale
P. O. Box 187
St. Joseph, Missouri 64504
Tim Burtner, President

DESCRIPTION OF OPERATION: The Mark-It Stores franchise system consists of retail stores in regional malls. We specialize in imprinted sportswear and accessory items. Average store size of 700 square feet. We operate a complete screen-printing plant.

NUMBER OF FRANCHISEES: 28 in 17 states

IN BUSINESS SINCE: 1975

EQUITY CAPITAL NEEDED: $35,000–$85,000

FINANCIAL ASSISTANCE AVAILABLE: None.

TRAINING PROVIDED: 2 days in store, 2 days in office. Available for assistance when needed.

MANAGERIAL ASSISTANCE AVAILABLE: Monthly newsletters, product location service, advertising assistance, store display.

INFORMATION SUBMITTED: April 1990

SALLY WALLACE BRIDES SHOP, INC.
2210 Pine Terrace
Scotch Plains, New Jersey 07076
John Van Drill, President

DESCRIPTION OF OPERATION: Sally Wallace Brides Shops offer a complete bride shop and bridal service. Wedding gowns, bridesmaids, mothers, party, cocktail, dance, and formals plus all accessories. Inventory consists of all the leading designers and manufacturers. Advertised in *Brides* and *Modern Bride Magazine*.

NUMBER OF FRANCHISEES: 12 in 5 states

IN BUSINESS SINCE: 1955

EQUITY CAPITAL NEEDED: $50,000

FINANCIAL ASSISTANCE AVAILABLE: A total investment of approximately $50,000 is needed for a complete turnkey operation including inventory and $5,000 operating fund backup. We will finance 30 percent if franchisee has good credit reference.

TRAINING PROVIDED: 3-week mandatory training course in one of our shops. Trainer spends 1 week with franchisee to open new shop. 6 months follow-through by trainer with close supervision via written reports and telephone.

MANAGERIAL ASSISTANCE AVAILABLE: Continuous. Consultant buyer and merchandise manager supervision on a weekly basis, checking sales, money, inventory, and cost controls. Field personnel available as needed, to visit shops and assist in solving problems. Buying service supplies as part of franchise agreement.

INFORMATION SUBMITTED: May 1990

WILD TOPS
NATIONAL DEVELOPMENT GROUP, INC.
74 Main Street
Framingham, Massachusetts 01701
Richard Gold, President

DESCRIPTION OF OPERATION: Wild Tops T-Shirt Stores are contemporary in design and are located in major regional malls. Average location size is 400 to 1,000 square feet. Wild Tops features an extensive selection of imprinted sportswear highlighted by T-shirts, sweatshirts, custom flock lettering, numbers, transfers, trendy fashion tops, sweaters, infant wear, and related items.

NUMBER OF FRANCHISEES: 37 franchised and 3 company-owned

IN BUSINESS SINCE: Predecessor: 1980; current company 1985

EQUITY CAPITAL NEEDED: $40,000 and leasehold improvements.

FINANCIAL ASSISTANCE AVAILABLE: The total investment of $40,000 and construction (if any) includes all equipment and fixtures such as heat press, cash register, press table, cash and wrap table counter, glass shelving, decal display book, promotional advertising, lease negotiation, home office training, and inventory.

TRAINING PROVIDED: Intensive on-the-job training at Wild Tops training center will last 1 week and cover the following topics: store opening and closing, transfer application, purchasing, store setup, advertising, hiring procedures, customer relations, etc.

MANAGERIAL ASSISTANCE AVAILABLE: Wild Tops representatives will be present for all franchisees' grand openings, and home office personnel are available on a daily basis to assist franchisees on a consultancy basis. A manual is also provided that outlines all policies, forms and procedures.

INFORMATION SUBMITTED: May 1990

CONSTRUCTION/REMODELING MATERIALS/ SERVICES

ABC SEAMLESS, INC.
3001 Piechtner Drive, SW
Fargo, North Dakota 58103
Jerry Beyers, President

DESCRIPTION OF OPERATION: ABC franchise sales for seamless steel siding, seamless gutters. All products manufactured on location. ABC seamless steel siding replaces the obsolescent method of applying siding in 12-foot lengths. Factory-direct suppliers.

NUMBER OF FRANCHISEES: 410 in 22 states and Canada

IN BUSINESS SINCE: 1973

EQUITY CAPITAL NEEDED: $30,000–$50,000

FINANCIAL ASSISTANCE AVAILABLE: Leasing available for equipment to qualified buyers, through national lease companies.

TRAINING PROVIDED: Training in sales, product information, and application.

MANAGERIAL ASSISTANCE AVAILABLE: Accounting services, product service, equipment service.

INFORMATION SUBMITTED: May 1990

* ACRYSYL INTERNATIONAL CORPORATION (AIC)
11 South 11th Street
P. O. Box 7858
Reading, Pennsylvania 19603
Dr. Donald G. Snyder, President

DESCRIPTION OF OPERATION: AIC is engaged in franchising nationwide a unique patent-pending 3-stage elastomeric roofing and siding coating system called AcrySyl.

NUMBER OF FRANCHISEES: 20 in Pennsylvania, New Jersey, North Carolina, and South Carolina

IN BUSINESS SINCE: 1982

EQUITY CAPITAL NEEDED: License fee minimum $15,000 plus $20,000 initial operating capital.

FINANCIAL ASSISTANCE AVAILABLE: None.

TRAINING PROVIDED: Technical aspects of the AcrySyl line of products; estimates; evaluations; application procedures; customer service and relations; marketing, management, and administrative procedures. Individual training in the field. Ongoing assistance on unusual roofing/siding service-related matters. Group meetings or training sessions to exchange marketing, administrative, and technical know-how among franchisees and for the transfer of specialized and advanced technical information and procedures from AIC to franchisee personnel.

MANAGERIAL ASSISTANCE AVAILABLE: See above.

INFORMATION SUBMITTED: May 1990

ADD-VENTURES OF AMERICA, INC.
38 Park Street Station
Medfield, Massachusetts 02052
Thomas D. Sullivan, President

DESCRIPTION OF OPERATION: Add-Ventures of America, Inc., specializes in remodeling construction for both residential and commercial tradesman. Developed business system and documentation for assisting carpenters/general contractors in administrating their operations. Regional franchise owners have exclusive rights to sell local franchises in defined territories.

NUMBER OF FRANCHISEES: 2 regional franchise owners, 12 local franchise owners

IN BUSINESS SINCE: 1977

EQUITY CAPITAL NEEDED: Regional franchise, $45,000; local franchise, $2,500

FINANCIAL ASSISTANCE AVAILABLE: Will assist in arranging financing.

TRAINING PROVIDED: Initial 10-day training, spread over 2–3 different sessions at regional franchise owner's location.

MANAGERIAL ASSISTANCE AVAILABLE: Assistance in preparation of business plan and ongoing management training.

INFORMATION SUBMITTED: May 1990

AMERICAN LEAK DETECTION
1750 East Arenas, Suite 7
Palm Springs, California 92262
Dick Rennick, Chief Executive Officer

DESCRIPTION OF OPERATION: Electronically locates leaks in pools, spas, fountains, under concrete slabs of homes, and commercial buildings. Locates hidden and concealed sewer lines, septic tanks, etc. Building energy loss, roof moisture analysis by the use of infrared thermography. Locate and repair drain, waste and sewer leaks.

NUMBER OF FRANCHISEES: 110 in 10 states, and 2 in Australia

IN BUSINESS SINCE: 1975, franchising since 1985

EQUITY CAPITAL NEEDED: $20,000

FINANCIAL ASSISTANCE AVAILABLE: Franchises start at $40,000—a portion can be financed in-house by franchisor with good credit rating.

TRAINING PROVIDED: 4- to 6-week training—50 hours plus per week—very intensive course. Ongoing quarterly training.

MANAGERIAL ASSISTANCE AVAILABLE: Ongoing public relations and marketing support given periodically or upon special request. Yearly training conventions and sales meetings, continual equipment and technique updates.

INFORMATION SUBMITTED: April 1990

ARCHADECK WOODEN PATIO DECKS
P. O. Box 5185
Richmond, Virginia 23220
Richard Provost, President

DESCRIPTION OF OPERATION: Archadeck (R-KA-DEK) markets, sells, and builds custom-designed, stick-built wooden patio decks for residential, builder, and commercial clients.

NUMBER OF FRANCHISEES: 32 in 15 states and Japan

IN BUSINESS SINCE: 1980, franchising since 1984

EQUITY CAPITAL NEEDED: $40,000–$60,000

FINANCIAL ASSISTANCE AVAILABLE: None.

TRAINING PROVIDED: Minimum 10 days' intensive training covering the areas of office management; marketing and advertising; sales; construction documentation and management; and design and estimating.

MANAGERIAL ASSISTANCE AVAILABLE: Unlimited managerial support via telephone and mails. Regular on-site services include support in all facets of business with special emphasis on sales support and business management. We provide working drawings for each project with specs, details, and material takeoffs. We also have an architectural rendering service and an in-house advertising agency.

INFORMATION SUBMITTED: May 1990

BASEMENT DE-WATERING SYSTEMS, INC.
162 East Chestnut Street
Canton, Illinois 61520
Robert Beckner, Marketing Director

DESCRIPTION OF OPERATION: Basement De-Watering Systems, Inc. (BDW), is the nation's largest network of professionally trained and authorized professionals, servicing residential and commercial waterproofing and radon testing and mitigation markets in 36 states and Canada. BDW offers a 2-in-1 business opportunity through year-round installations of both water seepage control systems and the Safe-Aire Patented Radon Mitigation System. The patented Safe-Aire System employs an Environmental Protection Agency–proven method that is capable of removing high concentrations of radon gas and structural water seepage in a single system application. Both the Basement De-Watering and Safe-Aire Systems utilize a unique method of interior perimeter baseboard channelization that is marketed and installed by our authorized dealers exclusively.

NUMBER OF FRANCHISEES: 23 franchises, plus 1 company store, plus over 100 dealers

IN BUSINESS SINCE: 1978

EQUITY CAPITAL NEEDED: $24,000–$45,000 is the approximate cost of original start-up; includes extensive training, specialized tools, marketing materials, inventory, and supplies. Initial product inventory is structured to recoup all or a large portion of original investment.

FINANCIAL ASSISTANCE AVAILABLE: Franchisor does not at present offer any specific kind or amount of financing.

TRAINING PROVIDED: The intial 1-week course is conducted at the home office in both water seepage control and radon testing and mitigation. Ongoing training is available for franchisee and future employees at the home office, at no additional cost for course studies.

MANAGERIAL ASSISTANCE AVAILABLE: Advertising, marketing, and management materials are initially provided during training. Ongoing support materials are provided throughout the year. Additionally, dealers are supported through in-house products catalog, in-house advertising layout support, radio and TV program support, and ongoing marketing materials support. Franchisor serves as continual technical consultant for franchisee via toll-free service hotline. Continual market awareness and research are provided bimonthly to all authorized dealers through BDW/SA Newsletter.

INFORMATION SUBMITTED: April 1990

BATHCREST INC.
2425 South Progress Drive
Salt Lake City, Utah 84119
Scott Peterson, President

DESCRIPTION OF OPERATION: Specializing in porcelain resurfacing on bathtubs, sinks, ceramic wall tile, kitchen appliances, chip repair on new tubs, fiberglass, and acrylic spa repair. Bathcrest Inc. services motels, hotels, apartment houses, homeowners, contractors, and repairs for manufacturers of new porcelain bathroom fixtures.

NUMBER OF FRANCHISEES: 153 in 35 states, 3 in Canada

IN BUSINESS SINCE: 1979

EQUITY CAPITAL NEEDED: $24,500

FINANCIAL ASSISTANCE AVAILABLE: None.

TRAINING PROVIDED: 5 days of on-the-job training by trained technicians. Complete equipment, printed materials, supplies, advertising, and enough Glazecote to return investment. Yearly dealers' meetings and newsletters. Protected territory.

MANAGERIAL ASSISTANCE AVAILABLE: Continual support.

INFORMATION SUBMITTED: April 1990

BATH GENIE, INC.
69 River Street
Marlborough, Massachusetts 01752
John J. Foley, President

DESCRIPTION OF OPERATION: The franchisor, through a uniquely developed and refined process, offers the service of restoring and resurfacing bathroom fixtures. This service includes the restoration, recoloring, and recoating of standard bathroom fixtures, which include bathtubs, sinks, wall tiles, fiberglass, and acrylic and chip repair.

NUMBER OF FRANCHISEES: 27 in 9 states and Canada

IN BUSINESS SINCE: 1978

EQUITY CAPITAL NEEDED: $24,500

FINANCIAL ASSISTANCE AVAILABLE: The franchisor does not offer any specific kind or amount of financial assistance to prospective franchisees. Assistance is rendered to prospective franchisees with regard to mode and method of financing where needed.

TRAINING PROVIDED: Prior to the start of the franchise business, the franchisor has the obligation to provide full training for a period of approximately 4 to 5 days in all phases of the business to include on-the-job training, revelation of all technical aspects and procedures of the business, and instruction with regard to marketing, public relations, and accounting procedures. Training is mandatory.

MANAGERIAL ASSISTANCE AVAILABLE: Beyond the training period, the franchisor keeps a continual liaison with the franchisee with regard to all details pertaining to training of personnel, public relations, marketing, and advertising. In addition, the franchisor provides the franchisee with periodic newsletters and newsworthy items pertaining to doings in the industry and also with regard to pertinent changes in the law and other factors that affect the conduct of the franchisee's problems, of any kind or nature, with the home office of the franchisor. All such communications are attended to by the franchisor's office immediately upon notification from the franchisee.

INFORMATION SUBMITTED: April 1990

* B-DRY SYSTEM, INC.
1341 Copley Road
Akron, Ohio 44320
Joseph Garfinkel, Vice President

DESCRIPTION OF OPERATION: Franchisor has developed and formulated unique procedures and techniques for the operation of a basement waterproofing business. Franchisor provides to franchisee a uniform system of procedures for the operation of a B-Dry franchise including the right to use the B-Dry patented process and the use of B-Dry logos and trademarks.

NUMBER OF FRANCHISEES: 80 franchises in 25 states and Canada

IN BUSINESS SINCE: 1958

EQUITY CAPITAL NEEDED: $20,000–$45,000

FINANCIAL ASSISTANCE AVAILABLE: Up to 50 percent of

the initial franchisee fee may be extended up to 24 months at no interest.

TRAINING PROVIDED: Franchisor provides the complete initial training on all aspects of technical, marketing, and adminsitrative phases of the operation. Initial training approximately 10 days. Regular follow-up training provided at no charge.

MANAGERIAL ASSISTANCE AVAILABLE: During operation of franchise, regular managerial and technical assistance is provided on an ongoing basis.

INFORMATION SUBMITTED: May 1990

CHIMNEY RELINING INTERNATIONAL, INC.
105 West Merrimack Street
P. O. Box 4035
Manchester, New Hampshire 03108
Cifford R. Martel, President

DESCRIPTION OF OPERATION: Using the PermaFlu Chimney Lining System, the PermaFlu franchisee can reline cracked, crooked, or deteriorated chimney flues and restore them to safe, efficient use with any heating fuel, including wood, oil, gas, and coal. Complete contractor package includes a mortar mixer mounted on a hopper that flows into a pump. Special PermaFlu Mix pumped into chimney around inflated rubber flue-former. When mix hardens, former is deflated and removed. New round flue. All cracks sealed.

NUMBER OF FRANCHISEES: 35 in 21 states and Canada; affiliate in United Kingdom

IN BUSINESS SINCE: 1981

EQUITY CAPITAL NEEDED: $14,700, $11,700, or $6,900

FINANCIAL ASSISTANCE AVAILABLE: Will provide model business plan.

TRAINING PROVIDED: 1-week intensive training in actual on-the-job chimney relining work; also classroom work reviewing operations guidelines, marketing, estimating, profit, and cost analysis; warehouse instructions on maintenance of PermaFlu Chimney Lining System.

MANAGERIAL ASSISTANCE AVAILABLE: Guidance in advertising and publicity, office operations, use of programmed estimating computer (provided by CRI); letters of introduction on franchisee's behalf sent with complete testing and descriptive package to franchisee's local (1) building inspectors, (2) insurance adjusters, (3) fire marshals, (4) real estate brokers, and (5) local newspapers. Advertising and publicity sales lead program on monthly basis—PermaFlu information sent to franchisee's customer, with copy to franchisee. Full package of franchisee identity materials provided—business cards, letterheads, invoices, envelopes, and brochures, all custom printed with the franchisee name, address, etc.

INFORMATION SUBMITTED: May 1990

CLASSIC STORAGE
12 Sterling Lane
Scotts Valley, California 95066
Bart L. Ross, CEO

DESCRIPTION OF OPERATION: CLASSIC STORAGE, the premier builder of quality residential and commercial storage buildings, offers a unique opportunity in owning your own business. No previous experience required; we completely train you in manufacturing, marketing, sales, and day-to-day operations. Exclusive territory, sales assistance, technical support, strong ongoing marketing support, low investment, low overhead. Take charge of your future.

NUMBER OF FRANCHISEES: 7 in California

IN BUSINESS SINCE: 1988

EQUITY CAPITAL NEEDED: Investment ranges between $24,500 and $50,000.

FINANCIAL ASSISTANCE AVAILABLE: Financial assistance is available up to $9,000.

TRAINING PROVIDED: 1 week at home office and 1 week at franchisee's location.

MANAGERIAL ASSISTANCE AVAILABLE: Continuous in all phases of management including lease negotiations, site selection, and all business services.

INFORMATION SUBMITTED: April 1990

COLLEGE PRO PAINTERS (U.S.), LTD.
(student franchise)
College Pro's PAINTERS PLUS
(full-time franchise contractor)
400 Riverside Avenue
Medford, Massachusetts 02155
Kenneth J. Cleary, Vice President

DESCRIPTION OF OPERATION: Student Division: Students are selected each fall to participate in the program. They are given territories in which they are to operate their own painting franchise; these territories are usually their own hometown area. During the winter and spring they are taught all the aspects of operating a painting business through attending 2 3-day classroom sessions and 1 3-day practical on-site training session. These are weekend sessions. After school is complete they begin operations and paint between 40 to 50 homes before going back to school. Full-time Franchise: Any person willing to operate a hands-on painting business year round will receive all the benefits of an association with the world's largest painting company. Training, financial assistance, marketing program, insurance, and expert support are all included.

NUMBER OF FRANCHISEES: Students: 295 in 20 states; full-time: 17 in 4 states

IN BUSINESS SINCE: 1971

EQUITY CAPITAL NEEDED: None.

FINANCIAL ASSISTANCE AVAILABLE: $2,500 is prepaid expenses and advertising.

TRAINING PROVIDED: 6 days of classroom, 8 days of in-the-field training.

MANAGERIAL ASSISTANCE AVAILABLE: Ongoing advice and assistance are available from experienced people at any time to the franchisee.

INFORMATION SUBMITTED: March 1990

EUREKA LOG HOMES INC.
Industrial Park, Commercial Avenue
Box 426
Berryville, Arkansas 72616
Bill Smith, President

DESCRIPTION OF OPERATION: Wholesaling through an international network of distributors and dealers.

NUMBER OF FRANCHISEES: 300 in 38 states, Japan, and Switzerland

IN BUSINESS SINCE: 1976

EQUITY CAPITAL NEEDED: $19,700 for 2,000-square-foot log home display model.

FINANCIAL ASSISTANCE AVAILABLE: None.

TRAINING PROVIDED: Excellent training manual and constant assistance from international marketing and production division.

MANAGERIAL ASSISTANCE AVAILABLE: Same as above.

INFORMATION SUBMITTED: June 1990

FERSINA WINDOWS, INC.
14201 F & G South Lakes Drive
South Point Business Park
Charlotte, North Carolina 28217
Chuck McGill

DESCRIPTION OF OPERATION: Sales/manufacture of solariums/windows.

NUMBER OF FRANCHISEES: Over 2,500 in 21 countries

IN BUSINESS SINCE: 1980

EQUITY CAPITAL NEEDED: Cash requirements $30,000–$35,000. Total investment up to $100,000.

FINANCIAL ASSISTANCE AVAILABLE: Up to 70 percent financing available.

TRAINING PROVIDED: Training provided.

MANAGERIAL ASSISTANCE AVAILABLE: Ongoing.

INFORMATION SUBMITTED: April 1990

KITCHEN SAVERS, INC.
715 Rose Street
La Crosse, Wisconsin 54603
Cliff LeCleir, President

DESCRIPTION OF OPERATION: Kitchen Savers remodels kitchen cabinets by first removing the existing doors and drawer fronts. Then we reface the existing framework with 1/8-inch, 3-ply oak paneling. The old doors and drawer fronts are then replaced with new, 3/4-inch solid oak doors and drawer fronts.

NUMBER OF FRANCHISEES: 11 plus 1 company-owned

IN BUSINESS SINCE: 1982

EQUITY CAPITAL NEEDED: Total investment: $11,000–$40,000, franchise fee: $7,500–$12,500

FINANCIAL ASSISTANCE AVAILABLE: Assistance and advice.

TRAINING PROVIDED: 2 days of extensive training at home office and 3 days at franchisee's location.

MANAGERIAL ASSISTANCE AVAILABLE: Ongoing training and consultation will be provided upon request.

INFORMATION SUBMITTED: April 1990

KITCHEN TUNE-UP
131 North Roosevelt
Aberdeen, South Dakota 57401
David Haglund, President

DESCRIPTION OF OPERATION: Kitchen Tune-Up offers wood care and maintenance for the home and office. Our 9-step process revitalizes and rejuvenates tired-looking cabinets. Our franchises also offer door replacement built to specifications and closet systems available in over 300 colors. Kitchen Tune-Up is a home-based business that requires no inventory.

NUMBER OF FRANCHISEES: 62 in 24 states

IN BUSINESS SINCE: 1988

EQUITY CAPITAL NEEDED: $11,495–$11,995; this includes $9,995 franchise fee.

FINANCIAL ASSISTANCE AVAILABLE: None.

TRAINING PROVIDED: Complete 3-day training program at franchisor location and an additional 2-day follow-up training at franchise location.

MANAGERIAL ASSISTANCE AVAILABLE: Kitchen Tune-Up offers a complete management training program including use of our operations and marketing manual. Kitchen Tune-Up visits its franchisees on a regular basis and offers regional training schools to update them on industry trends and improvements.

INFORMATION SUBMITTED: April 1990

LINDAL CEDAR HOMES, INC.
P. O. Box 24426
Seattle, Washington 98124
Sir Walter Lindal, Chairman

DESCRIPTION OF OPERATION: Manufacture and sale of Cedar Homes including precut Cedar Homes and Cedar Log Homes.

NUMBER OF FRANCHISEES: 346 in all 50 states

IN BUSINESS SINCE: 1945

EQUITY CAPITAL NEEDED: $5,000 minimum, none to Lindal (no franchise fee).

FINANCIAL ASSISTANCE AVAILABLE: Long-term mortgage financing for homes sold.

TRAINING PROVIDED: 5-day training seminar initially; 1-day seminars 3 times a year.

MANAGERIAL ASSISTANCE AVAILABLE: Area representative continually assists.

INFORMATION SUBMITTED: May 1990

MAGNUM PIERING INC.
720 A. West Fourth Street
Eureka, Montana 63025
Tom Zagel, Vice President

DESCRIPTION OF OPERATION: Raising, leveling, and stabilizing settled buildings, foundations, using steel piers to bedrock.

NUMBER OF FRANCHISEES: 8 in 7 states

IN BUSINESS SINCE: 1985

EQUITY CAPITAL NEEDED: $35,000 includes one-half of franchise fee, supplies, equipment, materials, and training.

FINANCIAL ASSISTANCE AVAILABLE: Partial financing of the franchise fee with no interest charged.

TRAINING PROVIDED: Complete training in office procedure, advertising, estimating presentation of contracts, closing and all facets of piering, including "hands-on" field work.

MANAGERIAL ASSISTANCE AVAILABLE: Franchisor features thorough training in both managerial and technical aspects and offers ongoing support without reservation.

INFORMATION SUBMITTED: April 1990

MR. BUILD HANDI-MAN SERVICES, INC.
628 Hebron Avenue
Glastonbury, Connecticut 06033
Thomas Tyska, President/CEO

DESCRIPTION OF OPERATION: Mr. Build Handi-Man Services offers residential and commercial property owners a central source for small repair maintenance and renovation work. Each franchisee has a protected territory and is tied into a regional central dispatch by computer.

NUMBER OF FRANCHISEES: 20

IN BUSINESS SINCE: 1989

EQUITY CAPITAL NEEDED: $30,000–$40,000

FINANCIAL ASSISTANCE AVAILABLE: None.

TRAINING PROVIDED: 1 week initial and then ongoing 1-day workshop.

MANAGERIAL ASSISTANCE AVAILABLE: Pre-opening and opening, central data processing, central purchasing, field operations evaluation, inventory control, regional or national meetings.

INFORMATION SUBMITTED: May 1990

NATURE LOG HOMES
Rt. 2, Box 164, South Kings Highway
Noel, Missouri 64854
Ernest Bramlett, President

DESCRIPTION OF OPERATION: International log home manufacturer.

NUMBER OF FRANCHISEES: 137 in 23 states

EQUITY CAPITAL NEEDED: $40,000–$50,000 (log model home)

FINANCIAL ASSISTANCE AVAILABLE: 50 percent is provided to qualified applicants.

TRAINING PROVIDED: Expense-free at our national office, excluding travel.

MANAGERIAL ASSISTANCE AVAILABLE: Technical manual, blueprints, and etc.

INFORMATION SUBMITTED: April 1990

NOVUS PLATE GLASS REPAIR, INC.
10425 Hampshire Avenue, South
Minneapolis, Minnesota 55438
Gerald E. Keinath, President

DESCRIPTION OF OPERATION: Using the exclusive NOVUS patented process, professionally trained franchisees repair, rather than replace, BB and stone-damaged plate-glass windows. NOVUS franchisees are the experts in plate-glass repair, and offer a money-saving service to contractors, store owners, banks, and other businesses that use plate-glass windows. Franchisees work out of their home or from a fixed location. This company is affiliated with NOVUS Windshield Repair, which has over 1,500 dealers worldwide.

NUMBER OF FRANCHISEES: 6

IN BUSINESS SINCE: 1972 (franchising since 1982)

EQUITY CAPITAL NEEDED: Approximately $12,000 (depending on size of exclusive area).

FINANCIAL ASSISTANCE AVAILABLE: None.

TRAINING PROVIDED: 3-day factory training at the NOVUS international headquarters includes technical training, sales and marketing classes, and seminars on general business operations.

MANAGERIAL ASSISTANCE AVAILABLE: Ongoing technical and sales assistance provided by professional staff. Newsletters, conventions, regional meetings, and ongoing research and development are included.

INFORMATION SUBMITTED: May 1990

PERMA CERAM ENTERPRISES, INC.
65 Smithtown Boulevard
Smithtown, New York 11787
Joseph Tumolo, President

DESCRIPTION OF OPERATION: Resurfacing and repair of porcelain and fiberglass bathroom fixtures such as tubs, sinks, and wall tile with Perma Ceram's Porcelaincote. Process used in private homes, apartments, hotels/motels, institutions, etc. Available in white and all colors. Established national accounts.

NUMBER OF FRANCHISEES: Approximately 175 in 39 states, Bermuda, Bahamas, Canada, and Puerto Rico

IN BUSINESS SINCE: 1975

EQUITY CAPITAL NEEDED: $19,500 total investment. Includes all equipment, materials, supplies, and training.

FINANCIAL ASSISTANCE AVAILABLE: 100 percent financing available through independent lending institutions.

TRAINING PROVIDED: 5 days' training at established location. All expenses included in cost of dealership. Technical training, sales training, management, marketing, etc. Operations manual provided.

MANAGERIAL ASSISTANCE AVAILABLE: Advertising, sales, and promotional materials; ongoing managerial and technical assistance provided. Continual updating of information provided through bulletins, newsletters, personal contact. Return visits to training facility available if necessary.

INFORMATION SUBMITTED: May 1990

PERMA-GLAZE, INC.
1200 North El Dorado Place, Suite A-110
Tucson, Arizona 85715
Dale R. Young, President

DESCRIPTION OF OPERATION: Perma-Glaze specializes in the restoration and refinishing of bathroom and kitchen fixtures such as bathtubs, sinks, and ceramic wall tiles. Materials to be refinished consist of porcelain, fiberglass, acrylic, cultured marble, Formica, kitchen appliances, whirlpool tubs, shower enclosures, and most building materials. Service includes chip repair, fiberglass and acrylic spa repairs, restoration and recoating of fixtures. Available in any color including white. All work under complete warranty. Perma-Glaze services homeowners, apartments, hotels/motels, institutions, hospitals, contractors, property managers, plumbing contractors, and many more.

NUMBER OF FRANCHISEES: 97 in 28 states and 3 countries

IN BUSINESS SINCE: 1978; sale of franchise began in 1983

EQUITY CAPITAL NEEDED: $16,500 to $19,500 includes all training, equipment, and supplies with enough product to earn back your initial investment.

FINANCIAL ASSISTANCE AVAILABLE: Franchisor does not offer any specific kind or amount of financial assistance to prospective franchises. Assistance is rendered to prospective franchises with regard to mode and method of financing and payment where a small amount of assistance is needed.

TRAINING PROVIDED: 5-day (hands-on) training session by trainer-technician at established location. Lodging and air fare included in cost of franchise. Technical training provided with operations manual, hotline service, and newsletter.

MANAGERIAL ASSISTANCE AVAILABLE: Info provided for support in advertising, sales, promotional sales, mailing lists, business contacts. Advertising format for Yellow Pages, newspapers, and magazines.

THE SCREENMOBILE CORP.
457 West Allen #107
San Dimas, California 91773
Monty M. Walker, President

DESCRIPTION OF OPERATION: Mobile window and door screening and rescreening service.

NUMBER OF FRANCHISEES: 40 in California, Arizona, Idaho, and Texas

IN BUSINESS SINCE: 1982

EQUITY CAPITAL NEEDED: $33,000

FINANCIAL ASSISTANCE AVAILABLE: None.

TRAINING PROVIDED: Field training, shop training, classroom training, approximately 2 weeks.

MANAGERIAL ASSISTANCE AVAILABLE: Ongoing 24-hour telephone and field assistance.

INFORMATION SUBMITTED: April 1990

TIMBERMILL STORAGE BARNS, INC.
P. O. Box 218
Sonoma, California 95476
Thomas N. Hoover, President

DESCRIPTION OF OPERATION: Timbermill Storage Barns, Inc., prefabricates, sells, and constructs on-site storage barns. These barns are constructed of top-quality materials purchased locally by the franchisee. Some prefabrication is required before construction takes place at the job site.

NUMBER OF FRANCHISEES: 26 nationwide

IN BUSINESS SINCE: 1985

EQUITY CAPITAL NEEDED: $18,000

FINANCIAL ASSISTANCE AVAILABLE: None.

TRAINING PROVIDED: Extensive 5-day training program at franchisee's location designed to educate him in all aspects of the Timbermill business plan. The loan of the Timbermill operations manual that includes such topics as material inventory, purchasing and construction procedures, marketing, bookkeeping, and much more.

MANAGERIAL ASSISTANCE AVAILABLE: Total training and ongoing assistance with advertising, technical bulletins, and managerial support. Conducts market research to aid franchisees in promoting their products. Timbermill Storage Barns, Inc., provides all assistance necessary to achieve and maintain the high quality that is becoming a trademark with our barns.

INFORMATION SUBMITTED: April 1990

THE WINDOWS OF OPPORTUNITIES, INC.
711 Rigsbee Avenue
Durham, North Carolina 27701
Conrad Harris

DESCRIPTION OF OPERATION: The Windows of Opportunities offers franchises in "The Window Man," for exclusive solid vinyl replacement windows and new construction vinyl windows, sun and garden room enclosures, and state-of-the-art wireless security systems.

NUMBER OF FRANCHISEES: 24 in North Carolina, South Carolina, Georgia, and Virginia

IN BUSINESS SINCE: 1983

EQUITY CAPITAL NEEDED: Varies from $15,000 to $35,000.

FINANCIAL ASSISTANCE AVAILABLE: Financing assistance to qualified applicants.

TRAINING PROVIDED: Extensive 1-week training at corporate training center in Durham, North Carolina. On-site start-up support and continual ongoing training and operational support.

MANAGERIAL ASSISTANCE AVAILABLE: Assistance in management, sales and marketing, business operations, advertising, lead operations, etc.

INFORMATION SUBMITTED: April 1990

* WORLDWIDE REFINISHING SYSTEMS, INC.
P. O. Box 3146
Waco, Texas 26207

DESCRIPTION OF OPERATION: Refinishing specialists of bathtubs and bath fixtures including antique leg tubs and unique sinks. We can change the color of an entire bathroom including the tile. We also refinish fiberglass benches (fast-food restaurants), chip repair on new and used fixtures. We refinish more other surfaces and market a line of bath and kitchen accessories.

NUMBER OF FRANCHISEES: Over 200 in 30 states

IN BUSINESS SINCE: 1970

EQUITY CAPITAL NEEDED: $11,000

FINANCIAL ASSISTANCE AVAILABLE: None.

TRAINING PROVIDED: 5-day intensive classroom and on-the-job training. Also includes training videotapes and TV commercials.

MANAGERIAL ASSISTANCE AVAILABLE: Complete backup and support system via the telephone for technical and marketing advice. Complete advertising and bookkeeping program.

INFORMATION SUBMITTED: May 1990

COSMETICS/TOILETRIES

ELIZABETH GRADY FACE FIRST, INC.
One West Foster Street
Melrose, Massachusetts 02176
John P. Walsh, Executive Vice President

DESCRIPTION OF OPERATION: With emphasis on individual consultation and clinical analysis, treatments by professional estheticians and a prescribed home care program, Elizabeth Grady Face First's goal has always been to promote the healthiest skin for all people. Our commitment to serve the best interests of our customers is reflected in the quality of our complete line of products, many of which are specifically developed for Elizabeth Grady salons.

NUMBER OF FRANCHISEES: 13 franchises, 14 company-owned stores available for purchase as franchises

IN BUSINESS SINCE: 1974

EQUITY CAPITAL NEEDED: Franchise fee of $15,000. $10,000 approximate total investment.

FINANCIAL ASSISTANCE AVAILABLE: No, but we will provide assistance in securing third-party financing.

TRAINING PROVIDED: Everything you need to know to operate is included in our training program. The tuition is included in your franchise fee. Furthermore, one of our representatives will work with you for 1 week during your first month of operation. Franchisees will also receive an operations manual covering all areas of importance.

MANAGERIAL ASSISTANCE AVAILABLE: Training includes periodic updates on all industry trends, new products and services, as well as new advertising and promotional techniques. In addition, franchisee will be provided with total ongoing supervision and support in the form of periodic visits by our experienced staff to consult with your staff on all aspects of operations. Other assistance provided on as needed basis.

INFORMATION SUBMITTED: April 1990

EDUCATIONAL PRODUCTS/SERVICES

* BARBIZON INTERNATIONAL, INC.
950 Third Avenue
New York, New York 10022
B. Wolff, President

DESCRIPTION OF OPERATION: Barbizon operates modeling and personal development schools for teenage girls, homemakers, and career girls. The schools also offer a male modeling program, acting course, and makeup artistry, and sell Barbizon cosmetics. We are the largest organization in this field.

NUMBER OF FRANCHISEES: 91 in 40 states

IN BUSINESS SINCE: 1939

EQUITY CAPITAL NEEDED: $25,000–$50,000

FINANCIAL ASSISTANCE AVAILABLE: Franchisee can finance 50 percent of franchise fee with franchisor. Total franchise fee is $19,500 to $35,000.

TRAINING PROVIDED: Intensive 1-week training program for franchisee and his/her director at corporate office. Extensive on-site field visits at franchisee's location by home office staff during first 6 months. Periodic staff visits and conferences at home office thereafter on a continuing basis.

MANAGERIAL ASSISTANCE AVAILABLE: In addition to initial training indicated above, Barbizon makes available continuing staff programs, sales aids, new programs, brochures, direct mail pieces, etc.

INFORMATION SUBMITTED: April 1990

* GYMBOREE CORPORATION
577 Airpost Blvd., #400
Burlingame, California 94010
Bob Campbell, Director of Franchise Sales

DESCRIPTION OF OPERATION: Gymboree, a quality developmental play program, offers weekly classes to parents and their children, age 3 months to 4 years, on custom-designed equipment for infants, toddlers, and preschoolers. The program is based on sensory integration theory, positive parenting, child development principles, and the importance of play.

NUMBER OF FRANCHISEES: Over 292 Gymboree centers in operation (including 5 company-owned). Franchises have been granted to over 146 franchisees covering market plans for the development of over 408 centers in 35 states and Canada, Australia, France, Israel, Mexico, and Taiwan.

IN BUSINESS SINCE: 1976

EQUITY CAPITAL NEEDED: $8,000–$18,000 fee per site depending on number of sites. Approximately $9,000 per site for equipment and supplies; $4,000–$6,000 working capital.

FINANCIAL ASSISTANCE AVAILABLE: None.

TRAINING PROVIDED: All franchisees attend a 9-day training seminar with a follow-up visit to their location(s) after opening and once a year thereafter. Regional training programs are held on an ongoing basis.

MANAGERIAL ASSISTANCE AVAILABLE: There is an annual seminar for ongoing training. All franchisees are visited annually. Phone contact regularly.

INFORMATION SUBMITTED: April 1990

* JOHN ROBERT POWERS FINISHING, MODELING & CAREER SCHOOL WORLD HEADQUARTERS
9 Newbury Street
Boston, Massachusetts 02116
Barbara J. Tyler, Executive Vice President

DESCRIPTION OF OPERATION: John Robert Powers School offers finishing, self-improvement, drama, modeling, executive grooming, fashion merchandising, interior design, makeup arts, TV acting/drama, flight attendants, preteen and communications in today's world to women and men of all ages. Classes are held year round—day and evening.

NUMBER OF FRANCHISEES: 70 in 26 states and Singapore; Manila, Philippines; Jakarta, Indonesia; Bangkok, Thailand; Sidney and Adelaide, Australia; and Japan

IN BUSINESS SINCE: 1923

EQUITY CAPITAL NEEDED: $25,000

FINANCIAL ASSISTANCE AVAILABLE: None.

TRAINING PROVIDED: 3 weeks of teaching and administrative training plus semiannual seminars.

MANAGERIAL ASSISTANCE AVAILABLE: We provide managerial and technical assistance during the life of the franchise by visiting field personnel. Accounting assistance is provided by home office personnel. Conferences are held during the year.

INFORMATION SUBMITTED: May 1990

KINDERDANCE INTERNATIONAL, INC.
2150 Atlantic St., P. O. Box 510881
Melbourne Beach, Florida 32951
Bernard Friedman, Vice President

DESCRIPTION OF OPERATION: "Education through Dance." A home-based dance/gymnastics/motor development program designed for boys and girls, ages 2 to 5. Preschoolers learn basics of ballet, tap, modern dance, gymnastics, blended with vocabulary, numbers, colors, shapes. A full-service program allows franchisees to teach in local nursery schools, day care centers, similar settings.

NUMBER OF FRANCHISEES: 16 franchisees, 22 units in 11 states

IN BUSINESS SINCE: 1979

EQUITY CAPITAL NEEDED: $7,000 total, includes $5,000 franchise fee.

FINANCIAL ASSISTANCE AVAILABLE: None.

TRAINING PROVIDED: An intensive 7-day training program is provided at company headquarters in Melbourne Beach, Florida, in all aspects of the business for quick start-up in local area and quick return on investment. Training includes a complete operations manual, initial start-up supplies, dancewear, videotapes, cassette tapes, classroom and on-site instruction with preschoolers.

MANAGERIAL ASSISTANCE AVAILABLE: Kinderdance provides a follow-up visit to franchisee's area by company personnel, free accounting systems, toll-free hotline, newsletters, discounted insurance, discounted hotel rates while training, annual conventions, continuing education, complete line of marketing, advertising, and public relations tools, site selection assistance, grand opening procedures.

INFORMATION SUBMITTED: April 1990

PERKINS FIT BY FIVE, INC.
1606 Penfield Road
Rochester, New York 14625
Betty Perkins-Carpenter, President

DESCRIPTION OF OPERATION: Athletically oriented preschool program for children 2½ to 5 years. The fundamental approach to instruction is through development of physical skills as the key to the acquisition of self-confidence, social interaction, tolerance, self-discipline, and verbal-conceptual understandings. The above purpose is accomplished through a revolutionary new idea in preschool education, using unique teaching techniques, special equipment, and unusual activities. Exercises, music, and basic motor skills are but some of the tools of instruction, which is success oriented, heavily flavored with kindness, consideration, respect, and love.

NUMBER OF FRANCHISEES: 1 in Maryland, 2 in New York, and 1 in Pennsylvania, not including company-owned

IN BUSINESS SINCE: 1969

EQUITY CAPITAL NEEDED: $35,000–$40,000 fee per site depending on number of sites, approximately $6,000 per site for equipment and supplies.

FINANCIAL ASSISTANCE AVAILABLE: Financial assistance is not provided.

TRAINING PROVIDED: All franchisees attend a 2-week training program. Follow-up visits to their location(s). Also additional training in Rochester, New York, as needed on ongoing basis.

MANAGERIAL ASSISTANCE AVAILABLE: All franchisees are visited once annually. Phone contact as needed, written communications monthly.

INFORMATION SUBMITTED: May 1990

PLAYORENA, INC.
125 Mineola Avenue
Roslyn Heights, New York 11577
Fred Jaroslow, Executive Vice President

DESCRIPTION OF OPERATION: Playorena is a recreational and exercise program for children 3 months to 4 years old who attend weekly sessions with a parent. Activities and equipment are custom designed and time tested for the rapidly shifting stages of motor development. Program is based on learning through natural play.

NUMBER OF FRANCHISEES: 64 in 6 states

IN BUSINESS SINCE: 1981

EQUITY CAPITAL NEEDED: From $14,000 to $7,000 fee pre site depending on number of sites. Approximately $8,000 per site for equipment. Additional working capital required.

FINANCIAL ASSISTANCE AVAILABLE: Up to 50 percent of franchise fee may be financed by qualified applicants.

TRAINING PROVIDED: 8-day training program encompassing the business as well as program aspects of Playorena. Upgrading and refresher training on a continuing basis.

MANAGERIAL ASSISTANCE AVAILABLE: Complete manuals provided. On-site visits by management. Seminars and franchisee meetings. Ongoing bulletin service. Public relations assistance. Marketing direction and advice.

INFORMATION SUBMITTED: May 1990

EMPLOYMENT SERVICES

* AAA EMPLOYMENT FRANCHISE, INC.
4910K Creekside Drive
Clearwater, Florida 34620
Stacy Madhu, Franchise Operations Director

DESCRIPTION OF OPERATION: AAA Employment Franchise, Inc., offers a highly ethical and professional service to both applicants and employers. AAA offices do not limit themselves to specialized areas of employment. Full service is available—executive to domestic placement—both temporary and permanent employment. The low-discount placement fee of only 3 weeks' salary has proven to be in great demand for the past 33 years. Coast-to-coast, border-to-border territories available on a first-to-qualify basis.

NUMBER OF FRANCHISEES: 40 in 19 states plus 85 company-owned offices in 4 states

IN BUSINESS SINCE: AAA Employment, Inc.—1957; AAA Employment Franchise, Inc.—1977

EQUITY CAPITAL NEEDED: Down payment depends on size of territory selected (minimum $4,000, maximum $15,000) and approximately $4,000 (includes office space, furnishings, office supplies, and licensing).

FINANCIAL ASSISTANCE AVAILABLE: Once down payment is made, the balance of the fee is paid $50 per week until paid off.

TRAINING PROVIDED: The franchisor's staff will provide the franchisee with an intensive 2-week training program at the corporate headquarters in St. Petersburg, Florida. Additional on-the-job training will be conducted in the field for the franchisee and employees. A representative from the home office will spend the first week of operation in the franchisee's office to offer assistance. Seminars are held semiannually to keep franchisees updated on new ideas and techniques.

MANAGERIAL ASSISTANCE AVAILABLE: The staff of the franchisor will provide the franchisee with continual support and assistance. Some of the services provided by the franchisor are (1) aid in selecting a prime location, (2) aid in negotiating a lease, (3) providing information and research requirements for city, county, and state licenses, (4) selection of office furniture and supplies, (5) establishing an advertising schedule, (6) establishing a budget schedule, (7) hiring and training employees, and (8) record keeping. In addition to the continual communication between the franchisee and franchisor by phone, and the continued furnishing of information through the mail, visits will be made periodically in the field by a representative of the corporation. The franchisee will also be provided with a detailed operations manual as well as other reference guides. Every effort will be made by AAA Employment Franchise, Inc.

INFORMATION SUBMITTED: April 1990

BAILEY EMPLOYMENT SYSTEM, INC.
51 Shelton Road
Monroe, Connecticut 06468
Sheldon Leighton, President

DESCRIPTION OF OPERATION: Profitable, nationally scoped, placement techniques augmented with a centralized, electronically computerized, data retrieval system. Centrally filed applicants and centrally filed job specifications, registered by individual Bailey Employment System offices, allow all franchisees a constant pool of qualified applicants and employers with which to work at all times. Bailey offers extensive training in the use of the intelligent computer Bailey provides to each franchisee. This computer permits instant retrieval of valuable candidate and/or company data in order for Bailey offices to hold a competitive advantage.

NUMBER OF FRANCHISEES: 15 in 3 states

IN BUSINESS SINCE: 1960

EQUITY CAPITAL NEEDED: $40,000

FINANCIAL ASSISTANCE AVAILABLE: If desired, purchase price may be financed at going bank rates.

TRAINING PROVIDED: Complete training in the profitable operation of a Bailey Employment Service office is given to each franchise operator before a new office is opened for business. Our training courses may be attended again and again by the franchise operator and his or her staff at their convenience. Additional training in advanced techniques of professional placement is offered 52 weeks a year. All such additional training is free of charge to all franchise operators and personnel. Conventions are offered at least 4 times a year to ensure continued interoffice cooperation, camaraderie, and profits.

MANAGERIAL ASSISTANCE AVAILABLE: Every conceivable service to ensure the owner a profitable return on his or her investment is offered.

INFORMATION SUBMITTED: April 1990

* DUNHILL PERSONNEL SYSTEM, INC.
1000 Woodbury Road
Woodbury, New York 11797

DESCRIPTION OF OPERATION: Dunhill Personnel System is an international company offering 3 different franchises in personnel services. The Full Service franchise is recruitment and search, for management and professional personnel on a national level, the Office Personnel franchise specializes in the high-demand area of executive and legal secretaries, word processing operators, and other office personnel job classifications; and the Temporary Service franchise contracts out office and light industrial staff for both short- and long-term assignments.

NUMBER OF FRANCHISEES: 268

IN BUSINESS SINCE: 1952

EQUITY CAPITAL NEEDED: The Full Service franchise requires minimum capital of $50,000, exclusive of personal needs. The Office Personnel combines O/P with the Temporary Service franchise, depending on the size or scope of the operation, requires $53,000 to $116,000. These amounts include the down payment of the franchise fee.

FINANCIAL ASSISTANCE AVAILABLE: Dunhill System will finance up to 60 percent of the franchise fee over a 4-year period, commencing 10 months after opening at 8 percent interest.

TRAINING PROVIDED: Dunhill Personnel System provides intensive, continuous, and updated training. The initial training provides 2 weeks of hands-on training in New York covering the search and placement cycle and the managerial aspects of the business. Extensive follow-up training is continuously provided on a regional and national basis. Motivational training and special industry training in the form of workshops and seminars are provided for franchisees and their consultants.

MANAGERIAL ASSISTANCE AVAILABLE: Follow-up support is provided through our qualified field representatives, both in the franchisee's office and through constant telephone contact. Audiovisual programs and resource material for in-house training are also available.

INFORMATION SUBMITTED: May 1990

* MANAGEMENT RECRUITERS INTERNATIONAL, INC.
1127 Euclid Avenue, Suite 1400
Cleveland, Ohio 44115-1638
Alan R. Schonberg, President

DESCRIPTION OF OPERATION: Search and recruiting service business under the names of Management Recruiters, Sales Consultants, OfficeMates/5, and CompuSearch. Also refer to the listing under Sales Consultants International.

NUMBER OF FRANCHISEES: 583 offices (including company-owned offices) in 45 states, the District of Columbia, and Puerto Rico

IN BUSINESS SINCE: 1957

EQUITY CAPITAL NEEDED: Minimum $35,500 to $62,400 depending on location.

FINANCIAL ASSISTANCE AVAILABLE: None.

TRAINING PROVIDED: The franchisor's staff will provide the licensee with an intensive initial training program of approximately 3 weeks conducted at the franchisor's corporate headquarters in Cleveland, Ohio, plus an initial on-the-job training program of approximately 3 additional weeks conducted in the licensee's first office. In addition to the above, the franchisor's staff will assist and advise the licensee in (1) securing suitable office space and the negotiation of the lease for same, (2) the design and layout of the office, (3) the selection of office furniture and equipment and the negotiation of the purchase or lease agreement for same, and (4) the establishment of a suitable telephone system for the licensee's office.

MANAGERIAL ASSISTANCE AVAILABLE: The licensee is provided with a detailed operations manual containing information, procedures and know-how for operating the business, account executive, accounting and administrative assistant's manuals. In addition, the licensee receives a VCR/color TV set plus franchisor's complete video training film series (21 cassettes), and a 90-day supply of all necessary operating forms, brochures, etc. The franchisor will furnish the licensee with continuing advice, guidance, and assistance through national and regional meetings, seminars, correspondence, video training films, and telephone and personal instruction with respect to the licensee's personnel placement service operations and procedures and their improvement and revision.

INFORMATION SUBMITTED: April 1990

* NORRELL TEMPORARY SERVICES, INC.
3535 Piedmont Road, N.E.
Atlanta, Georgia 30305
Stan Anderson, Regional Vice President of Franchise Sales

DESCRIPTION OF OPERATION: Temporary help industry catering to all segments of business. Vertical marketing programs designed for the banking, insurance, financial services, and office automation industries. Unique facilities staffing concept to address clients' changing personnel needs. Uses a consultive approach to the temporary help industry.

NUMBER OF FRANCHISEES: 141 in 40 states plus 189 units company-owned

IN BUSINESS SINCE: 1963

EQUITY CAPITAL NEEDED: $50,000–$80,000, no up-front franchise fee.

FINANCIAL ASSISTANCE AVAILABLE: Payroll financing and amounts receivable financing.

TRAINING PROVIDED: Initially, both field training and 5-day classroom courses are provided. Continuing classroom training and seminars in the franchisee's area are provided quarterly. Cassette tapes, manuals, and other written programs are available for each individual franchise office.

MANAGERIAL ASSISTANCE AVAILABLE: Field-dedicated regional managers and district managers assist in making sales calls with the franchisee, teaching proper pricing, assisting in recruiting, etc. Norrell supplies computer payrolling, customer billings, operations manuals, forms, brochures, national advertising, and direct mail promotion.

INFORMATION SUBMITTED: April 1990

THE OLSTEN CORPORATION
1 Merrick Avenue
Westbury, L.I., New York 11590
Robert J. Lemenze, Assistant Vice President

DESCRIPTION OF OPERATION: A national public company operating branch, franchise, and licensed offices. Provides temporary office and industrial personnel for as long as needed by businesses, government, industry, and institutions.

NUMBER OF FRANCHISEES: 105 franchise offices and 90 licensed offices

IN BUSINESS SINCE: 1950

EQUITY CAPITAL NEEDED: $40,000 minimum, includes working capital required to cover start-up costs and general operating expenses plus living expenses. No up-front money.

FINANCIAL ASSISTANCE AVAILABLE: Temporary payroll funded by The Olsten Corporation.

TRAINING PROVIDED: Comprehensive on-the-job training and field training as well as periodic visits covering every phase of business operations.

MANAGERIAL ASSISTANCE AVAILABLE: Full operating manuals, forms, printed sales material, and basic supplies provided at no charge. In addition, provides continuous, ongoing assistance in all facets of the business including technical assistance, insurance, marketing, sales, advertising, and other areas of temporary help. National sales leads also supplied whenever possible.

INFORMATION SUBMITTED: April 1990

* PERSONNEL POOL OF AMERICA, INC.
Personnel Pool Division
2050 Spectrum Boulevard
Fort Lauderdale, Florida 33309
John J. Marquez, Director, Market Development

DESCRIPTION OF OPERATION: International firm providing temporary help services to commercial, industrial, and governmental clients. Personnel services include clerical, word/data processing, marketing, telemarketing, paralegal, paratechnical, light industrial, and industrial work skills. Franchise opportunities available nationwide.

NUMBER OF FRANCHISEES: 156 franchisees, 80 company-owned

IN BUSINESS SINCE: 1946

EQUITY CAPITAL NEEDED: $50,000–$65,000 including working capital to cover start-up costs and general operating expenses, plus living expenses.

FINANCIAL ASSISTANCE AVAILABLE: Temporary employee payroll, taxes, and insurance funded by Personnel Pool.

TRAINING PROVIDED: 2 weeks at company's corporate service center in Ft. Lauderdale; includes owner/management training in financial, back office, and sales/marketing, plus 2 weeks on-the-job training at franchisee's office. Owner and staff training ongoing via seminars, regional training, teletraining, video and audio training programs.

MANAGERIAL ASSISTANCE AVAILABLE: Dedicated franchise operations director assists and consults owner on all facets of operating the business including sales, advertising, insurance, legal, risk management, market development, data processing, finance, national accounts, and recruitment.

INFORMATION SUBMITTED: May 1990

WESTERN TEMPORARY SERVICES, INC.
301 Lennon Lane
P. O. Box 9280
Walnut Creek, California 94598
A. Terry Slocum, Vice President, Corporate Development

DESCRIPTION OF OPERATION: Western operates over 350 offices in the United States and overseas, both company-owned and franchised. We provide a full line of temporary personnel services, including clerical office support, industrial, marketing, technical, medical/dental, pharmacy, and Santa/Photo.

NUMBER OF FRANCHISEES: 110 in 31 states

IN BUSINESS SINCE: 1948

EQUITY CAPITAL NEEDED: Initial franchise fee based on population, ranging from $10,000 to $25,000 for most cities, plus sufficient working capital to cover initial operating and living expenses.

FINANCIAL ASSISTANCE AVAILABLE: Western finances the temporary payroll and accounts receivable completely. Western also provides a special start-up incentive for the franchised operation for the first 6 months and offers additional incentives for volume thereafter.

TRAINING PROVIDED: Western provides initial training in 3 phases: (1) 1 week of operational and sales classroom training at corporate headquarters; (2) 2–3 days sueprvised hands-on experience in an operating field office; and (3) 2 days on-site training and orientation after the new franchise office has opened. Ongoing training through annual workshops is also made available.

MANAGERIAL ASSISTANCE AVAILABLE: Western supplies complete operating manuals to all franchisees and provides an experienced manager for on-site sales and operational assistance during training. In addition, franchisees receive ongoing management and technical assistance, which includes field meetings, publications, training tapes, sales bulletins, sales leads and referrals, public relations and direct mail assistance, promotional events, accounting support, credit and collection assistance, and national advertising. Western's corporate staff is always available for advice and consultation.

INFORMATION SUBMITTED: April 1990

EQUIPMENT/RENTALS

NATION-WIDE GENERAL RENTAL CENTERS, INC.
1684 Highway 92 West, Suite A
Woodstock, Georgia 30188
I. N. Goodvin, President

DESCRIPTION OF OPERATION: Nation-Wide General Rental Center operates a full-line consumer-oriented rental center including items for the contractor and do-it-yourself homeowner—items such as baby equipment, camping supplies, contractors equipment and tools, concrete tools, carpenters tools, invalid needs, lawn and yard tools, mechanics' tools, painters' equipment, moving needs, party and banquet needs, plumbers' tools, sanding machines, trailer hitches, household equipment, and local trucks and trailers. Building required is 1,800 to 3,000 square feet with outside fenced storage area, good traffic flow, and parking for 6 to 10 cars.

NUMBER OF FRANCHISEES: 196 in 38 states

IN BUSINESS SINCE: 1976

EQUITY CAPITAL NEEDED: $25,000 plus $7,500–$10,000 working capital. No franchise fees.

FINANCIAL ASSISTANCE AVAILABLE: With the down payment of $25,000, franchisee will get $98,500 worth of equipment and opening supplies. The balance can be financed over 5 years with local banks—company assistance to qualified applicants. No franchise or royalty fees; down payment goes toward equipment cost. All risk liability, conversion, group health, accident, and life insurance coverage available to franchisee. We also have a buy-back agreement and exclusive area agreement.

TRAINING PROVIDED: On-the-job training for 5 full days at no charge to the franchisee. Training covers everything you need from familiarization with and maintenance of equipment, accounting computerized system, advertising and promotion, purchasing add-on equipment, rental rates, insurance, inventory control, and operations manual covering much more.

MANAGERIAL ASSISTANCE AVAILABLE: Consultation on location and market feasibility studies; assistance in securing and negotiation building lease; a monthly computerized financial report giving balance sheet/income statement, and a list of all equipment in inventory with a month rental income per item. A rate guide book giving rental rates for each item and for your area. 100 percent financing for growth inventory or new equipment. Franchisees can buy all their equipment at 3 to 10 percent over cost, which offers great purchasing power and discounts to each store owner. Buy-back agreement gives you full credit on equipment. At the grand opening we will be there to help establish the franchisee in the community. We also mail 9,000 promotions to every home around a new center at grand opening time.

INFORMATION SUBMITTED: April 1990

PCR PERSONAL COMPUTER RENTALS
2557 Route 130
Cranbury, New Jersey 08512
Dan Bayha or Joe Laudisdo, Vice President, Franchise Development

DESCRIPTION OF OPERATION: Business-oriented rental center operated from office space. Each outlet provides short-term microcomputers and peripherals to all segments of the business community. Owners stress value-added customer service and cater to the needs of the client including free delivery, installation and maintenance, extensive training, and personal support.

NUMBER OF FRANCHISEES: 49 in 8 states plus 1 company-owned unit

IN BUSINESS SINCE: 1983

EQUITY CAPITAL NEEDED: $40,000–$50,000

FINANCIAL ASSISTANCE AVAILABLE: None.

TRAINING PROVIDED: Minimum 2-week comprehensive training for owner-operator and assistant manager. Additional week available (optional) to strengthen hardware, software knowledge.

MANAGERIAL ASSISTANCE AVAILABLE: After initial training, ongoing support and training are provided for the term of the franchise agreement. Complete manuals, forms, and instructions are furnished. In addition, franchisees will be informed of new products with evaluations, price changes, and improved software and hardware to market. A continuous research and development program will thoroughly test and evaluate products before they are recommended. Ongoing advertising will serve to create awareness of franchise and develop preference level.

INFORMATION SUBMITTED: April 1990

FOOD—DONUTS

DIXIE CREAM FLOUR COMPANY
P. O. Box 180
St. Louis, Missouri 63166
Attention: Franchise Director

DESCRIPTION OF OPERATION: Franchised privately owned doughnut and coffee shops, with both walk-in and drive-through stores. Retail and wholesale selling of over 50 varieties of freshmade yeast raised and cake doughnuts, as well as coffee and other beverages.

NUMBER OF FRANCHISEES: 42 in 11 states

IN BUSINESS SINCE: 1929

EQUITY CAPITAL NEEDED: Franchise and training fee $5,000. No overrides, royalties, or percentages. Equipment cost $15,000 to $40,000.

FINANCIAL ASSISTANCE AVAILABLE: None.

TRAINING PROVIDED: As part of the franchise fee, we have an extensive hands-on, in-shop training program of approximately 2 weeks' duration. Our company technicians work with you in your shop during this period. A comprehensive training manual is provided for production assistance. Additionally, information concerning new products as well as pertinent new ideas in helping your doughnut shop operate as efficiently as possible are available from our St. Louis office.

MANAGERIAL ASSISTANCE AVAILABLE: Continuous communication by correspondence, direct toll-free phone, and in-store visits by qualified home office personnel. There is also a procedures manual provided for everyday use in your doughnut shop. This manual, along with our technical assistance, will help each franchise attain its ultimate goal of profit and success.

INFORMATION SUBMITTED: May 1990

* DUNKIN' DONUTS OF AMERICA, INC.
P. O. Box 317
Randolph, Massachusetts 02368
Lawrence W. Hantman, Senior Vice President

DESCRIPTION OF OPERATION: Franchised and company-owned coffee and doughnut shops with drive-through and walk-in units. Sales of over 52 varieties of doughnuts, munchkin doughnuthole treats, muffins, cookies, brownies, and related bakery items, at retail, along with soup, coffee, and other beverages. Franchises are sold for individual shops and, in selected markets, multiple license agreements may be available. Franchisor encourages development of real estate and building by the franchisee, subject to approval of Dunkin' Donuts of America, Inc. Franchisor also develops locations for franchising and for company supervisions.

NUMBER OF FRANCHISEES: 1,714 units in 39 states, Canada, Japan, the Philippines, Thailand, Bahamas, Korea, Singapore, Colombia, Venezuela, Chile, Brazil, Indonesia, Saudi Arabia, and Taiwan

IN BUSINESS SINCE: 1950

EQUITY CAPITAL NEEDED: Franchise fee, $27,000–$40,000, depending on geographical area and whether franchisee owns or controls the real estate. Working capital, approximately $18,000.

FINANCIAL ASSISTANCE AVAILABLE: Financing assistance for real estate acquisition and development. Equipment and sign financing assistance is available to qualified franchisees.

TRAINING PROVIDED: 6-week training course for franchisees at Dunkin' Donuts University in Braintree, Massachusetts, consisting of production and shop management training. Initial training of doughnut-makers and managers for franchises and retraining are carried out at Dunkin' Donuts University without additional charge.

MANAGERIAL ASSISTANCE AVAILABLE: Continuous managerial assistance is available from the district sales manager assigned to the individual shop. The company maintains quality assurance, research and development, and new products programs. The franchisee-funded marketing department provides marketing programs for all shops. The marketing programs are administered by a field marketing manager who develops plans on a market basis.

INFORMATION SUBMITTED: June 1990

* MISTER DONUT OF AMERICA, INC.
P. O. Box 317
Randolph, Massachusetts 02308
Ralph Gabellieri, President

DESCRIPTION OF OPERATION: Franchised doughnut and coffee shops—drive-in and walk-in units. Retail selling of more than 55 varieties of doughnuts, baked goods, and nonalcoholic beverages, primarily coffee. Located on well-traveled streets, near schools, churches, shopping centers, amusements, and entertainment. Each shop produces its own doughnuts in its own kitchen.

NUMBER OF FRANCHISEES: Over 500 in United States and 2 countries

IN BUSINESS SINCE: 1955

EQUITY CAPITAL NEEDED: Franchise fee $25,000. Cost of real estate and building are responsibility of franchisee, but location is subject to Mister Donut's approval.

FINANCIAL ASSISTANCE AVAILABLE: None.

TRAINING PROVIDED: Continuous professional 4-week training program, consisting of practical as well as classroom training at company school in St. Paul, Minnesota.

MANAGERIAL ASSISTANCE AVAILABLE: An area representative is permanently located at company expense in each area of the United States and Canada for managerial assistance to franchise operators. The company maintains a quality-control service as well as a research and development department, marketing and advertising services to assist franchise owners. Location analysis, lease negotiation, and assistance with building design and construction are also provided by Mister Donut personnel.

INFORMATION SUBMITTED: June 1990

* WINCHELL'S DONUT HOUSE
16424 Valley View Avenue
La Mirada, California 90637
Chuck Tortorice

DESCRIPTION OF OPERATION: Winchell's is an established and highly recognized retail doughnut shop chain that offers a large variety of doughnuts, brownies, croissants, muffins, cookies, and related bakery items, as well as coffee and other beverages. Retail units are normally freestanding or strip shopping center, walk-in and drive-through locations.

NUMBER OF FRANCHISEES: 617 company-owned and 84 franchised locations in 13 Western states. Also, 34 locations in Japan, Korea, Philippines, and Guam.

IN BUSINESS SINCE: 1948

EQUITY CAPITAL NEEDED: $55,000 minimum with the ability to secure financing for the remaining portion of investment. (Initial franchise fee $25,000–$30,000.)

FINANCIAL ASSISTANCE AVAILABLE: Franchisees to arrange own financing. Winchell's provides a list of approved lenders.

TRAINING PROVIDED: A comprehensive 6-week franchisee training course where you'll receive extensive instruction in areas from the production of doughnuts to retail sales management, as well as personal development and communication. Additional training and supervision by a qualified company representative for approximately 7 days during store opening.

MANAGERIAL ASSISTANCE AVAILABLE: Franchisee will receive operations support through effective operating methods, systems, and procedures that begins at the grand opening and continues with periodic store visits throughout the term of the franchise. Also marketing support, developed by qualified professionals, through high-impact advertising materials and promotions, and Winchell's television and radio advertising, as well as research and development of new products and sales building promotions.

INFORMATION SUBMITTED: June 1990

FOOD—GROCERY/SPECIALTY STORES

CHEESECAKE, ETC.
400 Swallow Drive
Miami Springs, Florida 33166
Bill Wolar, Jr., Vice President, Franchise Director

DESCRIPTION OF OPERATION: Cheesecake, Etc., offers franchise owners a sound profit potential in the ever-increasing specialty dessert industry. Each unit is beautifully decorated for eat-in or take-home retail business. The wholesale market allows for outstanding long-term growth. All varieties and flavors of cheesecake, gourmet chocolates, and many other specialty desserts. A simple "pour and bake" system; other desserts supplied ready-to-serve.

NUMBER OF FRANCHISEES: 4 in 3 states

IN BUSINESS SINCE: 1974

EQUITY CAPITAL NEEDED: None

TRAINING PROVIDED: 7 days at home office and on-site support for opening. Extensive operations manual from baking to customer relations to wholesale selling.

MANAGERIAL ASSISTANCE AVAILABLE: Assistance with site selection, design of unit, lease negotiations, advertising materials, and continual home office support.

INFORMATION SUBMITTED: May 1990

* DAIRY MART CONVENIENCE STORES, INC.
240 South Road
Enfield, Connecticut 06082
Leonard F. Crogan, Vice President

DESCRIPTION OF OPERATION: Dairy Mart Convenience Stores, Inc., operates retail convenience stores in southern New England and the Midwest. Dairy Mart/Lawson stores are open 7 days a week from 18 to 24 hours per day, depending on location. Stores average approximately 1,800 to 2,000 square feet in size. Dairy Mart/Lawson typically provides the physical location and all equipment necessary to operate a convenience store.

NUMBER OF FRANCHISEES: 167 in 6 states

IN BUSINESS SINCE: 1957

EQUITY CAPITAL NEEDED: Minimum of $15,000

FINANCIAL ASSISTANCE AVAILABLE: No direct financial assistance is provided by franchisor. However, franchisor will make banking contract and assist franchisee in obtaining bank financing.

TRAINING PROVIDED: Typically, a 2-week training period is provided, primarily at the store location.

MANAGERIAL ASSISTANCE AVAILABLE: After the initial training period, regular store visits are made by Dairy Mart area supervisors. Dairy Mart also sponsors periodic meetings covering various aspects of store management including personnel, merchandising, and theft prevention.

INFORMATION SUBMITTED: June 1990

DIAL-A-GIFT, INC.
2265 East 4800 South
Salt Lake City, Utah 84117
Clarence L. Jolley, President

DESCRIPTION OF OPERATION: National gift wire service (like florists). National delivery of fancy gift baskets—fresh fruit, gourmet foods, cheeses, wines and champagne, decorated cakes, bouquets of balloons, steaks, smoked ham, turkey, and salmon.

NUMBER OF FRANCHISEES: 115 in 28 states

IN BUSINESS SINCE: 1980

EQUITY CAPITAL NEEDED: $15,000

FINANCIAL ASSISTANCE AVAILABLE: None.

TRAINING PROVIDED: Intensive 3-day training at home office.

MANAGERIAL ASSISTANCE AVAILABLE: Perpetual assistance.

INFORMATION SUBMITTED: June 1990

LAURA CORPORATION
dba FRONTIER FRUIT & NUT COMPANY
3823 Wadsworth Road
Norton, Ohio 44203
Alex E. Marksz, Vice President

DESCRIPTION OF OPERATION: The Frontier Fruit & Nut Company offers a unique retail store operation in regional malls featuring the retail sales of bulk dried fruits, nuts, candies, and gifts.

NUMBER OF FRANCHISEES: 6 franchisees, 58 locations in 6 states and Canada

IN BUSINESS SINCE: 1977

EQUITY CAPITAL NEEDED: $25,000 minimum

FINANCIAL ASSISTANCE AVAILABLE: None.

TRAINING PROVIDED: On-site training by full-time Frontier Fruit & Nut employee at time of opening.

MANAGERIAL ASSISTANCE AVAILABLE: Frontier provides continual assistance for the life of the franchise in such areas as bookkeeping, advertising, and inventory control. Complete manual of operations, product knowledge, forms, and directions are provided.

INFORMATION SUBMITTED: April 1990

JAKE'S TAKE N' BAKE PIZZA, INC.
620 High Street
San Luis Obispo, California 93401
Willis Reeser, President

DESCRIPTION OF OPERATION: The selling of unbaked pizzas, salads, cookie dough, soft drinks, and ice cream novelties.

NUMBER OF FRANCHISEES: 17

IN BUSINESS SINCE: 1984, first franchisee 1986

EQUITY CAPITAL NEEDED: Approximately $35,000–$45,000

FINANCIAL ASSISTANCE AVAILABLE: None.

TRAINING PROVIDED: 2 weeks of comprehensive training in all aspects of operation provided to 1 management person per store to be opened.

MANAGERIAL ASSISTANCE AVAILABLE: Site selection, equipment lists, preliminary drawings on store, inventory lists and specifications, opening procedures manual, 5-day in-store training when new location opens, operations manual, ongoing supervision for the operation of the business.

INFORMATION SUBMITTED: April 1990

* KID'S KORNER FRESH PIZZA, INC.
P. O. Box 9288
Waukegan, Illinois 60079-9288
Kathleen Gulko, Vice President

DESCRIPTION OF OPERATION: Custom-made pizza you take home to bake.

NUMBER OF FRANCHISEES: 30 in Wisconsin, Minnesota, Illinois, Georgia, and Louisiana

IN BUSINESS SINCE: 1977

EQUITY CAPITAL NEEDED: Approximately $30,000 to $40,000 including franchise fee, equipment, and inventory.

FINANCIAL ASSISTANCE AVAILABLE: None—company can assist in preparing financial presentation for use with lenders.

TRAINING PROVIDED: On-site training at home office and outlet site. Help with site selection, equipment selection, and decor and layout.

MANAGERIAL ASSISTANCE AVAILABLE: Help with advertising, promotion, seminars, bookkeeping, and product research.

INFORMATION SUBMITTED: April 1990

LI'L PEACH CONVENIENCE FOOD STORES
101 Billerica Avenue
North Billerica, Massachusetts 01862
Francis X. Kearns, President

DESCRIPTION OF OPERATION: Li'l Peach offers fully equipped and stocked convenience food stores averaging approximately 1,800 to 2,400 square feet. All stores are open 7 days a week, most from 7:00 A.M. until midnight.

NUMBER OF FRANCHISEES: 42 plus 2 company-owned in Massachusetts

IN BUSINESS SINCE: 1972

EQUITY CAPITAL NEEDED: Minimum of $8,000

FINANCIAL ASSISTANCE AVAILABLE: Financial assistance is available toward purchase of the store inventory. The franchisor does not extend financial assistance in regard to the initial investment.

TRAINING PROVIDED: In-store training totaling 3 weeks in one of our special training stores and in the new franchisee's own store.

MANAGERIAL ASSISTANCE AVAILABLE: Continual management service in such areas as accounting, payroll preparation, loss prevention. All manuals and forms are provided. Li'l Peach works closely with its franchisees through regularly scheduled visits by field representatives.

INFORMATION SUBMITTED: June 1990

T F M CO.
dba OKY DOKY FOOD MARTS
1250 Iowa Street—P. O. Box 300
Dubuque, Iowa 52001
John F. Thompson, President

DESCRIPTION OF OPERATION: Stores average from 1,200 square feet to 4,000 square feet—convenient parking required—open daily 7 A.M. to 11 P.M.—inventory selected for maximum turnover—equipment and building may be leased. Regional franchises now available to qualified individuals. Renovating gas stations or other existing good locations our specialty. No franchise fees charged on gas.

NUMBER OF FRANCHISEES: 21 in Iowa, Wisconsin, and Illinois. Company operations presently centered in the tristate region of Iowa, Illinois, and Wisconsin. However, other regional franchises are available.

IN BUSINESS SINCE: 1947

EQUITY CAPITAL NEEDED: Minimum $15,000 plus $25,000.

FINANCIAL ASSISTANCE AVAILABLE: None.

TRAINING PROVIDED: On-job training at home office or on site is required before franchisee is considered. This is at no expense to franchisee.

MANAGERIAL ASSISTANCE AVAILABLE: Expertise always available at home office upon request.

INFORMATION SUBMITTED: April 1990

PAPA ALDO'S INTERNATIONAL, INC.
9600 S.W. Capital Highway
Portland, Oregon 97219
John A. Gundle, President

DESCRIPTION OF OPERATION: Take-out pizza. Fresh unbaked pizza to be baked at home.

NUMBER OF FRANCHISEES: 85 in 6 states

IN BUSINESS SINCE: 1981

EQUITY CAPITAL NEEDED: $15,000–$25,000

FINANCIAL ASSISTANCE AVAILABLE: None.

TRAINING PROVIDED: 2 weeks total—1 week at corporate company store, 1 week in franchisee's store.

MANAGERIAL ASSISTANCE AVAILABLE: Ongoing field support.

INFORMATION SUBMITTED: June 1990

TOM'S FOODS INC.
900 Eighth Street
P. O. Box 60
Columbus, Georgia 31994
Al Davis, Vice President, Distributor Development
Charles Gosa, Director, Distributor Franchise Development

DESCRIPTION OF OPERATION: Route distribution of snack food products through national accounts, independent accounts, and vending accounts.

NUMBER OF FRANCHISEES: 330 in 46 states

IN BUSINESS SINCE: 1925

EQUITY CAPITAL NEEDED: $7,500–$100,000

FINANCIAL ASSISTANCE AVAILABLE: Assistance in financing through outside financial institutions.

TRAINING PROVIDED: On-the-job training plus classroom training provided, accounting procedures, merchandising, and marketing training.

MANAGERIAL ASSISTANCE AVAILABLE: Home office, field sales organization, advertising materials, and promotions.

INFORMATION SUBMITTED: April 1990

* WHITE HEN PANTRY, INC.
660 Industrial Drive
Elmhurst, Illinois 60126
James O. Williams

DESCRIPTION OF OPERATION: A White Hen Pantry is a convenience food store of approximately 2,500 square feet. There is generally up-front parking for 10 to 15 cars. Stores are usually open 24 hours (some operate a lesser number of hours) 365 days a year. Product line includes a service deli, fresh bakery, fresh produce, and a wide variety of the most popular staples. White Hen Pantry stores are franchised to local residents who become owner/operators of this "family business."

NUMBER OF FRANCHISEES: 365 in Illinois, Wisconsin, Indiana, Massachusetts, and New Hampshire

IN BUSINESS SINCE: 1965

EQUITY CAPITAL NEEDED: $20,000–$25,000 (varies by location)

FINANCIAL ASSISTANCE AVAILABLE: Total investment averages $41,300 to $48,000. Investment includes approximately $24,000 merchandise, $5,000 security deposit, $3,000 supplies, $200 cash register fund, and $10,000 training and processing fee. A minimum investment of $20,000 is required. Financial assistance available.

TRAINING PROVIDED: Classroom and in-store training precede store opening. Follow-up training provided after taking over store. Detailed operation manuals are provided.

MANAGERIAL ASSISTANCE AVAILABLE: This is a highly organized and comprehensive program. Other services provided include merchandising, accounting, promotions, advertising, and business insurance. (Group health and plate-glass insurance are optional.) Store counselor visits are regular and frequent.

INFORMATION SUBMITTED: June 1990

FOODS—ICE CREAM/YOGURT/CANDY/POPCORN/BEVERAGES

* BASKIN-ROBBINS, INCORPORATED
31 Baskin-Robbins Place
Glendale, California 91201
Jim Earnhardt, President, B-R USA, CO.

DESCRIPTION OF OPERATION: High-quality, multiflavored, hand-dipped retail ice cream store. Franchisor normally selects site and negotiates a lease; the store is completely equipped, stocked, and brought to a point where it is ready to open. The complete store is then sold to a qualified individual under a franchise after intensive training.

NUMBER OF FRANCHISEES: Over 3,000 stores in 895 cities throughout the United States, Canada, Japan, and Europe

IN BUSINESS SINCE: 1945

EQUITY CAPITAL NEEDED: Approximately $50,000 plus, depending on retail location.

FINANCIAL ASSISTANCE AVAILABLE: Yes.

TRAINING PROVIDED: A complete training program is provided plus on-the-job training in operating store under the guidance of experienced supervisors.

MANAGERIAL ASSISTANCE AVAILABLE: Continuous merchandising program, accounting procedures, business counsel, and insurance program (source optional).

INFORMATION SUBMITTED: April 1990

* BRESLER'S INDUSTRIES, INC.
999 East Touhy Avenue, Suite 333
Des Plaines, Illinois 60018
Howard Marks, Director of Franchise Development

DESCRIPTION OF OPERATION: Multiflavor specialty ice cream and yogurt shops—featuring ice cream cones, hand-packed ice cream, soft-serve yogurt, complete soda fountain, and made-to-order ice cream specialty items.

NUMBER OF FRANCHISEES: Approximately 300 in 30 states

IN BUSINESS SINCE: 1962

EQUITY CAPITAL NEEDED: Approximately $40,000

FINANCIAL ASSISTANCE AVAILABLE: At present, total investment of approximately $90,000 to $105,000 required plus working capital. Franchisee may obtain own financing, or at his request franchisor will attempt to obtain third-party financing for qualified applicant.

TRAINING PROVIDED: Classroom and in-store training lasting at least 3 weeks.

MANAGERIAL ASSISTANCE AVAILABLE: Franchisor assists franchisee in all aspects of shop operation, record keeping, advertising, and promotion and selling techniques. Manuals of operations and counseling are provided. Area licensees and home office field personnel are available to visit stores regularly.

INFORMATION SUBMITTED: May 1990

* GELATO CLASSICO FRANCHISING, INC.
369 Pine Street, Suite 900
San Francisco, California 94104
Janet Willis, Director of Franchising

DESCRIPTION OF OPERATION: Gelato Classico Italian ice cream manufactures a complete line of Italian ice cream, sorbetto, and yogurt, and supplies these products to its franchisees who retail to the public. Franchisees are part of a nationwide program for franchised shops.

NUMBER OF FRANCHISEES: 43 franchise locations plus 2 company-owned stores in 11 states

IN BUSINESS SINCE: 1976

EQUITY CAPITAL NEEDED: $50,000 per shop

FINANCIAL ASSISTANCE AVAILABLE: No financial assistance provided by franchisor.

TRAINING PROVIDED: Intensive 2-week program prior to opening, and additional training in franchisee's shop during first 5 days at opening. Complete operations manual also provided.

MANAGERIAL ASSISTANCE AVAILABLE: In addition to above, franchisor visits periodically to provide in-shop assistance. Other assistance provided on as-needed basis.

INFORMATION SUBMITTED: April 1990

GORIN'S HOMEMADE ICE CREAM AND SANDWICHES
158 Oak Street
Avondale Estates, Georgia 30002
Robert Solomon, President

DESCRIPTION OF OPERATION: Upscale homemade ice cream and sandwich shop featuring gourmet ice cream and a wide selection of grilled deli sandwiches.

NUMBER OF FRANCHISEES: 32 in Georgia, North Carolina, and Alabama

IN BUSINESS SINCE: 1981

EQUITY CAPITAL NEEDED: $35,000–$50,000, total investment of $100,000–$150,000.

FINANCIAL ASSISTANCE AVAILABLE: Lease equipment assistance available.

TRAINING PROVIDED: 3–4 weeks of comprehensive training in all aspects of operation for 3 management personnel per store to be opened.

MANAGERIAL ASSISTANCE AVAILABLE: Site selection, equipment lists, preliminary drawings on store, inventory lists and specifications, ongoing supervision for the operation of the business.

MISTER SOFTEE, INC.
901 East Clements Bridge Road
P. O. Box 313
Runnemede, New Jersey 08078
James F. Conway, Vice President and General Manager

DESCRIPTION OF OPERATION: Retailing soft ice cream products from a mobile unit, a complete dairy bar on wheels. Dealer is given a franchised area to operate. Mister Softee, Inc., maintains a supply department plus a service and parts department. Franchisees are supported with a merchandising, promotional, and advertising program.

NUMBER OF FRANCHISEES: 860 in 20 states

IN BUSINESS SINCE: 1956

EQUITY CAPITAL NEEDED: $22,000

FINANCIAL ASSISTANCE AVAILABLE: Financing can be arranged for qualified individuals.

TRAINING PROVIDED: Franchisee is trained on his mobile unit in his franchised area for 1 week in merchandising, route planning, operation of the mobile unit, sanitation, and maintenance.

MANAGERIAL ASSISTANCE AVAILABLE: Area representative visits franchisee for continuing assistance periodically and suggests improvements when needed. Standard operating procedure manual, service manual, accounting ledgers. Inventory control forms are provided to each franchisee.

INFORMATION SUBMITTED: June 1990

NIBBLE-LO'S
5300 West Atlantic Avenue
Delray Beach, Florida 33484
Michael L. Slope, Director of Franchising

DESCRIPTION OF OPERATION: Nibble-Lo's features a delicious, healthful, fat-free, cholesterol-free frozen dessert that rivals the taste of premium ice cream. Unlike other frozen desserts currently on the market, Nibble-Lo's is made from 98 percent skim milk. The unique traffic pattern, variety of novelty items, and marketing concept creates a year-round business with take-home products accounting for 45 percent of sales since the dessert can be frozen without the threat of freezer burn or loss of taste and texture.

NUMBER OF FRANCHISEES: 5 franchise locations, plus 1 company-owned store

IN BUSINESS SINCE: 1988

EQUITY CAPITAL NEEDED: $35,000–$50,000. Total investment of $110,000–$150,000.

FINANCIAL ASSISTANCE AVAILABLE: Company will assist the franchisee in applying for financing.

TRAINING PROVIDED: Complete, hands-on training is provided for owners and managers for 2 weeks at the corporate office. 1 additional week is spent with franchisee at his store during the first week of operation. Franchisee also receives training guides and manuals for the employees at their store.

MANAGERIAL ASSISTANCE AVAILABLE: Nibble-Lo's provides ongoing management support and technical assistance.

INFORMATION SUBMITTED: April 1990

STEVE'S HOMEMADE ICE CREAM, INC.
200 Bulfinch Drive
Andover, Massachusetts 01820
Michael Newport

DESCRIPTION OF OPERATION: Steve's offers the highest-quality super-premium ice cream in over 50 flavors yet still maintaining the old-fashioned store look.

NUMBER OF FRANCHISEES: 100 franchise-owned stores

IN BUSINESS SINCE: 1974

EQUITY CAPITAL NEEDED: 10 percent of total investment of $75,000.

FINANCIAL ASSISTANCE AVAILABLE: Steve's consults with franchisees regarding financing of project costs by independent financial institutions.

TRAINING PROVIDED: A 1-week training program is provided at a company training store in all phases of store operation.

MANAGERIAL ASSISTANCE AVAILABLE: Ongoing operational assistance will include visits by an operations representative to monitor quality control and store appearance. Complete manuals of operations, advertising, and promotion are provided. Other services include site approval, store design, approved suppliers, cooperative advertising assistance, ongoing proven menu enhancements, and the availability of a unique equipment package.

INFORMATION SUBMITTED: June 1990

WHIRLA WHIP SYSTEMS, INC.
9359 "G" Street
Omaha, Nebraska 68127
Duke Fischer, Director of Marketing

DESCRIPTION OF OPERATION: The custom blending of vanilla and chocolate ice cream or yogurt with the customer's choice of candy bars, fruits, cookies, nuts, or candy. Done in seconds at the point of sale.

NUMBER OF FRANCHISEES: 108 in 17 states and Washington, D.C., Canada, Japan, Australia, Singapore, Korea, Malaysia, Puerto Rico, Venezuela, and all of Europe.

IN BUSINESS SINCE: 1981

EQUITY CAPITAL NEEDED: $13,000–$80,000

FINANCIAL ASSISTANCE AVAILABLE: None.

TRAINING PROVIDED: Initial training 3 days, continued training as needed.

MANAGERIAL ASSISTANCE AVAILABLE: Initial training 3 days, opening assistance as needed, continued assistance as needed.

INFORMATION SUBMITTED: April 1990

FOODS—RESTAURANTS/DRIVE-INS/CARRY-OUT

APPETITO'S, INC.
5517 North 7th Avenue
Phoenix, Arizona 85013
Richard L. Schnakenberg, Chairman and President

DESCRIPTION OF OPERATION: Appetito's, Inc., is a fast service Italian restaurant. The average store size is 1,800 square feet, although restaurant sizes range from 900 square feet to 3,000 square feet and are in-line, in shopping centers, or standalone buildings. The menu consists of hot and cold submarines, pizza by the slice or pie, salads, and hot dinners of spaghetti, lasagna, and ravioli. The company stresses quick service including drive-through, take-out and delivery, cleanliness, and high-quality food products. Total turnkey operation. Selling individual restaurants and multiple unit territory franchises.

NUMBER OF FRANCHISEES: 19 plus 1 company-owned

IN BUSINESS SINCE: 1974

EQUITY CAPITAL NEEDED: $40,000–$50,000

FINANCIAL ASSISTANCE AVAILABLE: Equipment financial package.

TRAINING PROVIDED: Minimum of 160 hours of training at company facility in Phoenix, Arizona, for franchisee's managers and assistant managers.

MANAGERIAL ASSISTANCE AVAILABLE: Operations, training, maintenance, accounting, and financial planning. Company provides grand opening package, multifranchise territory package, central advertising and promotion.

INFORMATION SUBMITTED: June 1990

BARRO'S PIZZA, INC.
401 North LaCadena Drive
Colton, California 92324
Larry R. Polhill, President
John C. Martinez, Vice President/Franchising Director

DESCRIPTION OF OPERATION: Making and selling of pizza, sandwiches, and other complementary items. Beer and wine at our larger eat-in locations.

NUMBER OF FRANCHISEES: 40 in California, Arizona, Colorado, and Illinois

IN BUSINESS SINCE: 1969

EQUITY CAPITAL NEEDED: $25,000

FINANCIAL ASSISTANCE AVAILABLE: Equipment leasing and equipment packages.

TRAINING PROVIDED: 2 weeks to 1 month training.

MANAGERIAL ASSISTANCE AVAILABLE: Owner's manual and on-the-job training. Operation is simplified. Training is required as an on-the-job process.

INFORMATION SUBMITTED: April 1990

BREADEAUX PISA
Frederick Avenue at 23rd Station
P. O. Box 158 Fairleigh Station
St. Joseph, Missouri 64506
Jerry G. Banks, Director of Franchise Development

DESCRIPTION OF OPERATION: High-quality pizza outlet. Operating throughout the Midwest in small to large towns. Extensive menu, Buy one, Get one free pizzas, quality products. Operate in 800-to-1,800-square-foot existing buildings and strip centers.

NUMBER OF FRANCHISEES: 98

IN BUSINESS SINCE: 1985

EQUITY CAPITAL NEEDED: $20,000–$40,000 cash. Total investment range $65,000 to $100,000. Including equipment, remodeling, franchise, and other start-up costs.

FINANCIAL ASSISTANCE AVAILABLE: Possible equipment leasing.

TRAINING PROVIDED: 2 weeks extensive training at headquarters. 1 week on location at opening. Ongoing support, training, and assistance.

MANAGERIAL ASSISTANCE AVAILABLE: Design, site selection, marketing, accounting, services, general management consultation.

INFORMATION SUBMITTED: April 1990

BUBBA'S BREAKAWAY FRANCHISE SYSTEMS, INC.
2738 West College Avenue
State College, Pennsylvania 16801
Joseph I. Shulman, Executive Vice President, Franchise Development

DESCRIPTION OF OPERATION: Bubba's Breakaway offers the franchisee a unique opportunity in the area of home delivery of subs and cheesesteaks. Quality, variety, and free delivery are the fundamentals stressed in each store unit. A complete menu of sandwiches, cheesesteaks, pierogies, tacos, chips, salads, and soups are offered to the public through free home delivery.

NUMBER OF FRANCHISEES: 20 in 6 states plus 4 company-owned

IN BUSINESS SINCE: 1981

EQUITY CAPITAL NEEDED: $28,500 minimum

FINANCIAL ASSISTANCE AVAILABLE: A total investment of approximately $70,000 is necessary to open a Bubba's Breakaway store unit. Bubba's Breakaway Franchise Systems, Inc., provides no direct financing. However, the corporation will assist the franchisee in securing outside financing through the franchisee's own sources or one suggested by the franchise corporation.

TRAINING PROVIDED: Intensive, 21-day, mandatory training course is scheduled for all new franchisees and their personnel. 14 days are conducted at the home office school and at corporately owned stores; 7 days at franchisee's store unit under the supervision of full-time Bubba's Breakaway Franchise Systems, Inc., employees.

MANAGERIAL ASSISTANCE AVAILABLE: Bubba's Breakaway Franchise Systems, Inc., provides continual management service for the life of the franchise in such areas as record keeping, advertising, inventory control, and store operations. A complete manual of operations, forms, directions, and advertising is provided. District operations managers are available in all regions to work closely with franchisees and visit stores regularly to assist in solving problems. Bubba's Breakaway sponsors a franchise advisory council and conducts marketing and product research to maintain high Bubba's Breakaway consumer acceptance.

INFORMATION SUBMITTED: June 1990

CAJUN JOE'S
325 Bic Drive
Milford, Connecticut 06460
Donald G. Fertman, Franchise Director

DESCRIPTION OF OPERATION: Premium fried or roasted chicken available with "Hot" or "Mild" seasoning. Cajun-style side orders include beer-batter onion rings, chicken gumbo, fried okra, corn on the cob, and fresh-baked buttermilk biscuits and corn muffins. Take-out facilities in all units and seating available in many. Simple, low-cost operation.

NUMBER OF FRANCHISEES: 35 in 12 states and Canada

IN BUSINESS SINCE: 1985

EQUITY CAPITAL NEEDED: Approximately $45,000. Total investment: $57,900 to $94,100.

FINANCIAL ASSISTANCE AVAILABLE: Equipment leasing available depending on analysis of financial statements.

TRAINING PROVIDED: Cajun Joe's provides 2 weeks of comprehensive classroom and practical training at Cajun Joe's headquarters for store owners and store managers. The classroom curriculum includes training in location selection, store construction, accounting procedures, management theory as well as instruction in business analysis, product formulas, and control mechanisms specific to Cajun Joe's. In addition to classroom study, practical training is provided in one of the local Cajun Joe's stores to develop skills in sandwich making along with the day-to-day operation and management of a successful Cajun Joe store.

MANAGERIAL ASSISTANCE AVAILABLE: During store construction, which takes between 20 to 60 days, managerial and technical assistance is provided for each franchisee by a development agent and an office coordinator assigned to handle his/her file. Areas covered in this assistance include site selection, store design and layout, interior construction, equipment purchasing, arrangement of suppliers, and initial inventory ordering. When a store is scheduled to open, a development agent is available to help oversee the operation and provide backup support for the store owner in areas of employee training and successful operational procedure. After store opening, periodic inspections and field visits are conducted in each unit by the assigned development agent. Continual office support is made available to each franchisee through frequent contact with one's assigned coordinator. The coordinator development agent system for service provides continual assistance and support for each franchisee through the life of the franchise (20 years). A weekly newsletter comprised of articles written by department heads is sent to all franchisees. With receipt of this newsletter, all franchisees are kept continually apprised of new company policies and developments across the country. Also included in this publication are sections dealing with store management. Ongoing assistance in advertising is provided by the franchise advertising fund, which is directed by a board of directors comprised of 11 store owners elected by the franchisees.

INFORMATION SUBMITTED: April 1990

COZZOLI PIZZA SYSTEMS, INC.
555 N.E. 15th Street, Suite 33-D
Miami, Florida 33132
Merrill I. Lamb, President

DESCRIPTION OF OPERATION: Regional mall in line or food court unit. We now ship a complete equipment package for an individual to go into business anywhere in the world. 750 to 1,200 square feet.

NUMBER OF FRANCHISEES: 51 in 9 states and Guatemala

IN BUSINESS SINCE: 1951

EQUITY CAPITAL NEEDED: $40,000 cash—cost of units $60,000 to $125,000 depending on size.

FINANCIAL ASSISTANCE AVAILABLE: Complete financial assistance above the minimum amount of $40,000.

TRAINING PROVIDED: 2 weeks in existing store and at least 1 week in his/her store under supervision. Training center is in Miami, Florida.

MANAGERIAL ASSISTANCE AVAILABLE: We are available on any problem for as long as he/she wishes.

INFORMATION SUBMITTED: May 1990

* DAIRY ISLE CORPORATION
P. O. Box 273
Utica, Michigan 48087
David K. Chapoton, President
Shirley Chapoton, Corporate Secretary

DESCRIPTION OF OPERATION: Soft ice cream stores and fast-food operation.

NUMBER OF FRANCHISEES: 42 in 7 states

IN BUSINESS SINCE: 1942

EQUITY CAPITAL NEEDED: Minimum $35,000

FINANCIAL ASSISTANCE AVAILABLE: Dairy Isle Corporation does not provide direct financing to franchisees at the present time. However, it does provide assistance in obtaining financing, such as assisting the franchisee in preparing his proposal for bank financing and meeting with potential lenders.

TRAINING PROVIDED: 3 days or more depending on individuals being trained plus calls during the operating season.

MANAGERIAL ASSISTANCE AVAILABLE: Operations of unit and follow-up promotional ideas and equipment purchasing.

INFORMATION SUBMITTED: June 1990

* EVERYTHING YOGURT INC./BANANAS
Franchise Division
304 Port Richmond Avenue
Staten Island, New York 10302
Richard Nicotra, Chairman

DESCRIPTION OF OPERATION: Everything Yogurt restaurants are fast service retail operations featuring soft frozen yogurt sundaes and shakes, salads, quiche, hot and cold vegetable entrees, assorted pasta salads, fresh-squeezed fruit juices, and related healthful food and beverage items.

NUMBER OF FRANCHISEES: Over 300 plus 5 company-owned

IN BUSINESS SINCE: 1976, offering franchises since 1981.

EQUITY CAPITAL NEEDED: $56,000, total investment $175,000–$225,000.

FINANCIAL ASSISTANCE AVAILABLE: No company financing offered. Administrative assistance offered by company in providing necessary information to local banks for financing.

TRAINING PROVIDED: 2-week initial training program provided at company headquarters and at other stores in chain. Additional on-site training at franchisee's store for one week prior to opening. Follow-up training provided on a continuing basis as directed by company.

MANAGERIAL ASSISTANCE AVAILABLE: Operational and merchandising assistance provided as needed through headquarters office. Area representatives visit franchisees for continuing assistance, periodically suggesting improvements when needed. Comprehensive operations manual provided.

INFORMATION SUBMITTED: June 1990

RANDALL ENTERPRISES, INC.
dba FAMILIES ORIGINAL SUBMARINE SANDWICHES
5376 Tomah Drive #204
Colorado Springs, Colorado 80918
Randall Smith, President

DESCRIPTION OF OPERATION: Families delivers a menu of 27 basic submarine sandwiches with complementary salads, soups, chili, desserts, and other specialties. Breakfast menu available in some shops. Success is based on unique methods of portion control using Families recipes and formulas, emphasizing nutritional quality and quantity of product delivered in a fast-service take-out or sit-down setting. Shop size is 1,000 to 2,500 square feet and can be incorporated in a Shoppette or in a free-standing facility depending on site availability and business potential. Shops are open 12 hours per day, 7 days per week. Families offers tailored cost-effective design and special equipment package resulting in a relatively low initial capital investment.

NUMBER OF FRANCHISEES: 31 in Colorado, Indiana, South Dakota, and New Mexico

IN BUSINESS SINCE: 1972

EQUITY CAPITAL NEEDED: Approximately $55,000 to $60,000 will provide franchise fee, equipment, fixtures, inventory, start-up capital, etc., depending on the extent of necessary or desired leasehold improvements or property ownership.

FINANCIAL ASSISTANCE AVAILABLE: Families will assist franchisee in developing projections and proposals for financing agencies, including SBA, and may meet with such representatives on your behalf, but provides no financial assistance as such.

TRAINING PROVIDED: A mandatory 80-hour training period for each of 2 persons is conducted in Colorado Springs or at a place approved by the franchisor. The course for owners and managers covers the entire operation including necessary accounting, record keeping, marketing, advertising, and personnel management. Also covered are food preparation, sandwich making, and the use and maintenance of standard equipment. Additional instruction for owners, managers, and subordinate personnel will be provided during the opening and grand opening of franchisee's shop.

MANAGERIAL ASSISTANCE AVAILABLE: Ongoing training, education, and assistance are provided regularly during the lifetime of the franchise agreement. The franchisee will be kept abreast of new developments in company and industry-wide advertising and marketing techniques as well as economic trends that affect profits. Franchisor will conduct periodic quality-control surveys and evaluation of shop operations, to include monthly financial management, costs, profits, use of personnel, governmental reporting, continuing education, and other pertinent areas of concern.

INFORMATION SUBMITTED: June 1990

JERRY'S SUB SHOP
15942 Shady Grove Road
Gaithersburg, Maryland 20877
Kathleen L. McDonald

DESCRIPTION OF OPERATION: The chain is famous for its "overstuffed" subs and pizza. The self-service concept is placed in high-volume, high-traffic locations in very pleasant, upscale surroundings; beer and wine complement the menu.

NUMBER OF FRANCHISEES: 70 in 5 states and Washington, D.C.

IN BUSINESS SINCE: 1954

EQUITY CAPITAL NEEDED: $19,500 franchise fee and approximately $50,000 additionally for deposits, etc.

FINANCIAL ASSISTANCE AVAILABLE: Assistance in loan preparation as well as contacts to particular SBA programs that franchise qualifies for.

TRAINING PROVIDED: Extensive training both in classroom as well as unit operation. Follow-up training in franchisee's own site is also provided.

MANAGERIAL ASSISTANCE AVAILABLE: When a new store opens, Jerry's places a start-up team of trained supervisors in the store to help with the opening. The franchisor then has site supervisors visit the store twice a month, more if necessary, to assist the franchisee in running an efficient operation.

INFORMATION SUBMITTED: April 1990

JOYCE'S SUBMARINE SANDWICHES, INC.
1527 Havana Street
Aurora, Colorado 80010
David Meaux, President

DESCRIPTION OF OPERATION: Fast-food franchise consisting of submarine and deli sandwiches, soup, chili, salad bar, soft drinks, snacks, and desserts. Operates in 1,000–1,500 square feet leased space. Open 7 days per week.

NUMBER OF FRANCHISEES: 41 in Colorado, Montana, Nebraska, and Wyoming.

IN BUSINESS SINCE: 1971

EQUITY CAPITAL NEEDED: $25,000 minimum down payment for turnkey store operation.

FINANCIAL ASSISTANCE AVAILABLE: The total cost of a Joyce's Sub Shop operation is $50,000. $25,000 is required for a down payment. Joyce's Submarine Sandwiches, Inc., will carry back note for balance of $25,000 to acceptable persons with good credit references. Franchisee has option to arrange own outside financing.

TRAINING PROVIDED: Joyce's Subs provides 3 weeks free, intensive training for up to 2 persons at company-owned training store. Franchisee trained in menu preparation, inventory ordering and portion control, customer and employee relations, expense control, and fast-food marketing techniques.

MANAGERIAL ASSISTANCE AVAILABLE: Periodic monitoring of store operations by Joyce's corporate staff to assure product quality control, hygiene, customer relations, inventory and portion control, expense control, marketing techniques, and development of advertising and promotion programs. Joyce's provides complete training manual and conducts periodic owners' meetings to assist in problem solving and assure quality in its operations.

INFORMATION SUBMITTED: April 1990

LINDY-GERTIE ENTERPRISES, INC.
8437 Park Avenue
Burr Ridge, Illinois 60521
Joseph P. Yesutis

DESCRIPTION OF OPERATION: A sit-down restaurant featuring two famous products in one attractive food service operation. Lindy's Chili was established in 1924 and is the oldest chili parlor in Chicago featuring its unique famous chili. Gertie's Ice Cream was established in 1901 and features old-fashioned ice cream creations. The franchise package offers a thoroughly modern, attractively designed restaurant, equipment operational support, and a complete operations manual to each franchisee.

NUMBER OF FRANCHISEES: 9

IN BUSINESS SINCE: 1985

EQUITY CAPITAL NEEDED: $50,000 in liquid equity and the ability to finance $90,500 or more depending on the size and location of the business property.

FINANCIAL ASSISTANCE AVAILABLE: None.

TRAINING PROVIDED: We will train you and your managers in a comprehensive program lasting up to 6 weeks. This training will take place at a Lindy's Chili/Gertie's Ice Cream Restaurant or other location we designate. We also offer opening assistance at your site.

MANAGERIAL ASSISTANCE AVAILABLE: Lindy-Gertie Enterprises provides ongoing quality control assurance through field operations management.

Marketing and advertising programs are implemented in conjunction with the franchisees.

INFORMATION SUBMITTED: April 1990

O! DELI
65 Battery Street
San Francisco, California 94111
Mike Kiiek, Director of Franchising

DESCRIPTION OF OPERATION: O! Deli offers quality sandwiches, salads, breakfast, and desserts at fast-food prices. Customers are primarily working people during working hours, with O! Deli's often open only 5 days per week. O! Deli quality and value build a loyal repeat clientele. Catering and delivery are used. O! Deli's are approximately 1,000 square feet.

NUMBER OF FRANCHISEES: 21

IN BUSINESS SINCE: 1985

EQUITY CAPITAL NEEDED: $35,000–$50,000

FINANCIAL ASSISTANCE AVAILABLE: O! Deli assists franchisees, when requested, in preparing business plans and obtaining financing.

TRAINING PROVIDED: O! Deli provides 2 weeks' training in an operating O! Deli. O! Deli staff provides training and assistance during franchisee store opening week. An extensive operations manual covers portion control, hiring and training, financial controls, and food preparation.

MANAGERIAL ASSISTANCE AVAILABLE: O! Deli helps with site selection, lease negotiation, restaurant layout, discounts on equipment and food purchases, and training in operations management and control. Ongoing assistance involves frequent contact with O! Deli operations people to fine-tune your operation, analyze sales trends, and help the business prosper.

INFORMATION SUBMITTED: May 1990

ORANGE BOWL CORPORATION
227 N.E. 17th Street
Miami, Florida 33132
Leonard Turkel, President

DESCRIPTION OF OPERATION: A bright, colorful snack bar designed exclusively for operation in shopping centers, having the advantage of a limited menu offering popular food products such as pizza, hot dogs, hamburgers, soft ice cream, and fruit drinks.

NUMBER OF FRANCHISEES: 40 nationwide

IN BUSINESS SINCE: 1965

EQUITY CAPITAL NEEDED: Approximately $50,000 to $60,000—total cost $95,000 to $135,000.

FINANCIAL ASSISTANCE AVAILABLE: The franchisor does not directly offer any financing to the franchisee; however, it does assist the franchisee in securing bank financing and/or SBA guaranteed financing.

TRAINING PROVIDED: 2 weeks of on-the-job training and orientation at the franchisor's training center for the franchisee, his designee or manager.

MANAGERIAL ASSISTANCE AVAILABLE: Complete turnkey opening provided, with continual home office and area assistance in every aspect of store operations, promotions, and store review.

INFORMATION SUBMITTED: April 1990

PIZZA RACK FRANCHISE SYSTEMS, INC.
2130 Market Avenue North
Canton, Ohio 44714
Wiliam Cundiff, President

DESCRIPTION OF OPERATION: Operate and franchise pizza, French bread pizza, chicken and submarine sandwich carry-outs, with delivery. Franchise is designed for small investors. Stores are designed with a Victorian atmosphere for family dining or carryout.

NUMBER OF FRANCHISEES: 15 stores in Ohio

IN BUSINESS SINCE: 1975

EQUITY CAPITAL NEEDED: $36,000–$45,000

FINANCIAL ASSISTANCE AVAILABLE: Assistance with bank presentation.

TRAINING PROVIDED: A new franchisee is required to train for a period of 6 weeks at one of our existing stores.

MANAGERIAL ASSISTANCE AVAILABLE: Pizza Rack provides continuing management service during the entire franchise period in the areas of quality control, advertising, inventory control, and new product development. A manual of operations and menu preparation is provided.

INFORMATION SUBMITTED: June 1990

PONY EXPRESS PIZZA
931 Baxter Avenue
Louisville, Kentucky 40204
Kenneth Lamb, President

DESCRIPTION OF OPERATION: Pizza delivery chain.

NUMBER OF FRANCHISEES: 16 in Kentucky and Indiana

IN BUSINESS SINCE: 1982

EQUITY CAPITAL NEEDED: $2,500 minimum

FINANCIAL ASSISTANCE AVAILABLE: Relative to location selection and financial stability.

TRAINING PROVIDED: Area supervisor provides complete training in the art of pizza making and business-related paperwork for all new franchisees and their personnel.

MANAGERIAL ASSISTANCE AVAILABLE: Pony Express provides continual management service for the life of the franchise in such areas as bookkeeping, advertising, food cost and inventory control. Complete manuals of operation, recipes, paperwork forms, and directions are provided. Area supervisors are available in all regions to work closely with franchisees and visit stores regularly to assist in solving problems.

INFORMATION SUBMITTED: June 1990

PORT OF SUBS, INC.
100 Washington Street, Suite 200
Reno, Nevada 89503
Patricia Larsen, President

DESCRIPTION OF OPERATION: Port of Subs, Inc., is a submarine sandwich restaurant operation. Sandwiches are made-to-order with highest-quality ingredients. Typical stores are approximately 1,200–1,500 square feet and seat 30–35 people. Simplicity of operation and efficiency are cornerstones of the Port of Subs system. A nautical theme with blue, yellow, and white interiors presents a crisp, clean environment.

NUMBER OF FRANCHISEES: 41 (plus 7 company-owned units) in Arizona, California, Nevada, and Washington

IN BUSINESS SINCE: 1975

EQUITY CAPITAL NEEDED: $35,000–$50,000

FINANCIAL ASSISTANCE AVAILABLE: A total investment of $120,000 is estimated for a Port of Subs franchise. Port of Subs, Inc., assists potential franchisees in preparing documents for financing and maintains relationships with several banking institutions. Port of Subs, Inc., does not provide any internal financing.

TRAINING PROVIDED: Port of Subs, Inc., provides a mandatory, intensive 16-day training course that will give the skills, the knowledge, and the confidence a franchisee needs to manage the business effectively and efficiently. Training is conducted at corporate headquarters and at a company-owned store location and covers all material aspects of the operation of a Port of Subs franchise.

MANAGERIAL ASSISTANCE AVAILABLE: Port of Subs, Inc., provides franchisees with reference manuals, business forms, purchasing power, accounting service (optional), and the benefits of creative advertising campaigns. Port of Subs, Inc., also provides opening assistance during the initial opening for at least 5 days, and provides guidance in creating an attention-getting grand opening. Ongoing support includes monthly visits by representatives who will provide new updates, merchandising concepts, idea exchanges, and two-way communication. The corporate staff is always available between visits to provide assistance.

INFORMATION SUBMITTED: May 1990

QUIZNO'S INTERNATIONAL, INC.
190 East 9th Avenue, Suite 190
Denver, Colorado 80203
Boyd R. Bartlett, Vice President

DESCRIPTION OF OPERATION: Fast-food franchise shops offering Classic Subs made of the finest, freshest ingredients. Quizno's compliments the Classic Subs with a unique salad and dessert menu.

NUMBER OF FRANCHISEES: 31 in 2 states

IN BUSINESS SINCE: 1981

EQUITY CAPITAL NEEDED: Minimum of $40,000 (depending on location)

FINANCIAL ASSISTANCE AVAILABLE: Financial assistance provided to qualified franchisees.

TRAINING PROVIDED: Franchisees complete a comprehensive training program in company store prior to franchise opening.

MANAGERIAL ASSISTANCE AVAILABLE: Management representatives spend first 2 weeks assisting new franchisees in shops. Comprehensive operations manual provided with appropriate adjustments made to keep manuals updated. Operation hours response service available to franchisees to call for advice and problem solving.

INFORMATION SUBMITTED: April 1990

RANELLI FRANCHISE SYSTEMS, INC.
dba RANELLIS DELI AND SANDWICH SHOPS
2134 Warrier Road
Birmingham, Alabama 35208
Frank A. Ranelli, President

DESCRIPTION OF OPERATION: Ranellis is a deli and sandwich shop operation specializing in deli-type sandwiches and pizza. Feature product is a 16-inch Poboy called a Richman. Also featured is homemade lasagna served every Thursday. Stores have a specialty grocery section as well as a by-the-pound deli case.

NUMBER OF FRANCHISEES: 8 in 3 states

IN BUSINESS SINCE: 1949, started franchising in 1979

EQUITY CAPITAL NEEDED: $7,500 franchise fee.

FINANCIAL ASSISTANCE AVAILABLE: Total investment is approximately $40,000 to $65,000 including franchise fee. Franchisor offers no financial assistance.

TRAINING PROVIDED: 2 weeks in company unit, 1 week at location. Continuing assistance with problems thereafter.

MANAGERIAL ASSISTANCE AVAILABLE: Operations manual provided, and assistance with problems. Continuing inspections to avert problems.

INFORMATION SUBMITTED: June 1990

SEAWEST SUB SHOPS, INC.
One Lake Bellevue Drive, Suite 107
Bellevue, Washington 98005
Jim Iseman, President

DESCRIPTION OF OPERATION: Limited menu submarine sandwich; the franchise takes a flat fee of $2,000 year one; $3,000 year two; $4,000 years 3 through 10; no percentage royalty.

NUMBER OF FRANCHISEES: 96, all franchised

IN BUSINESS SINCE: 1980, franchised since 1985

EQUITY CAPITAL NEEDED: Minimum $15,000 cash

FINANCIAL ASSISTANCE AVAILABLE: Franchisees must obtain their own financing.

TRAINING PROVIDED: 2 weeks at regional office or Seattle, regional developer in market before a franchise is sold.

MANAGERIAL ASSISTANCE AVAILABLE: Ongoing assistance.

INFORMATION SUBMITTED: April 1990

* SONIC INDUSTRIES, INC.
120 Robert S. Kerr Avenue
Oklahoma City, Oklahoma 73102
Robert P. Flack, Vice President of Corporate Development

DESCRIPTION OF OPERATION: Fast-food drive-in restaurant specifically designed for speed of service and freshness of food. Emphasis on hamburgers, hot dogs, onion rings.

NUMBER OF FRANCHISEES: 924 plus 91 company-owned in 22 states

IN BUSINESS SINCE: 1959

EQUITY CAPITAL NEEDED: $38,000 to $68,000, includes $15,000 franchise fee.

FINANCIAL ASSISTANCE AVAILABLE: None.

TRAINING PROVIDED: Franchisor requires classroom and on-location training and provides management seminars and periodic updates on new techniques and profit making.

MANAGERIAL ASSISTANCE AVAILABLE: Specifically designed and tested equipment; certain expertise in site selection; quality control recommendations and testing of food products; requirements of proper training, chain-wide inspection program. Helps to provide voluntary chain-wide advertising programs and purchasing co-ops. Sonic Industries, Inc., provides time-tested managerial and technical assistance to each franchise with the ultimate goal of profit and success.

INFORMATION SUBMITTED: June 1990

SPINNER'S PIZZA
910 KCK Way
Cedar Hill, Texas 75104
Dick Pryor

DESCRIPTION OF OPERATION: Spinner's Pizza provides management expertise to enable you to operate a pizza delivery and take-out business in a proven and profitable manner. The system includes a two-for-the-price-of-one marketing system backed up by the finest ingredients and best equipment available. Operates from 1,000-square-foot space with approximately 12 employees. A simple menu consisting of large or small pizza and a sub sandwich (three varieties).

NUMBER OF FRANCHISEES: 40

IN BUSINESS SINCE: 1984

EQUITY CAPITAL NEEDED: Cash requirements $35,000 to $65,000 depending on whether you lease or purchase equipment package.

FINANCIAL ASSISTANCE AVAILABLE: Equipment leasing program available, plus assistance in finding sources of financing.

TRAINING PROVIDED: Franchisee/operator receives practical, on-site training of up to 500 hours at company store in Dallas, Texas. Trainee must complete certification test at end of training.

MANAGERIAL ASSISTANCE AVAILABLE: Ongoing assistance and support with site selection, lease negotiation, equipment leasing or purchase, advertising and marketing.

INFORMATION SUBMITTED: April 1990

* SUBWAY
325 Bic Drive
Milford, Connecticut 06460
Donald G. Furtman, Franchise Director

DESCRIPTION OF OPERATION: Freshly prepared foot-long specialty sandwiches (submarines) and salads. Present menu includes 10 varieties of hot and cold sandwiches. No grilling is involved other than in a microwave oven. All stores have a take-out service and many stores have eat-in facilities. Stores are open late 7 nights per week. All franchisees make freshly baked bread and whole wheat bread.

NUMBER OF FRANCHISEES: 4,400 in 50 states, Washington, D.C., Canada, Puerto Rico, Bahrain, the Bahamas, and Australia

IN BUSINESS SINCE: 1965 (franchising since 1974)

EQUITY CAPITAL NEEDED: Approximately $35,000. Total investment $39,900 to $67,900.

FINANCIAL ASSISTANCE AVAILABLE: Equipment leasing available depending on analysis of financial statements.

TRAINING PROVIDED: Subway provides 2 weeks of comprehensive classroom and practical training at Subway headquarters for store owners and store managers. The classroom curriculum includes training in location selection, store construction, accounting procedures, and management theory as well as instruction in business analysis, product formulas, and control mechanisms specific to Subway system. In addition to classroom study, practical training is provided in one of the local Subway stores to develop skills in sandwich making along with the day-to-day operation and management of a successful Subway store.

MANAGERIAL ASSISTANCE AVAILABLE: During store construction, which takes between 20 and 60 days, managerial and technical assistance is provided for each franchisee by a development agent and an office coordinator assigned to handle their file. Areas covered in this assistance include site selection, store design and layout, interior construction, equipment purchasing, arrangement of suppliers, and initial inventory ordering. When a store is scheduled to open, a development agent is available to help oversee the operation and provide backup support for the store owner in areas of employee training and successful operational procedure. After store opening, periodic inspections and field visits are conducted in each unit by the assigned development agent. Continual office support is made available to each franchisee through frequent contact with one's assigned coordinator. The coordinator development agent system for service provides continual assistance and support for each franchisee through the life of the franchise (20 years). A weekly newsletter comprised of articles written by department heads is sent to all franchisees. With receipt of this newsletter all franchisees are kept continually apprised of new company policies and developments across the country. Also included in this publication are sections dealing with store management. Ongoing assistance in advertising is provided by the franchise advertising fund, which is directed by a board of directors comprised of 11 store owners elected by the franchisees.

INFORMATION SUBMITTED: April 1990

TACO CASA INTERNATIONAL, LTD.
P. O. Box 4542
Topeka, Kansas 66604
James F. Reiter, President

DESCRIPTION OF OPERATION: Taco Casa International, Ltd., is the operator and franchisor for Taco Casa restaurants. Taco Casa is a fast-food Mexican restaurant featuring a limited menu and quick courteous service in an attractive atmosphere. Taco Casa International, Ltd., operates both free-standing and enclosed mall locations. Normal operating hours are from 11 A.M. to 12 midnight, 7 days a week.

NUMBER OF FRANCHISEES: 20 in 8 states plus 2 company-owned

IN BUSINESS SINCE: 1963

EQUITY CAPITAL NEEDED: The total franchise package is approximately $85,000, which includes equipment, inventory, start-up costs, starting capital, plus leasehold improvements.

FINANCIAL ASSISTANCE AVAILABLE: May assist in methods for arranging financing.

TRAINING PROVIDED: An initial 2 weeks for new licensees at our training school. 1-week assistance upon opening the new unit. Complete operations manual provided to unit. Continuous counseling and assistance with routine inspections by company representative. Monthly newsletter updating current events in Taco Casa and restaurant industry.

FINANCIAL ASSISTANCE AVAILABLE: T.F.I. does not provide direct financing to franchisees at the present time. However, it does provide assistance in obtaining financing, such as assisting the franchisee in preparing his proposal for bank financing and meeting with potential lenders.

TRAINING PROVIDED: Training course for all new licensees conducted at company training center and/or licensee's own store. Source covers managerial, accounting, promotional, food preparation, and operational phases under actual operating conditions. Continuous in-field counseling thereafter, covering merchandising, quality control, advertising and promotion by company regional store supervisors.

MANAGERIAL ASSISTANCE AVAILABLE: Regional territorial franchisees and/or state supervisors continue to counsel licensee in cost controls, new operational methods, advertising, merchandising, and quality control. In addition, company conducts national convention once each year for all licensees to exchange ideas on merchandising, advertising, management, and new food preparation methods.

INFORMATION SUBMITTED: May 1990

2 FOR 1 PIZZA ENTERPRISES
736 East Lincoln
Orange, California 92665
John T. Murray, President

DESCRIPTION OF OPERATION: 2 for 1 Pizza Company, take-out and delivery pizza, with buy 1 and get 1 free offer always in effect. We require approximately 1,100 square feet with ample store front parking and open 12–14 hours per day.

NUMBER OF FRANCHISEES: 19 franchised and 24 units company-owned in California, South Carolina, and Hawaii

IN BUSINESS SINCE: 1982

EQUITY CAPITAL NEEDED: $35,000

FINANCIAL ASSISTANCE AVAILABLE: A total of $70,000 is necessary to open a 2 for 1 Pizza Co. franchise. We offer assistance in locating lenders.

TRAINING PROVIDED: 6 weeks in training store.

MANAGERIAL ASSISTANCE AVAILABLE: Location and construction assistance, store supervision, bookkeeping, and QSC supervision.

INFORMATION SUBMITTED: June 1990

YOUR PIZZA SHOPS, INC.
1177 South Main Street
North Canton, Ohio 44720
John Purney, Jr., President

DESCRIPTION OF OPERATION: Carry-out, dining-room operation with salad bar and/or smorgasbord available.

NUMBER OF FRANCHISEES: 20 in Ohio, Arizona, and Florida

IN BUSINESS SINCE: 1949

EQUITY CAPITAL NEEDED: $40,000–$60,000

FINANCIAL ASSISTANCE AVAILABLE: None directly but source information available.

TRAINING PROVIDED: 1 month training in one of our operating shops, then training in franchisee's own shop until we feel franchisee can handle his/her own operation.

MANAGERIAL ASSISTANCE AVAILABLE: We are always available to our franchisees if they have any problems or questions of any kind, be it legal, accounting, managerial, or operational, for as long as they remain franchisees.

INFORMATION SUBMITTED: June 1990

HEALTH AIDS/SERVICES

* DIET CENTER, INC.
220 South 2nd West
Rexburg, Idaho 83440
General Manager of Franchise

DESCRIPTION OF OPERATION: The Diet Center business includes administration of the 5-phase Diet Center Weight Control Program through private, daily counseling and weekly classes, and sales of various vitamin, food, and nutritional products, generally under the Diet Center brand name. The Diet Center organization has grown, since its inception, to become the number-one franchised weight-control program in North America. With more than 2,200 locations throughout the United States and Canada, Diet Center continues to expand the scope of its organization to meet the needs of today's market.

NUMBER OF FRANCHISEES: There are over 2,315 in all states of the United States and Canada.

IN BUSINESS SINCE: 1972

EQUITY CAPITAL NEEDED: Initial franchise fee is $12,000 U.S. and $24,000 U.S. (includes starter kit, complete training program, necessary equipment, and franchise rights in exclusive territory). Minimum $10,000 additional operating capital essential.

FINANCIAL ASSISTANCE AVAILABLE: None.

TRAINING PROVIDED: A 1-week training seminar is provided to prepare operators for responsibilities of administering the Diet Center program and running a Diet Center business. Included in the seminar are courses providing instruction in every aspect necessary to the successful operation of a Diet Center.

MANAGERIAL ASSISTANCE AVAILABLE: In addition to refresher courses provided at counselor training school at the corporate headquarters, continuing education is conducted throughout the year at regional counselor-training seminars across the country and at annual international Diet Center conventions. Counselors and franchisees are also informed of new information through the monthly publications of the *AdVantage* magazine, the franchisee forum newsletter, and the Diet Center newsletter.

INFORMATION SUBMITTED: June 1990

* FORMU-3 INTERNATIONAL, INC.
4790 Douglas Center N.W.
Canton, Ohio 44718
Walter Poston, Vice President, Franchise Development

DESCRIPTION OF OPERATION: We offer unique franchise opportunities throughout the United States in the field of weight loss.

NUMBER OF FRANCHISEES: 300 plus in 26 states

IN BUSINESS SINCE: 1982

EQUITY CAPITAL NEEDED: $32,000

FINANCIAL ASSISTANCE AVAILABLE: None.

TRAINING PROVIDED: Franchisee training consists of 3-day owner's training, 4-day manager's class, and 5-day owner/employee training class, plus 1-week grand opening assistance.

MANAGERIAL ASSISTANCE AVAILABLE: Monthly area meetings, seminars, ongoing 5-day employee training classes held at corporate headquarters and in the field and 4-day manager training classes held at corporate headquarters. Corporate personnel assistance available.

INFORMATION SUBMITTED: May 1990

* FORTUNATE LIFE WEIGHT LOSS CENTERS
P. O. Box 5604
Charlottesville, Virginia 22905
Thomas Beslin, President

DESCRIPTION OF OPERATION: The Fortunate Life Center is a supervised weight control program. The program is scientifically based and focuses on the key ingredients of successful weight control—controlling caloric intake, modifying behavior, and working with a committed individual. The program is unique within the weight control industry.

NUMBER OF FRANCHISEES: 67 in 15 states

IN BUSINESS SINCE: 1984; JenDale, Inc., purchased franchise in June 1986.

EQUITY CAPITAL NEEDED: $6,000 plus working capital and initial franchise fee.

FINANCIAL ASSISTANCE AVAILABLE: None.

TRAINING PROVIDED: 3–5 days of extensive marketing and clinical training.

MANAGERIAL ASSISTANCE AVAILABLE: Physician and consulting dietician at home office. Marketing and clinical training updates provided through field visits and conventions.

INFORMATION SUBMITTED: June 1990

HEALTH CLUBS OF AMERICA
Box 4098
Waterville, Connecticut 06714
Gregg Nolan, Franchise Director

DESCRIPTION OF OPERATION: Health and slenderizing salons with separate facilities for men and women.

NUMBER OF FRANCHISEES: 18 in Connecticut, New York, and New Jersey

IN BUSINESS SINCE: 1961

EQUITY CAPITAL NEEDED: Minimum of $35,000, depending on equipment.

FINANCIAL ASSISTANCE AVAILABLE: Financing may be arranged through Horizons of America, Inc., parent company.

TRAINING PROVIDED: 1-week management training in main office in New York. At least 3 weeks of day-to-day operational training at own club.

MANAGERIAL ASSISTANCE AVAILABLE: Company is always available for counseling.

INFORMATION SUBMITTED: May 1990

JAZZERCISE, INC.
2808 Roosevelt Street
Carlsbad, California 92008

DESCRIPTION OF OPERATION: Jazzercise is a dance fitness program using choreographed dance fitness routines to music. The franchisee must successfully complete a training workshop and be proficient in dance and exercise in order to qualify for a franchise.

NUMBER OF FRANCHISEES: 4,000 franchised instructors in the USA plus 29 foreign countries.

IN BUSINESS SINCE: 1974

EQUITY CAPITAL NEEDED: Approximately $3,000

FINANCIAL ASSISTANCE AVAILABLE: None.

TRAINING PROVIDED: A 4-day workshop.

MANAGERIAL ASSISTANCE AVAILABLE: Jazzercise provides the services of agents who supervise and assist franchisees in all facets of their business on an ongoing basis.

INFORMATION SUBMITTED: June 1990

MED-WAY MEDICAL WEIGHT MANAGEMENT
1375 South Voss
Houston, Texas 77057
Jerry O. Cooksey, Executive Vice President

DESCRIPTION OF OPERATION: The Med-Way Medical Weight Management franchise is a proven weight-loss program offering sound nutrition, education, and behavior modification to the general public. The program is administered by physicians and nurses in a professional, clinical atmosphere. Franchise ownership is available to nurses and nonmedical investor owners. Med-Way provides complete assistance with site selection, center layout, personnel selection, training, advertising support, and comprehensive ongoing support.

NUMBER OF FRANCHISEES: 8 in Texas, 35 additional agreements have been signed. Franchising in other states also.

IN BUSINESS SINCE: 1987

EQUITY CAPITAL NEEDED: The total capital requirement to get a typical Med-Way Weight Management center open is from a low of $27,000 to $40,000, which includes the franchise fee. Average $36,000.

FINANCIAL ASSISTANCE AVAILABLE: Franchisor does not provide financial assistance at this time.

TRAINING PROVIDED: Franchisor provides free training to the franchisee and franchisee's employees at franchisor's headquarters in Houston, Texas. Franchisor will train franchisee's employees at no cost to franchisee for as long as franchisee owns the franchise. The franchisee is responsible for paying all costs of travel, food, and lodging to and from Houston, Texas. Franchisor provides 5 days of training in Houston and up to 5 days of training at franchisee's center.

MANAGERIAL ASSISTANCE AVAILABLE: In addition to the above training at franchisor headquarters, franchisor provides ongoing advice and assistance with advertising, promotions, seminars, written advisories, bulletins, and meetings at franchise headquarters. Franchisor has staff available during normal working hours to assist all franchisees with routine questions. Franchisor has "Area Nurse Managers" to advise and assist all franchise locations. Franchisor provides all franchisees with an operations manual, supply lists, and preprinted forms lists. Franchisor can supply all items used in each center, but franchisees do not have to purchase anything from franchisor.

INFORMATION SUBMITTED: June 1990

NATIONAL HEALTH ENHANCEMENT SYSTEMS, INC.
3200 N. Central Avenue, Suite 1750
Phoenix, Arizona 85012
Jeffrey T. Zywicki, Vice President of Finance

DESCRIPTION OF OPERATION: National Health Enhancement Systems, Inc., offers health care providers, through a business system, an innovative way of generating additional revenue, through the marketing of health evaluations to prevention-conscious consumers. Its comprehensive medical assessment program, designed to determine the relative health of an apparently well individual, was developed in 1979 by Dr. Edward B. Diethrich, and has evolved into five distinct systems that may be used as stand-alone or complementary products. Each program analyzes life-style, nutritional habits, and physical condition as they relate to cardiovascular disease risk factor and overall fitness.

NUMBER OF FRANCHISEES: 169 in 31 states

IN BUSINESS SINCE: 1983, formerly AHI, Limited

EQUITY CAPITAL NEEDED: Approximately $22,200, including initial fee.

FINANCIAL ASSISTANCE AVAILABLE: In certain situations the initial license fee is payable one-third down upon execution of a franchise agreement with the balance (plus interest) due in 12 equal monthly payments. The investment pays for all start-up materials and software product. (Does not include personal computer hardware equipment.)

TRAINING PROVIDED: An intensive 4-day mandatory training program held in Phoenix, Arizona; subsequent and follow-up training as often as franchisee requests under the direct supervision of full time NHES employees.

MANAGERIAL ASSISTANCE AVAILABLE: National Health provides continual marketing and technical support for the life of the franchise in the administration of the medical assessment and evaluation programs it provides to its franchisees.

INFORMATION SUBMITTED: May 1990

SLENDER CENTER, INC.
6515 Grand Teton Plaza, Suite 241
Madison, Wisconsin 53719
Jean Geurink, President

DESCRIPTION OF OPERATION: Weight-loss consultation. Individualized. No prepackaged foods. Use of 3-Step Breakthrough Program that increases intake at three stages using normal, regular foods for guaranteed loss. Behavior System training called Breakthrough Thinking that personalizes behavior change appropriate for gender/career/life-style/weight history. No drugs, no products. Comprehensive program manual provided to all clients. Programs for men, women, adolescents, nursing mothers, vegetarians. Audio cassettes on affirmations, relaxation, exercise, and self-esteem. Cookbook.

NUMBER OF FRANCHISEES: 34 centers in 6 states

IN BUSINESS SINCE: 1979

EQUITY CAPITAL NEEDED: $5,000–$10,000 plus franchise fee $12,000–$27,000.

FINANCIAL ASSISTANCE AVAILABLE: None.

TRAINING PROVIDED: Initial 5-day training at corporate headquarters. Procedure and policy manuals provided to owner and staff without cost.

MANAGERIAL ASSISTANCE AVAILABLE: Grand opening assistance for 5 days without fee. Support phone staff available ongoing. All print copy. TV commercials, and radio scripts provided. Monthly newsletter, regional meetings, franchise advisory board, annual award convention.

INFORMATION SUBMITTED: April 1990

TONING & TANNING CENTERS
% FITNESS SYSTEMS, INC.
106 West 31st Street
Independence, Missouri 64055
Glen Henson

DESCRIPTION OF OPERATION: We feature toning tables, tanning beds and isokinetic treadmills, bicycles with a line of isokinetic exercises for muscle toning. The program is designed for all ages of women and men alike. Our centers are priced so they may be adapted to any town of 5,000 to 10,000 or 20,000, as well as the larger communities. Our phone number is (816) 254-0805.

NUMBER OF FRANCHISEES: 300 in 30 states

IN BUSINESS SINCE: 1975

EQUITY CAPITAL NEEDED: $10,000 and up

FINANCIAL ASSISTANCE AVAILABLE: Leasing possible.

TRAINING PROVIDED: 1 week optional in Independence, Missouri, and on-site training when opening at no charge.

MANAGERIAL ASSISTANCE AVAILABLE: Total training on all aspects of the business at no charge. Managerial and technical assistance provided in use of all equipment, office forms, bookkeeping, etc.

INFORMATION SUBMITTED: April 1990

WOMEN AT LARGE SYSTEMS, INC.
dba WOMEN AT LARGE FITNESS SALONS
1020 South 48th Avenue
Yakima, Washington 98908
Sharlyne R. Powell, President & C.E.O.

DESCRIPTION OF OPERATION: Well-appointed exercise clubs provide a highly professional dance-exercise program directed toward the 35–40 million plus-size women shunned by today's physical fitness industry. These sophisticated, service-intensive clubs cater to the fitness, beauty, and self-esteem needs of larger women by offering members a state-of-the-art exercise regime, fitness analysis, wellness system for weight reduction and weight management, support groups, seminars on fashion, wardrobing, hair design, makeup application, and image enhancement. Exercise 101 classes teach and educate exercise programming and lifetime commitment to fitness. A full line of workout wear, custom made for larger women under the Women at Large label, is available in the pro shop along with the usual athletic gear for an extended profit base.

NUMBER OF FRANCHISEES: 24 in 14 states and Canada

IN BUSINESS SINCE: 1983, franchising since 1986

EQUITY CAPITAL NEEDED: $45,000–$60,000

FINANCIAL ASSISTANCE AVAILABLE: None.

TRAINING PROVIDED: Study and body conditioning begin weeks before arrival at home office. Owner arrives 1 week prior to staff for concentrated operations and business training. 5 staff members join the owner for 2 additional weeks of intensive fitness training, body conditioning, choreography memorization, study, and testing in areas as diverse as exercise physiology, kinesiology, and external promotions. Video, audio cassettes, written guides, log books, training, and operations manuals provide owner and staff continued means of training and polishing until the Women at Large specialist's arrival 2 days prior to grand opening for final inspection, training, and review.

MANAGERIAL ASSISTANCE AVAILABLE: New exercise routines and programs with written backups are sent via videotape to keep exercise programming current. Operations specialists are in constant contact with owners via on-site visits and telephone. Regional seminars, national conventions, international aerobic championship meets provide continuing education and advanced training. Corporate newsletters provide a continuous information flow and industry updates.

INFORMATION SUBMITTED: April 1990

HOME FURNISHINGS/FURNITURE RETAIL/REPAIR/SERVICES

AMITY QUALITY RESTORATION SYSTEMS, INC.
1571 Ivory Drive
P. O. Box 148
Sun Prairie, Wisconsin 53590
George Cash

DESCRIPTION OF OPERATION: Amity offers a unique furniture stripping and restoration system of equipment and chemicals for the stripping and restoration of antiques and furniture. The system to be located in purchaser's rented shop. There are no purchase requirements. No fee, all funds paid are for equipment and merchandise. All chemicals nonflammable. Also sells paint remover, spray equipment, and finishes, wholesale to the trade.

NUMBER OF FRANCHISEES: 700 in all states except Alaska and Hawaii

IN BUSINESS SINCE: 1971

EQUITY CAPITAL NEEDED: $1,800–$10,000

TRAINING PROVIDED: Training provided at home office for 2 days on use and application. Free consulting advice, conventions, seminars, newsletters. Training includes stripping, finishing, and repair.

MANAGERIAL ASSISTANCE AVAILABLE: Technical advice provided on restoration, stripping, finishing, repairing, business management.

INFORMATION SUBMITTED: April 1990

CHEM-CLEAN FURNITURE RESTORATION CENTER
P. O. Box 577
Elmira, New York 14902
Dr. R. G. Esposito, President

DESCRIPTION OF OPERATION: Patented nonwater systems for furniture stripping and refinishing.

NUMBER OF FRANCHISEES: 77 in 16 states, Canada, and Europe

IN BUSINESS SINCE: 1967

EQUITY CAPITAL NEEDED: $7,000–$25,000 total required.

FINANCIAL ASSISTANCE AVAILABLE: Lease purchase or financing plans available. No royalties; licensee owns all equipment outright. Equipment and solvents covered by U.S. and Canadian patents.

TRAINING PROVIDED: Up to 2 weeks of complete instruction in licensee-owned shop, plus follow-up. Environmental assistance.

MANAGERIAL ASSISTANCE AVAILABLE: Complete operating procedures, including technical and managerial techniques. Annual meetings of licensees. Newsletters.

INFORMATION SUBMITTED: June 1990

CHEM-DRY CARPET CLEANING
HARRIS RESEARCH, INC.
3330 Cameron Park Drive, #700
Cameron Park, California 95682
Robert Harris, President

DESCRIPTION OF OPERATION: Chem-Dry offers a unique, patented (#4219333) cleaning process utilizing a completely safe, nontoxic solution in conjunction with carbonation. The carbonated cleaner has opened the door for innovative approach to carpet cleaning and franchising. Carpets are guaranteed against damage, are left with no dirt-attracting residues, and generally dry in less than 1 hour.

NUMBER OF FRANCHISEES: 2,406 in 50 states and 22 countries.

IN BUSINESS SINCE: 1977

EQUITY CAPITAL NEEDED: $5,000–$12,500

FINANCIAL ASSISTANCE AVAILABLE: The down payment pays for equipment and solutions, office supplies, an advertising package, and training. Balance financed by Harris Research, Inc.

TRAINING PROVIDED: A 4-day training program includes on-the-job training where carpet cleaning skills will be taught, as well as the necessary business management aspects. A franchisee, his/her managers or employees may obtain as much additional training as they desire at no charge. Training can also be done by a videotape program that includes a written test.

MANAGERIAL ASSISTANCE AVAILABLE: A franchisee, his managers or employees may obtain as much additional training as they desire at no charge.

INFORMATION SUBMITTED: May 1990

* DECORATING DEN SYSTEMS, INC.
7910 Woodmont Avenue, Suite 200
Bethesda, Maryland 20814
Jim Bugg, President

DESCRIPTION OF OPERATION: The retailing of custom-made draperies, window treatments, floor coverings, wallcoverings, furniture, and other related decorating products. All merchandise sold from samples and catalogues in the customer's home on an appointment basis. Business does not require inventory or a retail store. This is a professional service business with competitive pricing on quality products.

NUMBER OF FRANCHISEES: 800

IN BUSINESS SINCE: 1970

EQUITY CAPITAL NEEDED: Franchise fee of $15,900 to $18,900 plus working capital of $4,800 minimum.

FINANCIAL ASSISTANCE AVAILABLE: Franchise fee cash. Lease available on ColorVan.

TRAINING PROVIDED: Decorating Den's initial training takes approximately 6 months. It combines classroom work, home study, meetings, seminars, on-the-job experience, and an internship with an experienced decorator. Secondary, advanced, and graduate training continue throughout the owner's career with Decorating Den. Decorating Den decorators are trained to identify life-style, personality, color preferences, and a comfortable budget. Emphasis is on the "feeling," the way people live more than historical period stylings.

MANAGERIAL ASSISTANCE AVAILABLE: Grand opening preparation and attendance. Planning and sales projection meeting. Post-opening progress checks. Ongoing services in marketing, sales, business operations, and business expansion as part of fee.

INFORMATION SUBMITTED: June 1990

DIP 'N STRIP, INC.
2141 South Platte River Drive
Denver, Colorado 80223
E. Roger Schuyler, President

DESCRIPTION OF OPERATION: Franchised and company-owned operations providing the household community, antique dealers, furniture refinishers, industrial and commercial accounts in the removal of finishes from wood and metal. Operation requires approximately 2,000 square feet of warehouse space with concrete floor, drain, cold water tap, 220 single-phase power, overhead door, and small office space. The removal is accomplished with a cold stripping formula in chemical solutions. Dip 'N Strip is a federally registered trademark since April 13, 1970. Dip 'N Strip trademark is registered in France, Germany, the Benulux countries, and the United Kingdom.

NUMBER OF FRANCHISEES: 214 in 36 states, Canada, and 57 in Europe.

IN BUSINESS SINCE: 1970

EQUITY CAPITAL NEEDED: $12,500—no franchise fee required.

FINANCIAL ASSISTANCE AVAILABLE: $3,000 will be financed up to 3 years, simple 10 percent interest, and will be carried by the franchisor for those who qualify.

TRAINING PROVIDED: A complete training program is provided for 5 days of actual job and office training in all aspects of the business at the franchisee's own location prior to the grand opening. In Europe, the same training is provided at the master licensee pilot location.

MANAGERIAL ASSISTANCE AVAILABLE: A complete operations manual and technical assistance is supplied during the training program, and in order to keep the franchisees current on the corporation and other franchisee's activities, a monthly newsletter, *Dip 'N Script*, is published. All advertising mats, layouts, and slicks are provided without charge to the franchisees on request.

INFORMATION SUBMITTED: April 1990

* DURACLEAN INTERNATIONAL
2151 Waukegan Road
Deerfield, Illinois 60015

DESCRIPTION OF OPERATION: On-location cleaning of carpet, rugs, upholstery, and drapery fabrics using exclusive, patented processes, plus ceiling cleaning, stain repelling, soil-retarding, static removal, spot removal, mothproofing, and minor carpet repair.

NUMBER OF FRANCHISEES: 610 in all 50 states, throughout Canada, and 20 countries overseas

IN BUSINESS SINCE: 1930

EQUITY CAPITAL NEEDED: $14,800 for training and $8,000 for equipment.

FINANCIAL ASSISTANCE AVAILABLE: For standard dealership Duraclean will finance balance of cost after $6,900 down payment for qualified applicants. Financing also available for other options.

TRAINING PROVIDED: 1-week resident training school, transportation, tuition; room and board at no cost to new dealers. Also, training with experienced dealer.

MANAGERIAL ASSISTANCE AVAILABLE: Advertising, sales promotion, bookkeeping, laboratory services on cleaning and technical spotting. Regional meetings throughout the U.S. and Canada. International conventions.

INFORMATION SUBMITTED: June 1990

FABRI-ZONE INTERNATIONAL, INC.
375 Bering Avenue
Toronto, Ontario, Canada M8Z3B1
David Collier, President

DESCRIPTION OF OPERATION: Establish cleaning service franchisees, total service including carpet, upholstery, drapery, ceiling, smoke and fire damage, water restoration, odor removal, and retail product sales.

NUMBER OF FRANCHISEES: 15 in 7 states

IN BUSINESS SINCE: 1981

EQUITY CAPITAL NEEDED: $2,500–$19,500

FINANCIAL ASSISTANCE AVAILABLE: Complete business plan for start-up, territory study, complete program, financing to qualified individuals.

TRAINING PROVIDED: 1 week at corporate office, videotape, and manuals.

MANAGERIAL ASSISTANCE AVAILABLE: Complete technical and systems support, advertising and marketing promotions, monthly newsletters, regional seminars, management support, and monthly bulletins.

INFORMATION SUBMITTED: April 1990

* FLOOR COVERINGS INTERNATIONAL
5182 Old Dixie Highway
Forest Park, Georgia 30050
Joseph R. Lunsford, President

DESCRIPTION OF OPERATION: Floor Coverings International (FCI) is a mobile carpet retail franchise that provides "mill direct" floor covering to residential homes and businesses from coast to coast. Member International Franchise Association.

NUMBER OF FRANCHISEES: 103 offices in 38 states. Franchises available in remainder of states, Canada, and abroad.

IN BUSINESS SINCE: 1985

EQUITY CAPITAL NEEDED: Total cost of franchise $9,700.

FINANCIAL ASSISTANCE AVAILABLE: Yes.

TRAINING PROVIDED: Mandatory Carpet College® is the finest in the carpet industry. Total training 1 week at company headquarters.

MANAGERIAL ASSISTANCE AVAILABLE: Our franchise includes carpet samples, printing, continual ongoing assistance through upgraded training sessions, monthly newsletters, constant contact with suppliers and manufacturers, and a toll-free help line.

INFORMATION SUBMITTED: June 1990

HILLSIDE BEDDING
700 Havemeyer Avenue
Bronx, New York 10473
Robert Martire, President

DESCRIPTION OF OPERATION: Largest chain of bedding shops offers franchised stores featuring mattresses, brass headboards, convertible sofas, and most other sleep products. National brand names such as Seally sold at discount prices.

NUMBER OF FRANCHISEES: 72 in New York, New Jersey, Connecticut, and Pennsylvania

IN BUSINESS SINCE: 1973

EQUITY CAPITAL NEEDED: $39,150–$54,000

FINANCIAL ASSISTANCE AVAILABLE: Will assist in obtaining financing.

TRAINING PROVIDED: 1 week of formal classroom training and 1 week with store manager of a company store. 1-week quarterly and 2-day monthly refresher courses available as continuing education.

MANAGERIAL ASSISTANCE AVAILABLE: Each region has a local supervisor of operations available at all times. Each month, a vice president of operations visits each store for an entire day to assist owner with problem solving and implementation of new products and promotional campaigns. Monthly marketing meeting in local areas and quarterly franchise meeting at company headquarters.

INFORMATION SUBMITTED: June 1990

LANGENWALTER INDUSTRIES, INC.
4410 East LaPalma Avenue
Anaheim, California 92807
Roy Langenwalter, President

DESCRIPTION OF OPERATION: Langenwalter-Harris Chemical Co., Inc., offers a unique carpet and upholstery dye process franchise, a breakthrough in dye chemistry in which the liquid dye is solubilized to produce a stable color. The dye sets instantly and permanently and allows the dyer to guarantee the color against color fade or lift from cleaning, etc., for 2 years. The dyer can control any color (an array of 18 brilliant colors) with perfect uniformity over extremely large areas of carpet and upholstery. Langenwalter-Harris Chemical Co., Inc., offers two distinct franchises. One is for the businessman who would enjoy providing the dye service for carpet and upholstery. The other is for the entrepreneur who would like to become a subfranchisor in a region and/or territory wherein he supplies all dye, chemicals, and equipment to the dyers. Both franchises now available for marketing overseas.

NUMBER OF FRANCHISEES: 243 and 32 subfranchises in 24 states

IN BUSINESS SINCE: 1972

EQUITY CAPITAL NEEDED: $16,500

FINANCIAL ASSISTANCE AVAILABLE: None.

TRAINING PROVIDED: An intensive, comprehensive, 5-day mandatory training course. The training program is held in the Langenwalter Dye Concept School facility in Anaheim, California. Franchisor provides test book, operational and technical manuals.

MANAGERIAL ASSISTANCE AVAILABLE: Franchisor provides continual technical, chemical, and management update seminars and workshops for all franchisees. A continuous marketing and product research and development program for all franchises.

INFORMATION SUBMITTED: April 1990

* MR. MINIBLIND
17985-F Skypark Circle
Irvine, California 92714
Scott Holt, Vice President, Franchise Sales

DESCRIPTION OF OPERATION: Window covering, sale and installation via mobile vans.

NUMBER OF FRANCHISEES: 50 plus 2 company-owned

IN BUSINESS SINCE: 1987, franchising since 1988

EQUITY CAPITAL NEEDED: $28,000 total investment

FINANCIAL ASSISTANCE AVAILABLE: None.

TRAINING PROVIDED: Complete training program.

MANAGERIAL ASSISTANCE AVAILABLE: Managerial assistance is continuously provided.

INFORMATION SUBMITTED: June 1990

NAKED FURNITURE, INC.
1099 Jay Street
Building 3
Rochester, New York 14611
Peter Judd

DESCRIPTION OF OPERATION: A Naked Furniture store franchise is a specialty retail store selling better-quality solid wood ready-to-finish furniture, custom finishing service, and custom-tailored upholstery.

NUMBER OF FRANCHISEES: 50 plus 2 company-owned in 15 states

IN BUSINESS SINCE: 1972

EQUITY CAPITAL NEEDED: $50,000 minimum; total package $130,000–$200,000.

FINANCIAL ASSISTANCE AVAILABLE: Franchisor will assist in perparing financing proposal for presentation to lending institutions.

TRAINING PROVIDED: Complete operator training and support provided through intensive 1- to 2-week training program as well as full field support on a continuing basis.

MANAGERIAL ASSISTANCE AVAILABLE: Naked Furniture, Inc., provides continual management service for the length of the franchise and provides an operations manual, a full bookkeeping package, forms, inventory selection assistance, regional warehousing, advertising, and professional floor display plan. Periodic visits from regional field representatives will provide help in every area of store management and operation.

INFORMATION SUBMITTED: June 1990

NETTLE CREEK INDUSTRIES, INC.
Peacock Road
Richmond, Indiana 47374

DESCRIPTION OF OPERATION: Home furnishings retail stores specializing in semi-custom-made bedspreads, window treatments, and decorative pillows. These are located in high-income shopping areas and cater to people who need advice and assistance in interior decorating. The stores are about 1,500 square feet, and feature Nettle Creek products.

NUMBER OF FRANCHISEES: 48 in 25 states

IN BUSINESS SINCE: 1950

EQUITY CAPITAL NEEDED: $50,000 investment including one-time franchise fee of $5,000.

FINANCIAL ASSISTANCE AVAILABLE: None.

TRAINING PROVIDED: Manuals and operating systems, on-site training of 1 week's duration, in-factory training of 2 to 3 days' duration, and continuing support and advice after the franchise is opened.

MANAGERIAL ASSISTANCE AVAILABLE: Nettle Creek provides bookkeeping systems, complete stationery supplies, advertising materials, and operating manuals. Full-time franchise coordinators assist in location research, store layout, setup, merchandise selection, and co-op advertising. Our entire executive staff is available for consultation.

INFORMATION SUBMITTED: June 1990

* PROFESSIONAL CARPET SYSTEMS, INC.
5182 Old Dixie Highway
Forest Park, Georgia 30050
Joseph R. Lunsford, President

DESCRIPTION OF OPERATION: Professional Carpet Systems is the leader in on-site carpet redyeing, servicing thousands of apartment complexes, hotels, motels, and residential communities. Worldwide services also include carpet cleaning, rejuvenation, repair, water and flood damage restoration, Kool-aid® removal, and "guaranteed odor control" for pet odor removal. "A total carpet care concept." Member American Association of Textile Chemists and Colorists and International Franchise Association.

NUMBER OF FRANCHISEES: 394 offices in 47 states. Franchises available in remainder of states, Canada, and abroad.

IN BUSINESS SINCE: 1978

EQUITY CAPITAL NEEDED: Total cost of franchise $13,500; franchisor requires $8,500 down, balance financed after the $8,500 down.

FINANCIAL ASSISTANCE AVAILABLE: The balance of $5,000 is company financed, using territory as collateral, 6 percent royalty.

TRAINING PROVIDED: 60 hours intensive technical/sales training and 20 hours office and bookkeeping managerial skills. Total training 2 weeks at our company headquarters.

MANAGERIAL ASSISTANCE AVAILABLE: Our franchise includes equipment package, supplies, printing, continual ongoing assistance through upgraded training sessions, monthly newsletters, toll-free hotlines, and national account acquisition and sales program.

INFORMATION SUBMITTED: June 1990

RAINBOW INTERNATIONAL CARPET DYEING AND CLEANING COMPANY
1010 University Park Drive
Waco, Texas 76707
Donald J. Dwyer, President

DESCRIPTION OF OPERATION: Carpet and upholstery dyeing and tinting—carpet and upholstery cleaning, deodorization services, fire and water restoration, fire retardant—fiber guard.

NUMBER OF FRANCHISEES: 1,000 in United States, Canada, France, Nassau, St. Croix, Guam, Ireland, Singapore, Taiwan, and Australia

IN BUSINESS SINCE: 1981

EQUITY CAPITAL NEEDED: $12,000

FINANCIAL ASSISTANCE AVAILABLE: Will finance 70 percent.

TRAINING PROVIDED: 1 week classroom and on-the-job-ongoing training via WATS line—mailing—regional seminars.

MANAGERIAL ASSISTANCE AVAILABLE: Continuous backup and support via toll-free telephone number.

INFORMATION SUBMITTED: April 1990

* RUG DOCTOR PRO
2788 North Larkin Avenue
Fresno, California 93727
Fred Thompson, National Director

DESCRIPTION OF OPERATION: Carpet upholstery, drapery, and specialty cleaning service.

NUMBER OF FRANCHISEES: 34 plus 1 company-owned

IN BUSINESS SINCE: 1987

EQUITY CAPITAL NEEDED: Equipment packages start at $6,500 to $22,000.

FINANCIAL ASSISTANCE AVAILABLE: 50 percent financing on franchise fee of $6,000 minimum and up to 90 percent on equipment.

TRAINING PROVIDED: Full training program.

MANAGERIAL ASSISTANCE AVAILABLE: Ongoing.

INFORMATION SUBMITTED: June 1990

* SERVICEMASTER RESIDENTIAL AND COMMERCIAL CORPORATION
855 Ridge Lake Boulevard
Memphis, Tennessee 38119
Joseph S. Kirday, Director, Market Expansion

DESCRIPTION OF OPERATION: ServiceMaster Residential and Commercial Corporation, a subsidiary of the ServiceMaster Company L.P. offers franchising in On Location Residential Services, Contract Services, Carpet/Upholstery Services, Small Business Contract Services, and On Location/Contract Services in small market. This encompasses carpet, rug, furniture, smooth-floor surface, housewide cleaning, wall cleaning, disaster restoration, and odor removal in homes and commercial buildings as well as complete janitorial services.

NUMBER OF FRANCHISEES: 4,029 in 50 states and worldwide

IN BUSINESS SINCE: 1948

EQUITY CAPITAL NEEDED: Initial franchise fee for the On Location franchise is $19,000, including training manuals and aids plus an additional $8,000 for a recommended package of promotional materials, professional equipment, supplies and tools, and professional chemicals for a total of $27,000. Initial franchise fee for the Contract Services franchise is $19,000, including manuals and aids plus an additional $9,000 for a recommended package of promotional materials, professional equipment, supplies and tools, and professional chemicals for a total of $28,000. Initial franchise fee for the Carpet/Upholstery franchise is $9,200 including training manuals and aids plus an additional $7,500 for a recommended package of professional materials, professional equipment, supplies and tools, and professional chemicals for a total of $16,700. Initial franchise fee for On Location/Contract Service in a small market area is $10,000, including training manuals and aids plus an additional $7,500 for a recommended package of promotional materials, professional equipment, supplies and tools, and professional chemicals for a total of $17,500. Initial franchise fee for Small Business Contract Service in buildings less than 5,000 square feet is $8,000, including training manuals and aids plus an additional $6,500 for a recommended package of promotional materials, professional equipment, supplies and tools, and professional chemicals for a total of $14,500.

FINANCIAL ASSISTANCE AVAILABLE: Yes.

TRAINING PROVIDED: Comprehensive home study, on-the-job training, setup training, and classroom training. Continuous training program provided for all licensees.

MANAGERIAL ASSISTANCE AVAILABLE: Managerial assistance is available on a continuous basis, from the company and from area-based distributors in the field. The company makes available advertising, sales promotions, formal training laboratory services, regional and international meetings.

INFORMATION SUBMITTED: June 1990

* SPRING CREST COMPANY, INC.
505 West Lambert Road
Brea, California 92621
Jack W. Long, President

DESCRIPTION OF OPERATION: Spring Crest Drapery Centers retail draperies and other window treatments such as blinds, shades, verticals, drapery hardware, and accessories.

NUMBER OF FRANCHISEES: 319 in 38 states, Canada, New Zealand, Australia, South Africa, Saudi Arabia, and the United Kingdom

IN BUSINESS SINCE: 1955, franchising since 1968

EQUITY CAPITAL NEEDED: $50,000 for total package.

FINANCIAL ASSISTANCE AVAILABLE: Yes.

TRAINING PROVIDED: Initial training at headquarters with additional training at franchise location.

MANAGERIAL ASSISTANCE AVAILABLE: Site selection, store design, fixtures and equipment, field staff support, operations manual, regional and national conference, newsletter.

INFORMATION SUBMITTED: April 1990

* STANLEY STEEMER INTERNATIONAL, INC.
5500 Stanley Steamer Parkway
P. O. Box 156
Dublin, Ohio 43017
Wesley C. Bates, President

DESCRIPTION OF OPERATION: A complete franchise system for on-location carpet and furniture cleaning, water damage cleanup, and odor removal services. Company manufactures patented in-truck and portable equipment—maintains complete supplies to provide backup for franchises.

NUMBER OF FRANCHISEES: Over 200 in 31 states, plus 19 company operations

IN BUSINESS SINCE: 1947, carpet and furniture cleaning. 1972, manufacturing and franchise sales.

EQUITY CAPITAL NEEDED: Variable, minimum $20,000

FINANCIAL ASSISTANCE AVAILABLE: Lease program available on equipment and new truck.

TRAINING PROVIDED: 2 weeks or longer, depending on need, at company headquarters. Training conducted by training director with a great amount of OJT with experienced cleaning crews. Periodic review and retraining provided where necessary. All manuals are provided.

MANAGERIAL ASSISTANCE AVAILABLE: Bimonthly newsletter and periodic technical and service bulletins issued. Specific department head help available on an individual basis. A complete advertising department is maintained for franchise support. Annual convention and regional meetings for franchisees. Group liability insurance and major medical and hospitalization insurance programs are available. Continuous research and development for improvement of cleaning methods and equipment.

INFORMATION SUBMITTED: April 1990

* STEAMATIC INCORPORATED
1601 109th Street
Grand Prairie, Texas 75050
John Gellatly, Vice President of Franchising

DESCRIPTION OF OPERATION: Steamatic provides 11 diversified cleaning and restoration services for the insurance, commercial, and residential market segments. These include air duct cleaning; fire, smoke, and water damage restoration; carpet, furniture, ceiling, wall, and drapery cleaning; deodorization and decontamination; wood restoration and corrosion control.

NUMBER OF FRANCHISEES: 225 (primarily in the United States and Canada)

IN BUSINESS SINCE: 1948

EQUITY CAPITAL NEEDED: $10,000–$50,000

FINANCIAL ASSISTANCE AVAILABLE: If franchisee qualifies, one-half of franchise fee can be financed through bank in Fort Worth.

TRAINING PROVIDED: Extensive 2-week training course. This includes 1 week of on-location experience in homes and offices, followed by a 1-week minibusiness school.

MANAGERIAL ASSISTANCE AVAILABLE: Insurance, commercial, and residential marketing; advertising; financial management; regional and national seminars; continuous field support services; operational assistance; Steamatic Executive Council and technical bulletins to franchise owners.

INFORMATION SUBMITTED: April 1990

TOWN & COUNTRY OFFICE & CARPET CARE
2580 San Ramon Valley Boulevard, Suite B-208
San Ramon, California 94583

DESCRIPTION OF OPERATION: State-of-the-art dry extractor carpet cleaning and professional office care.

NUMBER OF FRANCHISEES: 90 throughout the United States

IN BUSINESS SINCE: 1971, began franchising in 1986

EQUITY CAPITAL NEEDED: $3,000–$10,000

FINANCIAL ASSISTANCE AVAILABLE: None.

TRAINING PROVIDED: 3–5 days' training provided.

MANAGERIAL ASSISTANCE AVAILABLE: Continuous managerial assistance available.

INFORMATION SUBMITTED: April 1990

* WASH ON WHEELS-HY-DRY
5401 South Bryant Avenue
Sanford, Florida 32773
George Louser

DESCRIPTION OF OPERATION: Carpet, furniture, and drapery cleaning.

NUMBER OF FRANCHISEES: 40

IN BUSINESS SINCE: 1987

EQUITY CAPITAL NEEDED: $5,400

FINANCIAL ASSISTANCE AVAILABLE: Financial assistance available to those with good credit. Total investment $16,000.

TRAINING PROVIDED: 5 days' intensive training, then constant ongoing manuals, seminars, newsletters, hotlines, and direct mail.

MANAGERIAL ASSISTANCE AVAILABLE: Ongoing

INFORMATION SUBMITTED: April 1990

LAUNDRIES, DRY CLEANING/SERVICES

* DUDS 'N SUDS
CLEAN DUDS INC.
3401 101st Street, Suite E
Des Moines, Iowa 50322
Philip G. Akin

DESCRIPTION OF OPERATION: Self-serve laundry, snack bar, and cleaning services. We call it "Good, Clean, Fun." A full-service laundry that is energy efficient and also has a soda fountain that serves pop, coffee, and even beer. It also has a big-screen TV, pool table, and video games. Approximately 3,000 square feet.

NUMBER OF FRANCHISEES: 85 in 27 states

IN BUSINESS SINCE: 1983

EQUITY CAPITAL NEEDED: $60,000; total system price $80,000

FINANCIAL ASSISTANCE AVAILABLE: We have a loan guide and loan proposal that we present to financial institutions. We also work with the SBA. Limited financial assistance available. Equipment lease programs.

TRAINING PROVIDED: On-site training in store during the opening. Also a week training prior to opening at Des Moines, Iowa. Also operations manuals and instructional videotapes are provided.

MANAGERIAL ASSISTANCE AVAILABLE: Full promotional and management support, manuals, design and layout of store, all signage, videotapes, financial evaluations, inspections, maintenance program, regional and national franchisor meetings.

LONDON INDUSTRIES INC.
2510 Metropolitan Drive
Trevose, Pennsylvania 19047
Ronald London, President

DESCRIPTION OF OPERATION: Offering complete professional drycleaning plants and coin laundry stores. All stores are custom-designed for maximum efficiency and profitability.

NUMBER OF FRANCHISEES: 265 in 6 states and Washington, D.C.

IN BUSINESS SINCE: 1963

EQUITY CAPITAL NEEDED: $35,000 minimum

FINANCIAL ASSISTANCE AVAILABLE: Up to 90 percent financing of equipment through financial institutions.

TRAINING PROVIDED: In-house training as required, service clinics.

MANAGERIAL ASSISTANCE AVAILABLE: Field inspection and assistance in all phases of management on a continuing basis.

INFORMATION SUBMITTED: May 1990

* MARTIN FRANCHISES, INC.
2005 Ross Avenue
Cincinnati, Ohio 45212
Franchise Director

DESCRIPTION OF OPERATION: Comprehensive start-up assistance including locations/site assistance with NDS computerized demographics, mapping capabilities, full plant layout and mechanical drawings, 3-week training program, in-store start-up assistance, equipment shakedown and ongoing local store and marketwide promotional programs, field and operations assistance.

NUMBER OF FRANCHISEES: 904 in 49 states and 4 countries

IN BUSINESS SINCE: 1949

EQUITY CAPITAL NEEDED: $65,000 start-up cash; $157,000–$230,000 total investment.

FINANCIAL ASSISTANCE AVAILABLE: Associated with SBA financial lender and leasing company; however, there is no direct financing.

TRAINING PROVIDED: 3 weeks of comprehensive managerial and technical classroom and in-plant training at Martinizing National Training Center; start-up assistance in franchisee's plant, as well as the comprehensive support listed under "Description of Operation."

MANAGERIAL ASSISTANCE AVAILABLE: Supervision and guidance provided by local representative and franchisor.

INFORMATION SUBMITTED: April 1990

LAWN CARE SERVICES

BAREFOOT GRASS LAWN SERVICE, INC.
1018 Proprietors Road
Worthington, Ohio 43085
John E. Dunham, Vice President for Franchising

DESCRIPTION OF OPERATION: Barefoot Grass provides professional granular lawn care to residential and commercial lawns. Fertilizers, weed controls, insect controls, and disease controls are applied on a scheduled basis following prescribed programs. Enjoyable outdoor work environment.

NUMBER OF FRANCHISEES: 30 in 21 states

IN BUSINESS SINCE: 1975

EQUITY CAPITAL NEEDED: $25,000

FINANCIAL ASSISTANCE AVAILABLE: None.

TRAINING PROVIDED: Technical agronomic training, sales training, and business training are provided. Training is conducted at the franchisee's site or at the franchisor's headquarters in Worthington, Ohio, a Columbus, Ohio suburb. Formal introductory training programs last at least 4 days, with follow-up provided as needed.

MANAGERIAL ASSISTANCE AVAILABLE: Barefoot Grass provides continuing management services for the duration of the franchise in such areas as computer services, including customer records; bookkeeping, including accounts receivable, payroll; marketing and advertising; purchasing and inventory control. Operating and technical manuals and updates are provided. Forms and supplies are available. Regional managers are available to work closely with franchisees and visit regularly to assist with problem solving and quality control. Barefoot Grass sponsors meetings of branch and franchise managers to maintain high levels of training and performance.

INFORMATION SUBMITTED: April 1990

* LAWN DOCTOR INCORPORATED
P. O. Box 512142 Highway #34
Matawan, New Jersey 07747
Ed Reid, National Franchise Sales Director

DESCRIPTION OF OPERATION: Professional automated lawn services.

NUMBER OF FRANCHISEES: Over 300 in 27 states

IN BUSINESS SINCE: 1967

EQUITY CAPITAL NEEDED: Minimum of $30,500

FINANCIAL ASSISTANCE AVAILABLE: Yes.

TRAINING PROVIDED: Extensive 2-week managerial, sales, and technical training at the home office. Technical training for each employee at the home office. Weekly workshops. Management seminars.

MANAGERIAL ASSISTANCE AVAILABLE: All necessary initial bookkeeping, advertising, and sales promotional materials supplied. Close follow-up after initial training with service representatives available for both telephone and in-the-field assistance whenever required. Public relations consultation available. Extensive TV advertising campaigns in major markets.

INFORMATION SUBMITTED: May 1990

LIQUI-GREEN LAWN CARE CORPORATION
9601 North Allen Road
Peoria, Illinois 61615
B. C. Dailey, President

DESCRIPTION OF OPERATION: Lawn spraying of fertilizer and weed control, plus many additives. Tree spraying, deep feeding, and injection. Each franchise is owner operated, using a new 1-ton truck, mounted with 300- and 500-gallon tank with injectors for special products.

NUMBER OF FRANCHISEES: 25 in Illinois, Iowa, and Pennsylvania

IN BUSINESS SINCE: 1953

EQUITY CAPITAL NEEDED: $10,000

FINANCIAL ASSISTANCE AVAILABLE: Possible to qualified persons.

TRAINING PROVIDED: Extensive on-the-job training in technique, material handling, sales and advertising.

MANAGERIAL ASSISTANCE AVAILABLE: Liqui-Green sponsors seminars to introduce new ideas, products, and advertising ideas. Liqui-Green is staffed with turf and tree experts for counsel to all its franchises.

INFORMATION SUBMITTED: April 1990

NITRO-GREEN CORPORATION
2791 F.N. Texas Street, Suite 300
Fairfield, California 94533
Roger Albrecht, President

DESCRIPTION OF OPERATION: Lawn fertilizing, weed control, insect control, disease control for turf. Tree and shrub care.

NUMBER OF FRANCHISEES: 39 in 14 states

IN BUSINESS SINCE: 1977

EQUITY CAPITAL NEEDED: $25,000

FINANCIAL ASSISTANCE AVAILABLE: On equipment only.

TRAINING PROVIDED: 10 days' training and ongoing. Seminars at various times during the year. Monthly newsletters, toll-free telephone assistance.

MANAGERIAL ASSISTANCE AVAILABLE: Bookkeeping and related lawn technology.

INFORMATION SUBMITTED: May 1990

* SERVICEMASTER LAWN CARE
855 Ridge Lake Boulevard
Memphis, Tennessee 38119
Dan Kellow, Vice President

DESCRIPTION OF OPERATION: Professional lawn, tree, and shrub care for residential and commercial clients.

NUMBER OF FRANCHISEES: 175 in United States

IN BUSINESS SINCE: 1985

EQUITY CAPITAL NEEDED: $10,000–$12,000

FINANCIAL ASSISTANCE AVAILABLE: Up to $15,300 financing through ServiceMaster and leasing arrangements.

TRAINING PROVIDED: Technical agronomic, licensing preparation, and marketing training is provided during 6-day academy. On-site training at licensee's business is provided through the regional manager and master franchise coordinator.

MANAGERIAL ASSISTANCE AVAILABLE: Continuous support is available throughout the franchise agreement. This support is provided through the master franchise coordinator for the area.

INFORMATION SUBMITTED: April 1990

* SPRING-GREEN LAWN CARE CORP.
P. O. Box 908
Naperville, Illinois 60566
Thomas W. Hoter, President

DESCRIPTION OF OPERATION: Professional lawn, tree, and shrub care service to residential and commercial customers. Spring-Green uses state-of-the-art equipment and techniques in a modern and rapidly growing industry. Extremely high annual customer renewal plus complete marketing programs help franchisee to realize solid growth. Customer programs generally include 4 to 6 applications per year.

NUMBER OF FRANCHISEES: 137 in 22 states

IN BUSINESS SINCE: 1977

EQUITY CAPITAL NEEDED: Total initial investment of $17,595 plus $8,000 working capital.

FINANCIAL ASSISTANCE AVAILABLE: In addition, a national equipment lease program is available. Assistance is provided in obtaining financing through private sources.

TRAINING PROVIDED: 1-week intensive modular training at beginning of franchise operation with ongoing guidance and support. Periodic instructional meetings as well as seminars are provided at various times during the year. Biweekly newsletter and toll-free telephone assistance are available to all franchisees.

MANAGERIAL ASSISTANCE AVAILABLE: S-G provides managerial and technical assistance to the franchisees on an ongoing basis. Training manuals as well as various publications are provided for each franchise. Field representatives visit each franchisee on a regular basis to provide assistance in an area where the franchisee may need help. Seminars are also held during the year covering such items as cash flow projections, selling skills, and technical assistance. S-G also provides assistance in advertising, marketing and business management, using video and other modern training techniques. For more information call (800) 435-4051.

INFORMATION SUBMITTED: April 1990

MAID SERVICES/HOME CLEANING/PARTY SERVICING

* AMERICA'S MAID SERVICE—THE MAIDS
THE MAIDS INTERNATIONAL, INC.
4820 Dodge Street
Omaha, Nebraska 68132
Danielle Bishop

DESCRIPTION OF OPERATION: Your investment accesses you to a multibillion-dollar market positioned for 20 percent annual growth into the 1990s. We've led the way for 10 years with a proven system featuring low-investment, up-front cash flow, high customer demand, small inventory with volume discounts on your supply and equipment, total advertising to target your customers and complete management training (featured in *USA Today* as one of America's top franchise training programs).

NUMBER OF FRANCHISEES: 200 in 38 states and 2 countries

IN BUSINESS SINCE: 1980

EQUITY CAPITAL NEEDED: Franchise fee $16,900; other capital requirements $20,000 plus.

FINANCIAL ASSISTANCE AVAILABLE: Yes.

TRAINING PROVIDED: 6-week pre-training counseling. 12-day corporate training (administrative and technical) with complete hands-on computer training. 90-day post-training follow-up.

MANAGERIAL ASSISTANCE AVAILABLE: Monthly newsletter, toll-free phone support, regional seminars and annual meetings. Accounting staff, advertising, PR program, tech staff.

INFORMATION SUBMITTED: April 1990

* MERRY MAIDS
11117 Mill Valley Road
Omaha, Nebraska 68154
Bob Burdge/Paul Hogan

DESCRIPTION OF OPERATION: Merry Maids is the largest professional home cleaning service in the nation. With over 500 franchise offices, the company dominates important metropolitan markets. Compared with others, Merry Maids has the strongest business control system, the lowest cost structure on equipment and supplies, the most comprehensive employee recruiting and training tools, highly aggressive marketing and PR programs, and an unmatched depth of corporate office management and staff.

NUMBER OF FRANCHISEES: 500

IN BUSINESS SINCE: 1980

EQUITY CAPITAL NEEDED: Affordable $18,500 franchise fee plus $10,000 to $15,000 to cover start-up expenses including office furnishings, required IBM computer and video equipment, and working capital.

FINANCIAL ASSISTANCE AVAILABLE: Yes, up to $10,000 of $18,500 franchise fee.

TRAINING PROVIDED: Comprehensive, all-inclusive 5-day training program at Merry Maids' Omaha training center is included in the franchise fee. Curriculum covers all the necessary procedures, program, and tools necessary to develop, manage, and operate a successful franchise.

MANAGERIAL ASSISTANCE AVAILABLE: No one in the industry provides a greater commitment—and ongoing support—to new and established franchise owners. A network of regional coordinators, a corporate staff, and the company's unique "Franchise Buddy System" of established owners all contribute to monitoring, counseling, and guiding the growth and success of each Merry Maids franchise operation. Individual support is further enhanced through regional franchise owners' meetings, specialized field seminars, and the company's national convention, which is annually attended by more than 80 percent of Merry Maids franchise owners.

INFORMATION SUBMITTED: May 1990

MINI MAID SERVICES, INC.
1855 Piedmont Road, Suite 100
Marietta, Georgia 30066
Leone Ackerly, President

DESCRIPTION OF OPERATION: Mini Maid pioneered the residential team cleaning concept in 1973 and has been franchising since 1976, longer than anyone else. We have been cited as one of America's top 101 service companies. Our concept delivers the quality of service desired by today's consumer. Our unique flat-rate royalty system, low initial investment, and the industry's most comprehensive training program allow our franchisees the industry's best profit opportunity.

NUMBER OF FRANCHISEES: 133

IN BUSINESS SINCE: 1973—first franchised in 1976

EQUITY CAPITAL NEEDED: $12,000–$20,000

FINANCIAL ASSISTANCE AVAILABLE: None.

TRAINING PROVIDED: Intensive 5-day headquarters production/administrative training. Complete pre- and post-opening program including additional 55 days at established franchises.

MANAGERIAL ASSISTANCE AVAILABLE: Ongoing training, consultation, regional field managers, headquarters staff field visits, toll-free number, regional and national meetings, newsletters, complete supervisory certification programs.

INFORMATION SUBMITTED: April 1990

* MOLLY MAID, INC.
707 Wolverine Tower Building
3001 South State Street
Ann Arbor, Michigan 48108
David G. McKinnon, President

DESCRIPTION OF OPERATION: A team of two uniformed maids arrives in a company car with their own cleaning supplies and equipment at the customer's home. Cleaning includes dusting baseboards, pictures, lampshades, knickknacks, windowsills, furniture, fixtures, and vacuuming throughout. Kitchen and bathrooms are sanitized, walls are spotcleaned, cabinet fronts and floors professionally washed. All maids are bonded, insured, and professionally trained.

NUMBER OF FRANCHISEES: 280

IN BUSINESS SINCE: Started in Canada in 1978 and licensing in the United States since 1984.

EQUITY CAPITAL NEEDED: $16,900 plus approximately $10,000 in start-up costs, along with the ability to support self outside of business for at least 1 year.

FINANCIAL ASSISTANCE AVAILABLE: Yes.

TRAINING PROVIDED: Prior to the commencement of the Molly Maid business by the franchisee, the franchisor will provide a 5-day training program guiding through methods, procedures, standards, and techniques of the Molly Maid system and in the basic marketing, management, and bookkeeping system. The training day starts in the early morning and continues through the evening with lectures, discussions, assignments, and actual hands-on training.

MANAGERIAL ASSISTANCE AVAILABLE: The franchisor may from time to time hold training seminars, workshops, and conferences concerning sales techniques, purchasing, training of personnel, performance standards, advertising and promotion programs, and merchandising procedures for the franchisee and the franchisee's managerial staff.

INFORMATION SUBMITTED: May 1990

MAINTENANCE—CLEANING/SANITATION—SERVICES/SUPPLIES

* AMERICLEAN
Americlean Franchising Corporation
6602 South Frontage Road
Billings, Montana 59101
Mark Taverniti, Vice President of Franchise Development

DESCRIPTION OF OPERATION: Disaster restoration services and specialty cleaning.

NUMBER OF FRANCHISEES: 105 in 35 states

IN BUSINESS SINCE: 1979

EQUITY CAPITAL NEEDED: $28,000–$124,000

FINANCIAL ASSISTANCE AVAILABLE: Assistance with securing financing through third parties.

TRAINING PROVIDED: 2-week classroom and in-field training. Installation and opening support. Operations manuals, support staff visits, and toll-free support line, certified restorer on staff.

MANAGERIAL ASSISTANCE AVAILABLE: See above.

INFORMATION SUBMITTED: April 1990.

* COUSTIC-GLO INTERNATIONAL, INC.
7111 Ohms Lane
Minneapolis, Minnesota 55435
Everett C. Smith, President

DESCRIPTION OF OPERATION: The Coustic-Glo concept offers a unique opportunity for an individual to achieve a high degree of financial independence in a virtually untapped industry. The need for ceiling cleaning is all around you in every structure you enter on a daily basis, and as a Coustic-Glo franchisee you will be provided with all the equipment, products, chemicals, and training necessary to prosper in this field.

NUMBER OF FRANCHISEES: 165 throughout the United States, Canada, and Europe

IN BUSINESS SINCE: 1980

EQUITY CAPITAL NEEDED: $9,750–$25,000 depending on area assigned.

FINANCIAL ASSISTANCE AVAILABLE: None.

TRAINING PROVIDED: Each new franchise is provided with a very intensive 2–3-day training program that takes place in their respective exclusive areas under the direct supervision of an experienced franchisee that is brought in from their area to assist in the establishment of the new franchisee's business. Also available to the new franchisee is option of training course provided at home office under direct supervision of home office personnel.

MANAGERIAL ASSISTANCE AVAILABLE: The home office of Coustic-Glo International, Inc., provides continual support in all areas of this business. Toll-free phones are maintained to give direct and constant access to the home office and assistance with field problems, technical questions, etc. Complete test reports on all products are provided with updating as necessary. A very aggressive national advertising campaign is pursued. Local ad mats and all product identification provided. Complete manuals, forms, and customer lists are supplied each new franchisee. New national accounts are being added, and you will have available to you a field man to assist in your area with questions. Company also sponsors meetings of franchisees and continues to maintain market and research and development departments to find further outlets for its products and services.

INFORMATION SUBMITTED: June 1990

* JANI-KING, INC.
4950 Keller Springs, Suite 190
Dallas, Texas 75248
James Cavanaugh, President
Jerry Crawford, National & International Marketing Director

DESCRIPTION OF OPERATION: World's largest commercial cleaning franchisor. Franchisees provide professional cleaning programs to commercial and industrial buildings on a long-term contract basis. Franchisees follow proven business plan and benefit from national advertising, excellent references coast-to-coast, and support from the industry leader.

NUMBER OF FRANCHISEES: 1,500 in the United States and Canada

IN BUSINESS SINCE: 1969

EQUITY CAPITAL NEEDED: $3,000–$14,500 plus

FINANCIAL ASSISTANCE AVAILABLE: A total investment of $6,500 is necessary to start a Jani-King franchise. Jani-King will finance part of the total investment depending on the location desired.

TRAINING PROVIDED: Training is provided for all new franchisees through a designated center. The training is conducted under the supervision of a full-time Jani-King employee.

MANAGERIAL ASSISTANCE AVAILABLE: A complete manual of operations, forms, and directions are provided for each new franchise. Jani-King also provides continual management service for the life of the franchise, such as contract negotiations, bookkeeping, hiring and training procedures, securing new business, and public relations. Regional and service managers are available to work closely with franchisees and visit service locations to provide technical advice and assist in solving problems.

INFORMATION SUBMITTED: April 1990

MR. MAINTENANCE
21401 South Norwalk Boulevard
Hawaiian Gardens, California 90716
Philip A. Syphers, President

DESCRIPTION OF OPERATION: ABC Maintenance development corporation has developed a complete system for providing commercial building maintenance services under the tradename of Mr. Maintenance. The company sales force develops as many customers as are desired by the franchisee. Customers are located in an area chosen by the franchisee. Area subfranchising rights are available to qualified individuals who wish to sell Mr. Maintenance franchises in selected regions of the country.

NUMBER OF FRANCHISEES: 53 plus 13 company-owned units in California

IN BUSINESS SINCE: 1971

EQUITY CAPITAL NEEDED: $2,000–$25,000 (proportional to the $ volume of customers provided)

FINANCIAL ASSISTANCE AVAILABLE: Partial financing available.

TRAINING PROVIDED: Complete training is provided, which lasts from 3 days to 2 weeks for the service franchisee to 1 month for area subfranchisors. In either program the training consists of both classroom and field training.

MANAGERIAL ASSISTANCE AVAILABLE: The company provides complete ongoing managerial services including computerized bookkeeping systems, billing, collecting, employee referrals; technical advice, sales assistance, company supervision, and continuous management counseling. Payroll services, tax deposit, and full computerized accounting services are an available option to the franchisee.

INFORMATION SUBMITTED: June 1990

MR. ROOTER CORPORATION
P. O. Box 3146
Waco, Texas 76707

DESCRIPTION OF OPERATION: Mr. Rooter has developed improved equipment and marketing materials and techniques in the sewer and drain cleaning business. Each licensee has access to the management skills of generations of master plumbers, the use of five U.S. patent office registered servicemarks, and an extensive national advertising program designed to increase business. Mr. Rooter is a step-by-step integrated business system geared for success.

NUMBER OF FRANCHISEES: 47 in 15 states

IN BUSINESS SINCE: 1968, incorporated 1970

EQUITY CAPITAL NEEDED: Initial equipment and supply package is $6,000.

FINANCIAL ASSISTANCE AVAILABLE: None by company.

TRAINING PROVIDED: No special training is required prior to owning a franchise.

MANAGERIAL ASSISTANCE AVAILABLE: Mr. Rooter corporation maintains a continuous home office advisory service for the lifetime of the agreement. This includes guidance in both managerial and technical aspects of the business. Dealers may take refresher training at any time at their convenience.

INFORMATION SUBMITTED: June 1990

* ROTO-ROOTER CORPORATION
300 Ashworth Road
West Des Moines, Iowa 50265
Paul W. Carter

DESCRIPTION OF OPERATION: Sewer and drain cleaning service.

NUMBER OF FRANCHISEES: 650 plus 50 company-owned

IN BUSINESS SINCE: 1935

EQUITY CAPITAL NEEDED: $7,000–$60,000

FINANCIAL ASSISTANCE AVAILABLE: None.

TRAINING PROVIDED: Training available at home office, but most new franchisees prefer training at an operating franchise near their homes.

MANAGERIAL ASSISTANCE AVAILABLE: Continued assistance in all phases of operation through field staff, manuals, bulletins, advertising, etc.

INFORMATION SUBMITTED: June 1990

SPARKLE WASH, INC.
26851 Richmond Road
Bedford Heights, Ohio 44146
Wallace Nido, President

DESCRIPTION OF OPERATION: Sparkle Wash, Inc., operates and directs successful international network of mobile power cleaning licensees. These individuals, partnerships, and corporations provide power cleaning services for a diverse market, including truck fleets; mobile and residential homes; commercial, governmental, and industrial buildings; industrial and farm machinery, boats; etc. Power cleaning services are provided using company-developed patented mobile cleaning units and marketing programs. Services include washing, waxing, historical restoration, masonry cleaning and sealing, paint and graffiti removal, etc.

NUMBER OF FRANCHISEES: 176 in 49 states, Canada, Japan, and Austria

IN BUSINESS SINCE: 1965

EQUITY CAPITAL NEEDED: $10,000 minimum initial, $37,000–$55,000 total.

FINANCIAL ASSISTANCE AVAILABLE: Various financing plans available through company-assisted, GMAC and FMC unit financing plans. Cost includes complete start-up package, mobile equipment, van, and training program.

TRAINING PROVIDED: Initial training in equipment operation, maintenance, chemicals, marketing and sales provided at company headquarters or regional offices. In-field training uses licensee's unit and operators. Company representative visits licensee's area to conduct training and generate initial accounts.

MANAGERIAL ASSISTANCE AVAILABLE: Company provides regular publications containing up-to-date marketing and technical information. Company also provides computer printouts of truck fleet operators, market surveys, advertising materials, sales, and business consultation on general or specific needs. Company provides technical assistance programs and periodic regional and international meetings.

INFORMATION SUBMITTED: June 1990

VALUE LINE MAINTENANCE SYSTEMS
A Division of WESTERN MAINTENANCE COMPANY
3801 River Drive North
Great Falls, Montana 59401
William D. Blackhall

DESCRIPTION OF OPERATION: Value Line Maintenance Systems offers a unique service business, specializing in flexible cleaning programs for supermarkets, large retail outlets, and other types of facilities. Franchise areas are protected within the Value Line operations.

NUMBER OF FRANCHISEES: 35 in 18 states

IN BUSINESS SINCE: 1959, franchising since 1982

EQUITY CAPITAL NEEDED: $23,000 minimum

FINANCIAL ASSISTANCE AVAILABLE: A total minimum investment of $42,200, consisting of $25,000 franchise fee, $8,800 equipment, $3,000 inventory, $5,400 working capital and miscellaneous, is required. A minimum down payment of $13,000 for franchise fee, plus $10,000 certifiable investment capital, is required. Financing arrangements are available for $12,000 of the franchise fee, and equipment purchases. The inventory can be financed on a 30-60-90-day interest-free payment plan.

TRAINING PROVIDED: An intensive 5-day mandatory training course is scheduled for all new franchisees at the home office. An additional 14 days' training is provided in the field, on-site at the franchisee's contracts.

MANAGERIAL ASSISTANCE AVAILABLE: Value Line provides continuing management and technical assistance as required for the life of the franchise. An operating guide, employee handbooks, video training tape, and many other management aids are provided. Regional marketing representatives are available to assist in marketing and problem solving. Value Line also conducts national and regional marketing and product research. The MASCO Sales Division provides supplies and equipment at specially reduced prices.

INFORMATION SUBMITTED: June 1990

* WASH ON WHEELS-WOW
5401 South Bryant Avenue
Sanford, Florida 32773
George Louser

DESCRIPTION OF OPERATION: Mobile power cleaning franchise providing cleaning services for a diverse market, including government, industrial, commercial buildings, residential homes, and more.

NUMBER OF FRANCHISEES: 52 nationwide

IN BUSINESS SINCE: 1965, franchising since 1987

EQUITY CAPITAL NEEDED: $7,500–$9,000

FINANCIAL ASSISTANCE AVAILABLE: Financial assistance to qualified persons with good credit. Total investment $23,000 to $33,000.

TRAINING PROVIDED: 5 days' intensive training, then ongoing. Manuals, seminars, newsletters, hotlines, and direct mail.

MANAGERIAL ASSISTANCE AVAILABLE: Ongoing.

INFORMATION SUBMITTED: April 1990

WEST SANITATION SERVICES, INC.
25100 South Normandie Avenue
Harbor City, California 90710
G. H. Emery, President

DESCRIPTION OF OPERATION: Route odor control and washroom service.

NUMBER OF FRANCHISEES: 25 in 8 states

IN BUSINESS SINCE: Franchise operations since 1978—wholly owned subsidiary of West Chemical Products, Inc., formed in 1882 up to August 1984 when the subsidiary was sold to present owners.

EQUITY CAPITAL NEEDED: $9,600 (maximum)

FINANCIAL ASSISTANCE AVAILABLE: Franchisor will finance approximately 80 percent of total cost, except inventory and supplies.

TRAINING PROVIDED: Full operational training on-the-job including accounting, administration, customer relations, etc. 1 to 2 weeks' duration.

MANAGERIAL ASSISTANCE AVAILABLE: Continuous.

INFORMATION SUBMITTED: April 1990

PET SHOPS

DOCKTOR PET CENTERS, INC.
355 Middlesex Avenue
Wilmington, Massachusetts 01887
Leslie Charm, Chairman
Joe Hedl, Director/Franchise Development

DESCRIPTION OF OPERATION: Retail pets, supplies, and pet accessories in regional shopping malls and major strip center locations.

NUMBER OF FRANCHISEES: 270 stores in 37 states

IN BUSINESS SINCE: 1966

EQUITY CAPITAL NEEDED: Approximately $50,000–$60,000. ($150,000–$211,000 total investment.)

FINANCIAL ASSISTANCE AVAILABLE: Docktor Pet Centers will assist with the preparation and presentation of financing applications; SBA loans available to qualified applicants.

TRAINING PROVIDED: 3 weeks at franchisor's headquarters; subjects covered include store operations, care and maintenance of pets, accounting management, inventory, personnel selection, merchandising, promotions, advertising, etc. Regional and national seminars.

MANAGERIAL ASSISTANCE AVAILABLE: Advice on stocking, fixture arrangement, receipt of livestock, maintenance procedures, and profit control, site selection, lease negotiation, store planning, etc. On-the-site advisor guides franchisee during first 2 weeks of operations. Advertising materials, accounting forms, and seasonal signs furnished. Consultants make frequent visits to stores to assist franchisees.

INFORMATION SUBMITTED: April 1990

* PETLAND, INC.
195 North Hickory Street
P. O. Box 1606
Chillicothe, Ohio 45601-5606
Edward R. Kunzelman, President
Linda H. Heuring, Vice President, Marketing

DESCRIPTION OF OPERATION: Full-service retail pet stores carrying pets and pet supplies, specializing in innovative pet care, housing, and customer education.

NUMBER OF FRANCHISEES: 185 plus 2 company-owned stores in the United States, Canada, France, and Japan

IN BUSINESS SINCE: 1967

EQUITY CAPITAL NEEDED: $40,000–$60,000, depending on store size and location. Total investment $125,000 to $300,000.

FINANCIAL ASSISTANCE AVAILABLE: Franchisor will assist in preparation of financial presentation package.

TRAINING PROVIDED: Complete classroom at Ohio main office, hands-on in-store training, plus training in franchisee's store. Additional assistance in-store after opening. Ongoing training on specific topics related to business management, livestock care, product knowledge, advertising, and sales.

MANAGERIAL ASSISTANCE AVAILABLE: Assistance in merchandising, livestock management, and maintenance procedures. On-site advisor guides franchisee during first week of operation. Advertising manual, ongoing promotion, and standardized accounting and reporting forms furnished. Area field supervisors make regular visits and provide assistance in problem areas. Advertising manual, operations manual, employee training manuals, videotapes, counter reference book, all forms for operations provided.

INFORMATION SUBMITTED: April 1990

PRINTING

* AMERICAN SPEEDY PRINTING CENTERS, INC.
Corporate Offices
32100 Telegraph Road, Suite 110
Birmingham, Michigan 48010
Vernon G. Buchanan, President

DESCRIPTION OF OPERATION: American Speedy Printing Centers, Inc., offers franchise owners an outstanding profit potential in the fast-growing quick printing industry. A center is set up with all the necessary equipment for offset printing, bindery, and photo copying as well as all other accessories needed to operate a successful quick printing center. For additional information call (800) 521-4002 (in Michigan [800] 482-0421; in Canada [800] 544-8405).

NUMBER OF FRANCHISEES: More than 650 in United States, Canada, Japan, and England

IN BUSINESS SINCE: 1977

EQUITY CAPITAL NEEDED: $40,000 minimum cash requirement

FINANCIAL ASSISTANCE AVAILABLE: Financing available to qualified applicants.

TRAINING PROVIDED: Completion of an extensive 4-week training course that includes bookkeeping and reporting system, equipment operation and maintenance, marketing, pricing, work scheduling, and management of employees. Franchisor's representative assists franchisee in his or her location during his or her first week of operation.

MANAGERIAL ASSISTANCE AVAILABLE: American Speedy Printing Centers provides a continuing support system to all of its franchisees through the home office as well as several regional offices for the life of the franchise agreement. This includes national conventions, conferences, and miniseminars, advertising; management consultation; employment services; negotiation of national contracts for supply and equipment discounts; equipment, maintenance, and repair seminars; sales seminars; press and camera services; technical and supply bulletins; monthly newsletter; and continuing research of new equipment and supplies. The home office staff is available for personal assistance and counseling by telephone and in person.

INFORMATION SUBMITTED: June 1990

* FRANKLIN'S COPY SERVICE, INC.
135 International Boulevard
Atlanta, Georgia 30303
Hal Collins, President

DESCRIPTION OF OPERATION: Full-service quick printing and office supply stores featuring printing, typesetting, high-speed copy reproduction, and a complete line of office supplies.

NUMBER OF FRANCHISEES: 83 stores in 15 states and Canada

IN BUSINESS SINCE: 1971

EQUITY CAPITAL NEEDED: $40,000–$50,000, which includes working capital.

FINANCIAL ASSISTANCE AVAILABLE: Franklin's will assist franchise owner in obtaining bank financing.

TRAINING PROVIDED: 3 weeks and ongoing as necessary.

MANAGERIAL ASSISTANCE AVAILABLE: Franklin's provides support to the franchisee in hiring, marketing, advertising, purchasing, and receivables control. The franchisor is available for assistance in any area necessary for the operation of the stores.

INFORMATION SUBMITTED: May 1990

* THE INK WELL, INC.
2323 Lake Club Drive
Columbus, Ohio 43232
Gerard Ales, Vice President, National Development

DESCRIPTION OF OPERATION: The Ink Well printing centers are positioned in the market to provide high-quality printing and related services to the business community through retail printing operations. Our owners benefit from the industry's most experienced management team and an exceptional business system. We offer you complete support: continual training, financial guidance, marketing programs, business management programs, and all the other operational support you'd expect from a franchise. Investor opportunities available for regional master franchise expansion program.

NUMBER OF FRANCHISEES: 356 locations in 41 states, Washington, D.C., Puerto Rico, and Canada

IN BUSINESS SINCE: 1965

EQUITY CAPITAL NEEDED: $88,000 minimum cash requirement.

FINANCIAL ASSISTANCE AVAILABLE: A total investment of $132,500 is necessary in order to open an Insty-Prints store. Insty-Prints provides no financial assistance to the franchise owner at this time.

TRAINING PROVIDED: To expedite opening, Insty-Prints provides 1 week of business training at Minneapolis headquarters. This training covers desktop publishing using state-of-the-art Apple Macintosh hardware and software, advertising and marketing systems, sales techniques, job flow systems, bookkeeping, estimating, paper, health and safety on the job, inventory control, the role of the owner, and other management skills. 1 week of additional training in the franchise owner's store is offered immediately following the headquarters training. This phase of training provides the franchise owner assistance in putting into practice those systems and programs learned previously. Additional follow-up training is also scheduled at this time.

MANAGERIAL ASSISTANCE AVAILABLE: Annual convention seminars and workshops, annual regional workshops, continuing management advice and counsel, instant in WATS telephone communications, continuing advertising and marketing programs, regularly scheduled newsletters/bulletins, informational mailings, national advertising fund.

INFORMATION SUBMITTED: April 1990

* KWIK-KOPY CORPORATION
1 Kwik-Kopy Lane
P. O. Box 777
Cypress, Texas 77429
Director—Marketing

DESCRIPTION OF OPERATION: A Kwik-Kopy Center franchise offers a system for production and sale of high-quality printing, duplicating, copying, bindery, and attendant services on rapid time schedules tailored to meet the customers' desire. The franchise includes volume buying discounts on the purchase of equipment, microcomputer hardware with specialized business systems software, furniture, fixtures and supplies, market research, site selection, negotiation of real estate leases, equipment operation, public relations, sales and advertising programs, start-up assistance, and continued support service in technical and business management problems over the entire 25-year term of the franchise agreement.

NUMBER OF FRANCHISEES: Approximately over 1,000 in 42 states, Canada, United Kingdom, Australia, South Africa, and Israel

IN BUSINESS SINCE: 1967

EQUITY CAPITAL NEEDED: Minimum cash requirement of approximately $40,000 to $50,000.

FINANCIAL ASSISTANCE AVAILABLE: Third-party financing available.

TRAINING PROVIDED: Completion of an intensive 2-week training course is provided by Kwik-Kopy Corporation at its management training center and is required prior to opening a Kwik-Kopy Center. Additional 1-week on-the-job training in the franchise owner's place of business during and after start-up is also provided. Training includes equipment operation, accounting, advertising sales and business methods in Kwik-Kopy Center operations. Pre- and post-training videotapes on business procedures, operation and maintenance of equipment, sales, and advertising programs are supplied to each franchise owner.

MANAGERIAL ASSISTANCE AVAILABLE: The company provides continued support services to its franchise owners for the term of the franchise agreement, including management counsel, advertising, and training of new employees. Assistance and counseling is available to all franchise owners by telephone through nationwide toll-free WATS lines available to all franchise owners.

INFORMATION SUBMITTED: June 1990

* MINUTEMAN PRESS INTERNATIONAL, INC.
1640 New Highway
Farmingdale, New York 11735
Roy W. Titus, President

DESCRIPTION OF OPERATION: Minuteman Press International, Inc., offers a unique approach to the instant printing franchise through its full-service printing centers. Not only the ability to produce high-quality instant printing, but also the versatility of the equipment enable the owners with no previous printing or graphics experience to produce multicolor printing, photostats, overhead visuals, and the screening of halftones. A complete package is offered that includes all the necessary equipment for printing, cutting, folding, padding, collating, stapling, plus the initial supply of ink, film, paper, stationery, and promotional materials for marketing. Also included in the package is the research of the proposed area, securing an acceptable location, and assistance in the negotiation of the lease as well as overseeing the compete renovations of the location, including the installation of fixtures, signs, furniture, and all accessories needed to operate a successful Minuteman Press Full Service Printing Center.

NUMBER OF FRANCHISEES: Over 900 in 44 states and Canada

IN BUSINESS SINCE: 1973

EQUITY CAPITAL NEEDED: Approximately $22,500–$32,500

FINANCIAL ASSISTANCE AVAILABLE: $94,586 to $116,742 total investment, with financing available through the 3M Company (Minnesota Mining and Manufacturing Company).

TRAINING PROVIDED: There is an intensive 2-week training program held at the Minuteman Press Training Center in Farmingdale, New York, covering all aspects of the business, plus a minimum of 40 hours of continued training at the franchisee's own location under home office field supervision. Training covers use of all equipment, advertising, pricing, bookkeeping, sales promotion, counter procedures, inventory, and cost control and general management. The owner is also trained in a marketing program developed by the company, which has been one of the keys to the success of the Minuteman Press franchises.

MANAGERIAL ASSISTANCE AVAILABLE: The company has regional offices under the supervision of an officer of the company in Atlanta, Baltimore, Birmingham, Boston, Chicago, Cleveland, Dallas, Denver, Ft. Lauderdale, Los Angeles, Minneapolis, New York, Philadelphia, Pittsburgh, San Francisco, Seattle, St. Louis, and Canada to provide continued support services and guidance to its franchisees, including management, marketing, advertising, and training of new employees. Franchise owners are kept current with results of research and new equipment through periodic meetings and seminars and visits by field representatives who provide assistance as required. Continuous guidance and support are available to all franchise owners through the regional or home office.

INFORMATION SUBMITTED: April 1990

PRINT SHACK
Intracoastal Building, 5th Floor
3000 NE 30th Place
Ft. Lauderdale, Florida 33305

DESCRIPTION OF OPERATION: Print Shack has established itself as the most unique franchise opportunity in the instant printing industry. Our centers market a full range of printed paper products including multicolor work, full typesetting services, and related services. Additionally, Print Shack centers offer over 50,000 different advertising specialty products to the same customer base, combining the $3 billion instant printing industry with the $4 billion advertising specialty industry. We offer single-store, multistore, and regional opportunities.

NUMBER OF FRANCHISEES: 100 in 30 states

IN BUSINESS SINCE: 1982

EQUITY CAPITAL NEEDED: Franchise fee $30,000; no charge for second franchise; $46,000–$65,000 total cash.

FINANCIAL ASSISTANCE AVAILABLE: Financing available for all equipment and a portion of the franchise fee to qualified individuals. SBA also available.

TRAINING PROVIDED: All franchisees receive a full 2 weeks of comprehensive training at our home office in Ft. Lauderdale, Florida, and 2 weeks on location. In addition, training classes are continuous, and you may enroll members of your staff or yourself in any ongoing class at no extra charge for the term of the franchise. Instruction covers every aspect of equipment training, marketing, accounting procedures, personnel, advertising, public relations, proper management, and systems control.

MANAGERIAL ASSISTANCE AVAILABLE: Continuous, ongoing, and comprehensive for the life of our agreements. Your success is our success!

INFORMATION SUBMITTED: April 1990

* PRINT THREE FRANCHISING INC.
600 Central Avenue, Suite 333
Highland Park, Illinois 60035
Cliff Richler, Vice President, Franchise Development

DESCRIPTION OF OPERATION: Full-service electronic printing centers featuring a leading-edge desktop publishing system using proprietary laser printing equipment with superior resolution of 1,200 × 600 d.p.i. A high-tech operation with print-link communications, offering instantaneous transmittal of text, data, and graphics across the continent.

NUMBER OF FRANCHISEES: 175 in 17 states and 2 countries

IN BUSINESS SINCE: 1970

EQUITY CAPITAL NEEDED: $50,000

FINANCIAL ASSISTANCE AVAILABLE: 100 percent

TRAINING PROVIDED: 3-week comprehensive business training, with 1 week on-site after center opening. Ongoing management and computer training, professional marketing support, and periodic business evaluation.

MANAGERIAL ASSISTANCE AVAILABLE: All owners are trained in Print Three business operations and customer service techniques. On-site opening assistance, frequent visits, ongoing support and consultation, toll-free operations and technical support hotlines, annual convention, retraining for new staff at no charge.

INFORMATION SUBMITTED: April 1990

* SIR SPEEDY, INC.
23131 Verdugo Drive
LaGuna Hills, California 92653
Dave Collins, Vice President Franchising

DESCRIPTION OF OPERATION: Sir Speedy, Inc., is a leading franchisor of printing centers, providing full-service printing and the highest average gross sales volume per store in the industry. Centers are franchisee-owned, using established system, procedures, and techniques. Franchise package includes equipment, supplies, signage, graphics, market survey, and training programs. Prior printing experience not required.

NUMBER OF FRANCHISEES: Approximately 900 in 46 states

IN BUSINESS SINCE: 1968

EQUITY CAPITAL NEEDED: Total franchise package is $120,000 plus working capital of $50,000. Initial investment as low as $50,000.

FINANCIAL ASSISTANCE AVAILABLE: Financing available for entire package to qualified individuals, excluding working capital.

TRAINING PROVIDED: Total of 4 weeks' initial training. This in-depth initial training includes advertising and marketing strategy, bookkeeping and record keeping, computer graphic design, shop organization and work flow, pricing, employee relations, and more. Ongoing regional and national seminars and conventions to keep franchisees informed of trends in the industry.

MANAGERIAL ASSISTANCE AVAILABLE: In-depth market surveys, site selection, assistance in lease negotiations, national contract purchasing power, marketing and advertising support, accounting system, communication with all franchisees, profit management seminars, equipment evaluations, plus royalty rebate program.

INFORMATION SUBMITTED: April 1990

REAL ESTATE

* BETTER HOMES AND GARDENS REAL ESTATE SERVICE
2000 Grand Avenue
Des Moines, Iowa 50312
Randy Schwager

DESCRIPTION OF OPERATION: A national marketing program licensing the Better Homes and Gardens trademarks to selected real estate firms in assigned exclusive market territories. The variety of programs available to licensees includes a national and local advertising program, a referral service, mortgage origination capability (in states where available), a corporate relocation program, a concurrent licensing program, management seminars, training materials, a home warranty program (in states where available), client promotion materials, a building support program, and the benefits of belonging to a national network of professional real estate firms.

NUMBER OF FRANCHISEES: Over 685 in all 50 states

IN BUSINESS SINCE: 1978

EQUITY CAPITAL NEEDED: The initial joining fee is an applied percentage of the annual residential gross commission income of each firm. The minimum joining fee is $11,000.

FINANCIAL ASSISTANCE AVAILABLE: A down payment of 50 percent of the joining fee is due when the contract is executed. The remaining 50 percent is due at the opening date. The opening date is the date that the firm first publicly uses the Better Homes and Gardens marks or 120 days after the effective date of the contract, whichever is earlier.

TRAINING PROVIDED: Better Homes and Gardens Real Estate Service provides a management orientation session for members at Better Homes and Gardens corporate headquarters. In addition, Better Homes and Gardens provides an orientation for the agents of each new firm at its primary office without charge. Better Homes and Gardens provides periodic regional training seminars for the management of its members at reasonable cost.

MANAGERIAL ASSISTANCE AVAILABLE: Better Homes and Gardens maintains a service staff with assigned territories to provide each firm with personal contact and consultation on the effective use of the programs. Toll-free inbound WATS lines access the service department for improved communication. Regional groups have been established and sponsored by Better Homes and Gardens to provide for periodic meetings of all members in each geographic area to discuss common ideas.

INFORMATION SUBMITTED: June 1990

BETTER HOMES REALTY
1556 Parkside Drive
P. O. Box 8181
Walnut Creek, California 94596
Clifford R. Fick, Senior Vice President/CEO

DESCRIPTION OF OPERATION: Better Homes Realty is a network of independently owned and operated real estate offices. A dual-identity program allows brokers to retain their established identity, plus combine with Better Homes Realty brand-name awareness, mass marketing, national relocation services, continuous management and associate training and education programs, and consumer-service preferred treatment programs, including a unique in-house Preferred Financing program. Better Homes Realty is the franchisor of Better Homes Realty.

NUMBER OF FRANCHISEES: Better Homes Realty currently has 1,200 associates in over 90 offices.

IN BUSINESS SINCE: Founded in Walnut Creek, California, as an all-broker cooperative during the 1960s, Better Homes Realty began franchise expansion in 1974.

EQUITY CAPITAL NEEDED: Under the Better Homes Realty franchise agreement, a one-time initial franchise fee of $9,950 allows a franchisee to assume the established Better Homes Realty trademark and support services. A substantial amount of the initial franchise fee is returned to the franchisee in office setup materials. Service fees are equal to 6 percent of the gross commissions for transactions requiring a real estate license. No additional advertising fees or assessments are charged.

FINANCIAL ASSISTANCE AVAILABLE: Franchisor may agree to accept deferred payments totaling $11,190 with a $3,000 down payment and monthly installments of $455.

TRAINING PROVIDED: The Better Homes Realty Institute of Real Estate programs begin with recruitment career nights, and cover a sales training course at no cost to associates, a continuing education program for license renewal credit, and regular management and associate conferences over a 4- to 10-day period.

MANAGERIAL ASSISTANCE AVAILABLE: Representatives of the Better Homes Realty business development department make regular visits to Better Homes Realty associate offices to discuss the uses of all business development materials and to counsel management decisions. Bethome Media, the professionally staffed in-house advertising agency, prepares and produces continuous advertising and marketing campaigns within each regional area.

INFORMATION SUBMITTED: April 1990

* BY OWNER, INC.
Lochaven Square, Suite A
North 8884 Government Way
Hayden Lake, Idaho 83835
Jerry L. Wall, President

DESCRIPTION OF OPERATION: BY OWNER franchises feature professional photo property displays in a retail environment, offering marketing and real estate services with no percentage commissions. Our federally trademarketed BY OWNER logo and franchise locations attract sellers and buyers who want to save thousands of dollars. Franchisee income is derived from very reasonable BY OWNER fees that are based on services rendered, rather than on the property's sales price.

NUMBER OF FRANCHISEES: 12 in 3 states and Canada

IN BUSINESS SINCE: 1985

EQUITY CAPITAL NEEDED: Approximately $15,000, plus cost of franchise, which is currently $16,500.

FINANCIAL ASSISTANCE AVAILABLE: BY OWNER, INC., does not offer financing at this time.

TRAINING PROVIDED: Master Franchises: 1 week at corporate headquarters plus on-site follow-up. Unit franchises: 1 week on-site, and follow-up. Training includes computer introduction and application. Ongoing support.

MANAGERIAL ASSISTANCE AVAILABLE: Provided by subfranchisor and/or training.

INFORMATION SUBMITTED: April 1990

* CENTURY 21 REAL ESTATE CORPORATION
International Headquarters
Century Centre, 2601 S.E. Main Street
P. O. Box 19564
Irvine, California 92713-9564
Vice President, Franchise Sales

DESCRIPTION OF OPERATION: World's largest real estate franchising organization, established to provide a marketing support system for independently owned and operated real estate brokerage offices, offering international advertising, VIP referral system, residential and commercial sales training, management training, national accounts center, client follow-up, and other real estate related services. Insurance, mortgage brokerage, and securities and syndication services are available in selected regions through subsidiary companies in Century 21 Real Estate Corporation. Subsidiary of Metropolitan Insurance Company.

NUMBER OF FRANCHISEES: Over 7,000 offices in United States, Canada, and Japan

IN BUSINESS SINCE: First offices opened in 1972.

EQUITY CAPITAL NEEDED: Cash investment $12,000–$25,000

FINANCIAL ASSISTANCE AVAILABLE: Some financing may be available.

TRAINING PROVIDED: The exclusive Century 21 CareerTrak program offers training and accreditation in all major real estate disciplines: office management, investment and residential sales, sales management, and relocation services. The program links educational standards with productivity for a systemwide method of motivation and career development.

MANAGERIAL ASSISTANCE AVAILABLE: New franchisees attend the international management academy, a 3½-day orientation/management training seminar held in Irvine, California. Other courses offered through the regions include the property management support system, principles of sales management, and commercial property series.

INFORMATION SUBMITTED: June 1990

* HELP-U-SELL, INC.
57 West 200 South
Salt Lake City, Utah 84101
Carter Knapp

DESCRIPTION OF OPERATION: Help-U-Sell is a merger of real estate marketing, counseling and traditional real estate. The Help-U-Sell marketing system generates hundreds of buyer and seller leads for each office without canvassing, farming, or holding open houses. The Help-U-Sell counseling method assists home buyers and sellers for a set fee instead of a percentage commission, payable at closing. Help-U-Sell franchisees are real estate brokers and membership in the local multiple listing service is required, where available. This concept provides more benefits to buyers, sellers, brokers, and agents than does traditional real estate. It is ideally suited to the changing real estate market. For more information, call (800) 669-4357 or (800) 366-1177. Ask for a Franchise Specialist.

NUMBER OF FRANCHISEES: 567 in 42 states and Canada

IN BUSINESS SINCE: 1976

EQUITY CAPITAL NEEDED: Franchise fee is $8,500 and up.

FINANCIAL ASSISTANCE AVAILABLE: Terms may be available.

TRAINING PROVIDED: 5-day intensive initial training at corporate headquarters in Salt Lake City. Ongoing support and training through a personal Operations Consultant and through *live* semimonthly satellite broadcasts.

MANAGERIAL ASSISTANCE AVAILABLE: Management consultant assigned to each office.

INFORMATION SUBMITTED: May 1990

HOMEOWNERS CONCEPT, INC.
3508 W. Galbraith Road
Cincinnati, Ohio 45239
Jeffrey C. Knab, President

DESCRIPTION OF OPERATION: Alternative avenue in selling real estate. Homeowner shows own property and pays flat fee for professional real estate consulting. Homeowners Concept is a corporation in Ohio.

NUMBER OF FRANCHISEES: 70 in 18 states

IN BUSINESS SINCE: 1982

EQUITY CAPITAL NEEDED: $25,000–$30,000—initial fee $9,000.

FINANCIAL ASSISTANCE AVAILABLE: Neither the franchisor nor any affiliated persons offer direct or indirect financing to franchisees.

TRAINING PROVIDED: 14 hours on-the-job training.

MANAGERIAL ASSISTANCE AVAILABLE: Continuous consulting from franchisor and periodic seminars.

INFORMATION SUBMITTED: June 1990

RECREATION/ENTERTAINMENT/TRAVEL—SERVICES/SUPPLIES

* ASK MR. FOSTER ASSOCIATES, INC.
7833 Haskell Avenue
Van Nuys, California 91406
Kelly Nelson, Chief Operating Officer

DESCRIPTION OF OPERATION: Licensing opportunities to established travel agencies in geographical areas not presently covered by Ask Mr. Foster's 500 plus owned and operated branch offices.

NUMBER OF FRANCHISEES: 500 plus in 50 states

IN BUSINESS SINCE: 1984 (parent company since 1888)

EQUITY CAPITAL NEEDED: None.

FINANCIAL ASSISTANCE AVAILABLE: None.

TRAINING PROVIDED: Initial orientation and ongoing consultation; specific training programs available.

MANAGERIAL ASSISTANCE AVAILABLE: Licensee ("Associate") becomes a part of the Ask Mr. Foster branch network and thereby participates in all company marketing programs and proprietary service systems. Licensees have a dedicated company staff to assist them in using company programs to their fullest.

INFORMATION SUBMITTED: April 1990

COMPLETE MUSIC
8317 Cass Street
Omaha, Nebraska 68114
G. E. Maas, President

DESCRIPTION OF OPERATION: Complete Music is the leader in disc jockey entertainment, providing dance music for over 1 million people each year. The uniqueness of this business allows owners, who need not be entertainers, to use their skills in management to hire and book their own Complete Music trained D.J.s for all types of special events.

NUMBER OF FRANCHISEES: 76 franchises covering 22 states, plus 1 company-owned location

IN BUSINESS SINCE: 1974, franchising since 1982

EQUITY CAPITAL NEEDED: $13,000 for franchise fee, training, materials, and supplies. $2,500–$8,000 for lighting and sound equipment.

FINANCIAL ASSISTANCE AVAILABLE: Partial assistance available.

TRAINING PROVIDED: Franchisor trains and educates franchisee for 10 days at their home office. During this time, business is generated for the new franchise. Four days of training in franchisee's city is also included.

MANAGERIAL ASSISTANCE AVAILABLE: Annual visit to franchisee location plus annual owners' meeting. Video training tapes and manuals are all provided as well as 24-hour access to the franchise office for ongoing support.

INFORMATION SUBMITTED: April 1990

CRUISE HOLIDAYS INTERNATIONAL, INC.
4740 Murphy Canyon Road, Suite 200
San Diego, California 92123
David Pava, Vice President, Franchise Marketing

DESCRIPTION OF OPERATION: North America's largest franchisor of cruise-only travel agencies. Complete start-up assistance, use of proprietary software, national advertising, and marketing support. Franchisor negotiates volume discounts with major cruise lines. A perfect opportunity in the most profitable segment of the travel industry.

NUMBER OF FRANCHISEES: 84 in 21 states and 2 Canadian provinces

IN BUSINESS SINCE: 1984

EQUITY CAPITAL NEEDED: $25,000 franchise fee, $20,000 start-up expenses, and $30,000 working capital, total $75,000.

FINANCIAL ASSISTANCE AVAILABLE: None.

TRAINING PROVIDED: 2 weeks, conducted in selected port cities nationally, includes ship inspections and cruise.

MANAGERIAL ASSISTANCE AVAILABLE: Cruise Holidays provides ongoing management consulting, cruise line negotiation, and advisory services. Manuals, forms, data control systems, and inventory control guidance are provided. Centralized purchasing of printing supplies is available. Advertising on a regional basis is coordinated by the corporate office.

INFORMATION SUBMITTED: April 1990

CRUISE SHOPPES AMERICA, LTD.
115 Metairie Road, Suite E
Metairie, Louisiana 70005
Bill Worden, CTC/Admiral
Gary P. Brown, Vice Admiral/Franchise & Associate Development

DESCRIPTION OF OPERATION: Franchisor of cruise-only travel agencies offering initial entry and associate programs for existing travel agencies. Each location is approximately 1,000 square feet with designated motif.

NUMBER OF FRANCHISEES: 28 in 15 states

IN BUSINESS SINCE: 1985

EQUITY CAPITAL NEEDED: Entry level $22,500

FINANCIAL ASSISTANCE AVAILABLE: A total investment of between $87,000 and $93,000 (including working capital) is needed. Some financing available through franchisor.

TRAINING PROVIDED: Intensive 7-day home office training for owner and personnel. Additional on-site training as well as seminars, ship inspections, and familiarization cruises.

MANAGERIAL ASSISTANCE AVAILABLE: C.S.A. provides continuous managerial services, including marketing and promotional support through its Marketing Center in New Orleans, Louisiana. In addition C.S.A. provides complete operational, sales, and marketing manuals.

INFORMATION SUBMITTED: April 1990

GO-KART TRACK SYSTEMS
5954 Brainerd Road
Chattanooga, Tennessee 37421-3598
Jay Grant

DESCRIPTION OF OPERATION: 12 to 15 concession-type go-karts that are rented for a 4- to 5-minute ride on approximately 800-foot curved track at a speed of 18–20 mph.

NUMBER OF FRANCHISEES: 82 in 20 states

IN BUSINESS SINCE: 1972

EQUITY CAPITAL NEEDED: $45,000–$70,000

FINANCIAL ASSISTANCE AVAILABLE: None.

TRAINING PROVIDED: Training on-the-job until operator is completely satisfied he can handle the job. Manager's manual will cover most questions that come up.

MANAGERIAL ASSISTANCE AVAILABLE: Site selection, complete track and building layout, and construction planning.

INFORMATION SUBMITTED: April 1990

GOLF PLAYERS, INC.
5954 Brainerd Road
Chattanooga, Tennessee 37421
Earl Magrath, President

DESCRIPTION OF OPERATION: Miniature golf courses with very large, colorful, and distinctive figures and caricatures—some animated. Operation under the name Sir Goony Golf.

NUMBER OF FRANCHISEES: 49 in 12 states

IN BUSINESS SINCE: 1964

EQUITY CAPITAL NEEDED: $36,800

FINANCIAL ASSISTANCE AVAILABLE: None.

TRAINING PROVIDED: Training at home office and on-the-job. Continuing help by personal visits, newsletters, and phone calls. A complete operational manager's manual is provided.

MANAGERIAL ASSISTANCE AVAILABLE: Course design and construction planning, continuing management service and advice.

INFORMATION SUBMITTED: April 1990

LOMMA MINIATURE GOLF
1120 South Washington Avenue
Scranton, Pennsylvania 18505
Gary Knight, Executive Vice President

DESCRIPTION OF OPERATION: The Lomma Miniature Golf Company, the world's oldest and largest designer and builder of miniature golf courses, offers a dynamic noncommodity, easily run, high cash flow recreational business. The modular golf courses are designed for maximum flexibility of layout, and the portability allows usage indoors and outdoors for year-round revenue.

NUMBER OF FRANCHISEES: 5,108 in 50 states and 15 countries around the world

IN BUSINESS SINCE: 1960

EQUITY CAPITAL NEEDED: $5,900

FINANCIAL ASSISTANCE AVAILABLE: As little as 10 percent down payment is needed and the balance payable up to 5 years. Complete and concise free franchise program with no franchise or royalty fees to pay.

TRAINING PROVIDED: We conduct seminars at our offices for small groups and/or regionally at your location.

MANAGERIAL ASSISTANCE AVAILABLE: We supply a detailed manager's guide and operating manual.

INFORMATION SUBMITTED: April 1990

MINI-GOLF, INC.
202 Bridge Street
Jessup, Pennsylvania 18434
Joseph J. Rogari, Director of Marketing

DESCRIPTION OF OPERATION: The world's largest builder of prefab miniature golf courses. Company's owners have almost 70 years experience in miniature golf. Each operator gets a layout to scale tailor-made for their area. Courses are designed for an unlimited clientele with very animated, moving, flashing, and challenging obstacles. Easy to set up outdoors or indoors. Theme courses available. Courses shipped within 5 days. High cash flow, noncommodity, easy business to run.

NUMBER OF FRANCHISEES: 957 in 50 states in 11 countries

IN BUSINESS SINCE: 1981

EQUITY CAPITAL NEEDED: 4,000–$19,900

FINANCIAL ASSISTANCE AVAILABLE: Cash plan: 10 percent discount; financing: 35 to 50 percent down with 2 years remaining on balance.

TRAINING PROVIDED: Training sessions conducted at home office. Weekends also available.

MANAGERIAL ASSISTANCE AVAILABLE: Extensive operator's manual with press releases, promotions, parties, and major tournaments. Support includes periodic follow-up after installation.

INFORMATION SUBMITTED: April 1990

RETAILING—ART SUPPLIES/FRAMES

ART MANAGEMENT SERVICES, INC.
Franchisor of the KOENIG ART EMPORIUMS
265 Old Gate Lane
Milford, Connecticut 06460

DESCRIPTION OF OPERATION: Koenig Art Emporiums are retail artists', drafting supply, picture frame stores selling to the creative person, amateur, professional, hobbyist, and the general public. Each Emporium's merchandise has a broad appeal to the general public through items such as fine writing instruments, framed posters, and custom framing. Inventory is complemented by a full-line catalogue. Average store size is 2,000 square feet.

NUMBER OF FRANCHISEES: 86 in 21 states plus 30 company-owned stores

IN BUSINESS SINCE: 1933 (started franchising 1979).

EQUITY CAPITAL NEEDED: Start-up franchises require a minimum cash investment of $50,000.

FINANCIAL ASSISTANCE AVAILABLE: The total investment for a Koenig Art Emporium franchise is approximately $175,000 to $225,000; included in the total investment is a franchise fee of $25,000. A.M.S. offers no financing arrangements directly to the franchisee, but will assist prospective franchisees with obtaining suitable financing from established lending institutions.

TRAINING PROVIDED: Training is of a minimum of 2 weeks' duration at A.M.S. headquarters, and will include familiarization with merchandise and its application, operating systems, do-it-yourself, and custom picture framing techniques, computer reports, etc. In addition the franchisee will gain experience in store operations at an existing Koenig Art Emporium. Finally, A.M.S. will have a field representative on-site prior to and at the time of opening to instruct and assist the franchisee.

MANAGERIAL ASSISTANCE AVAILABLE: A.M.S. provides a unique computerized inventory control system by interfacing its computer with the franchisee electric cash register. The computer will monitor inventory movement, generating orders automatically for timely stock replacement while providing meaningful reports to A.M.S. and the franchisee. A.M.S. also serves the franchisee as a continuing source of expertise in all facets of the store operation. The franchisee will also receive operations and employee manuals necessary for effective store procedures. A.M.S. will also offer advice with regard to the efficient and economical operation of the franchising Koenig Art Emporium.

INFORMATION SUBMITTED: April 1990

FRAME AND SAVE
1126 Dixie Highway
Eranger, Kentucky 41018
Charles Karlosky, President

DESCRIPTION OF OPERATION: Frame and Save offers to the public a "Do-It-Yourself and Custom Picture Framing Shop." Each store is approximately 1,600 square feet with a setup of 8 individual working booths. Frame and Save has a line of quality moldings and mats.

NUMBER OF FRANCHISEES: 40 in 7 states

IN BUSINESS SINCE: 1973

EQUITY CAPITAL NEEDED: $35,000

FINANCIAL ASSISTANCE AVAILABLE: None.

TRAINING PROVIDED: Intensive 2-week mandatory training course is scheduled for all new franchisees at one of our locations. This training involves learning the techniques of cutting and assembling molding, mats, glass, and conservation of valuable artwork. Also, Frame and Save gives the franchisee 1 week of professional supervision at your location.

MANAGERIAL ASSISTANCE AVAILABLE: Frame and Save provides continual contact with each individual franchisee with all update pricing and new techniques of the framing industry. District managers are available in all regions to work closely with the franchisees and visit the stores regularly to assist solving problems.

INFORMATION SUBMITTED: June 1990

* THE GREAT FRAME UP SYSTEMS, INC.
9335 Belmont Avenue
Franklin Park, Illinois 60131
Walter Wolnik, Director of Marketing

DESCRIPTION OF OPERATION: Nation's largest do-it-yourself franchise frame shops; also include custom, commercial framing with art and preframed galleries.

NUMBER OF FRANCHISEES: 110 in 25 states

IN BUSINESS SINCE: 1975

EQUITY CAPITAL NEEDED: $28,000–$33,000

FINANCIAL ASSISTANCE AVAILABLE: Total investment is approximately $110,000 including a $19,500 franchise fee. The Great Frame Up will assist in obtaining suitable financing through SBA guaranteed loans or other institutions.

TRAINING PROVIDED: The training provides franchisee with complete working knowledge of framing techniques, customer service, business management, and the Great Frame Up system. Hands-on, classroom and in-store training are part of the comprehensive program.

MANAGERIAL ASSISTANCE AVAILABLE: In addition to site selection, design, layout, and construction, the Great Frame Up provides advertising, field support and product, as well as vendor buying assistance, in addition to publications and an annual conference.

INFORMATION SUBMITTED: April 1990

RETAILING—COMPUTER SALES/SERVICES

CONNECTING POINT OF AMERICA, INC.
5240 Souh Quebec Street, Suite 300
Englewood, Colorado 80222
Peter Sherry

DESCRIPTION OF OPERATION: The Connecting Point retail store is a single source for all computer hardware, software, training, and services.

NUMBER OF FRANCHISEES: Over 300

IN BUSINESS SINCE: 1982

EQUITY CAPITAL NEEDED: At least $5,000 in liquid capital, plus $50,000 line of credit.

FINANCIAL ASSISTANCE AVAILABLE: No direct financial assistance.

TRAINING PROVIDED: Customized sales and management training in all facets of store management, product knowledge, personnel management, inventory control, and sales techniques. All on-site.

MANAGERIAL ASSISTANCE AVAILABLE: Pre-opening assistance includes site selection, lease negotiation, store design, construction management, staff recruitment, recommended inventory planning, and extensive training. Ongoing support includes monthly advertising and promotional planning, inventory recommendations, and new product awareness.

INFORMATION SUBMITTED: June 1990

RETAILING/MISCELLANEOUS

ANNIE'S BOOK STOP, INC.
15 Lackey Street
Westborough, Massachusetts 01581
Anne Adams

DESCRIPTION OF OPERATION: Franchisor sells franchises to establish bookstore centers for the sale and exchange of preread paperback books, for the sale of new books, both paperback and hardcover editions, and for the sale of other book-related or gift items.

NUMBER OF FRANCHISEES: 95 in 23 states

IN BUSINESS SINCE: 1981

EQUITY CAPITAL NEEDED: $35,000–$50,000

FINANCIAL ASSISTANCE AVAILABLE: None.

TRAINING PROVIDED: On-hand training plus detailed manual, duration 2 weeks plus.

MANAGERIAL ASSISTANCE AVAILABLE: Ongoing through phone and mail for life of franchise.

INFORMATION SUBMITTED: May 1990

* BATHTIQUE INTERNATIONAL, LTD.
Carnegie Place—247 North Goodman Street
Rochester, New York 14607
Don A. Selpel, President

DESCRIPTION OF OPERATION: A retail bath, bed, and gift specialty shop offering the latest products and accessories.

NUMBER OF FRANCHISEES: 67 in 30 states, Puerto Rico, and the Virgin Islands including 16 company-owned shops

IN BUSINESS SINCE: 1969

EQUITY CAPITAL NEEDED: $35,000. No direct financing, but assistance in acquiring funding through local banks.

FINANCIAL ASSISTANCE AVAILABLE: No direct financing but assistance in acquiring financing through local banks.

TRAINING PROVIDED: A concentrated 1-week training period is conducted for all new franchisees. Individuals for each franchise participate in a 1-week manager training program. This program includes a classroom and on-the-job training under experienced managers. An additional 2 weeks of on-site location assistance is provided by the home office staff at the time the franchisee's shop opens. A follow-up briefing session is conducted on-site after opening.

MANAGERIAL ASSISTANCE AVAILABLE: Bathtique International provides continuing review and feedback concerning shop operations in areas such as sales, purchasing, advertising, and labor schedule. Merchandising is recommended to franchisees after testing in company shop. Merchandise is bought directly from recommended suppliers; quantity discounts available. A continuous personnel training program is strongly emphasized. Advertising materials and co-op funds are provided regularly including direct mail books. Annual and regional conferences are offered throughout the country.

INFORMATION SUBMITTED: April 1990

BIGHORN SHEEPSKIN COMPANY
11600 Manchaca Road
Austin, Texas 78748
Barry Silverman, President

DESCRIPTION OF OPERATION: Bighorn Sheepskin Company franchises the operation of temporary retail locations in regional shopping malls during the Christmas season, selling genuine sheepskin gift items, apparel, and automotive accessories. Typical locations are 100-square-foot kiosks located in the common areas of shopping malls and are open during November and December.

NUMBER OF FRANCHISEES: 67 locations in 22 states

IN BUSINESS SINCE: 1983

EQUITY CAPITAL NEEDED: $2,500 plus $20,000 letter of credit.

FINANCIAL ASSISTANCE AVAILABLE: None.

TRAINING PROVIDED: 3-day seminar each October in Austin, Texas.

MANAGERIAL ASSISTANCE AVAILABLE: Site selection, lease negotiation, comprehensive operations manual, computerized ordering system, and promotional materials.

INFORMATION SUBMITTED: April 1990

BOOK RACK MANAGEMENT, INC.
2703 E. Commercial Boulevard
Ft. Lauderdale, Florida 33308
Fred M. Darnell

DESCRIPTION OF OPERATION: Used paperback books and new books.

NUMBER OF FRANCHISEES: 248 in 34 states

IN BUSINESS SINCE: 1963

EQUITY CAPITAL NEEDED: $12,000

FINANCIAL ASSISTANCE AVAILABLE: None.

TRAINING PROVIDED: 1 or 2 weeks' training and site location. Help supply inventory, yearly meeting, and monthly newsletter.

MANAGERIAL ASSISTANCE AVAILABLE: Ongoing assistance.

INFORMATION SUBMITTED: April 1990

THE BOX SHOPPE, INC.
7165 East 87th Street
Indianapolis, Indiana 46256
Duke Smith

DESCRIPTION OF OPERATION: We are a retail and wholesale business involved in the sale of gift boxes, moving boxes, storage boxes, bows, ribbons, gift wrap, etc.

NUMBER OF FRANCHISEES: 63 in Indiana, Illinois, Kentucky, Ohio, North and South Carolina, and Michigan

IN BUSINESS SINCE: 1984

EQUITY CAPITAL NEEDED: $30,700

FINANCIAL ASSISTANCE AVAILABLE: Yes.

TRAINING PROVIDED: Extensive 3-day training program at franchisor's headquarters, additional on-site assistance as necessary.

MANAGERIAL ASSISTANCE AVAILABLE: None required.

INFORMATION SUBMITTED: April 1990

CREATE-A-BOOK
6380 Euclid Road
Cincinnati, Ohio 45236
Robert Young

DESCRIPTION OF OPERATION: Create-A-Book is a company that prints and sells personalized children's books. Any child can have his/her name printed throughout colorful storybooks along with friends, relatives, pets, age, hometown, etc. It takes four minutes from start to finish to print, bind, and place a book in a hard cover. Franchisees have the equipment to completely print and bind the books. There are many, many different ways to sell and market the books. Training provided. Excellent home business.

NUMBER OF FRANCHISEES: 400

IN BUSINESS SINCE: 1980

EQUITY CAPITAL NEEDED: $2,995 plus approximately $1,200 for equipment.

FINANCIAL ASSISTANCE AVAILABLE: We do not offer any financial assistance.

TRAINING PROVIDED: Training is provided in Cincinnati, Ohio. For those people unable to attend the training, we provide a manual and videotape. Additional training is provided through seminars and meetings.

MANAGERIAL ASSISTANCE AVAILABLE: Seminars and meetings are provided to update franchisees. Newsletters are sent to all franchisees throughout the year.

INFORMATION SUBMITTED: April 1990

* FLOWERAMA OF AMERICA, INC.
3165 West Airline Highway
Waterloo, Iowa 50703
Chuck Nygren, Vice President

DESCRIPTION OF OPERATION: Flowerama of America, Inc., offers a unique and innovative approach to retail floral merchandising. Flowerama offers prime regional mall locations of about 600 to 1,000 square feet and free-standing locations of between 2,000 and 3,000 square feet situated on high vehicular traffic sites. Flowerama offers fresh flowers, floral arrangements, green and blooming plants, silk products, and related gift and accessory items at prices dramatically below conventional florist. Flowerama offers a comprehensive franchise package including site selection, lease negotiations, store design, training, supplier programs, and continued operational support.

NUMBER OF FRANCHISEES: 74 in 23 states plus 14 company-owned shops.

IN BUSINESS SINCE: 1966

EQUITY CAPITAL NEEDED: Mall locations: $20,000–$40,000. Free-standing: $50,000–$110,000.

FINANCIAL ASSISTANCE AVAILABLE: Assists franchisee in obtaining financing from local lending institutions; however, no direct funding is available.

TRAINING PROVIDED: Mall locations: 9 days' training in classroom and on-the-job training. Free-standing: 4 weeks including classroom and on-the-job training.

MANAGERIAL ASSISTANCE AVAILABLE: Flowerama provides continual management service for the life of the franchise in such areas as bookkeeping, advertising, store operations, and inventory control. Complete manuals of operations, forms, and directions are provided. Field representatives and staff personnel are continually available to provide franchise owners with assistance in the operation of their retail floral shop.

INFORMATION SUBMITTED: April 1990

FRIEDMAN FRANCHISORS
2301 Broadway
Oakland, California 94612
Arthur Friedman, General Partner

DESCRIPTION OF OPERATION: Friedman's Microwave Ovens, microwave specialty stores selling only microwave ovens and accessories enhanced by microwave cooking schools. A unique business with a focus on complete customer satisfaction by offering 60-day free exchange, competitive prices, free schools for life, and discounts on accessories.

NUMBER OF FRANCHISEES: 49 in 23 states

IN BUSINESS SINCE: 1976, franchising since 1979

EQUITY CAPITAL NEEDED: $25,000–$35,000

FINANCIAL ASSISTANCE AVAILABLE: None.

TRAINING PROVIDED: Weeklong training session held at Oakland, California, headquarters, on-site training prior, during, and after opening; telephone assistance always available.

MANAGERIAL ASSISTANCE AVAILABLE: Included in the above.

INFORMATION SUBMITTED: June 1990

HOBBYTOWN USA
5930 South 58th Street
Lincoln, Nebraska 68516
James E. Hogg, Franchise Operations Manager

DESCRIPTION OF OPERATION: HobbyTown USA is America's largest chain of franchised hobby stores. HobbyTown USA stores are full-line retail hobby stores with product offerings in 8 to 10 hobby categories including model railroad supplies, radio controlled cars, trucks, airplanes, and helicopters, plastic model kits, games, sports cards, stamps and coins, and paints and tools.

NUMBER OF FRANCHISEES: 25 franchise locations in 11 states

IN BUSINESS SINCE: 1969, franchising since 1985

EQUITY CAPITAL NEEDED: $25,000–$30,000 of total $80,000–$100,000 investment.

FINANCIAL ASSISTANCE AVAILABLE: None.

TRAINING PROVIDED: Franchisor trains and educates franchisees for 1 to 2 weeks in its home office in Lincoln, Nebraska. Further training is provided at the franchisee's location during the first 1 to 2 weeks that the store is open.

MANAGERIAL ASSISTANCE AVAILABLE: Full assistance is provided in site selection, lease negotiation, store layout and design, and all operational procedures of the store. Additionally, franchisor representatives visit each store 4 times a year, and the franchisor is available at all times to offer assistance to the franchisee.

INFORMATION SUBMITTED: April 1990

KITS CAMERAS, INC.
6051 South 194th
Kent, Washington 98032
Corporate Development Manager

DESCRIPTION OF OPERATION: A Kits Camera franchise system offers a unique opportunity in the operation of a specialty photographic equipment, video, and supplies store. Most stores are located in enclosed shopping centers. The store carries an extensive line of brand-name and private label merchandise.

NUMBER OF FRANCHISEES: 33 on the West Coast

IN BUSINESS SINCE: 1975

EQUITY CAPITAL NEEDED: Total investment of approximately $135,000 of which $50,000 has to be cash.

FINANCIAL ASSISTANCE AVAILABLE: Franchisor will assist franchisee in arranging the balance from a commercial bank.

TRAINING PROVIDED: 4–6-week course at the home office and company stores. Successful completion of training course a prerequisite to obtaining a franchise.

MANAGERIAL ASSISTANCE AVAILABLE: Kits Cameras provide continuous management service for the life of the franchise in areas of bookkeeping, advertising, merchandising, and store operations. Coordinators visit stores regularly to provide assistance. Semiannual conventions are sponsored by Kits Cameras.

INFORMATION SUBMITTED: May 1990

LEMSTONE BOOKS
1123 Wheaton Oaks Ct.
Wheaton, Illinois 60187
Lynn P. Wheaton, Sales Manager

DESCRIPTION OF OPERATION: Christian bookstores located in large regional shopping malls that stock a unique variety of books, Bibles, Bible study material, gifts, music, greeting cards designed to meet the needs of the family as well as the institutional church market. Telephone (708) 682-1400.

NUMBER OF FRANCHISEES: 37 in 14 states

IN BUSINESS SINCE: 1981

EQUITY CAPITAL NEEDED: Approximately $40,000

FINANCIAL ASSISTANCE AVAILABLE: Lemstone Books will assist franchisee in obtaining outside local financing if needed.

TRAINING PROVIDED: 1-week manager's training class prior to opening at franchise headquarters. 400-page manual of operation detailing every aspect of store operations and procedure. On-site training during 5 days of new store setup. Ongoing regular field visits throughout the year by member of franchise team. Regional advanced management seminars annually. Annual franchise convention in Chicago area.

MANAGERIAL ASSISTANCE AVAILABLE: Will assist franchisee to hire sales staff. Regular field visits by franchise operations staff as well as regular franchise seminars. Comprehensive marketing and promotion program plus computerized inventory control and accounting systems provided. All aspects of financial accounting reviewed including monthly open to buy, cash flow projections, and actual to budget performance tracked monthly.

INFORMATION SUBMITTED: April 1990

* LITTLE PROFESSOR BOOK CENTERS, INC.
110 North Fourth Avenue, Suite 400
Ann Arbor, Michigan 48104
Carla Garbin, Senior Vice President

DESCRIPTION OF OPERATION: Little Professor Book Centers are full-line, full-service retail book stores.

Each store (most are approximately 2,400 square feet) carries a complete selection of hardcover and papercover titles, magazines, and newspapers. Franchisor provides complete assistance and counsel needed to open and operate a book store, from site selection to store opening and throughout the life of the franchise agreement.

NUMBER OF FRANCHISEES: 135 stores in 35 states

IN BUSINESS SINCE: 1969

EQUITY CAPITAL NEEDED: $35,000–$45,000 liquid, total investment $150,000 plus.

FINANCIAL ASSISTANCE AVAILABLE: Little Professor Book Centers, Inc., will assist in the loan application process, but provide no direct financial assistance.

TRAINING PROVIDED: Little Professor Book Center franchise owners participate in an established training program to learn the important aspects of retailing including inventory control, general operations, financial management, advertising, and other forms of sales promotion. The training program is conducted for 15 days: 10 days at company headquarters in Ann Arbor, Michigan, 5 days onsite in the new store.

MANAGERIAL ASSISTANCE AVAILABLE: Little Professor Book Centers, Inc., provides continuous assistance and counsel in bookstore operation throughout the length of the franchise. Periodic visits are made by representatives of Little Professor Book Centers, Inc. Performance and results are evaluated and recommendations are offered on improving sales and profits. Experienced personnel are always available to assist in the solution of any problems. Comprehensive marketing and inventory management programs are provided.

INFORMATION SUBMITTED: April 1990

* ONE HOUR MOTO PHOTO
4444 Lake Center Drive
Dayton, Ohio 45426
Michael Adler, President

DESCRIPTION OF OPERATION: One Hour Moto Photo is the world's largest franchisor of imaging services. A variety of imaging services is offered including on-site color negative film processing, color enlargements, portrait studios, video transfer, color copying, and merchandising of frames, mats, and albums. The concept is expanding to include, among other things, video camera rental and commercial account development.

NUMBER OF FRANCHISEES: 356 in the United States, Canada, Norway, and Sweden

IN BUSINESS SINCE: 1981

EQUITY CAPITAL NEEDED: $40,000

FINANCIAL ASSISTANCE AVAILABLE: Franchisor assists in obtaining financing. Franchisor has secured various financing packages to assist qualified franchisees with their first store. Franchisor also offers a comprehensive financing package for additional stores.

TRAINING PROVIDED: Company provides up to 4 weeks of initial training. The training program includes 2 weeks' in-store training and 2 weeks at franchisor's corporate training facility. A comprehensive on-site training program, including videotapes and manuals, is provided to franchisees to assist the ongoing training of their store associates.

MANAGERIAL ASSISTANCE AVAILABLE: Moto Photo has over 100 corporate associates and a host of independent franchisees to assist a new franchisee with his/her business. Moto Photo offers support in training, marketing, business/operating systems, store design and construction, and real estate/site selection. Moto Photo provides franchisees with a proven marketing, promotion, in-store selling, and monitoring system. A Moto Photo marketing manager will work with you to develop a marketing and advertising plan tailored to your store and market area. Moto Photo will keep you up to date with the latest technology and trends so that you can take advantage of new profit opportunities. Moto Photo continues to develop complete training and marketing programs, not only for 1-hour processing but also for portrait studios, merchandising, commercial account development, and many other imaging products and services. Moto Photo's exclusive franchise accounting and point-of-sale system creates a data base with customer, marketing, and accounting information. The system provides all accounting functions, including inventory control, income and balance statements, invoicing, etc.

INFORMATION SUBMITTED: May 1990

PLAY IT AGAIN SPORTS
1550 Utica Avenue South
Suite 775
Minneapolis, Minnesota 55416
Craig Smock

DESCRIPTION OF OPERATION: Retail sporting goods stores, new and used merchandise.

NUMBER OF FRANCHISEES: 35

IN BUSINESS SINCE: 1983, franchising since 1988

EQUITY CAPITAL NEEDED: $30,000

FINANCIAL ASSISTANCE AVAILABLE: None.

TRAINING PROVIDED: 1 week of training provided in all operations of store.

MANAGERIAL ASSISTANCE AVAILABLE: Ongoing support.

INFORMATION SUBMITTED: April 1990

PORTRAIT AMERICA, INC.
22511 Telegraph Road, Suite 205
Southfield, Michigan 48034
Edward R. Schlager, Director of Franchise Development

DESCRIPTION OF OPERATION: Full-service professional photography specializing in children's and family portraits, weddings, executive portraits, sports teams, and special events. Excellent equipment and training allow franchisees to produce top-quality work, resulting in referral and repeated business.

NUMBER OF FRANCHISEES: 24 franchised locations, 2 company-owned locations

IN BUSINESS SINCE: 1987

EQUITY CAPITAL NEEDED: Capital requirements are approximately $23,000.

FINANCIAL ASSISTANCE AVAILABLE: Available for qualified franchisees.

TRAINING PROVIDED: An initial 1 week of training in all areas of portrait photography and business operations including marketing, sales, pricing, bookkeeping, financial control, public relations, and employee training provided. Ongoing training thereafter includes on-site, technical updates and seminars on various topics.

MANAGERIAL ASSISTANCE AVAILABLE: The franchisor's department of operations provides ongoing managerial assistance in all technical and nontechnical areas of the business.

INFORMATION SUBMITTED: April 1990

THE TINDER BOX INTERNATIONAL, LTD.
Franchise Development Office
19060 Dominguez Hills Drive
Compton, California 90220
Wayne Best, Director, Franchise Development

DESCRIPTION OF OPERATION: Specialty retail mall chain with product mix consisting of unique gifts as well as pipes, cigars, and tobaccos.

NUMBER OF FRANCHISEES: 154 stores in 37 states plus 20 company-owned stores.

IN BUSINESS SINCE: 1928

EQUITY CAPITAL NEEDED: Minimum $50,000—total investment $135,000 to $200,000, including inventory.

FINANCIAL ASSISTANCE AVAILABLE: Financing assistance or direct financing available through company.

TRAINING PROVIDED: 5-day intensive training for franchisee and/or manager at franchisor's headquarters plus in-store setup and training.

MANAGERIAL ASSISTANCE AVAILABLE: Franchisor provides ongoing merchandising, advertising, marketing and accounting assistance. Also available are site selection, store design and lease assistance, operations manuals, training videos, and various fliers and publications. Annual convention and/or regional seminars including a private gift and tobacco show.

INFORMATION SUBMITTED: April 1990

VIDEO GALAXY FRANCHISE, INC.
P. O. Box 1033
East Granby, Connecticut 06026
William D. Corbin

DESCRIPTION OF OPERATION: Video Galaxy Franchise began in the video rental and retail business in Connecticut in 1981 and has been franchising since 1985. Currently ranked number 8 in top 100 video companies in sales volume. Video Galaxy is actively seeking new franchisees in selected markets.

NUMBER OF FRANCHISEES: 45

IN BUSINESS SINCE: 1981

EQUITY CAPITAL NEEDED: $50,000

FINANCIAL ASSISTANCE AVAILABLE: None.

TRAINING PROVIDED: Yes.

MANAGERIAL ASSISTANCE AVAILABLE: Yes.

INFORMATION SUBMITTED: April 1990

VIDEOMATIC INTERNATIONAL, INC.
1060 West Covina Parkway
West Covina, California 91790
Harold E. Brown, President

DESCRIPTION OF OPERATION: Videomatic is a fully automated video store, operating 24 hours per day, with no employees and using an on-line computerized credit card system rather than cash to rent top hits and new releases. Requires only a few spare hours to operate. Seeking regional franchisors.

NUMBER OF FRANCHISEES: 48 plus 1 company-owned in 10 states.

IN BUSINESS SINCE: 1988

EQUITY CAPITAL NEEDED: Approximately $40,000 of total investment of $160,000.

FINANCIAL ASSISTANCE AVAILABLE: The company will assist franchisee in locating and applying for financing. The company does not make direct loans.

TRAINING PROVIDED: 2 days on-site.

MANAGERIAL ASSISTANCE AVAILABLE: Continuous

INFORMATION SUBMITTED: May 1990

WEE WIN TOYS AND ACCESSORIES, INC.
15340 Vantage Parkway E., Suite 250
Houston, Texas 77032
James D. Flanagan

DESCRIPTION OF OPERATION: Wholesale 2 lines of toys, Christian toys and wholesome toys.

NUMBER OF FRANCHISEES: 181 in entire United States

IN BUSINESS SINCE: 1984

EQUITY CAPITAL NEEDED: $9,500 initial investment

FINANCIAL ASSISTANCE AVAILABLE: None.

TRAINING PROVIDED: 3-day training meeting held once each month. We encourage distributors to come as often as possible.

MANAGERIAL ASSISTANCE AVAILABLE: Continued, ongoing training by Wee Win managers.

INFORMATION SUBMITTED: April 1990

* WICKS 'N' STICKS DIVISION
WNNS, INC.
P. O. Box 4586
Houston, Texas 77210-4586
Paul Klatsky, Senior Vice President

DESCRIPTION OF OPERATION: Wicks 'N' Sticks is the nation's largest specialty retailer of candles, room fragrancing products, and related home decorating accessories. Merchandise, including private label and exclusive products, comes from vendors worldwide. Stores are located in major regional malls, today's most desirable retail setting.

NUMBER OF FRANCHISEES: 274 in 43 states

IN BUSINESS SINCE: 1968

EQUITY CAPITAL NEEDED: $65,000–$75,000

FINANCIAL ASSISTANCE AVAILABLE: Some financing may be available.

TRAINING PROVIDED: Extensive 1-week classroom training prepares franchisee for the daily operation of the store. Field staff continues training the franchisee and employees once the store is open, and ensures successful operation during the first critical weeks in business.

MANAGERIAL ASSISTANCE AVAILABLE: Wicks 'N' Sticks provides extensive assistance, including site selection guidelines, construction specifications and plans; merchandise selection, pricing guidelines, and visual presentation recommendations; national buying power; marketing support materials. Field staff makes frequent store visits, supplemented by telecommunications, publications, regional meetings, and an annual convention.

INFORMATION SUBMITTED: June 1990

WILD BIRDS UNLIMITED, INC.
1430 Broad Ripple Avenue
Indianapolis, Indiana 46220
James R. Carpenter, President

DESCRIPTION OF OPERATION: Wild Birds Unlimited, Inc., offers unique retail shops that specialize in supplying birdseed, feeders, and gift items for the popular hobby of backyard bird feeding. The franchise package includes assistance in site selection and store layout, and includes each store in a discount purchasing program for both feeders and birdseed. Franchises are currently available throughout the United States and Canada.

NUMBER OF FRANCHISEES: 48 in 16 states and Canada

IN BUSINESS SINCE: 1981

EQUITY CAPITAL NEEDED: $35,000–$50,000

FINANCIAL ASSISTANCE AVAILABLE: No financial assistance is provided by the franchisor.

TRAINING PROVIDED: The franchisor provides 3 days of training at a company-owned store and provides 2 training manuals, 1 for store operations, 1 for knowledge about bird feeding and sales techniques. Additional visits to the franchisee's store once opened will concentrate on displays, inventory, and advertising techniques.

MANAGERIAL ASSISTANCE AVAILABLE: Wild Birds Unlimited, Inc., provides continuing management assistance in areas such as group purchasing, advertising, new product information and help with any problems in the operation of the store.

INFORMATION SUBMITTED: April 1990.

SECURITY SYSTEMS

* DYNAMARK SECURITY CENTERS, INC.
P. O. Box 2068
Hagerstown, Maryland 21742-2068
Wayne E. Alter, Jr., President and Chief Executive Officer

DESCRIPTION OF OPERATION: Dynamark Security Centers, over the past 13 years, has developed a unique program and method of marketing residential and light commercial security and fire protection devices. Using standardized trade names, service marks, and trademarks, and advertising plus training and instructions in operating an exclusive DSC business, franchisees purchase from DSC at bonafide wholesale prices, then sell, install, and service devices at retail prices in their marketing territories. Central station monitoring services are available through a DSC subsidiary, DynaWatch, Inc.

NUMBER OF FRANCHISEES: Approximately 150 in 33 states

IN BUSINESS SINCE: 1977 as Amtronics, Inc.; in 1984 changed name to Dynamark Security Centers, Inc.

EQUITY CAPITAL NEEDED: $50,000. This includes franchise fees, initial classroom and on-the-job training, opening inventory, working capital, and miscellaneous costs.

FINANCIAL ASSISTANCE AVAILABLE: DSC does not guarantee to obtain or provide financing for franchisee.

TRAINING PROVIDED: 5-day mandatory initial training course scheduled at national training center for all new franchisees and/or their operations managers. Ongoing advanced training conducted at national training center and at regional locations.

MANAGERIAL ASSISTANCE AVAILABLE: DSC provides management services in such areas as marketing and sales, advertising and public relations, and bookkeeping. A complete manual of operations, forms, guidelines, and directions is provided. Corporate staff as well as technical advisors work via phone in the field with franchise organizations for training and problem solving purposes. DSC sponsors national and regional meetings of franchisees in addition to conducting ongoing marketing research and development to maintain leadership position with the consumer public.

INFORMATION SUBMITTED: April 1990

THE SECURITY ALLIANCE CORPORATION
1865 Miner Street
Des Plaines, Illinois 60016
Ron Davis, President

DESCRIPTION OF OPERATION: Security Alliance Corporation is a franchisor of companies that wish to be in the residential and minicommercial security systems business. Using state-of-the-art, supervised wireless systems, Security Alliance members are provided with a broad range of training, advertising, and promotional support.

NUMBER OF FRANCHISEES: 110 in 25 states

IN BUSINESS SINCE: 1974

EQUITY CAPITAL NEEDED: $15,000

FINANCIAL ASSISTANCE AVAILABLE: Financing is available on a limited basis, although support is provided to obtain SBA assistance to qualified franchisees.

TRAINING PROVIDED: 1 week of initial training, followed by 1 week of sales training plus quarterly regional training seminars plus monthly visitations.

MANAGERIAL ASSISTANCE AVAILABLE: Franchisor provides ongoing telephone, in-person support, and managerial assistance through seminars. Three separate types of seminars are offered every 45 days, ranging from technical and sales support to sales management and management seminars. In addition, 5 field marketing people are available for in-field visitations, usually on a monthly basis.

INFORMATION SUBMITTED: May 1990

TOOLS/HARDWARE

MAC TOOLS, INC.
P. O. Box 370
South Fayette Street
Washington Court House, Ohio 43160
Rick Cote, Vice President Sales

DESCRIPTION OF OPERATION: Distributors carrying complete inventory of over 9,000 tools, calling directly on mechanics and light industry. These tools consist of a complete assortment of all small hand tools, sockets, wrenches, punches, chisels, screwdrivers, tool boxes, pneumatic tools, as well as special tools designed for the automotive market.

NUMBER OF FRANCHISEES: Over 1,800 throughout the United States and Canada

IN BUSINESS SINCE: 1938

EQUITY CAPITAL NEEDED: $45,000

FINANCIAL ASSISTANCE AVAILABLE: The $45,000 starting amount includes a basic starting inventory, initial deposit on a new tool truck, business supplies, and backup capital. There are no franchise fees, and the original investment is protected by a buyback agreement. Financing for the starter inventory is available for qualified applicants.

TRAINING PROVIDED: After new distributor training in Ohio, each distributor is assigned to a district manager who lives in the local area and does all necessary follow-up training. He will aid in displaying the trucks, establishing bookkeeping systems, and technical knowledge, and spend approximately 3 weeks with any new distributor and then maintain a monthly contact. Also will continue to work with the distributor as he deems necessary.

MANAGERIAL ASSISTANCE AVAILABLE: Same as above.

INFORMATION SUBMITTED: April 1990

VENDING

FORD GUM & MACHINE COMPANY, INC.
Division of LEAF, INC.
New and Hoag Streets
Akron, New York 14001
George H. Stege, Vice President

DESCRIPTION OF OPERATION: Manufacturer and distributor of chewing gum, candy, and candy-coated confections for sale through self-service vending machines, also manufactured and distributed to franchisees by the company.

NUMBER OF FRANCHISEES: 183 in all states, Canada, and Puerto Rico

IN BUSINESS SINCE: 1934 with manufacturing plant in Akron, New York.

EQUITY CAPITAL NEEDED: $5,000–$30,000 depending on area.

FINANCIAL ASSISTANCE AVAILABLE: Extended credit to new franchisees for expansion of franchised territory, purchase of existing franchise from retiring franchisee, and purchase of equipment and supplies.

TRAINING PROVIDED: On-the-job training in machine and service operation in franchisee's area.

MANAGERIAL ASSISTANCE AVAILABLE: See above.

INFORMATION SUBMITTED: May 1990

WATER CONDITIONING

* RAINSOFT WATER CONDITIONING CO.
2080 Lunt Street
Elk Grove Village, Illinois 60007
John R. Grayson, President

DESCRIPTION OF OPERATION: Sell, lease, and rent water treatment equipment to homes, businesses, and industry.

NUMBER OF FRANCHISEES: Over 200 in most states

IN BUSINESS SINCE: 1953

EQUITY CAPITAL NEEDED: Varies from $15,000 minimum.

FINANCIAL ASSISTANCE AVAILABLE: Assist in establishing retail financing. Financing of rental equipment to qualified dealers on selected basis.

TRAINING PROVIDED: On-plant and field training in sales, service, and operation.

MANAGERIAL ASSISTANCE AVAILABLE: Continuing contact for training and assistance through national and regional seminars, plus regular person-to-person contact from regional field representatives.

INFORMATION SUBMITTED: April 1990

WATERCARE CORPORATION
1520 North 24th Street
Manitowoc, Wisconsin 54220
William K. Granger, President

DESCRIPTION OF OPERATION: Water conditioning sales and service, domestic, industrial, institutional, and commercial. Method of service and sales is portable exchange water conditioners; permanently installed water conditioners on a rental basis and outright sales.

NUMBER OF FRANCHISEES: 135 dealers in 35 states

IN BUSINESS SINCE: 1946

EQUITY CAPITAL NEEDED: $15,000

FINANCIAL ASSISTANCE AVAILABLE: After initial financing Water-Care provides dealer growth money on plant equipment and rental water conditioners.

TRAINING PROVIDED: Includes techniques of water conditioning, water analysis, sales and service of equipment, office procedures, and management, all of which is done at our home office and plant in Manitowoc, Wisconsin, and our Dealer Lab company-owned retail operation at Green Bay, Wisconsin. Time is approximately 1 week in Wisconsin and 1 week by dealer counselor at the franchisee's place of operation. In addition, monthly call on franchisee by dealer counselor and semiannual area work seminars.

MANAGERIAL ASSISTANCE AVAILABLE: Same as above.

INFORMATION SUBMITTED: April 1990

MISCELLANEOUS WHOLESALE AND SERVICE BUSINESS

BALLOON BOUQUETS, INC.
69 Kilburn Road
Belmont, Massachusetts 02178

DESCRIPTION OF OPERATION: Balloon delivery and decorating and special events service.

NUMBER OF FRANCHISEES: 16 in 12 states and Washington, D.C.

IN BUSINESS SINCE: 1976

EQUITY CAPITAL NEEDED: None.

FINANCIAL ASSISTANCE AVAILABLE: None.

TRAINING PROVIDED: 2 days: business management, office operations, balloon delivery, and balloon decorating.

MANAGERIAL ASSISTANCE AVAILABLE: Continuing technical assistance. Advertising, purchasing, nationwide customer referrals to franchisees through toll-free 800 lines: (800) 424-2323.

INFORMATION SUBMITTED: April 1990

CROWN TROPHY, INC.
1 Odell Plaza
Yonkers, New York 10701
Chuck Wersenfeld, President

DESCRIPTION OF OPERATION: Manufacturer of all types of awards, signs, trophies, plaques, medals, ribbons, desk accessories, and advertising specialties.

NUMBER OF FRANCHISEES: 13 in 4 states

IN BUSINESS SINCE: 1978

EQUITY CAPITAL NEEDED: $48,000–$60,000

FINANCIAL ASSISTANCE AVAILABLE: 100 percent financing for qualified buyers.

TRAINING PROVIDED: 2 weeks' training: 1 week at home office and 1 week on-site.

MANAGERIAL ASSISTANCE AVAILABLE: We will assist the buyer until he has enough knowledge on all the aspects of running his business.

INFORMATION SUBMITTED: April 1990

* HEEL/SEW QUIK!
1720 Cumberland Point Drive, Suite 15
Marietta, Georgia 30067

DESCRIPTION OF OPERATION: Instant shoe repair, high-speed monogramming (computerized), and clothing alterations. Our objective is to create a one-stop service center to meet today's needs and demands. High-tech equipment and machinery means improved service/speed. Consistent quality work at very competitive prices. Specialty retail items related to all three services.

NUMBER OF FRANCHISEES: 314 in 27 states and 5 countries

IN BUSINESS SINCE: 1984

EQUITY CAPITAL NEEDED: $15,000–$25,000

FINANCIAL ASSISTANCE AVAILABLE: None.

TRAINING PROVIDED: 2 to 3 weeks' training at company training center, operations manuals, video training tapes, continuing consulting support, in-the-field training, refresher and technical update sessions.

MANAGERIAL ASSISTANCE AVAILABLE: In addition to training described above, licensor provides established total concept system of while-you-wait shoe repair methodology, sales, marketing techniques, trademarks and ongoing supervision and support, advertising package, training manuals, and videotapes.

INFORMATION SUBMITTED: April 1990

MEISTERGRAM
3517 West Wendover Avenue
Greensboro, North Carolina 27407
Stephen R. Gluskin, Vice President/General Manager

DESCRIPTION OF OPERATION: Established in 1931, Meistergram, Inc., is the most comprehensive source of computerized, single-head monogramming and embroidery equipment. Meistergram owners include department stores, manufacturers, and entrepreneurs who establish a business in their home or storefront. New products include the Meistergram Embroidery Design System (MED), a computerized digitizing system for creating custom embroidery designs. Additional products include the ETCH-MASTER 2,000 and ETCH-MASTER 3,000, personalization equipment for glass and other hard-surfaced items including ceramics and acrylics. Comprehensive parts and supplies for monogramming/embroidery and etching systems, with a toll-free customer service hotline. Technical service in-house. On-site training by a certified Meistergram instructor.

NUMBER OF FRANCHISEES: 8,000 in United States and overseas

IN BUSINESS SINCE: 1931

EQUITY CAPITAL NEEDED: Monogramming/embroidery equipment: $19,750, ETCH-MASTER systems: $1,595–$1,995. MED equipment: $21,600–$27,400.

FINANCIAL ASSISTANCE AVAILABLE: Leasing available to qualified U.S. applicants.

TRAINING PROVIDED: On-site, conducted by a trained Meistergram instructor.

MANAGERIAL ASSISTANCE AVAILABLE: On-site training includes instruction in operation, techniques, and machine maintenance. Comprehensive manual includes marketing and promotional information.

INFORMATION SUBMITTED: April 1990

SHOE STOP, INC.
13625 N.E. 165th Place, Suite 430
Kirkland, Washington 98034
Mike Pula, Manager, Franchise Sales

DESCRIPTION OF OPERATION: Shoe Stop is an "instant" shoe-repair company that features quality repairs, outstanding customer service, and attractively designed stores. The outlets are located in shopping malls and other high-traffic sites; about 500 square feet of space is required.

NUMBER OF FRANCHISEES: 20

IN BUSINESS SINCE: 1984

EQUITY CAPITAL NEEDED: $30,000 initial investment, total from $60,000 to $100,000.

FINANCIAL ASSISTANCE AVAILABLE: Will work with franchisee to locate sources of capital.

TRAINING PROVIDED: Extensive training in shoe-repair skills and in the management of the business is provided. Shoe Stop has a training center and also uses company stores in the training process. The length of training is from 4 to 12 weeks, depending on the franchisee.

MANAGERIAL ASSISTANCE AVAILABLE: Site selection,

lease negotiations, turnkey store, operations manual, machine and equipment repairs, and promotion and sales support. Also able to purchase merchandise and materials directly from Shoe Stop.

INFORMATION SUBMITTED: April 1990

THE SPORTS SECTION PHOTOGRAPHY, INC.
3120 Medlock Bridge Road
Norcross, Georgia 30071
R. Daniel Burgner, President

DESCRIPTION OF OPERATION: TSS, a custom-color production facility, specializes in youth and youth sports photography. Franchisees with strengths in sales and marketing are trained in photography and become a part of our network of professionals offering unique photographic products and highly organized services to youth groups as a part- or full-time venture. Franchisees are encouraged to work from their homes. There is no merchandise to maintain; a protected territory of 500,000 to 1,000,000 population is worked year-round.

NUMBER OF FRANCHISEES: 54 in 23 states including Canada and South Africa

IN BUSINESS SINCE: 1983

EQUITY CAPITAL NEEDED: Protected territories, $9,500–$25,000.

FINANCIAL ASSISTANCE AVAILABLE: None.

TRAINING PROVIDED: Sales and marketing training in territory for 1 to 2 days and complete photography training in territory. Additional training available according to size of territory and needed assistance.

MANAGERIAL ASSISTANCE AVAILABLE: Turnkey operation provided, including all materials necessary for success. Sales and photography training provided in $20,000 franchise. Sales seminar in Atlanta headquarters for $7,900 franchise. Sales and photographic experts on call throughout United States.

INFORMATION SUBMITTED: April 1990

* STAINED GLASS OVERLAY, INC.
2325 Morse Avenue
Irvine, California 92714
Peter Shea, President

DESCRIPTION OF OPERATION: Franchisees are exclusive distributors of the patented "Overlay" process, which they apply to windows (without removing them from their mountings), mirrors, skylights, ceiling panels, etc. Just as beautiful as cut stained glass, Overlay has many benefits: it's seamless—no air or water leakage; it strengthens the glass; intricate designs are completed easily and quickly; over 200 colors coordinate with any decor; it can be used in residential and commercial markets anywhere—even where safety glass is specified. The corporation is continuously involved in market research and testing of new products and services. Complementary products available to franchisees now: oak doors and beveled glass, carved glass, and designer rugs.

NUMBER OF FRANCHISEES: 350 plus in United States, Australia, Canada, England, France, Germany, Switzerland, Japan, and Israel

IN BUSINESS SINCE: 1974; franchising since 1981.

EQUITY CAPITAL NEEDED: Franchise fee $34,000; start-up materials and supplies $11,000.

FINANCIAL ASSISTANCE AVAILABLE: Initial cash investment required $45,000.

TRAINING PROVIDED: Minimum 40 hours' training at corporate headquarters, including (but not limited to) Overlay application, marketing, and business administration. Ongoing updates and training through regional seminars and company newsletter.

MANAGERIAL ASSISTANCE AVAILABLE: Corporate office provides continuous assistance in all phases of business operations and management, finances and record keeping, marketing and personnel. Upon request, a corporate representative will provide assistance at franchisee's location.

INFORMATION SUBMITTED: June 1990

STARVING STUDENTS FRANCHISE CORPORATION
P. O. Box 351206
West Los Angeles, California 90035
Ethan H. Margalith, President

DESCRIPTION OF OPERATION: Moving and storage—local, intrastate, and interstate.

NUMBER OF FRANCHISEES: 21

IN BUSINESS SINCE: 1973

EQUITY CAPITAL NEEDED: $16,950–$40,000; $6,950–$15,000 capital to begin business.

FINANCIAL ASSISTANCE AVAILABLE: In some cases, for uniquely qualified individuals, franchisor will finance 100 percent under a partnership type arrangement. In some cases franchisor will accept a promissory note for $5,000 of the franchise fee.

TRAINING PROVIDED: Initial training lasts up to 8 weeks, depending on prior experience. Additionally, ongoing training is provided as necessary, for the duration of the franchise relationship.

MANAGERIAL ASSISTANCE AVAILABLE: All phases of operations, moving company accounting, advertising and promotion, etc. Duration of assistance will vary with individual's experience and background.

INFORMATION SUBMITTED: June 1990

Resources

Small Business Administration Regional and District Offices

REGIONAL OFFICES

Region 1
(Connecticut, Maine, Massachusetts, New Hampshire, Rhode Island, Vermont)

60 Batterymarch Street, Boston, MA 02110, Tel: (617) 451-2023

Region 2
(New Jersey, New York, Puerto Rico, Virgin Islands)

26 Federal Plaza, Room 31-08, New York, NY 10278, Tel: (212) 264-7772

Region 3
(Delaware, District of Columbia, Maryland, Pennsylvania, Virginia, West Virginia)

475 Allendale Road, King of Prussia, PA 19406, Tel: (215) 962-3750

Region 4
(Alabama, Florida, Georgia, Kentucky, Mississippi, North Carolina, South Carolina, Tennessee)

1375 Peachtree Street, N.E., Atlanta, GA 30367, Tel: (404) 347-2797

Region 5
(Illinois, Indiana, Michigan, Minnesota, Ohio, Wisconsin)

230 South Dearborn Street, Room 510, Chicago, IL 60604, Tel: (312) 353-0359

Region 6
(Arkansas, Louisiana, New Mexico, Oklahoma, Texas)

8625 King George Drive, Dallas, TX 75235, Tel: (214) 767-7643

Region 7
(Iowa, Kansas, Missouri, Nebraska)

911 Walnut Street, 13th Floor, Kansas City, MO 64106, Tel: (816) 426-2989

Region 8
(Colorado, Montana, North Dakota, South Dakota, Utah, Wyoming)

999 18th Street, Denver, CO 80202, Tel: (303) 294-7001

Region 9
(Arizona, California, Hawaii, Nevada, Pacific Islands)

Federal Building, 450 Golden Gate Avenue, Room 15307, San Francisco, CA 94102, Tel: (415) 556-7489

Region 10
(Alaska, Idaho, Oregon, Washington)

2615 4th Avenue, Room 440, Seattle, WA 98104, Tel: (206) 442-5676

DISTRICT OFFICES

Region 1

10 Causeway Street, Boston, MA 02222, Tel: (617) 565-5590

Federal Building, 40 Western Avenue, Room 512, Augusta, ME 04330, Tel: (207) 622-8242

55 Pleasant Street, Room 209, Concord, NH 03301, Tel: (603) 225-1400

330 Main Street, Hartford, CT 06106, Tel: (203) 240-7400

Federal Building, 87 State Street, Room 205, Montpelier, VT 05602, Tel: (802) 828-4474

380 Westminister Mall, Providence, RI 02903, Tel: (401) 528-4586

Region 2

Carlos Chardon Avenue, Hato Rey, PR 00918, Tel: (809) 753-4002

60 Park Place, Newark, NJ 07102, Tel: (201) 645-2434

100 State Street, Room 601, Rochester, NY 14614, Tel: (716) 263-6700

Federal Building, Room 1071, 100 South Clinton Street, Syracuse, NY 13202, Tel: (315) 423-5383

111 West Huron Street, Room 1311, Federal Building, Buffalo, NY 14202, Tel: (716) 846-4301

333 E. Water Street, Elmira, NY 14901, Tel: (607) 734-8130

445 Broadway, Albany, NY 12207, Tel: (518) 472-6300

Region 3

168 W. Main Street, Clarksburg, WV 26301, Tel: (304) 623-5361

960 Penn Avenue, Pittsburgh, PA 15222, Tel: (412) 644-2780

Federal Building, 400 North 8th Street, Room 3015, Richmond, VA 23240, Tel: (804) 771-2617

1111 18th Street, N.W., Washington, DC 20417, Tel: (202) 634-4950

100 Chestnut Street, Harrisburg, PA 17101, Tel: (717) 782-3840

20 N. Pennsylvania Avenue, Wilkes-Barre, PA 18702, Tel: (717) 826-6497

920 N. King Street, Room 412, Wilmington, DE 19801, Tel: (302) 573-6294

10 N. Calvert Street, Baltimore, MD 21202, Tel: (301) 962-2235

Region 4

2121 8th Avenue, N., Suite 200, Birmingham, AL 35203, Tel: (205) 731-1344

222 S. Church Street, Room 300, Charlotte, NC 29202, Tel: (704) 371-6563

1835 Assembly Street, Columbia, SC 29202, Tel: (803) 765-5376

100 West Capitol Street, Jackson, MS 39201, Tel: (601) 965-4378

Federal Building, 400 West Bay Street, Room 261, Jacksonville, FL 32202, Tel: (904) 791-3782

5601 Corporate Way, W. Palm Beach, FL 33407, Tel: (407) 689-3922

50 Vantage Way, Nashville, TN 37228, Tel: (615) 736-6850

501 E. Polk Street, Tampa, FL 33602, Tel: (813) 228-2594

1720 Peachtree Road, N.W., 6th Floor, Atlanta, GA 30309, Tel: (404) 347-2441

Region 5

511 W. Capital Street, Springfield, IL 62704, Tel: (217) 492-4416

1240 East 9th Street, Room 317, Cleveland, OH 44199, Tel: (216) 522-4180

85 Marconi Boulevard, Columbis, OH 43215, Tel: (614) 469-6860

Federal Building, 550 Main Street, Cincinnati, OH 45202, Tel: (513) 684-2814

477 Michigan Avenue, McNamara Building, Detroit, MI 48226, Tel: (313) 226-6075

575 N. Pennsylvania Avenue, Century Building, Indianapolis, IN 46204, Tel: (317) 269-7272

212 East Washington Avenue, Room 213, Madison, WI 53703, Tel: (608) 264-5261

100 North 6th Street, Minneapolis, MN 55403, Tel: (612) 370-2324

300 S. Front Street, Marquette, MI 49855, Tel: (906) 225-1108

310 W. Wisconsin Avenue, Room 400, Milwaukee, WI 53203, Tel: (414) 291-3941

500 South Barstow Street, Room 16, Federal Office Building and U.S. Courthouse, Eau Claire, WI 54701, Tel: (715) 834-9012

Region 6

625 Silver S.W., Albuquerque, NM 87102, Tel: (505) 766-1879

2525 Murworth, Houston, TX 77054, Tel: (713) 660-4401

320 West Capitol Avenue, Little Rock, AR 72201, Tel: (501) 378-5871

1611 Tenth Street, Lubbock, TX 79401, Tel: (806) 743-7462

222 East Van Buren Street, Harlingen, TX 78550, Tel: (512) 427-8533

505 E. Travis, Marshall, TX 75670, Tel: (214) 935-5257

1661 Canal Street, New Orleans, LA 70113, Tel: (504) 589-2354

200 N.W. 5th Street, Suite 670, Oklahoma City, OK 73102, Tel: (405) 231-4301

7400 Blanco Road, San Antonio, TX 78216, Tel: (512) 229-4535

1100 Commerce Street, Dallas, TX 75242, Tel: (214) 767-0605

10737 Gateway W., Suite 320, El Paso, TX 79902, Tel: (915) 541-7586

400 Main Street, Corpus Christi, TX 78401, Tel: (512) 888-3331

Region 7

New Federal Building, 210 Walnut Street, Room 749, Des Moines, IA 50309, Tel: (515) 284-4422

11145 Mill Valley Road, Omaha, NE 68154, Tel: (402) 221-3604

815 Olive Street, St. Louis, MO 63101, Tel: (314) 425-6600

110 East Waterman, Wichita, KS 67202, Tel: (316) 269-6571

Region 8

Room 4001, Federal Building, 100 East B Street, Casper, WY 82601, Tel: (307) 261-5761

301 S. Park, Room 528, Helena, MT 59626, Tel: (406) 449-5381

Federal Building, 657 2nd Avenue, North, Room 218, Fargo, ND 58102, Tel: (701) 239-5131

Federal Building, 125 South State Street, Room 2237, Salt Lake City, UT 84138, Tel: (801) 524-5800

101 South Main Avenue, Sioux Falls, SD 57102, Tel: (605) 336-2980

Region 9

300 Ala Moana Boulevard, Honolulu, HI 96850, Tel: (808) 541-2990

211 Main Street, San Francisco, CA 94105, Tel: (415) 744-6823

2005 N. Central Avenue, Phoenix, AZ 85004, Tel: (602) 379-3737

880 Front Street, San Diego, CA 92101, Tel: (619) 557-5440

301 E. Stewart, Las Vegas, NV 89121, Tel: (702) 388-6611

6477 Telephone Road, Ventura, CA 93003, Tel: (805) 642-1866

901 W. Civic Center Drive, Santa Ana, CA 92703, Tel: (714) 836-2494

660 J Street, Sacramento, CA 95814, Tel: (916) 551-1426

300 W. Congress Street, Tucson, AZ 85701, Tel: (602) 629-6715

Region 10

1020 Main Street, Boise, ID 83702, Tel: (208) 334-1696

222 S.W. Columbia, Portland, OR 97201, Tel: (503) 326-2682

W. 601 First Avenue, Spokane, WA 99204, Tel: (509) 353-2807

701 C Street, Anchorage, AK 99513, Tel: (907) 271-4022

Sources of Franchising Information

Below is a listing of various books, periodicals, and tapes that may be of interest to you. If the work is produced or published by the International Franchise Association, you can order it through the IFA's toll-free number. Here are the address and phone number of the IFA's executive offices:

International Franchise Association
1350 New York Avenue, N.W.
Washington, D.C. 20005
202-628-8000
800-543-1038

For other publishers, you can either write to the address shown and request ordering information or visit your local library. If the book is not on the shelf (and if you live in a small community, most books won't be), you can usually obtain the publication through an interlibrary loan.

Business Building Ideas for Franchises and Small Business. Med Serif. Pilot Industries, Inc., 347 Fifth Avenue, New York, NY 10016.

Business Franchise Guide. Commerce Clearing House, Inc., 4025 W. Peterson Avenue, Chicago, IL 60646. Monthly or more as required.

Checklist for Going into Business. Small Business Administration, Washington, DC 20416. Small Marketers Aids No. 71.

The Complete Handbook of Franchising. David D. Seltz. Addison-Wesley, Gen. Books Div., Reading, MA 01867. 1981.

Continental Franchise Review. 5000 S. Quebec, Suite 450, Denver, CO 80237. Biweekly.

Directory of Franchise Business Opportunities. Franchise Business Opportunities Publishing Co., Suite 205, 1725 Washington Road, Pittsburgh, PA 15241. Annual.

Directory of Franchising Organizations. Pilot Industries, Inc., 103 Cooper Street, Babylon, NY 11702. Annual.

Evaluation and Buying a Franchise. James A. Meaney. Pilot Industries, Inc., 103 Cooper Street, Babylon, NY 11702. 1988.

Financial Security and Independence Through a Small Business Franchise. Donald J. Scherer. Pilot Industries, Inc., 103 Cooper Street, Babylon, NY 11702. 1976.

The Franchise Advantage: Donald A. Borian and Patrick J. Borian. National BestSeller Corp., 955 American Lane, Schaumburg, IL 60173. 1987.

The Franchise Annual. Info Press, 736 Center Street, Lewiston, NY 14092. Annual.

Franchise Encyclopedia. Dr. Alfred J. Modica. Published by ADA Publishing, 28 Sandrock Avenue, Dobbs Ferry, NY 10522. 1986.

The Franchise Game. (Rules and Players.) Harold Nedell. Olempco, Dept. C., P.O. Box 27963, Houston, TX 77027.

Franchise Investigation: A Contract Negotiation. Harry Gross and Robert S. Levy. Pilot Industries, Inc., 103 Cooper Street, Babylon, NY 11702.

Franchise Law Bibliography. American Bar Association, 750 N. Lake Shore Drive, Chicago, IL 60611.

Franchise Manual. Dr. Alfred J. Modica and Dr. Anthony F. Libertella. Published by the National/International Institute for Franchise Research and Development, 3 Barker Avenue, White Plains, NY 10601. 1986.

Franchise Opportunities Guide. International Franchise Association, 1350 New York Avenue, Suite 900, Washington, DC 20005. Summer 1990.

The Franchise Option. DeBanks M. Henward, III, and William Ginalski. International Franchise Association, 1350 New York Avenue, Suite 900, Washington, DC 20005.

Franchise Restaurants. The National Restaurant Association, 311 1st Street, N.W., Washington, DC 20001.

Franchise Rights—A Self-Defense Manual for the Franchisee. Alex Hammond. Hammond & Morton, 54 Riverside Drive, New York, NY 10024. 1980.

Franchise Suitability Questionnaire. Dr. Alfred J. Modica. Published by ADA Publishing, 28 Sandrock Avenue, Dobbs Ferry, NY 10522. 1986.

Franchising. Gladys Glickman, Matthew Bender & Co., Inc., 1275 Broadway, Albany, NY 12201. 1979.

Franchising. Dr. Alfred J. Modica. Published by Quick Fox, distributed by ADA Publishing, 28 Sandrock Avenue, Dobbs Ferry, NY 10522. 1981.

Franchising: A Planning and Sales Compliance Guide. Commerce Clearing House, 4025 W. Peterson Avenue, Chicago, IL 60646.

Franchising—The How-to Book. Lloyd Tarbutton. International Franchise Association, 1350 New York Avenue, N.W., Suite 900, Washington, DC 20005.

Franchising: How to Successfully Select a Money Making Business of Your Own. Bruce Scher. Bay Publishing Co., 316 Fifth Avenue, New York, NY 10001.

New consumer guide written for the individual considering a career in franchising. Lists the eight major mistakes overlooked in the selection process. Shows how to investigate and evaluate all franchise opportunities.

Franchising: The Inside Story. John Kinch. International Franchise Association, 1350 New York Avenue, Suite 900, Washington, DC 20005.

Franchising: Regulation of Buying and Selling a Franchise. Philip F. Zeidman, Perry C. Ausbrook and H. Bret Lowell. Bureau of Nat'l Affairs, 9435 Key West Avenue, Rockville, MD 20850. (CPS Portfolio #34.)

Franchising in the Economy—1988–90. International Franchise Association, 1350 New York Avenue, Suite 900, Washington, DC 20005.

Franchising Opportunities. International Franchise Association, 1350 New York Avenue, N.W., Suite 900, Washington, DC 20005.

Franchising Realities & Remedies. Harold Brown. Law Journal Seminal Press, 111 Eighth Avenue, New York, NY 10011. Summer 1986.

FTC Franchising Rule: The IFA Compliance Kit. International Franchise Association, 1350 New York Avenue, N.W., Suite 900, Washington, DC 20005.

Government Regulation of Real Estate Franchising. Peter D. Baird, John L. Hay, and Judith M. Baily. Appears in American Bar Associaiton publication, *Real Property, Probate and Trust Journal,* Pates 580-619. Vol. 12, Fall 1977.

How to Be a Franchisor. Robert E. Kushell and Carl E. Zwisler III. International Franchise Association, 1350 New York Avenue, N.W., Suite 900, Washington, DC.

How to Franchise Your Business. Mack A. Lewis. Pilot Industries, Inc., 103 Cooper Street, Babylon, NY 11702. 1990.

How to Organize a Franchise Advisory Council. International Franchise Association, 1350 New York Avenue, N.W., Suite 900, Washington, DC 20005.

How to Organize and Operate a Small Business, 7th Ed. Clifford M. Baumback et al. Prentice-Hall, 200 Old Tappan Road, Old Tappan, NJ 07675. 1985.

How to Prepare Effective Business Program Blueprints. David D. Seltz. Addison-Wesley, Gen. Books Div., Reading, MA 01867. 1981.

How to Select a Franchise. Robert McIntosh. International Franchise Association, 1350 New York Avenue, N.W., Washington, DC 20005.

The Info Franchise Newsletter. Info Press, 736 Center Street, Lewiston, NY 14092. Monthly.

Investigate Before Investing: Guidance for Prospective Franchisees. Jerome L. Fels and Lewis G. Rudnick. International Franchise Association, 1350 New York Avenue, N.W., Suite 900, Washington, DC 20005. 1974.

Is Franchising for You? Robert K. McIntosh. International Franchise Association, 1350 New York Avenue, N.W., Suite 900, Washington, DC 20005.

Legal Aspects of Selling and Buying. Shepard's/McGraw-Hill, P.O. Box 1235, Colorado Springs, CO 80901.

Negotiate Your Way to Success. David D. Seltz and Alfred J. Modica. Published by Farnsworth Publishing Company, Inc., distributed by ADA Publishing, 28 Sandrock Avenue, Dobbs Ferry, NY 10522. 1980.

Own Your Own Franchise: Everything You Need to Know About the Best Franchise Opportunities in America. Ray Bard and Sheila Henderson. Addison-Wesley, Gen. Books Div., Reading, MA 01867. 1987.

The Perfect Business Plan. William R. Lasher. Doubleday, 1540 Broadway, New York, NY 10036. 1994.

Pilot's Question and Answer Guide to Successful Franchising. Pilot Industries, Inc., 103 Cooper Street, Babylon, NY 11702.

Protecting Your Franchising Trademark and Trade Secrets. Donald A. Kaul. International Franchise Association, 1350 New York Avenue, N.W., Suite 900, Washington, DC 20005.

Starting a Business After 50. Samuel Small. Pilot Industries, Inc., 103 Cooper Street, Babylon, NY 11702. 1990.

Twenty-One Questions. International Franchise Association, 1350 New York Avenue, N.W., Suite 900, Washington, DC 20005.

Understanding Franchise Contracts. David C. Hjelmselt. Pilot Books, Inc., 103 Cooper Street, Babylon, NY 11702.

A Woman's Guide to Her Own Franchised Business. Anne Small. Pilot Industries, Inc., 103 Cooper Street, Babylon, NY 11702.

INDEX